# Essays in
# Indian History

# Essays in Indian History

## Towards a Marxist Perception

### Irfan Habib

 Tulika

Published by **Tulika Books**
No. 44, first floor, Shahpur Jat, New Delhi 110 049, India

First edition (hardback) 1995
Second edition (paperback) 1997
Third edition 1998; Fourth edition 2000; Fifth edition 2001;
Sixth edition 2002; Seventh edition 2005; Eighth edition 2007;
Ninth edition 2010; Tenth edition 2011; Eleventh edition 2013;
Twelfth edition 2015; Thirteenth edition 2017

Fourteenth edition 2019

ISBN: 978-93-82381-69-3

Printed at Chaman Offset, Delhi 110 002

# Contents

# Preface

This collection of papers brings together material published over a span of some thirty years. What gives this collection such
unity as it possesses is my effort to interpret the main currents of our
country's history from a standpoint which belongs to the Marxist tradition of historiography. This is the justification for the sub-title given
to this collection.

I realize that the reader is not likely to be interested in how
the approach I use came to be adopted by me. What he may be expected to be interested in is whether we can understand our past as a
people better by giving due weight to the interaction of material
conditions, classes, ideas and class struggles, which it was the great
achievement of Marx to establish both in theory and in actual work
of description and analysis. One major requirement that Marx
always sought to fulfil was a combination of breadth of generaliza-
tion with rigour in detail. This is a requirement which is especially
hard to meet, and I have indicated any disavowal of definitiveness in
my effort by claiming for my work only an endeavour *towards* a
Marxist approach rather than the attainment and application of such
an approach in all its fullness.

I should make it clear, as the reader will soon judge for himself, that many recent trends in historiography, such as Namierism,
French 'New History', Subalternity and Postmodernism, have passed
me by. I do not deny the insights one can gain from some or all of these
(although I often find their terminology or theology difficult to follow), nor do I think that the Marxist approach necessarily excludes
them or cannot gain in knowledge or method by their study. Essentially, I would argue, the difference between their practitioners and

Marxists lies in the fact that they are asking different questions and do not share the same vision for humanity. When a reviewer, writing about my *Agrarian System of Mughal India*, wrote that I had a 'definitely socialist point of view', he meant, I am sure, that a person who did not feel that mankind needs socialism would have appraised even the Mughal empire quite differently.

Over the years I have gained immeasurably from the guidance and help of numerous friends and colleagues, and it is now impossible to thank them all. Some of them, alas, are no longer alive to receive my thanks. But throughout this period, I have had one source of correction, one hand by which my natural rigidities have been softened, a constant, critical companionship: I cannot thank Sayera enough.

*Aligarh*                                                   IRFAN HABIB

# Acknowledgements

Problems of Marxist Historiography
Text of the Second V.P. Chintan Memorial Lecture, Indian School of Social Sciences, Madras, September 1988. Published in *Social Scientist*, Vol. 16, No. 12, December 1988.

Marx's Perception of India
Paper read at the Marx Centenary Congress: Marx and the Third World, Friedrich-Ebert-Stiftung, Trier, March 1983. Published in *The Marxist*, Vol. I, No. 1, July–September 1983.

The Social Distribution of Landed Property in Pre-British India: A Historical Survey
Paper read at the International Economic History Conference, Munich, August 1965. Published in *Enquiry*, New Series, Vol. II, No. 3, 1965; and in R.S. Sharma and V. Jha (eds), *Indian Society: Historical Probings. In Memory of D.D. Kosambi*, New Delhi, 1974.

The Peasant in Indian History
Presidential Address, Indian History Congress, Kurukshetra, 1982. Published in *Social Scientist*, Vol. 11, No. 3, March 1983.

Caste in Indian History
Text of the Inaugural D.D. Kosambi Memorial Lecture, Bombay, March 1985. Published in *Caste and Money in Indian History*, Bombay, 1987.

Potentialities of Capitalistic Development in the Economy of Mughal India
Paper read at the International Economic History Congress,

Bloomington, 1968. Published in *Enquiry*, New Series, Vol. III, No. 3; and in *Journal of Economic History*, Vol. XXIX, 1969.

### Forms of Class Struggle in Mughal India
Paper originally prepared for a colloquium on International Labour Issues, McGill University, Canada, May 1980; also read at the Indian History Congress, Bombay, 1980.

### Processes of Accumulation in Pre-Colonial and Colonial India
An earlier version of this paper was delivered as the Asiatic Society of Bangladesh Lecture, Dhaka, January 1988. The complete version was published in *Indian Historical Review*, Vol. XI, Nos 1–2.

### Colonialization of the Indian Economy 1757–1900
Paper read at a seminar of the Tamilnadu Council for Historical Research, Madras, October 1974. Published in *Social Scientist*, Vol. 3, No. 8, March 1975.

### Studying a Colonial Economy—Without Perceiving Colonialism
An earlier version of this paper was presented at a conference on the *Cambridge Economic History of India*, Cambridge, 1984. Published in *Modern Asian Studies*, Vol. 19, No. 3, 1985; and in *Social Scientist*, Vol. 12, No. 12, December 1984.

We have made an attempt to trace the publication history of each article included in this volume as accurately as possible. Any lapse is inadvertent and regretted. To maintain stylistic uniformity, minor changes have been carried out in each article.

PUBLISHER

# Problems of Marxist Historiography

In one of his theses on Feuerbach Marx said: 'Philosophers have so far interpreted the world. The point is to change it.' Marxism sees an innate unity between perception of the past and present practice. This unity implies continuous interaction between the two: as time passes and history (human experience) lengthens, we draw greater lessons from it for the present; and as our present experience tells us more about the possibilities and limitations of social action, we turn to the past and obtain new comprehensions of it. Consider Marc Bloch's understanding of the French Revolution as mainly representing continuity and not a break in French agrarian history: an understanding reached *after* the Soviet Revolution of 1917 how much more radical revolutionary changes could be. Similarly our new perception of the limitations of Soviet peasant mobilization that followed the success of the Chinese Revolution (1949), a massive 'peasant revolution'. It is inherent in the unity of past and present that Marxist historiography must continuously turn to fresh aspects to explore and re-explore and seek fresh questions to answer. Nothing is more illustrative of this need than the history of socialist societies since 1917. This history cannot be meaningfully studied only from what the classics tell us socialism should be. The lengthening, complex history of socialism is of great significance not only for the peoples of socialist countries, but also for all those who aspire for socialism in their own countries.

There are other factors too which must cause continuous reconsiderations of positions previously taken. Research expands and exposes facts we did not know before: without undue modesty, we can say we know more about India's past than Marx did. Can his statements on India be accepted as the last word, even when we recognize that his information was limited? Naturally, extended knowledge imposes on us the task of testing our older interpretations against our information as it now stands. It has to be an unceasing process.

More: Marxism, as the ideology of the working class, does not exist alone and in isolation. There are rival interpretations arising all the time. The authors of these interpretations might not accept the basic premises of a class approach; and, therefore, for us to dismiss them as 'bourgeois' and ignore them brings no conviction. They have to be rationally analysed. In India every day we find ourselves face to face with chauvinistic, communal and regional approaches to history, which we must answer by detailed arguments. But there are other and more fundamental challenges too. Gramsci, in criticising Bukharin's *ABC of Communism* said that in the war of ideas, unlike ordinary war, you have to attack the enemy's strongest, and not weakest, points. This, of course, demands constant enquiry and self-examination, and the refining and extension of Marxist positions. This examination must cover everything from general principles to specific facts, because both are all the time being brought into question by others. We have to answer not by denunciation—that is always a bad counsellor—but by careful scrutiny and investigation.

Finally, I believe that scientific socialism requires constant debate within itself, without need for polemics from outside. Long before the current recognition of the virtues of 'plurality', Mao Tsetung had urged that truth could belong to a minority, and all truths are at first espoused only by a minority. This applies to a revolutionary party as well as society at large.

### 'Mind and Matter' in History

One of the common obscurities in popular understanding about Marxian historiography has been caused, I believe, by the textbook view of Marxism as 'determinism'. While Marxists have protested against this characterization, their own description of 'Historical Materialism' (as in Stalin's essay *Dialectical and Historical Materialism*) is often in fact couched in deterministic terms. We are told that the production technology ('forces of production') determines the social relationships ('relations of production'). These together constitute the 'mode of production', which determines the world of ideas and culture ('the superstructure'). For has not Marx said, 'It is their social being that determines their consciousness'? Clearly the relationship of technique—class relations and mode of production—and culture, is crucial, but in what way exactly does one part of the relationship 'determine' the configuration of the other part? It has been said that 'Marxism is a product of capitalism'. It could not have arisen before capitalism created the working class. But that the different aspects of Marx's thought were inevitably or automatically just what they were, having been directly formed by the conditions created by capitalism, would be a statement very difficult to substantiate.

One would rather propose that capitalism set the context, rather than the structure, for Marxism—and this is very different from determinism of any recognizable kind. (For the moment, I am not going into Althusser's discussion of 'determination' and 'over-determination'.)

Marxist textbooks often suggest that the 'mode of production', but especially the 'forces of production', represent the 'material' base, whereas ideas form a separate superstructure seated upon it. But long ago the archaeologist Gordon Childe in the very title of his work, *Man Makes Himself,* showed that production technology is after all inseparable from ideas. Matter does not create technology; human ideas, reflected in skill, dexterity and science, create it. When Maurice Dobb argues in his *Studies in the Development of Capitalism* that the inventions which triggered the English Industrial Revolution in the eighteenth century came not earlier, and only then, because the surrounding economic circumstances were not favourable earlier, is he not suggesting a reverse determination, of 'forces of production'—the supposedly material base—by social relationships?

Marx's view of historical development is clearly far more refined and persuasive than a mere extension of materialist determination to social evolution: 'Just as we cannot judge an individual by the opinion he has of himself, so we cannot judge a period of social transformation by its own consciousness.' This statement means that the intricacies of the contemporary modes of production and social relationships could not be seen in the earlier periods. Rather, they were always misconceived. To Marx such misconceptions or imperfect perceptions set limits on the growth of further ideas, or of action during the process of transformation. When he said that 'ideas become a material force once they have gripped the masses', he surely meant that consciousness once generalized delimits the range of ideas of individuals and social action. Religion, and race or community prejudices could also colour class struggles and shape their results (we can illustrate this from our own history). What happened in the epoch of capitalism and as a consequence of the simultaneous or attendant scientific revolution was the creation of a possibility, re-realized in Marxism, of an approximately closer perception of the mode of production and social relationships with a view to a far more resolute guidance of the 'transformation' or social revolution. It is in this sense that the achievement of the perception by the working class of the real world around it and the potentiality of its own revolutionary role—its 'class consciousness'—has been given such signal importance in Marxist practice. But this surely means that the role of ideas, compared with earlier periods, has been substantially enlarged: blind struggles have been replaced by sighted ones. Can we not go further and say that this has been a feature of human development, and that the bourgeoisie, which according to the *Communist Manifesto* had played such a 'revolutionary role', was responsible for the previous round of such intellectual enlargement? I believe that Marx believed that ideas would be attaining continuously greater importance in future. When he spoke of the future as one where mankind marched 'from the realm of necessity to the realm of freedom', I feel convinced (in spite of Engels' unfortunate gloss on 'freedom' as the 'recognition of necessity') that Marx looked forward to ideas at last gaining ascendancy over matter, not by any spiritualist exercise, but by the abundance of material wealth which communism would ultimately produce.

Far, therefore, from being a theory of materialist determinism, Marxism sees the past of humanity in its true relationship to the material world and aspires to achieve for it its ultimate sovereignty by progress through socialism and communism, the twin states, present and future, of social evolution that Marx confidently charted in the *Critique of the Gotha Programme*.

It goes without saying that for us today liberation from the 'inevitability' theory, erroneously ascribed to Marxism, is a major necessity. Capitalism and other exploitative systems are not going to break down by their own weight or by the 'General Crisis of Capitalism'. There is no alternative to entering the battle of ideas;

economic action is a help, but it is no substitute for class consciousness.

### Social Formations and Class Struggles

'The history of all hitherto existing societies is the history of class struggles.' These ringing words of the *Communist Manifesto* seem quite often lost in the long debates among Marxist historians over modes of production, social formations, and especially feudalism. I cannot protest too much over it, because I have also participated in these debates. Nor do I think that they are irrelevant, although it does seem to me that we should be careful not to lose sight of the wood for the trees.

The relevance of defining social formations arises because one cannot study class struggles without discerning classes; and classes must belong to structures which we call social formations. Social formations constitute successive organizations of society, so that the classic order of succession has been primitive communism–slavery–feudalism–capitalism. Whether the classic order is also universal is a question on which there has been much controversy. Marx did not think that pre-colonial India was 'feudal': it lacked serfdom, and there was identity between tax and rent. The 'Asiatic Mode', which Marx speculated on in the 1850s, has been resurrected as the Tributary Mode of Samir Amin; and sub-classified into 'feudal' (based on rent) and 'despotic' (based on tax) by Chris Wickham; D.D. Kosambi and R.S. Sharma have argued that India did not see the stage of slavery, but had forms of feudalism from the middle of the first millennium or thereabouts to the colonial conquest.

While the controversy is not likely to cease, I do not wish to discuss it here at length. My own views are against a universalization of 'feudalism' as an umbrella to cover all pre-capitalist systems whatever their actual modes of surplus extraction (class exploitation). I agree that failure to universalize feudalism would lead us to accept a multiplicity of social formations over different territories; but I see no scandal in this. I would reassert that this is also implicit in the *Communist Manifesto*, when it treats capitalism as the first universal mode of production, and speaks of complex class structures preceding it.

What I think needs correction is the view tacitly accepted by many Marxist historians that every social order is created exclusively by the internal contradictions of the previous one only at the apex of its development. Thus slavery–feudalism–capitalism form a unilinear succession, which if confined to Europe, would show that social evolution in its highest stages belonged to Europe alone. I would contest the premise. Marx and Engels were conscious, as shown by many of their statements, of the backwardness of European feudal society when compared with contemporary societies in other parts of the world. European feudalism was not necessarily—in terms of commodity production, productivity, etc.—the most advanced social formation in the world in its day. That it was ultimately transformed into capitalism was by no means due to the development of its internal contradictions alone. Joseph Needham has rightly emphasized the importance of Chinese technological discoveries, viz. paper, printing press, pedals, belt-transmission with fly-wheel, mariner's compass, gunpowder, etc., for the technological developments in late- and post-feudal Europe, without which the technological base for the Industrial Revolution would have been inconceivable. Clearly, while human advance has been on a universal scale, different regions in different periods have been ahead of others: China was so clearly ahead of Europe before 1200. And yet it could not for that reason generate capitalism. Other factors too were required for the genesis of capitalism, such as overseas plunder from the close of the fifteenth century onwards and the ravaging of Africa for slaves, on the one hand, and the Scientific Revolution, on the other. We may, by labelling India or China as 'feudal', lay claims to having possessed the potentiality of developing capitalism had colonialism not intervened. Despite the seductiveness of this notion, I hope we will resist it, not only because the factual base has been lacking (despite my colleague Iqtidar Alam Khan's firm arguments), but also because a universal feudal system would go so strikingly against the law of uneven development which is so vital a part of Marxist dialectics.

All social formations contain contradictions; the most important revolve around classes and express themselves in the form of class struggles. For Marxist historians it is not only important to rescue from oblivion the narratives of rebellions of the subjugated classes but also to analyse their nature and the extent to which their participants were aware of their true class affiliations. For there can be class struggles without the participants realizing that they are of this nature.

Unfortunately, since many of the uprisings are written about by their opponents, who were partisans of the ruling classes, we have often no means of knowing what the rebels really thought. Even so, one becomes aware that there was more class consciousness in the peasant rebellions of China or in England in 1381 than in the agrarian uprisings in India of the seventeenth century. The factors behind this backwardness, such as possibly the caste system, must be investigated; these may well have lessons for us today.

We should also not forget that class struggles appear on two planes: risings of the oppressed (e.g., peasant wars) and conflict between two ruling classes (e.g., the aristocracy versus the bourgeoisie in the French Revolution). The latter may involve the other classes in the roles of auxiliaries. We should consider if this has not been true of certain uprisings in India where, as in the case of Shivaji with his *bargis*, the peasants were used to establish a *zamindar*-style state.

In this connection, Gramsci's judgement that peasants cannot create an ideology of their own, is an interesting thesis to test. We may here remark that Ranajit Guha, and other scholars of the 'subaltern school' who use Gramsci's terminology (but in a peculiar way and with additions like 'elite classes'), lay particular stress on the 'autonomy' of the 'subaltern classes' in ideology and culture. Their 'subaltern classes', however, often appear to be not true classes, but merely castes, tribes and communities, where *zamindars* and peasants are seen and accepted as undifferentiated. The view that these composite groups necessarily developed 'autonomous' ideologies (as the working class does, in Marxism) is an unproven premise. If religion is the opium of the people, a religion that attaches itself only to the ruling class and does not command the loyalty of the subject people, would be of no use to the ruling class. The 'hegemony' of the ruling class, in any stable social formation, is only partly based on armed power; it must also be an ideological hegemony. To think that 'subaltern' classes in India have possessed deep-rooted subterranean ideologies of their own is belied by the universal prevalence of caste ideology, which these classes have shared with the ruling class. It is the prevalence of such ideas within the 'subaltern' groups that necessarily limited their protest or resistance and brought about their downfall. The subaltern scholars are happy narrators of tragedy; it is not their task to look for salvation. Such salvation can indeed come not with the oppressed protecting their 'autonomy' in a system of class exploitation, but with their rejecting their past parochialism, espousing the ideology of the working class and joining their peers in a common struggle for liberation.

### Capitalism and Colonialism

Marx in his contributions to the *New York Tribune*, and in *Capital* and other writings, gave special attention to the relationship between the colonies and the emergence of capitalism in England. He framed the theory of primary or primitive accumulation of capital to explain how the Industrial Revolution in England was generated by colonial plunder. Nationalist economists since the time of Dadabhai Naoroji rightly made the tribute or drain of wealth a major Indian grievance against Britain. Unfortunately, British Marxist historians, like Dobb and Hobsbawm, have either omitted a consideration of this aspect of colonial relationships or only assigned it a marginal role in the origins and sustenance of capitalist expansion in Britain. This lapse has surely to be rectified if the real significance of colonialism in the formation of a capitalist economy is to be properly assessed.

In still another matter, there has been a seeming lag in Marxist appraisals of nineteenth-century colonialism. Lenin's *Imperialism, The Highest Stage of Capitalism*, which was taken to suggest that imperialism, as a vehicle of capitalists' striving for territory and wealth abroad, came only with the development of finance capital and monopoly. Indeed, Lenin went so far as to say: 'When free competition in Great Britain was at its height, i.e. between 1840 and 1860, the leading British bourgeois politicians were opposed to colonial policy and were of the opinion that the liberation of the colonies and their complete separation from Great Britain was inevitable and desirable.' I am sure Lenin would not have written these words had he known that Marx himself had regarded the anti-colonial professions of the British free traders of that very period with healthy scepticism. When India had been in the process of annexation, everyone had kept quiet; once the 'natural limits' had been reached, they had 'become loudest with their hypocritical peace cant'. But, then, 'firstly, they had to get it [India] in order to subject it to their sharp philanthropy'. This was written in 1853. In 1859 Marx was writing that 'the "glorious" reconquest of India' after the Mutiny had been essentially carried out 'for securing the monopoly of the Indian market to the Manchester Free Traders'. He thus anticipated the conception of imperialism of free trade, which John Gallagher and Ronald Robinson put forward a hundred years later (1953), but without Marx's economic insights.

The importance of colonies for free-trade capitalism also poses for Marxists a simple theoretical problem. All surplus value is produced by the worker. Thus, surplus values of manufactured goods exported from Britain to India represented the exploitation of the English worker, not the Indian. Yet, these very exports caused vast unemployment and artisans' distress in India. Marx might have had this particular question in mind when he put forward the notion of 'unequal exchange' (without use of the particular term) and said that 'the richer country exploits the poorer one'. The precise mechanism, given Marx's theoretical framework, still remains only dimly illumined. Rosa Luxemburg came near to answering the question by asserting that there could be no 'extended reproduction' in capitalism without exchanges with the non-capitalist sectors (including colonies), through which the additional surplus value would be 'realized'. Whatever the theoretical weaknesses of Rosa Luxemburg's position (for which, see the sympathetic assessment by Joan Robinson and the harsher ones by Bukharin and Paul Sweezy), the question she poses does not go away. It is an area where Marx's own historical understanding of a phenomenon has yet to be appropriately accommodated within his theory of capitalist production and circulation.

It is also time that we reconsider the question of export of capital as an important element of the colonial relationship. Outside the railways, much of British capital in India was not imported, but generated in India from official salaries and mercantile activities of Englishmen. Its later transfer from India to Britain was not true repatriation, but another element of the drain.

### The National Movement
Since R.P. Dutt's *India Today* (1940/1946) there has been considerable writing on the Indian national movement by Marxists. There has been a recent detailed survey by E.M.S. Namboodiripad, *A History of India's Freedom Struggle*. It seems to me that there is now a general understanding that the national movement was a

united front of all classes of the Indian people, the peasantry, other petty bourgeoisie, the bourgeoisie an the working class, to the exclusion of the big landowners and princes. The major nationalist organization, the Indian National Congress, did not always reflect the united front, although, as in the late 1930s, it came very close to such a position.

It is, of course, important in the light of this understanding to review many harsh criticisms of the leaders of the national movement, which can be found in the documents of the communist movement till before the Dutt-Bradley thesis of 1936 and occasionally later. The correction of this attitude need not, however, mean that the communists or the other left groups were incorrect in all the basic positions they took, for example in 1942. An overwhelming preoccupation with the 'errors' of the left, as in the volume edited by Bipan Chandra, is unfortunate, since by this very preoccupation, it belittles the achievements of the left during the national movement and its contributions to it. After all, the creation of the organized kisan movement and the trade unions was mainly the handiwork of the communists and their allies; and that cannot be forgotten.

I would urge that we should treat the national movement (which was always larger than the Congress) as a common heritage. All assessment of individuals playing roles in it must be tempered by the realization that they stood up in opposition to British rule. Dadabhai Naoroji spoke for the silent millions when he brought the poverty of the Indian people and its removal as a major issue between imperialism and the Indian people. Gandhi succeeded in mobilizing those millions—though the forms of that mobilization may have remained limited. These were undying services to the cause of the Indian people. Marxist should be on guard against efforts to treat these as illusory, or insignificant, as in the writings of the Cambridge and subaltern schools, which, by the way, in effect treat the left also as part of the elite leadership.

Today, the positive aspects of the national movement, its bourgeois-democratic values such as secularism, women's rights, national unity, freedom of the press, and parliamentary democracy, need particular emphasis. These can form the initial points for a people's front, in which all classes may be united and can carry forward the cause of democracy and socialism. Such a front could be a worthy successor to our national movement.

### Historiography of Socialism

One of the admitted weaknesses of Marxist historiography lies in the limitations of its analysis of the history of socialist societies, whose existence began with the Russian Revolution of 1917. While in Marx's *Capital*, we have a theoretical framework for understanding 'the laws of motion' of capitalist society, no such framework is available for socialism. It was for long thought sufficient that the state should own industry and that agriculture should be collectivized so as to produce socialism. Not until 1952 did the Soviet Union possess, in Stalin's pamphlet, *Economic Problems of Socialism in the USSR*, an authoritative exposition of some of the most elementary questions relating to a socialist economy. But Stalin left many important problems unresolved or omitted them from view altogether. The only objective that he set for socialism was the enlargement of production on the basis of higher techniques. A more important breakthrough was made by Mao Tse-tung. Althusser commends Mao for making, in his essay *On Contradiction*, a basic addition to the Marxian theory of dialectics. And Oskar Lange commented as early as 1957 that 'it has been the merit of Mao Tse-tung to have re-called with emphasis that socialist society too develops through contradictions'. What Stalin's essay indeed lacked primarily was the spelling out of the contradictions that beset socialist society in the USSR in the particular stage he was dealing with. In his speeches *Correctly Handling Contradictions among the People* and *Ten Great Relationships* in the late 1950s, Mao had clearly begun to evolve a theoretical basis for the analysis of progress towards socialism. But unluckily, by the mid-1960s he seems to have altered his views so as to hold that the contradictions of socialism were being transformed in China into contradictions *between* socialism and capitalism; he thereupon initiated and led the Cultural Revolution, which our Chinese friends now hold to have been an error.

It is, therefore, important to consider what specific contradictions need resolution in a socialist society. These are obviously to be considered in two major stages within socialism: (1) transition to socialism; and (2) socialism, or what Marx called the lower stage of communism. In the first stage there are obvious class contradictions between the proletariat and the former capitalists and landlords, and between the proletariat and the petty bourgeosie (rich peasantry, etc.) There is little dispute involved here, although the time is past when we should accept all the measures actually taken in the USSR and other socialist countries as the only ones possible. A comparison between the Soviet methods of collectivization and the Chinese mobilization for cooperatives and communes suggests important differences in outlook towards the peasantry, which could have lessons for other countries building socialism.

For the second stage, in which the USSR and China now (1988) are, two basic contradictions may be defined by looking at the goals which Marx in his *Critique of the Gotha Programme* set for 'the higher stage of Communism', towards which socialist society would evolve.

(1) Contradiction between 'mental and physical labour': essentially the contradiction generated by higher incomes and authority for bureaucrats, managers, intellectuals, etc., which has to be maintained in socialism for quite a long time in the interest of higher production.

(2) Contradiction between town and country: this often arises in the socialist countries in the form of pressure of industry upon agriculture. It was the source of the theory of socialist primitive accumulation, abandoned in words, but often pursued in practice to promote industrialization.

There are other contradictions, which need also to be examined. Socialism has come about in a system of nation-states, and when one large economically powerful socialist nation deals with others, national contradictions are bound to arise.

How such contradictions are to be resolved, raises the problem of the political system of socialism. In an old controversy (where Stalin was on the side of the angels), the question was raised whether the dictatorship of the proletariat means the dictatorship of the party and whether they were the same. Clearly, there must always exist contradictions between the ruling party apparatus or leadership and the working class, which cannot be glossed over by a mere designation of the party as a working-class party.

There is no doubt that until the abundance of material wealth ushers in the period of communism, these contradictions would continue to exist. This has been proved amply by the Chinese measures after the Cultural Revolution, under which even individual farming has been restored: this is relevant to our Contradiction (2), since both communes and collective farms could be made to surren der surpluses for industry more easily than individual farmers, who may otherwise, apparently, produce more. In the Soviet Union there has recently been more concern with the contradictions between the party and the population, and measures similar to those of the Chinese are on the agenda, relating to both our Contradictions (1) and (2). And yet if what Marx called 'bourgeois rights' continue in socialism, it is also important that as production advances they should be contained. Distribution is as important as production (a point not touched upon by Stalin in his essay); and 'Equality, Liberty and Fraternity' should surely be more than mere slogans in a socialist society—far more than in revolutionary France which gave birth to them.

A Marxist historiography of socialism can be reconstructed on the basis of our comprehension of the various contradictions within socialism. The task can be eminently performed by historians of the socialist countries with direct access to archives and experience. But it is as crucial a task for Marxists outside the socialist countries. One would differ from Charles Bettelheim in the stand he takes, but the task of analysing the Soviet experience from a Marxist point of view, which he aims at in his *Class Struggles in the USSR*, is in principle an unexceptionable one. The gauntlet has been thrown to those who could do it with a different perception of the evolution of socialism. With socialism a reality for the last seventy years, the people's choice for it cannot be invoked on the basis of the inequities of capitalism alone. It is surely obligatory on us to frame our own independent analysis of the history of socialist societies in order to define the contours of the socialism that we aspire to build in India.

# Marx's Perception of India

The hundredth anniversary of the death of Karl Marx (1983) coincides with the hundred and thirtieth anniversary of two of his writings which originally appeared as the despatches of a London correspondent to a New York newspaper, and have since become celebrated documents of Indian history. In the two articles, 'The British Rule in India', and 'The Future Results of the British Rule in India', published in *New York Daily Tribune* (date-lines 10 June and 22 July 1853), Marx consciously set himself to interpret the basic mechanics of the pre-colonial civilization of India, the impact of British rule on India, and the future course of India's development and liberation. Brilliant as they are, and powerful as they have been as sources of inspiration for the Indian national movement, these writings do not yet constitute the complete statement of Marx's understanding of India. In part, this is because Marx wrote other pieces on India as well, and in part, because he continued to study and reflect after he had written these articles in 1853.

Through the 1850s, Marx wrote various articles for the same newspaper in which he made important observations on India; some supplementary statements also occur in the letters which Marx and Engels wrote to each other during the decade, and in articles which Engels wrote at the request of Marx.[1]

[1] The two collections used by me in which the articles of Marx and Engels have been published are Karl Marx and Frederick Engels, *On Colonialism*, Moscow, n.d.; and Karl Marx and Frederick Engels, *The First Indian War of Independence, 1857–1859*, Moscow, n.d.; cited respectively as *On Colonialism* and *FIWI*. For the few articles on India not included in either of the two collections, I have used *Karl Marx, On Colonialism and Modernization*, edited by Shlomo Avineri, New York, 1969 (cited as 'Avineri').

During 1857–58 Marx set down on paper the famous *Grundrisse*, his notes fur self-clarification preparatory to *Capital*, and here he tried to set India in his scheme of pre-capitalist formations.[2] But it is in *Capital* itself, notably in Volume I (1867), that Marx contributed a partial restatement (with important emendations, cautions and new elaborations) of his main theses on India, which obtains added significance by being placed within the classical presentation of his full-scale analysis of capitalism. Scattered statements of value also occur in the posthomous two volumes of *Capital* edited by Engels from Marx's notes.[3]

After 1867, references to India become relatively infrequent in Marx's published writings, but he did not cease to inform himself, as his extensive notes on Indian history taken some time after 1870 amply bear witness.[4] There was a renewed interest too in the village community arising out of Marx's reading of Morgan and Kovalevsky.[5]

Any assessment of Marx's views on India must take into account all his writings spread over practically three decades. We cannot, moreover, simply fix all the pieces together, since over time

---

An earlier publication, Karl Marx, *Articles on India*, introduction by R.P. Dutt, first Indian edition, Bombay, 1943, is now of historical interest only. For their letters, I have used Marx and Engels, *Selected Correspondence, 1846–1895*, edited by Dona Torr, Calcutta, 1945; other publications are cited wherever this collection omits a letter or truncates its text.

[2] I have used Karl Marx, *Grundrisse*, English translation, with foreword by Martin Nicolaus, London, 1973. The historical portion of *Grundrisse* was translated by Jack Cohen, with an introduction by E.J. Hobsbawn, as *Pre-Capitalist Economic Formations*, London, 1964. Where the reference is to the portion of *Grundrisse* contained in the latter, its translation has been followed.

[3] For *Capital*, Vol. I, I have cited the standard reprint of the Moore-Aveling translation edited by Dona Torr, London, 1938. For Vols II and III, I have used the translations published in Moscow: 1957 (Vol. II), 1959 (Vol. III).

[4] Karl Marx, *Notes on Indian History (1664–1858)*, Moscow, n.d. It is unluckily not made clear by the publishers when exactly Marx took down these notes. But it would be presumably after 1870, when Sewell's book, *The Analytical History of India*, was published. The other work used, Elphinstone's *History of India*, had been published as early as 1841, though a new edition appeared in 1874.

[5] On those two fresh sources of interest for Marx, see Daniel Thorner, 'Marx on India and the Asiatic Mode of Production', *Contributions to Indian Sociology*, IX (December 1966), pp. 58–63.

Marx's views might well have undergone change, this being especially true of his interpretation of pre-colonial India.

### Pre-Colonial Society
*The Inherited Generalizations*
When Marx wrote in 1853 of Indian society before the British conquest, he seems to have taken as his starting point the descriptive elements in Hegel's interpretation of the Indian civilization. 'The Hindoos have no history,' Hegel had said, 'no growth expanding into a veritable political condition.'[6] The admitted diffusion of Indian culture had been 'a dumb, deedless expansion'. Thus, 'the people of India have achieved no foreign conquests, but have on every occasion been vanquished themselves.'[7] It is essentially this judgement which is repeated by Marx in the well-known passage: 'Indian society has no history, at least no known history. What we call its history is but the history of successive intruders who founded their empires on the passive basis of that unresisting and unchanging society.'[8]

Hegel saw in the ideology of the Indian ('Hindoo') culture a pantheism of 'Imagination', expressed in the 'universal deification of all finite existence and degradation of the Divine', a deprivation of man 'of personality and freedom';[9] 'the morality which is involved in respect for human life is not found among the Hindoos.'[10] Marx, too, similarly speaks of 'murder itself [being] a religious rite in Hindustan— a brutalizing worship of nature, exhibiting its degradation in the fact that man, the sovereign of nature, fell down on his knees in adoration of Hanuman, the monkey, and Sabbala, the cow.'[11]

In the actual organization of society, the multiplication of divine forms was paralleled by the multiplicity of castes. This was

---

[6] G.W. Friedrich Hegel, *The Philosophy of History*, translated by J. Sibree, New York, 1956, p. 163.
[7] Ibid., p. 142.
[8] *Tribune*; article date-lined 22 July 1853; *On Colonialism*, p. 76. For a criticism of the historicity of this judgement, see D.D. Kosambi, *An Introduction to the Study of Indian History*, Bombay, 1956, p. 11.
[9] Hegel, *Philosophy of History*, p. 141.
[10] Ibid., p. 150.
[11] *Tribune*, article date-lined 10 June 1853; *On Colonialism*, pp. 36–37.

recognized by Hegel to be an advance over an undifferentiated society, but then was immediately condemned by him as establishing 'the most degrading spiritual serfdom'.[12] In the organization of the Indian village, he discerned a similar immutable rigidity:

> The whole income belonging to every village is, as already stated, divided into two parts, of which one belongs to the rajah, the other to the cultivators; but proportionate shares are also received by the provost of the place, the judge, the water-surveyor, the brahmin, who superintends religious worship, the astrologer (who is also a brahmin, and announces the days of good and ill omen), the smith, the carpenter, the potter, the washerman, the barber, the physician, the dancing girls, the musician, the poet. This arrangement is fixed and immutable, and subject to no one's will. All political revolutions, therefore, are matters of indifference to the common Hindoo, for his lot is unchanged.[13]

All this Marx repeats, giving an identical description of the village community for which he quotes *in extenso* from what was probably Hegel's authority as well, a passage in the celebrated *Fifth Report* of 1812.[14] Marx not only condemns these communities as being 'contaminated by distinctions of caste, and by slavery', but also stresses their isolation from political events. He writes indignantly of 'the barbarian egotism' of the Indian villages, which, 'concentrating on some miserable patch of land, had quietly witnessed the ruin of empires, the perpetration of unspeakable cruelties, the massacre of the population of large towns, with no other consideration bestowed upon them than on natural events.'[15]

The comparisons of Hegel in 1830 and Marx in 1853 are brought out not to show that Marx was simply repeating Hegel, but merely to underline the fact that in spite of his vastly different critical

---

[12] Hegel, *Philosophy of History*, p. 144.
[13] Ibid., p. 154.
[14] *Fifth Report from the Select Committee on the Affairs of the East India Company*, 1812, Photo-offset edition, Irish University Press Series of British Parliamentary Papers, Colonies: East India: 3, Shanon, 1969, p. 85. Marx reproduces the passage in *Tribune*, article date-lined 10 June 1853; *On Colonialism*, pp. 35–36.
[15] *Tribune*, article date-lined 10 June 1853; *On Colonialism*, pp. 36–37.

apparatus, Marx had to begin from such assessment of Indian culture as happened to be the accepted one among the best bourgeois thinkers of his day. What is of signal importance, of course, is how he later on revised it and set it in a totally different analytical framework.

For one thing, right from the beginning Marx accepted only those factual pillars of the Hegelian generalizations, which he believed to be sufficiently substantiated. Already in 1853 he had consulted the *Fifth Report*, a voluminous document; also Wilks' *Historical Sketches of South India* (1810), whose passage on the village communities he seems to have drawn on in a letter to Engels;[16] John Campbell's *Modern India* (1852) and James Mill's *History of British India* (1806–18);[17] and volumes of parliamentary debates and reports, especially those preceding the Charter Act of 1853. He refers to the *Manusmriti* ('Manu') which he might well have read in the translation of Sir William Jones;[18] and he specifically alludes to his recent reading of Francois Bernier's *Travels*, which contained a striking description of the Mughal empire in Aurangzeb's time.[19]

This was reasonably large reading, enough to check Hegel's more exorbitant pronouncements. Yet Marx's conception of India was by no means an edited restatement of Hegel. He did the same with the great philosopher's interpretation of India as he had done with his dialectics; that is, he 'inverted' it. He had already posed the question in a letter to Engels: 'Why does the history of the East *appear* as a

---

[16] Marx takes recourse to Wilks' passage (*Historical Sketches of South India*, I, edited by Murray Hammick, Mysore, 1930, pp. 136–39) to insert additions into the quotation from the *Fifth Report* that he gives in his letter to Engels, 14 June 1853; *On Colonialism*, pp. 279–80. Wilks is expressly cited as authority for the description of the village community in *Capital*, I, p. 352n.

[17] Quotations from Campbell occur more than once in the *Tribune* articles; *On Colonialism*, pp. 60, 68, 74, 75, 80. See also *Capital*, I, p. 352n. Mill's *History* is also quoted by Marx in 1853; *On Colonialism*, p. 43.

[18] Marx's reference to Manu occurs in a letter of 14 June 1853; *Selected Correspondence*, p. 62; *On Colonialism*, p. 281.

[19] *Selected Correspondence*, pp. 57–58. Marx also quotes Bernier in *A Contribution to the Critique of Political Economy*, English translation, Moscow, 1970, p. 130. Bernier well deserved Marx's admiration, since he consciously attempts an analysis of the factors behind the decline of the Mughal empire. For Engels' remarks on Bernier, see *Selected Correspondence*, p. 60.

history of religions?'[20] The religious peculiarities which Hegel saw at the foundations of the peculiarities of Indian culture were really themselves the consequences of Indian social organization, pre-eminently the village community.[21] This last, as Marx saw things in 1853, was the crucial institution and explained practically everything.

### The Village Community

Marx's excitement at his discovery of the Indian village community at this time is not surprising. Already in *The German Ideology*, prepared by him and Engels, there was a groping towards an elucidation of the main pre-capitalist forms of property. They had distinguished in order of sequence (a) 'tribal' property corresponding to the 'undeveloped stage of production'—hunting and fishing and early agriculture; (b) 'ancient communal and state ownership', generating class differentiation between citizens and slaves; and (c) 'feudal or estate property with an enserfed small peasantry'.[22] These forms had largely been hypothetical, though form (b) derived from Marx's understanding of Roman society, and form (c) from that of medieval western Europe. Now India too seemed to illustrate, through actual survivals, a system of property and economic and social relationships which broadly accorded with form (b);[23] and the descriptions of English observers themselves could be shown to reinforce the basic point that pre-capitalist societies moved according to 'laws of motion' different from those of the capitalist society.

In *Capital*, I (1867), Marx gives as the first feature of the Indian village community, the prevalence of 'possession in common of the land'.[24] What exactly did this mean? Marx often spoke as if it implied that the villagers in some places at least 'cultivated' the land 'in common'. His source for this seems to have been Wilks, who had

---

[20] Letter of 8 June 1853; *Selected Correspondence*, p. 57. Marx's emphasis.

[21] *Tribune*, article date-lined 10 June 1853; *On Colonialism*, pp. 36–37.

[22] Karl Marx and Frederick Engels, *The German Ideology*, Moscow, 1964, pp. 33–36.

[23] This is presumed in Engels' question (letter of 6 June): 'How does it come about that the orientals do not arrive at landed property even in its feudal form?' *Selected Correspondence*, p. 59.

[24] *Capital*, I, p. 350. In E. and C. Paul's translation, Part I, 1930, p. 377, 'communal ownership of the land'. See also *Capital*, I, p. 325, where Marx ascribes to the Indian communities 'ownership in common of the means of production'.

said: 'In some instances the lands of a village are cultivated in common, and the crop divided up in the proportion of the labour contributed, but generally each occupant tills his own field.'[25] This statement does not appear in the *Fifth Report*, which is quoted for the Indian village community in Marx's 1853 *Tribune* article; but he already shows knowledge of Wilks' description in a letter of 1853: 'In some of these communities the lands of the village are cultivated in common; in most cases each occupant tills his own field.'[26] In *Grundrisse* (1857–58) Marx refers to the 'common organization of labour' surviving in 'some tribes of India'.[27] In *Capital*, I, he follows Wilks closely, and indeed expressly cites him; he further assigns communal cultivation to village communities of the 'simplest form'.[28]

A formulation of the historical relationship between communal agriculture and communal ownership was already offered by Marx in *Grundrisse*: it was from communal agriculture that communal property originated; but once established, communal property tended to survive the development of individual peasant agriculture.[29]

In an article that Marx contributed to the *Tribune* while he was composing *Grundrisse*, he appealed to 'a more thorough study of the institutions of Hindustan' to support 'the opinion that by the original Hindu institutions, the property of the land was in the village corporations, in which resided the power for allotting it out to individuals for cultivation.'[30] Here Marx has obviously in mind the common practice of village headmen allotting wasteland for cultivation to outsiders or willing peasants. The right tended to establish, in Marx's eyes, corporate village ownership.

In *Grundrisse*, Marx argues that such ownership by the village community demarcated the 'Asiatic' form of the community from the two other developed forms of that institution, viz. the Roman (where land was owned by the urban community) and the

[25] Lt. Col. Wilks, *Historical Sketches of South India* (originally published in London, 1810), I, edited by Murray Hammick, Mysore, 1930, p. 137.
[26] Letter of 14 June 1853; *On Colonialism*, p. 280.
[27] *Pre-Capitalist Formations*, p. 70; *Grundrisse*, p. 473.
[28] *Capital*, I, p. 351.
[29] *Pre-Capitalist Formations*, pp. 68–69; *Grundrisse*, p. 472.
[30] Published 25 May 1858; *On Colonialism*, p. 163.

Germanic (where the unit of ownership was the homestead).[31]

Besides common land ownership, Marx saw in the Indian village community two phenomena which were apparently contradictory but were well integrated into it. On the one hand, there was a lack of development of division of labour, which resulted in 'the domestic union of agricultural and manufacturing pursuits'. This observation occurs in one of the *Tribune* articles of 1853, but it continued to occupy a central position in Marx's analysis and recurs in *Grundrisse* and in *Capital*, I, as well as elsewhere.[32] On the other hand, there was a development on the opposite extreme: the establishment of 'an unalterable division of labour'. This was realized through the caste system supplying, 'with the irresistible authority of the law of nature', the hereditary 'individual artificer, the smith, the carpenter, and so on'. The economic basis for this was the 'unchanging market' that the community provided to the artisan, prohibiting any alteration in the social division of labour once fixed.[33] Though the classic statement of this phenomenon is formulated in *Capital*, I, Marx had surely been from the beginning aware of the hereditary occupations and the system of caste within the community.[34]

Marx in 1853 spoke deprecatingly of the 'stagnatory, vegetative life' inherent in the Indian community.[35] In 1857–58, he went on to argue that the cause of this imperviousness to change lay within the community's structure, that is, within those elements of domestic industry and caste specialization which have just been described. He says:

> The Asiatic form [of the community, as against the Roman and Germanic] necessarily survives longest and most stubbornly. This is due to the fundamental principle on which it is based, that is, that the individual does not become independent of the community, that

---

[31] *Pre-Capitalist Formations*, pp. 71–82; *Grundrisse*, pp. 474–86.
[32] *On Colonialism*, pp. 35–36; *Pre-Capitalist Formations*, pp. 70, 83, 91; *Grundrisse*, pp. 473, 486, 493; *Capital*, I, p. 350.
[33] *Capital*, I, pp. 351–52. On castes as arising out of the 'conversion of fractional work into the life-calling of one man', see *Capital*, I, p. 331.
[34] See for example the reference to 'hereditary means of subsistence' and 'the distinctions of caste' in *Tribune*, article date-lined 10 June 1853; *On Colonialism*, pp 36–37.
[35] *Pre-Capitalist Formations*, p. 83; *Grundrisse*, p. 486.

the circle of production is self-sustaining, unity of agriculture and craft manufacture, etc.[36]

Elsewhere, Marx argues that conquests of one tribe by another, given different internal structures of the conquered society, have helped to alter the form of property, leading to either slavery or serfdom. But, owing to the internal solidity of the Indian community, subjugation does not subvert its basic nature: 'Slavery and serfdom are simply further developments of property based on tribalism. They necessarily modify all its forms. This they are least able to do in the Asiatic form.'[37]

What one must remember here is that Marx is speaking of the internal conditions of the community, not of society as a whole; and even within the village community, he had noticed the existence of slavery as early as the *Tribune* article of 1853.[38] What he means is that 'conquerors' could obtain larger surplus by exploiting the community, economically solidified as it was, than by exploiting directly the individuals who composed it.[39] To the system of exploitation to which the Indian village communities came to be subjected Marx gave the designation of despotism; and only with its description could his picture of pre-colonial Indian society be regarded as complete.

### Despotism, Surplus and Commodities

Marx had already read Bernier in 1853, and in a letter to Engels he quotes him extensively. Now Bernier's main thesis was that the Mughal empire and the other oriental states were decaying because there was no private property in the soil. Marx noted Bernier's statement that the king was 'the sole and only proprietor of the land', and added: 'Bernier rightly considers that the basic form of all phenomena in the East—he refers to Turkey, Persia, Hindustan—is

---

[36] Ibid.
[37] *Pre-Capitalist Formations*, p. 91; *Grundrisse*, p. 493.
[38] Date-lined 10 June 1853; *On Colonialism*, p. 37.
[39] See *Capital*, III, pp. 771–72, where Marx says that individual bondage in the form of serfdom is not necessary where, 'as in Asia', the state is the 'landlord'. 'Under such circumstances there need exist no stronger political or economic pressure than that common to all subjection to that state.'

to be found in the fact that *no private property in land existed*. This is the real key even to the oriental heaven.'[40]

But Bernier's description, while it showed that the Indian property system was quite different from that of Europe, could not be reconciled with the existence of communal property in India. Marx sought to resolve the problem in *Grundrisse*: whether the property resided in the community or the state, the individual 'is in fact propertyless'. Marx then introduces a distinction between 'property' and 'possession', so that 'the all-embracing unity which stands above all these small common bodies may appear as the higher or sole proprietor, the real communities only as hereditary possessors.'[41] Further:

> The despot here appears as the father of all the numerous lesser communities, thus realizing the common unity of all. . . . The surplus product . . . belongs to this highest unity. Oriental despotism therefore appears to lead to a legal absence of property. In fact, however, its foundation is tribal or common property.[42]

This rather mystical view of the property of the ruler was apparently abandoned by Marx within barely months of putting it down on paper. In a *Tribune* article of 1858, on Indian land tenures, he was willing to quote approvingly an opinion that the

> alleged property in the government [is] nothing more than the derivation of title from the sovereign, theoretically acknowledged in all countries the codes of which are based on the feudal law and substantially acknowledged in all countries whatever in the power of the Government to levy taxes on the land to the extent of the needs of the government.[43]

---

[40] Letter of 2 June 1853; *Selected Correspondence*, p. 58. Emphasis in original. The statement in question occurs in Francois Bernier, *Travels in the Mughal Empire, AD 1656–1668*, translated by A. Constable, edited by V.A. Smith, Oxford, 1916, pp. 5, 204, 226, 232, 238.

[41] *Pre-Capitalist Formations*, p. 69; *Grundrisse*, pp. 472–73.

[42] *Pre-Capitalist Formations*, pp. 69–70; *Grundrisse*, p. 473.

[43] Published 25 May 1858; *On Colonialism*, p. 162. In an article in *Tribune*, 3 April 1858, doubtfully attributed to Marx it is even stated: 'The land, however, in India did not belong to the government, the greater proportion of it being as much private property as in England many of the natives holding their estates by titles six or seven hundred years old.' (Avineri, p. 278.)

In the last words of this quotation Marx seems to suggest that the sovereign's property in land was related to the size of the land tax. If it accounted for the bulk of the surplus, if, that is, it was practically rent, then the king was, in fact, claiming what was the due of the land-owner.[44] It was this which was central to any recognition of the sovereign as the proprietor. The argument is made entirely explicit in *Capital*, III, the draft of which was composed by Marx in 1863–67:

> . . . in Asia . . . [where the state] stands over them [the direct producers] as their landlord and simultaneously as sovereign, then rent and taxes coincide, or rather, there exists no tax which differs from this form of ground-rent [labour rent converted into tributary relationship]. Sovereignty here consists in the ownership of land concentrated on a national scale. But on the other hand, no private ownership of land exists, although there is both private and common possession of the land.[45]

'Oriental despotism', in Marx's analysis, is therefore essentially rent-receiving sovereignty and stands practically divested of the other political features assigned to it in European liberal thought such as arbitrary and absolute monarchy.[46]

The 1858 article in the *Tribune* which we have quoted shows that Marx was aware of the actual complexities of the pre-British Indian society, where there existed not a simple 'tributary relationship' between peasant and state, but a triangular one, involving another class of claimants to the surplus, namely, the '*zamindars*'. Marx recognizes that the *zamindars* claimed to be land-owners (subject to certain assessments due to government), treating the peasants as mere 'tenants-at-will'. He, however, invoked the contrary official British view that 'the zamindars and talukadars were nothing but

---

[44] The claim that the king was the owner of the soil is not made by any Indian authority before the eighteenth century, whereas it was the usual statement on the lips of European observers from the sixteenth century onwards. It was clearly the land-tax, often termed by them 'rent', which suggested to them the existence of an all-embracing royal property in land. See Irfan Habib, *Agrarian System of Mughal India*, Bombay, 1963, pp. 112–13.

[45] *Capital*, III, pp. 771–72.

[46] Compare Macaulay who in his obituary of Lord William Bentinck contrasted 'British freedom' with 'oriental despotism'.

officers of the government appointed to look after, to collect, and to pay over to the prince the assessment due from the village.'[47] In other words, their claimed rights were a usurpation of those of the state. Yet 'prescription [was] in their favour'; and 'in Oudh these feudal land-holders had gone very far in curtailing alike the claims of the government and the rights of the cultivators.'[48]

The crucial implication of these observations is that to Marx the Asiatic state did not represent simply a single person or even only a simple 'higher community'; it implied the existence of a definite social class, which appropriated the surplus through the mechanism of the tax-rent. Only out of such a class, in the process of a territorial dispersal of the claims to surplus, could develop local magnates as those of Oudh, with such exercise of the rights of lordship as to obtain from even so careful a writer as Marx the designation of 'feudal land-owners'.

If it is once recognized that individual land-ownership could be created out of state landlordism by acts of usurpation, could not state landlordism itself have been created by acts of conquest, the supreme usurpation? In fact, in 1853, Marx thought that the institution of 'no property in land', i.e. of state property, might have been established by the Muslims 'throughout the whole of Asia'.[49] This piece of speculation had great potentiality, suggesting that in its fullest form the tax-rent was the particular characteristic of Islamic polities. This was never taken up by Marx later on; but it remains of singular value in suggesting that he was prepared to recognize even in 1853 that history could well have had a part to play, after all, in shaping the basic forms of structure of Indian or Asiatic societies.

In one major respect, Marx seems to have revised or refined his ideas during the ten years or so preceding the publication of *Capital*, I. This was the realm of exchange or commodity production within the pre-colonial Indian society, a fundamental issue for any understanding of its historical nature. In *Grundrisse*, Marx notes that in communities of all types (Indian, Roman, Germanic), 'the economic object is the production of use-values', so that the communities

---

[47] *Tribune*, 7 June 1858; *On Colonialism*, p. 123.
[48] *Tribune*, 7 June 1858; *On Colonialism*, pp. 163–64.
[49] Letter of 14 June 1853; *Selected Correspondence*, p. 62.

could have produced only little for exchange.[50] Indeed, the 'system of production founded on exchange' characterized the 'historic dissolution' of the communal form.[51] In *Capital*, III, the 'Indian community', like the society of European antiquity and the middle ages, is said to possess, through the union of agriculture and handicraft, a 'mode of production' able to sustain a 'natural economy'—or an economy without exchange.[52] In *Capital*, I, Marx shows that surplus could be exacted and consumed without any mediation of exchange. The case of the Indian magnate is cited as an illustration: he appropriates the agricultural 'surplus-product' as 'tribute or rent', and then sets out to partly consume the surplus in kind, partly have it used by 'non-agricultural labourers'. 'Production and reproduction on a progressively increasing scale go on their way here', not only without the intervention of capital, as Marx stresses, but in fact without any commodity circulation at all.[53]

Apparently Richard Jones is Marx's authority for this illustration; and if we had nothing else from Marx, we may well have supposed that the old Indian society was marked by an absence of commodity exchange in all its sectors, inside the community as well as outside. But the classic passage on the Indian community in the same volume of *Capital* dispels all doubts on the matter, and shows that Richard Jones's Indian magnate was not, in Marx's view, characteristic of the Indian society as a whole: he merely illustrated a possibility, and no more.

This is because in the passage of *Capital* we are speaking of, Marx contrasts the internal conditions of production of the village with 'the division of labour brought about in Indian society as a whole, by means of the exchange of commodities'. Thus, outside the village, it was the commodity and not the 'natural economy' that reigned. This is made explicit by the very words that Marx uses to qualify the domain of exchange in the society containing the communities: 'It is the surplus alone that becomes a commodity, and a portion of even that, not until it has reached the hands of the state into

---

[50] *Pre-Capitalist Formations*, pp. 80–81; *Grundrisse*, p. 485.
[51] *Grundrisse*, p. 882.
[52] *Capital*, III, p. 767.
[53] *Capital*, I, p. 610.

whose hands from time immemorial a certain quantity of these products has found its way in the shape of rent in kind.'[54]

These statements are of crucial significance, though their implications have been seldom recognized. These may be summed up as follows:

(a) The peasant raised a part of his produce for his own subsistence, and this did not go on the market. The combination of agriculture with handicraft ensured that the peasant did not buy anything on the market. He himself lived in a 'natural economy'.

(b) Of the remainder of the produce—the surplus product—the peasant parted with a portion in payment of rent-in-kind. This, Marx thought, was the normal mode of surplus acquisition in Asia.[55] The part of the product taken in rent, was put on the market after it had been obtained by the state, and thus was converted into commodities outside the village.

(c) Another portion of the surplus (presumably the smaller) became a commodity inside the village in that it was raised for sale on the market by the peasant who then paid money-rent; the market for the product, however, remained outside the village.

Natural economy was thus confined to the village; outside of it commodity circulation dominated, creating a division of labour based on its own operation. The contrast is striking between these conditions postulated for pre-colonial India and what Marx describes as the situation 'in many Roman latifundia, or upon the villages of Charlemagne, or more or less during the entire [European] Middle Ages', where not the whole or bulk of the surplus, but 'only a relatively small portion of that part of the product which represents the landlord's revenue' enters 'the process of circulation'.[56] Is it then possible that Marx was allowing a much higher level of monetization in pre-colonial India than in medieval Europe?

It is a pity that we have little means of knowing why Marx felt he had to introduce these general qualifications to allow for such a large realm of commodity circulation in Indian society. He may possibly have come across statements in the *Fifth Report* about

---

[54] Ibid., p. 351.
[55] *Capital*, III, p. 776.
[56] Ibid., p. 767.

Indian peasants paying the land tax or rents in money.[57] Moreover, he had spoken in a *Tribune* article of the original *zamindars* in Bengal being replaced wholesale by 'mercantile speculators', under the impetus of the Permanent Settlement. These speculators must have been present in the older society as possessors of large enough merchant capital if they could later buy over 'all the land of Bengal'.[58]

Marx also knew that the urban structure sustained by the agrarian surplus had within it an exchange economy. Richard Jones himself distinguishes, in a passage quoted by Marx, between the town artisan in India ('where the admixture of Europeans has not changed the scene'), who was dependent on the vagaries of the market, and the rural artisan directly maintained by the village.[59] In *Capital*, I, Marx quotes another authority for the description of the Indian weaver as 'merely a *detached* individual working a web when ordered by a customer'.[60] Caste here operated not to weld the artisan permanently into the community but essentially to enable 'special skill' to be 'accumulated from generation to generation'.[61] Here, then, the Indian caste system could be quite consistent with independent petty production in an environment of commodity circulation.

In 1853 Marx had derived the information from Bernier that the seventeenth-century Indian cities had been 'properly speaking, nothing but military camps'. Through a long quotation from Bernier he seems to emphasize the large numbers of soldiers and camp-followers and their ability to live at a bare subsistence level.[62] This tallied with Richard Jones's observation that the 'artisans of the towns' in India drew their wages from 'surplus revenue from land'— a fund the greater part of which was 'distributed by the state and its

---

[57] Sir John Shore in his famous Minute of 18 June 1789, forming Appendix I to the *Fifth Report*, says: 'In general throughout Bengal, the rents are paid by the ryots in money' (p. 192, paragraph 226).

[58] Date-lined 19 July 1853; *On Colonialism*, p. 73.

[59] *Theories of Surplus Value*, III, Moscow, 1971, pp. 434–35.

[60] *Capital*, I, pp. 331–32. The quotation (emphasis ours) is taken by Marx from Hugh Murray and James Wilson, *Historical and Descriptive Account of British India*, Vol. II, Edinburgh, 1832.

[61] *Capital*, I, pp. 331–32.

[62] *Selected Correspondence*, pp. 57–58. The quotations Marx gives appear to be taken from the French passages corresponding to Bernier, *Travels*, pp. 219–20, 251–52, 381–90. Marx makes a brief reference to Bernier in this context also in *Theories of Surplus Value*, III, p. 435.

officers'; the urban artisans thus had to migrate to whatever new seats their royal or aristocratic customers shifted to. In the quotation that Marx gives from Jones, the latter contrasted this migratory nature of the Indian artisan with the dependence of the European worker on the locales of 'fixed capital'.[63] But one may, perhaps, see the main difference between India and post-feudal Europe to lie in the nature of the market for urban craft-products: in India, it was confined to the aristocracy and its dependents, while in Europe it included the rural gentry as well as the emerging middle classes.

A question which Marx sought to answer from 1853 onwards was why the state in India or Asia should have succeeded in converting its tax into rent, while this did not happen in Europe. This could partly be explained by the 'unresisting' nature of the Indian community; but working upon a suggestion originally made by Engels, he found an economic factor behind the state's direct control over the produce. This was artificial irrigation which, on the scale needed in India, could only be undertaken by a centralized despotism.[64] The thesis, after being put forward in 1853, was repeated in *Grundrisse*, and then again—in a rather low key—in *Capital*, I.[65] Engels in 1878 was to set it forth again in *Anti-Duhring*.[66] The substantiation offered always remained rather slender, though it provided fuel enough for large-scale theorization about 'hydraulic' societies in subsequent literature, crowned by Karl A. Wittfogel's *Oriental Despotism*, 1957.[67]

### The 'Asiatic Mode': Reconsiderations

Well before 1867, Marx had thus evolved a comprehensive notion of the fundamental elements of the economic and political

[63] *Theories of Surplus Value*, III, p. 435.
[64] In a letter to Marx, 6 June 1853, Engels spoke of 'artificial irrigation' as 'the first condition of agriculture' in the large zone extending from the Sahara to 'India and Tartary'. He went on to distinguish three departments of oriental governments: finance, war and public works. *Selected Correspondence*, p. 59. Marx bodily incorporated these ideas in *Tribune*, article date-lined 10 June 1853; *On Colonialism*, pp. 33–34.
[65] *Pre-Capitalist Formations*, pp. 70–71; *Grundrisse*, pp. 473–74; and *Capital*, I, p. 523n.
[66] *Anti-Duhring*, Moscow, 1947, p. 269.
[67] I offered a critique of this work in *Enquiry*, No. 6, Delhi, pp. 54–73.

system of India and (as he thought) of much of Asia before the colonial incursion. In 1859 he appeared confident that the 'Asiatic' merited a separate place in the classification of the major 'modes of production' in human history.[68]

This system of production in Marx's conception clearly consisted, as we have seen, of two elements, the village community and Oriental despotism. The first was perhaps more crucial in that it defined the form of the labour process: self-sustaining petty production without individual bondage but with fixed occupations. The 'despotism' lay in the identity of tax with rent, that is, the appropriation of the surplus through the agency of the state. While 'natural economy' prevailed in the village, commodity circulation could still develop outside of it on the basis of the disposal of the surplus.

This being so, the pre-colonial Indian society (as the classic 'Asiatic' type) was clearly a developed class society, with a ruling class of surplus appropriators and a division of labour based on exchange outside the village community. Hobsbawm can, therefore, hardly be right when he supposes that Marx's 'Asiatic system is not yet a class society, or, if it is a class society, then it is the most primitive form of it.'[69] This not only runs counter to Marx's whole concept of the existence of surplus appropriation in the 'Asiatic system' but is also contradicted by what Engels says in *Anti-Duhring* (1878), a book whose text was checked and approved by Marx. There Engels expressly describes the emergence of 'an oriental despot or satrap' as part of the 'process of formation of classes' with 'the separate individual rulers [uniting] into a ruling class'.[70] The Asiatic society was, then, a full-fledged class society.

Persuasive as Marx's analysis of the pre-colonial economy set in the form of the 'Asiatic mode' may appear to us, there seems to

[68] 'In broad outlines, the Asiatic, the ancient, the feudal and the bourgeois modes of production may be designated as epochs marking the progress of the economic development of society.' Preface to *Contribution to the Critique of Political Economy*, p. 21.

[69] E.J. Hobsbawm, Introduction, *Pre-Capitalist Formations*, p. 34. If no classes then no class struggles. Thus Wittfogel: 'The history of hydraulic society suggests that class struggles far from being a chronic disease of all mankind, is the luxury of multi-centered and open [western] societies.' *Oriental Despotism*, p. 71.

[70] *Anti-Duhring*, pp. 268–69.

be good reason to believe that Marx developed considerable reservations about the 'Asiatic' concept after 1867. For one thing, there were too many questions that had been left unresolved.

The first question related to the place of the Asiatic system in the order of stages of social progress. In his 1859 preface to the *Critique of Political Economy*, Marx speaks as if the Asiatic system preceded classical antiquity. He also says in the same work that the 'Indian communal property' contained the 'various prototypes of Roman and German property'.[71] In the 1867 German text of *Capital*, I, Marx put the rise of the classical (Roman) community 'after the primitive oriental communal ownership of the land had disappeared'.[72] He reiterated the same view in his letters in 1868 and 1870.[73] But the classic Indian communities produced a surplus which was necessary to maintain Asiatic despotism, as we have seen, while the original primitive communities were unable to produce a surplus at all, as is made clear by Engels in *Anti-Duhring*: slavery originated as soon as the community began to produce a surplus.[74] The Asiatic system (i.e. the surplus-producing community and the rent-receiving state) could not therefore have preceded slavery; at best it could only have developed parallel to the formation of slave and feudal societies. Such seems to be Engels's own view (and since Marx gave his approval to his text, the view of Marx as well), since in *Anti-Duhring* the emergence of the 'oriental despot or satrap' is treated as part of the very process which also produced the division of society into master and slave.[75]

While the Indian or Asiatic society thus lost its primitive antiquity, Marx could not have been unaware of a process which he had so far assumed, but to whose implications he had previously paid

---

[71] *A Contribution to the Critique of Political Economy*, pp. 21, 33n.

[72] *Capital*, I, translated by E. and C. Paul, p. 351n. The word 'oriental' is omitted in the Moore-Aveling translation, *Capital*, I, p. 325n.

[73] 'The Asian or Indian forms of property constitute the initial ones everywhere in Europe', letter of 14 March 1868; *Pre-Capitalist Formations*, p. 139. In this letter Marx also says that Maurer's work had confirmed this view. In a letter of 17 February 1870, he says still more positively that 'communal property', whether Slavic or other, is 'of Indian origin'. Marx, *Letters to Kugelmann*, London, n.d. (1935?), p. 99.

[74] *Anti-Duhring*, pp. 267–71.

[75] Ibid., pp. 268–69.

little attention. If in the original form the Indian community had practised communal cultivation, then the change to individual petty production, which was now the dominant form,[76] must represent a fundamental alteration in the very essence of that 'unchanging' community. A contradiction must exist too between communal property and individual production. The matter was brought forcefully to Marx's notice in relation not to India, but to Russia: yet the logic applies to both. In the combination of 'common ownership [and] divided petty cultivation', 'mobile property, an element which plays an increasing part even in agriculture, gradually leads to differentiation among the members of the community, and therefore makes it possible for a conflict of interests to arise, particularly under fiscal pressure of the state.'[77]

This may be considered alongside the fact that Marx in his notes on Kovalevsky's work, *Communal Landholding* (1879), had already marked the emergence of private property within the Indian village community, leading to the genesis of contradictions within it.[78] It was, therefore, no longer possible to hold that the Indian community had been internally a totally stagnant institution.

In these same notes on Kovalevsky, Marx restates his view that the Indian communities belonged to a system different from that of Germano–Roman feudalism. What is interesting here is that the main points of difference marked are the absence of serfdom in India, and the lack of inalienability of land to 'non-members of the noble class'.[79] These are hardly features that could put the Indian commu-

---

[76] This is acknowledged to be the case by Marx right from his 1853 writings (see above).

[77] Second draft of letter to Vera Zasulich, 8 March 1881, *Pre-Capitalist Formations*, p. 143.

[78] See Daniel Thorner in *Contributions to Indian Sociology*, II, 1966, pp. 60–62. One wonders what Marx would have said if he had come across the earliest known description of the functioning of the Indian village community in the *Milindapanho* (c. first century AD). When the village headman summons all the villagers to assemble, it is only the 'heads of houses' who are expected to respond: 'There are many who do not come: women and men, slave girls and slaves, hired workmen, servants, peasantry [lit., villagers], sick people, oxen, buffaloes, sheep and goats and dogs—but all these do not count.' *Questions of King Milinda*, I, translated by Rhys Davids, pp. 208–9.

[79] Quoted in Hobsbawm, Introduction, *Pre-Capitalist Formations*, p. 58.

nities in a lower historical position even from the point of view of
development of commodity circulation and private property.

If the Indian community was subject to historical development, it was all the more the case with the economic and political
superstructure, the machinery of the so-called Oriental despotism. In
1853 Marx had touched upon the question whether the Islamic
polities had been responsible for the sovereign's claims to property in
land.[80] It is possible that later on Marx became aware of the controversy regarding this matter. Kovalevsky, in the same work of 1879
read by Marx, criticized the ascription to the 'Mahometan theory and
practice' of an alleged rejection of private property in land.[81] Thus,
even the notion of the state as the landed proprietor in Asia and the
absence of individual private property in land seemed to dissolve,
though this did not necessarily affect the practical identity of the tax
with the surplus ('rent').

Marx's further reading on India included Elphinstone's
*History of India*, from which some time during the 1870s he took
copious notes. Most of the facts taken down related to straight-
forward dynastic history; in respect of Akbar, the great Mughal emperor (1556–1605), however, Marx wrote down (and underlined) a
summary of his principal revenue measures. He noted that Akbar
fixed one-third of the produce as the tax-standard, and, still more important, that he took the tax in cash by averaging past prices for purposes of commutation.[82] As we have seen, Marx in *Capital*, I, had
already allowed for part-payment of land revenue in cash. But this
new information could also have modified the assumption, stated in
*Capital*, III, that the rent-in-kind was the mainstay of 'the stationary
social conditions' in Asia:[83] the introduction of the cash-nexus contradicted both elements in this assumption, one, of the dominance of
rent-in-kind, and the other, of 'stationary conditions'.

Finally, even the Asiatic 'despotism' began to lose its previous awesome individuality. A.L.H. Gunawardana points out that
in his notes on Henry Sumner Maine's *Lectures on the Early History*

---

[80] Letter of 14 June 1853; *On Colonialism*, p. 62.
[81] See Rosa Luxemburg, *The Accumulation of Capital*, translated by A.
Schwarzchild, London, 1951, pp. 372–73n.
[82] Karl Marx, *Notes on Indian History*, p. 42.
[83] *Capital*, III, p. 776.

*of Institutions* (1875), Marx expresses direct opposition to the idea of
the state standing above society and insists that everywhere it arose
out of social contradictions.[84]

There is thus enough evidence that Marx's continued reading on India after 1867 led him to reconsider the force of a number
of his earlier ideas on pre-colonial India. Moreover, the new theoretical formulation of primitive communism, reinforced by Morgan's
work, suggested a universalization of some characteristics of the
Indian community (notably the alleged original communal cultivation) and their relegation everywhere to an earlier epoch. Correspondingly, the basic mechanics of social evolution subsequent to that
primitive stage also tended to be universalized. The stagnant Asiatic
mode no longer fitted the theoretical framework as it was now
refined, just as more detailed investigations had suggested a reformu-
lation of some of the earlier theses on the Indian communities and
fiscal system. It is certain that Engels alone is not to blame for the
abandonment of the Asiatic mode.[85]

The reserve apparently entertained by Marx in his later years
in respect of the Asiatic category did not imply that he was willing to
overlook the specific features of Indian society and economy. This is
clear from his objection to any designation of the Indian communities
as 'feudal'. It is also best to remember that his analysis of the union
of agriculture and craft and the immutable division of labour, as the
twin pillars of the Indian village economy, is of lasting value. Furthermore, the economic historian today must ask the same questions as
Marx did, about the precise implications of the extraction of 'rent' in
the shape of land tax. The contrast that Marx drew between an
exchange economy based on the disposal of the surplus and the 'natural economy' within the village serving for its basis, must still stand,
though the intrusion of commodity production and differentiation

---

[84] *Indian Historical Review*, II (2), p. 387. Gunawardana infers from this
that the notes reflect 'Marx's dissatisfaction with his own formulation in
the *Grundrisse* on the nature of the oriental state.'

[85] When Engels wrote his *Origin of the Family, Private Property and the
State*, 1884, he made not the slightest allusion to this system. See especially
the passage where he speaks of 'the three great epochs of civilization',
English edition, Moscow, 1948, p. 240. Hobsbawm's explanation for this
omission is rather strained; see Introduction, *Pre-Capitalist Formations*,
p. 52n. See also Wittfogel, *Oriental Despotism*, p. 386.

within the village might yet have been more extensive than Marx had allowed for. In his view, the urban economy was largely parasitical; and here we have an important suggestion as to why the potentialities of capitalistic development in the Indian economy remained thwarted.[86] All these form an important legacy of ideas for Indian historians, who may thereby be inspired still more to explore the mechanics of change in a society which Marx himself had once thought rather unjustly to be unchanging.

### Colonialism and India

### The Tribute

The parliamentary debates preceding the Charter Act of 1853 provided Marx with considerable information on the English East India Company, and this he supplemented from other literature. He was able to trace the pre-colonial history of the Company from the beginning of the eighteenth century, when in England 'the old landed aristocracy [had] been defeated, and the bourgeoisie [was] not able to take its place except under the banner of moneyocracy, or the "haute finance".'[87] The East India Company was a great corporate organization of the latter class, claiming a monopoly of the East India trade and invoking commercial freedom to export treasure: Marx comments wryly on 'the curiosity' that 'the Indian monopolists were the first preachers of free trade in England'.[88]

Marx saw the conquest of India as emanating from the financiers' desire to enlarge their capital by the revenues of conquered

---

[86] This, of course, is an important subject of debate among Indian historians. I have presented my own views in 'Potentialities of Capitalistic Development in the Economy of Mughal India', *Enquiry*, NS, III (3), pp. 1–56; pp. 180–232 of the present volume. By designating the medieval Indian society as 'feudal', some Indian and Soviet historians tend to assume that there were possibilities of a growth of capitalism but that these were aborted owing to the British conquest. V.I. Pavlov surveys the debate with much direct use of evidence in his *Historical Premises for India's Transition to Capitalism*, Moscow, 1978, pp. 4–159.

[87] *Tribune*, article date-lined 24 June 1853; *On Colonialism*, p. 41.

[88] *Tribune*, article date-lined 24 June 1853; *On Colonialism*, p. 46. Marx especially refers to the two great partisans of the Company in the mercantilist controversy: Thomas Mun, author of *A Discourse of Trade, from England unto the East Indies* (1621), and Sir Josiah Child, who wrote *A Treatise wherein is demonstrated 1. That East India Trade is the Most National of all Foreign Trade* (1668).

territories. They 'had even as early as 1689 conceived the establishment of a dominion in India, and making territorial revenues one of
their sources of emolument'.[89] This direct plunder of India by taxation remained the key feature of the English regime in India: 'During
the whole course of the eighteenth century the treasures transported
from India to England were gained much less by comparatively insignificant commerce than by the direct exploitation of that country, and
by the colossal fortunes there extorted and transmitted to England.'[90]

By the 'direct exploitation' of the country was meant first of
all the appropriation of the income of the government. The Company
took over the sovereign's right to tax-rent already established in India
and greatly enlarged it. In *Capital*, III, Marx spoke of the disastrous
consequences for the direct producer, when the rent-in-kind 'is met
with and exploited by a conquering commercial nation, e.g., the
English in India'.[91] This urge for 'fiscal exploitation' naturally reduced the expenditure on public works to the barest minimum. Out of
gross revenues of £19.8 million in 1851–52, only £0.17 million were
spent on 'roads, canals, bridges and other works of public necessity'.[92]
As for the main object of expenditure, Marx noted that 'nowhere [else]
so extravagant is a provision made for the governing class itself' as
in India.[93]

The plunder of India was carried out not only through taxation, but also through the creation of personal fortunes. These in the
eighteenth century had been mainly created by extortion, bribery and
monopoly.[94] In *Capital*, I, Marx cited the estimated figure of £6
million for the value of 'gifts' obtained from Indians during the ten
years 1757–66; he also gave an illustration of how money was made

[89] *Tribune*, article date-lined 24 June 1853; *On Colonialism*, p. 44.

[90] *Tribune*, article date-lined 24 June 1853; *On Colonialism*, p. 47.

[91] *Capital*, III, p. 777.

[92] Marx is here referring to a speech by Bright, *Tribune*, article date-lined
22 June 1853; *On Colonialism*, pp. 27, 30. See also *Tribune*, article date-
lined 19 July 1853; *On Colonialism*, p. 72, for the low percentage of
revenue expended on public works in different provinces.

[93] *Tribune*, 23 July 1858; *On Colonialism*, p. 180.

[94] 'Did they [the English] not, in India, to borrow an expression of that great
robber, Lord Clive himself, resort to atrocious extortion when simple
corruption could not keep pace with their rapacity?' *Tribune*, article date-
lined 22 July 1853; *On Colonialism*, p. 81.

by favoured Englishmen through inland commercial monopoli:s.[95]
The large incomes continued into the nineteenth century, but now
mainly as the principal burden on the revenues. Investigating these in
1857, Marx found that 'the profits and benefits which accrue to
individual British subjects' were 'very considerable'; and 'their gain
goes on to increase the sum of the national wealth' of England. He,
however, noted that part of the costs of the possession of India had
now begun to be placed on the British tax-payer.[96]

Marx was, of course, not the first to speak of the drain of
wealth from India. It was recognized as the basis of the Indian
connection with Britain as early as the eighteenth century by parlia-
mentarians like Burke and administrators like Sir John Shore and
Lord Cornwallis.[97] The ruin of India through the levy of tribute continued to strain the consciences of English liberals such as James Mill
and Montgomery Martin.[98] Marx himself made use of Bright's criticisms of the financial exploitation of India, though he observed that
Bright's 'picture of India ruined by the fiscal exertions of the company
and government did not, of course, receive the supplement of India
ruined by Manchester and Free Trade.'[99]

Marx devoted an article in the *Tribune* to an analysis of
Bright's view of India as a very heavily taxed country. He expressed
some reserve about Bright's calculations, but made the important
point that:

> In estimating the burden of taxation, its annual amount must not
> fall heavier in the balance than the method of raising it, and the

---

[95] *Capital*, I, p. 777.
[96] *Tribune*, articles of 21 September 1857 (*On Colonialism*, pp. 140–44), and
30 April 1859; Avineri, pp. 366–74.
[97] Burke is quoted in R.C. Dutt, *Economic History of India in Early British
Rule*, second edition, London, 1906, pp. 49–50. Sir John Shore's observations are in his Minute of 18 June 1789, paragraphs 131–142; *Fifth Report*,
p. 183. Cornwallis in his Minutes of 10 February 1790, spoke of India's
value in 'furnishing a large annual investment to Europe', and of the
baleful effect on Indian agriculture and commerce of 'the heavy drains
of wealth' to England; *Fifth Report*, p. 493.
[98] See quotations in Dadabhai Naoroji, *Poverty and Un-British Rule in India*
(originally published in London, 1901), 1962, pp. iv, 35–36; also R.C.
Dutt, *The Economic History of India in the Victorian Age*, eleventh
edition, London, 1950, pp. 115–16.
[99] *Tribune*, 22 June 1853; *On Colonialism*, p. 29.

manner of employing it. The former is detestable in India, and in the branch of land-tax, for instance, wastes perhaps more produce than it gets. As to the application of the taxes, it will suffice to say that no part of them is returned to the people in works of public utility.[100]

In order to maximize the revenue collections, the English carried out 'agrarian revolutions', subverting the existing property relationships. They created various 'forms of private property in land—the great desideratum of Asiatic society'.[101] But the real purpose was, by this means, to sustain or increase the tax-paying capacity of the country: 'The zamindari and ryotwari settlements were both of them agrarian revolutions, effected by British ukases—both made not for the people, who cultivate the soil, nor for the holder, who owns it, but for the government that taxes it.'[102] The *zamindari* (or the permanent) settlement was merely 'a caricature of English land-lordism', the *ryotwari* of 'French peasant-proprietorship':

> A curious sort of English landlord was the zamindar, receiving only one-tenth of the rent, while he had to make over nine-tenths of it to the Government. A curious sort of French peasant was the ryot, without any permanent title in the soil, and the taxation changing every year in proportion to his harvest.[103]

There is undoubtedly an element of overstatement in these pronouncements. The standard of one-eleventh (not one-tenth) of rental for the share of the *zamindar* in the Permanent Settlement had little relevance since with the rise in prices and expansion of cultivation, the *zamindar's* share in the rent increased considerably. Indeed, Marx himself elsewhere recognized that the Settlement created a 'landed gentry' in Bengal, adversely affecting the interests of the government as well as 'the actual cultivators'.[104] These landlords were 'mercantile speculators' who had replaced the old *zamindars*, and had created 'a hierarchy of middle men' or *patnidars*, 'which

---

[100] *Tribune*, 23 July 1858; *On Colonialism*, pp. 175–80.
[101] *Tribune*, article date-lined 22 July 1853; *On Colonialism*, p. 77.
[102] *Tribune*, article date-lined 19 July 1853; *On Colonialism*, p. 73.
[103] Ibid. See also *Capital*, III, p. 328n.
[104] *Tribune*, article date-lined 7 June 1858; *On Colonialism*, p. 163.

presses with its entire weight on the unfortunate cultivator'.[105]

As for the *ryotwari* system, Marx's statement that the revenue varied every year according to harvests is only partly correct. If the *ryot* brought wasteland under cultivation, he had to pay more; and there was provision made for varying the tax according to changes in prices. Marx was right, however, in saying that the *ryotwari* system had often disregarded superior rights like 'mirassis, jagirs, etc.',[106] and the revenue assessed on the peasant was by no means light. Elsewhere Marx presented evidence of how the peasants were tortured by the Company's officials in the process of revenue collection in these same *ryotwari* areas.[107]

Marx felt that far from there being left any margin for saving or 'profit' for the 'direct producer', the rent burden imposed on him by the English made any 'expansion of production more or less impossible'; the peasant was reduced to 'the physical minimum of the means of subsistence'.[108] Moreover, though the *ryot* 'manages his farm as an independent producer', the usurer would 'not only rob him of his entire surplus by means of interest', but also eat into his 'wage'.[109]

As for the superior land-holding classes, it was not only that their claims suffered in the *ryotwari* settlements. As Marx shows in an article of 1858, these classes were under pressure in northern India as well, this being illustrated by the example of the Oudh *taluqdars*.[110]

Under the impulse of the same drive for revenue came the absorption of Indian princely states. The Company's policy towards them was that of the Romans: 'a system of fattening allies, as we fatten oxen, till they were worthy of being devoured.'[111] In a later article Marx, discussing a speech by Disraeli, showed how 'the forcible destruction of native princes' had accelerated owing to 'the financial difficulties' of the Company, which had reached a high point in 1843.[112]

[105] *Tribune*, article date-lined 5 August 1853; *On Colonialism*, p. 73.
[106] Ibid.
[107] *Tribune*, article date-lined 17 September 1857; *On Colonialism*, pp. 134–39.
[108] *Capital*, III, p. 777.
[109] Ibid., p. 211.
[110] *Tribune*, article date-lined 7 June 1858; *On Colonialism*, pp. 162–65.
[111] *Tribune*, article date-lined 25 July 1853; *On Colonialism*, p. 66.
[112] *Tribune*, article date-lined 25 July 1853; *On Colonialism*, pp. 127–28.

Marx did not harbour any particular sympathy for the Indian princes: most of them did not even possess 'the prestige of antiquity', and were 'the most servile tools of English despotism' to boot.[113] And yet he was aroused to indignation at the way British power dealt with its own creatures. Thus he wrote a scathing condemnation of the methods by which the annexation of Oudh (1856) was managed:

> This denying the validity of treaties which had formed the acknowledged base of intercourse for twenty years; this seizing violently upon independent territories in open infraction even of the acknowledged treaties; this final confiscation of every acre of land in the whole country;[114] all these treacherous and brutal modes of proceeding of the British toward the natives of India . . .[115]

Finally, the direct exploitation of India began to require for its continuance an intensified pressure upon China. The British government in India 'depends for full one-seventh of its revenue on the sale of opium to the Chinese' (1855).[116] Marx sketched an account of how opium, monopolized by the Company in India, was forced on China in increasingly larger quantities through organized smuggling and war.[117]

The opium monopoly was not only an indispensable pillar of the fiscal exploitation of India; the opium trade to China formed an important mode of realization of the Indian tribute by England. Marx gives figures to show that in 1858 Britain had a trade deficit of more than £6 million with China:

> Now this balance due to China by England, Australia and the United States is transferred from China to India, as a set-off against

---

[113] Nor was he unsympathetic to the argument that the princes were 'the stronghold of the present abominable English system and the greatest obstacles to Indian progress'; and he was plainly sceptical of the pleadings of Munro and Elphinstone on behalf of the 'native aristocracy'. *Tribune*, article date-lined 25 July 1853; *On Colonialism*, pp. 67–68.

[114] This refers to Canning's proclamation confiscating the *taluqdars'* lands in Oudh, 1857.

[115] *Tribune*, 28 May 1858; *On Colonialism*, p. 161.

[116] *Tribune*, 14 June 1853; *On Colonialism*, p. 21. In 1858 the ratio is given as one-sixth (see reference in the next note).

[117] *Tribune*, article of 25 September 1858; *On Colonialism*, pp. 190–91.

> the amount due by China to India, on account of opium and cotton. ... [The] imports from China to India have never yet reached the amount of £1,000,000 Sterling, while the exports to China from India realize the sum of nearly £10,000,000.[118]

Thus the large quantities of tea and silk which England obtained from China gratis were mainly received in payment of the Indian tribute—but at what an enormous moral and social cost to the Chinese people![119]

In addition, there was the excess of Indian exports over imports in the direct trade with England. Marx gives the figures from parliamentary enquiries, which showed that the excess amounted to £2,250,000 in 1855: 'England simply consumes this tribute without exporting anything in return.'[120] Marx, while writing this, seems to overlook the principal means of realization of the tribute, which in this period was via China, and which would naturally give a far higher remuneration to England for the 'good government' that it furnished, opium and all.[121]

In *Capital*, I, Marx views this drain of wealth from India as an important source of 'primary [primitive] accumulation', which he regarded as essential for the genesis of industrial capitalism.[122] This effect of the tribute is by no means widely admitted, even by British historians writing under the influence of the Marxist interpretation. In Maurice Dobb's *Studies in the Development of Capitalism*, the exploitation of the colonies appears as an element of mercantilist

---

[118] *Tribune*, 10 October 1859; *On Colonialism*, pp. 214–15.

[119] It is worth mentioning that India's great spokesman Dadabhai Naoroji, writing in 1880, saw the opium trade in the same light as Marx and was equally indignant: 'Because India cannot fill up the remorseless drain; so China must be dragged in to make it up, even though it be by being "poisoned". . . . This opium trade is a sin on England's head and a curse on India for her share in being the instrument. . . .' *Poverty and Un-British Rule in India*, p. 190.

[120] *Capital*, III, pp. 569–70.

[121] A question by Sir Charles Wood to a witness before a Parliamentary Committee (1857): 'Then, the export, which you state, is caused by the East India drafts, is an export of good government, and not of produce?' Quoted by Marx, *Capital*, III, p. 569.

[122] *Capital*, I, p. 777. The Moore-Aveling translation of *Capital*, I, has given currency to the term 'primitive', whereas a better rendering (as, for example, in E. and C. Paul's translation) would be 'primary'.

policy rather than as a source of primary accumulation.[123] This is surprising because the magnitude of the inflow of wealth from India and the West Indies is seldom denied.[124] It might have amounted to an apparently small part of British national income, say 4.8 per cent in 1801, but at that size, it would still have equalled nearly 70 per cent of the British annual net domestic investment.[125] The major argument seems to be mainly that the 'nabobs', and others who made colonial gains, are not known to have directly invested in industry.[126]

One cannot, of course, be confident about how Marx would have answered such objections. In *Capital*, I, he seems to suggest that in so far as the colonial plunder enlarged commercial capital, it cleared the path for British industrial growth: 'In the period of manufacture properly so called it is . . . the commercial supremacy that gives industrial dominance [and not vice versa]. Hence the preponderant role that the colonial system plays at that time.'[127] The matter may, however, be looked at a little differently as well. At the level of money capital, whether the 'nabobs' bought estates or houses, their acts of purchase would have released other funds to flow into industry. Again, in terms of goods received through colonial exploitation, England was enabled to obtain large quantities of raw materials and wage goods gratis from other countries; this in effect added to industrial capital in the same proportion as that capital increased its sway over British economy.

Given the possibility that the Indian tribute swelled primary accumulation in the eighteenth century, one must ask if it continued

[123] See Dobb, *Studies in the Development of Capitalism*, London, 1946, pp. 208–9, for colonial plunder; primitive accumulation is discussed on pp. 177–86. See also E.J. Hobsbawm, *Industry and Empire*, Pelican Economic History, Vol. 3, 1969, p. 54, where 'commerce with the underdeveloped world' is said to be an important factor behind the growth of 'our industrial economy'.

[124] Phyllis Deane and W.A. Cole (in *British Economic Growth, 1688–1959*, Cambridge, 1962, p. 34) state that in 1797–98 the colonies accounted for 9 per cent of English exports, but 24 per cent of imports (including re-exports).

[125] Sayera I. Habib in *Proceedings of the Indian History Congress*, 36th Session (Aligarh, 1975), Section IV, pp. XXII–XXIV.

[126] See Francois Crouzet (ed.), *Capital Formation in the Industrial Revolution*, London, 1972, pp. 175–77.

[127] *Capital*, I, p. 779.

to perform the same function in the nineteenth century as well. Taken literally, Marx's 'primary [or primitive] accumulation' was one that 'preced[ed] capitalist accumulation', being 'not the result of the capitalist mode of production, but its starting point.'[128] But it is not necessary to interpret Marx's definition in a purely chronological spirit.[129] Direct extraction of surplus from non-capitalist economies (the tax-rent and monopoly of sale of their products), 'the bleeding process' of which Marx spoke in a letter of 1881, must have gone on augmenting industrial capital within the metropolitan country:

> What the English take from them [the people of India] annually in the form of rent, dividends for railways useless to the Hindus, pensions for military and civil servicemen, for Afghanistan and other wars, etc.,—what they take from them *without any equivalent* and *quite apart* from what they appropriate to themselves annually within India—speaking only of the *value of the commodities* the Indians have gratuitously and annually to send over to England—it amounts to *more than the total sum of income of 60 million of agricultural and industrial labourers of India!* This is a bleeding process with a vengeance![130]

This was 'primary accumulation', pure and simple; and it was similar in many respects to the 'accumulation' obtained from the continuous political subjugation by capitalist countries of non-capitalist economies which Rosa Luxemburg described in 1913.[131] It

---

[128] Ibid., p. 739.

[129] As, for example, in Dobb, *Studies in the Development of Capitalism*, p. 178. That Marx himself was far from considering primary accumulation an obsolete process in his own day, is shown by his remarks in *Capital*, I, p. 790: 'In Western Europe, the home of political economy, the process of primitive [primary] accumulation is more or less accomplished. . . . It is otherwise in the colonies.' See also ibid., pp. 798–99, for a specific contemporary method of 'primitive accumulation' by the English government in the colonies.

[130] Letter to F. Danielson, 19 February 1881 (emphasis by Marx); *Selected Correspondence*, pp. 340–41.

[131] Rosa Luxemburg, *The Accumulation of Capital*, translated by A. Schwarzchild, London, 1951, especially pp. 369–70. Luxemburg too believed that Marx had thought primary accumulation to belong exclusively to the period of the genesis of capitalism; see ibid., pp. 364–65. This may have been due to her unfamiliarity with Marx's writings on India and China, notably in *Tribune*. She apparently did not know that her own

was not just the Indian market, but the Indian empire, which helped
to sustain the tempo of the British industrial revolution once it had
begun.

There was thus an ultimate unity underlying the conflict
which Marx saw between the interests of the British 'moneyocracy'
and oligarchy, which sought direct tribute, and of the 'millocracy',
which found its markets in India constricted by the burden of the
tribute.[132] Could one say that this visible conflict essentially represented the contradiction between the urge for primary accumulation and
the need simultaneously for an expanding market for British capitalism?
And could one not find in the actual resolution of this contradiction
the real secret of the 'Imperialism of Free Trade'?[133]

For, if the intensification of the revenue burden was to be
restrained in the interest of the market, the area on which the revenue
was levied had to be extended. Thus the years 1843–56, the very
period of the triumph of the free trade doctrines in England, saw also
the most relentless phase of British expansion in India.

It must be remembered that Marx was always healthily
sceptical of the anti-imperialist professions of the free traders. When
India was in the process of annexation, everyone had kept quiet: now,
when its 'natural limits' had been reached, they had 'become the loudest with their hypocritical peace-cant'. But, then 'firstly, of course,
they had to get it in order to subject it to their sharp philanthropy'.[134]
That philanthropy, as one may expect, consisted in the industrial
devastation of India, with Lancashire cloth in the van.

---

indignant account of the subjugation of the east by the colonial powers
was so much in the tradition of Marx himself.

[132] See especially, *Tribune*, article date-lined 24 June 1853; *On Colonialism*,
pp. 48–49. The contradiction had an early history; Marx speaks in the
same article of parliamentary intervention invoked by 'the industrial
class' against the East India Company's imports of Indian textiles and
refers to John Pollexfen's tract, *England and East-India Inconsistent in
their Manufactures* (1697)—a title, he says, 'strangely verified a century
and a half later, but in a very different sense'. *On Colonialism*, p. 46.

[133] For the phenomenon, not its causes, see the essay under this title by John
Gallagher and Robinson, *Economic Review*, second series, IV(1), 1953.
See also R.J. Moore, 'Imperialism and Free Trade Policy in India', ibid.,
XVII, 1946. Both essays are reprinted in A.G.L. Shaw, *Great Britain and
the Colonies, 1815–1865*, London, 1970, pp. 142–63, 184–96.

[134] *Tribune*, article date-lined 24 June 1853; *On Colonialism*, p. 45. In 1859

## *The Industrial 'Expropriation'*

Engels once wrote of how 'the conquest of India' pursued in search of 'imports'—the material form of tribute, that is to say—helped to transform the metropolitan country, creating within it the need for 'exports' and the development of large-scale industry. He seems to set 1800 as the dividing line between the 'import' and 'export' phases of British colonialism.[135] This was clearly in line with Marx's own perceptions. Marx put the change after 1813:

> After the opening of the trade in 1813 [by the Charter Act] the commerce with India more than trebled in a very short time. But this was not all. The whole character of the trade was changed. Till 1813 India had been chiefly an exporting country, while it now became an importing one. . . .[136]

Marx, in defining exports and imports, was clearly giving consideration to industrial goods alone: 'India, the great workshop of cotton manufacture for the world, since immemorial times, became now inundated with English twists and cotton stuffs.'[137] He gave precise quantitative data for the expansion of the British exports of cotton manufactures to India: 'From 1818 to 1836 the export of twist from Great Britain to India rose in the proportion of 1 to 5,200. In 1824 the export of British muslins to India hardly amounted to 1,000,000 yards, while in 1837 it surpassed 64,000,000 yards.'[138]

The importance of the trade for Britain rose in proportion to the expansion of British exports to India: in 1850, Marx tells us, Great Britain's exports to India amounted to one-eighth of its entire exports, and cotton exports to one-fourth of 'the foreign cotton

---

Marx wrote another significant article in which he examined the post-Mutiny financial crisis. To this crisis the payments pledged to railway companies—under the pressure of the free traders—had duly contributed. Marx summed it all up by saying sarcastically that 'these financial fruits of the "glorious" reconquest of India' had been incurred essentially 'for securing the monopoly of the Indian market to the Manchester free-traders'. *Tribune*, 30 April 1859; Avineri, p. 374.

[135] Engels, letter to Conrad Schmidt (27 October 1890); *Selected Correspondence*, pp. 420–21.

[136] *Tribune*, article date-lined 24 June 1853; *On Colonialism*, p. 47.

[137] *Tribune*, article date-lined 24 June 1853; *On Colonialism*, pp. 47–48.

[138] *Tribune*, article date-lined 7 June 1853; *On Colonialism*, p. 34.

trade'. After reminding the reader that cotton manufactures employed one-eighth of the population of Great Britain, he continues: 'At the same rate at which the cotton manufactures became of vital interest for the whole social frame of Great Britain, East India became of vital interest for the British cotton manufacture.'[139]

If such was the importance for England of its textile exports to India, what about their impact on India? Marx regarded these as the source of an immense transformation of social and economic conditions:

> English interference having placed the spinner in Lancashire and the weaver in Bengal, or sweeping away both Hindu spinner and weaver, dissolved these small semi-barbarian, semi-civilized communities, by blowing up their economical basis, and thus produced the greatest, and, to speak the truth, the only social revolution ever heard of in Asia.[140]

To understand the scale of economic disruption which Marx is speaking about, it may be recalled that according to Ellison, English cloth accounted for 3.9 per cent of Indian cloth consumption in 1813–35, but 35.3 per cent of it in 1856–60 and 58.4 per cent in 1880–81.[141] When one remembers that in addition to cloth, yarn also was imported, one may understand what Marx means by saying that the traditional 'union between agriculture and manufacturing industry' in India was radically disrupted.[142] The peasant would buy cloth produced in Lancashire, dispensing with the domestic spinner as well as with the village weaver. And the weaver would attempt to continue with the cheaper Lancashire yarn, dispensing in this case too with the home spinner. The earlier natural economy would collapse, and in order to buy the imported manufactures the peasant would have to raise for the market far beyond the surplus product, to which

[139] *Tribune*, article date-lined 24 June 1853; *On Colonialism*, p. 48.
[140] *Tribune*, article date-lined 10 June 1853; *On Colonialism*, p. 36.
[141] Thomas Ellison, *The Cotton Trade of Great Britain* (first edition, 1886), London, 1968, pp. 62–63.
[142] *Tribune*, article date-lined 10 June 1853; *On Colonialism*, p. 34; *Capital*, III, p. 328.

commodity circulation, according to Marx, had up till now been confined.[143]

Once agriculture was commercialized, peasants must raise raw materials for the world market instead of crops for domestic or direct village-level consumption: 'In this way East India was compelled to produce cotton, wool, hemp, jute and indigo for Great Britain.'[144] The transformation was naturally of deadly consequence for the weaver and spinner. First, the loss of the European market and then the influx of Lancashire cloth into India, brought about a 'decline of Indian towns celebrated for their fabrics'.[145] Marx quotes the Governor-General as reporting in 1833–34 that 'the bones of the cotton-weavers are bleaching the plains of India'.[146] And again: 'After 1833, the extension of the Asiatic markets is enforced by "destruction of the human race" (the wholesale extinction of Indian handloom weavers).'[147]

The ruin of Indian weavers was almost unanimously accepted for a fact until an American scholar initiated a debate by suggesting that the imported yarn reinforced the position of the Indian weaver, and that the total Indian demand expanded so as to absorb British imports without curtailing the consumption of Indian cloth.[148] By and large, there has been no factual substantiation of these arguments,

---

[143] See *Capital*, II, p. 34, for the effects of 'capitalist world commerce on such nations as the Chinese, Indians, Arabs, etc.'. The translation reads 'excess' where Marx clearly intended 'surplus'.

[144] *Capital*, I, p. 453.

[145] *Tribune*, article date-lined 10 June 1853; *On Colonialism*, p. 34. The population of Dacca fell, says Marx, from 150,000 to 20,000 inhabitants presumably between 1824 and 1837. These figures do not accord with those given in W.W. Hunter's official *Statistical Account of Bengal*, V, London, 1875, p. 68—1800: 200,000 inhabitants (Taylor's estimate); 1823: 300,000 (Hebert's estimate, probably inflated); 1830: 66,989 (town census); 1867: 51,656 (official estimate); 1872: 69,212 (census). The enormous decline in the town's population is quite as obvious from these figures as from Marx's.

[146] *Capital*, I, p. 432. I have not been able to trace the source from which Marx has taken this quotation.

[147] *Capital*, I, p. 461. Parentheses as in the original.

[148] Morris D. Morris, *Indian Economic and Social History Review (IESHR)*, V(1), pp. 8–9.

while the objections to the thesis have been formidable.[149] It may be recalled that according to Ellison's estimates the Indian production of cloth per head fell from 2.4 lb in 1831–35, to 1.6 lb in 1856–60, and to just above 1.0 lb in 1880–81; and by 1880–81 it already included Indian factory-made cloth.[150]

Ellison's figures bear out Marx's description of the destruction of the Indian craft industry; but they also bear out his insistence that 'the work of [its] dissolution proceeds very gradually' because 'the substantial economy and saving in time afforded by the association of agriculture with manufacture put up a stubborn resistance to the products of the big industries, whose prices include the faux frais of the circulation process which pervades them.'[151]

It is implicit in Marx's analysis of the impact of industrial goods on India that the unemployed artisans should have turned into landless labourers; moreover, the expansion of commodity production which he so greatly stressed, must inevitably have led to the subsidence of a large strata of the poorer peasants into the ranks of the rural proletariat. R.P. Dutt and Surendra J. Patel have adduced considerable evidence for the increase in the numbers of this class from the latter half of the nineteenth century.[152] Even the figures given

---

[149] Bipan Chandra, *IESHR*, V(1), pp. 52–68; Meghnad Desai, *IESHR*, VII(4), pp. 317–61. Marx, by the way, was aware of Lancashire yarn being used by the Indian weaver. See *Tribune*, article date-lined 10 June 1853; *On Colonialism*, p. 36. Yet he made fun of Thiers for saying that 'the inventor of the spinning machine has ruined India'; the real culprit, says Marx, was the powerloom; see *Capital*, I, p. 443n.

[150] Ellison, *The Cotton Trade of Great Britain*, p. 63 (table).

[151] *Capital*, III, p. 328. The point had been made by Marx earlier in 1859 as well: 'this combination of husbandry with manufacturing industry for a long time withstood, and still checks, the export of British wares to East India'. *Tribune*, article date-lined 3 December 1859; Avineri, p. 398. If the resistance in India, unlike in China, had at last weakened, it was because by the acquisition of political control and by becoming 'supreme landlords of the country', the British had been able to 'forcibly convert part of the Hindoo self-sustaining communities into mere farms, producing opium, cotton, indigo, hemp and other raw materials, in exchange for British stuffs'; ibid. We here encounter once again the close connection between imperialism and 'trade'.

[152] R.P. Dutt, *India Today*, Bombay, 1947, pp. 198–200; Surendra J. Patel, *Agricultural Labourers of India and Pakistan*, Bombay, 1952, pp. 1–20. Some of Patel's interpretations need to be refined, but it is nevertheless a pioneer work.

by Dharma Kumar, who otherwise disputes the thesis, tend to confirm the phenomenal growth of landlessness in the nineteenth century.[153]

Impressed with all such forms of dissolution of the older relationships and the suffering inherent in that dissolution, Marx always spoke very feelingly of 'India ruined by Manchester and Free Trade'.[154] Already in 1847 he drew the balance-sheet in very human terms when he spoke of 'the millions of workers who had to perish in the East Indies [India] so as to procure for the million and a half workers employed in England in the same [textile] industry, three years' prosperity out of ten.'[155] The sale of British goods thus accomplished in India what had already taken place in Britain—the large-scale 'expropriation' of the petty producer, summed up in that portentous chapter in *Capital*, I, on the 'Historical Tendency of Capitalist Accumulation'.[156]

But was there something much more fundamental still for metropolitan capitalism in this relationship? Rosa Luxemburg in 1913 published a critique of Marx's concept of capitalist accumulation in which surplus value seemed to be generated by labour within the capitalist economy alone. She argued, on the contrary, that surplus value in capitalist production could be 'realized' by the capitalists only through the enforced system of commodity exchange with pre-capitalist (colonial and peasant) economies.[157] (This is to be distinguished, of course, from the simple primary accumulation gained from India, which was certainly recognized and stressed by Marx down to 1881, as we have seen.) It is to the credit of Nikolai Bukharin that, while he criticized the basic premises of Luxemburg's theory, he drew attention to two passages in Marx, where he had amply acknowledged that the 'advanced' country in selling manufactures to a

[153] Dharma Kumar, *Land and Caste in South India*, Cambridge, 1965, pp. 166–82. She concedes an increase in the number of agricultural labourers from 17 or 19 per cent to 27 or 29 per cent of the total agricultural population in south India; yet she declines to see in it 'a radical transformation of the agrarian economy'.

[154] The words are from *Tribune*, 22 June 1853; *On Colonialism*, p. 29.

[155] Marx, *The Poverty of Philosophy*, Moscow, n.d., p. 113.

[156] *Capital*, I, pp. 786–89.

[157] Rosa Luxemburg, *The Accumulation of Capital*, with a sympathetic introduction by Joan Robinson. For a brief critique see Paul M. Sweezy, *The Theory of Capitalist Development*, London, 1946, pp. 202–7.

backward country (and in buying raw materials from the latter) obtains an advantage, a 'surplus-profit': 'In this case', Marx says, 'the richer country exploits the poorer one.'[158] Thus even if the surplus value was not 'realized' through the colonies, it was certainly continually enlarged through unequal exchange with the colonies. Industrial expropriation in India was thus a process of 'exploitation' of the colony, as much to Marx as to Luxemburg.

### Resistance

In 1853, in the first of the two well-known articles in the *Tribune*, Marx presented a particular dilemma. On the one hand, he realized how 'sickening to human feeling' must be the sight of 'the sea of woes' into which the Indian rural population had been plunged; the members of the village communities 'losing at the same time their ancient form of civilization and their hereditary means of subsistence'. On the other, it was impossible to demand that the old system should have continued, when it 'restrained the mind within the smallest possible compass', cultivated a 'barbarian egotism', and supported vile superstition, in effect depriving society of 'all grandeur and historical energies', of all capacity for change.[159] The old production system and culture had to be destroyed, just as petty production had to be annihilated upon the onset of modern industry.[160] Marx had, therefore, quoted Goethe to justify his approval of the entire dreadful process of change let loose by British rule.[161]

But when rebellion actually broke out in 1857, in total revulsion against British rule, Marx was unable to heed his own advice. His natural sympathies were on the side of the rebels; and with his usual acuteness he accurately analysed the unfolding of the events even when the material at his disposal was necessarily limited.

For one thing, Marx saw the rebellion as 'not a military

---

[158] *Capital*, III, pp. 232–33, and *Theories of Surplus Value*, III, pp. 105–6. See also Nikolai Bukharin, *Imperialism and the Accumulation of Capital*, English translation, edited by K.J. Tarbuck, New York, 1972, pp. 244–45.

[159] *Tribune*, article date-lined 10 June 1853; *On Colonialism*, pp. 36–37.

[160] 'To perpetuate it [petty production] would be, as Pecqueur rightly says, "to decree universal mediocrity".' *Capital*, I, p. 787.

[161] *Tribune*, article date-lined 10 June 1853; *On Colonialism*, p. 37.

mutiny, but a national revolt'.[162] 'As to the talk about the apathy of the Hindus [Indians], or even their sympathy with British rule, it is all nonsense.'[163] Indeed, the British forces were tending to become 'small posts planted on insulated rocks in a sea of revolution'.[164]

The real reason for British isolation was the absence towards them of 'the good feelings of the peasantry'.[165] The fact that the revolt did not originate with the peasants was explained by an analogy with the French Revolution:

> The first blow dealt to the French monarchy proceeded from the nobility, not from the peasants. The Indian revolt does not [similarly] commence with the ryots, tortured, dishonoured, stripped naked by the British, but with the sepoys, clad, fed, patted, fatted and pampered by them.[166]

The paragraph shows great insight, because the participation of the peasants, though hardly mentioned in the textbooks, excited the great ire of the British administrators.[167]

The higher agrarian classes were also involved. Marx wrote a long despatch on a speech by Disraeli in which he had shown how, apart from the deposed princes, 'the jagirdar' and 'the inamdar' too

---

[162] *Tribune*, article date-lined 28 July 1857 (approvingly citing Disraeli); *FIWI*, p. 53. Also article date-lined 31 July 1857; *FIWI*, p. 56.

[163] *Tribune*, article date-lined 14 August 1857; *FIWI*, p. 65. Marx's employment of the word 'Hindu' in the general sense of 'Indian' (apart from its specific sense) follows the English usage of his time.

[164] *Tribune*, editorial, 15 September 1857; *FIWI*, p. 85.

[165] *Tribune*, article date-lined 14 August 1857; *FIWI*, p. 65.

[166] *Tribune*, article date-lined 4 September 1857; *FIWI*, pp. 91–92; *On Colonialism*, p. 130. Here Marx could well claim to have been a true prophet, for in 1853 he had spoken of 'the native army organized and trained by the British drill-sergeant' as 'the sine qua non of the Indian self-emancipation'. *Tribune*, article date-lined 22 July 1853; *On Colonialism*, p. 77.

[167] 'However paradoxical it may appear it is a matter of fact that the agricultural labouring class—the class who above all others have derived the most benefit from our rule—were the most hostile to its continuance, while the large proprietors who have suffered under our rule, almost to a man stood by us.' The recipe for the British government: 'throw itself on the large proprietors and repress the peasantry'. Mark Thornhill, 15 November 1858, quoted by Eric Stokes, *The Peasant and the Raj*, Cambridge, 1978, pp. 195–96. The large proprietors, however, were by no means as universally loyal as Thornhill pictures them to be.

had been aggrieved by the British invasion of their rights.[168] Subsequently, he wrote an article on Canning's Oudh proclamation in which he spoke of the dispute about the *taluqdars'* rights after the annexation of Oudh. The resulting 'discontent on their part led them to make common cause with the revolted sepoys'.[169] He at least had a more realistic view of the rebellion than some later interpreters, one of whom has characterized it as 'a peasant war against indigenous landlordism and foreign imperialism'.[170]

Marx's sympathy for the rebels shows itself in a number of ways: his scornful scepticism of the claims of an early British capture of Delhi from the mutineers;[171] his detection of exaggeration in the horror stories of atrocities committed by the rebels and his justifications of these as events inescapable in such revolts anywhere;[172] and, finally, his denunciation of the atrocities committed by British officers and troops.[173]

However sympathetic, by natural instinct, Marx was with the 1857 rebels, he was clear enough in his mind that the rebellion was a response of the old classes to the process of pauperization of a large mass of the Indian people and the dissolution of a whole old way of life; it was not the product of the Indian 'regeneration' that he himself looked forward to. He admitted in respect of the mutiny that 'It is a curious quid pro quo to expect an Indian revolt to assume the features of a European revolution.'[174]

In 1853 Marx had criticized the English for tolerating religious superstition in India;[175] but it was precisely the apprehension

---

[168] *Tribune*, article date-lined 28 July 1857: *FIWI*, pp. 51–52; *On Colonialism*, pp. 128–29.

[169] *Tribune*, 7 June 1858; *FIWI*, p. 159.

[170] Talmiz Khaldun in *Rebellion 1857*, edited by P.C. Joshi, 1957, p. 52.

[171] *Tribune*, 29 August and 15 September 1857; *FIWI*, pp. 63–65, 78–82.

[172] *Tribune*, article date-lined 4 September 1857; *FIWI*, pp. 91, 93–94; *On Colonialism*, pp. 130, 132–33.

[173] *Tribune*, article date-lined 4 September 1857; *FIWI*, pp. 92–93; *On Colonialism*, pp. 131–32; and article published on 5 April 1858; Avineri, pp. 280–84. See also Engels, *Tribune*, 25 May and 26 June 1858; *FIWI*, pp. 145–48, 164–66; *On Colonialism*, pp. 151–53, 166–68.

[174] *Tribune*, 14 August 1857; *FIWI*, p. 65.

[175] *Tribune*, article date-lined 22 July 1853; *On Colonialism*, p. 81.

concerning British intentions towards their religion, that proved to be the immediate catalyst for the sepoy rebellion.[176] Moreover, except for the sepoys there was no modern element in the rank of the rebels that Marx could identify; and, as Engels said, 'even they [the sepoys] entirely lacked the scientific element, without which an army is nowadays hopeless.'[177] The rebellion was therefore doomed, much as Marx and Engels would have liked it to continue even in the form of a guerrilla war.[178]

### Regeneration

In 1853 Marx defined the dual historical character of British rule: 'England has to fulfil a double mission in India: one destructive, the other regenerating—the annihilation of old Asiatic society, and the laying of the material foundations of western society in Asia.'[179] The two roles were performed simultaneously, not in any distinct sequential stages: the creative was rooted in the destructive, and, therefore, apparently secondary and less visible: 'The work of regeneration hardly transpires through a heap of ruins. Nevertheless it has begun.'[180] The constructive 'mission' was in fact blind and unintended: Britain, like the bourgeoisie in general, created 'these material conditions of a new world in the same way as geological revolutions have created the surface of the earth'.[181]

The process of dissolution of the old Indian village economy

---

[176] *Tribune*, 15 July and 14 August 1857; *FIWI*, pp. 40, 50; *On Colonialism*, pp. 118, 127.

[177] Engels, *Tribune*, editorial, 5 December 1857; *FIWI*, p. 117. It is interesting, however, that Engels approved some of the plans for the defence of Delhi adopted by the sepoys, showing that 'some notions of scientific warfare had penetrated among the sepoys'. He even wondered if 'they originated with Indians, or with some of the Europeans that are with them'; there were, of course, no Europeans at all with the mutineers. *Tribune*, editorial, 5 December 1857; *FIWI*, p. 123.

[178] Engels, *Tribune*, 25 May, 15 and 26 June, and 6 July 1858; *FIWI*, pp. 149, 163, 166–68, 175–80.

[179] *Tribune*, article date-lined 22 July 1853; *On Colonialism*, p. 77. The duality was recognized by early nationalist spokesmen. Thus Dadabhai Naoroji, writing in 1870–71: 'If India is to be regenerated by England, India must make up its mind to pay the price.' Quoted by Bipan Chandra, *The Rise and Growth of Economic Nationalism in India*, New Delhi, 1966, p. 638.

[180] *Tribune*, article date-lined 22 July 1853; *On Colonialism*, p. 77.

[181] *Tribune*, article date-lined 22 July 1853; *On Colonialism*, p. 82.

laid the foundation for regeneration by loosening the strong grip of tradition and superstition over the Indian people.[182] The negative effect was supplemented by certain positive achievements: the political unification of the country reinforced by the electric telegraph; effective defence secured by a modern 'native army'; a new consciousness engendered by a 'free press'; the introduction of private landed property; the provision, on a limited scale, of western education; and railways and steam transport which brought the country closer still to the western world.[183] Here were thus the pre-requisites for the creation of an Indian bourgeoisie: 'From the Indian natives, reluctantly and sparingly educated at Calcutta, a fresh class is springing up, endowed with the requirements of government and imbued with European science.'[184]

Marx held that the laying of the network of railways inside the country was of crucial importance. At the time (1853), these were only just beginning to be laid out from the three great port towns of Calcutta, Bombay and Madras. But in a remarkable passage Marx thus foresaw the future:

> I know that the English millocracy intend to endow India with railways with the exclusive view of extracting at diminished expenses the cotton and other raw materials for their manufactures. But when you have once introduced machinery into the locomotion of a country, which possesses iron and coal, you are unable to withhold it from its fabrication. You cannot maintain a net of railways over an immense country without introducing all those industrial processes necessary to meet the immediate and current wants of railway locomotion, and out of which there must grow the application of machinery to those branches of industry not immediately connected with railways. The railway system will therefore become, in India, truly the forerunner of modern industry.[185]

And so it proved to be. Indian railway mileage exceeded 5,000 miles in 1871 and 10,000 in 1882. And already by March 1877

[182] This is implied in *Tribune*, article date-lined 10 June 1853; *On Colonialism*, pp. 36–37.
[183] *Tribune*, article date-lined 22 July 1853; *On Colonialism*, pp. 77–78.
[184] *Tribune*, article date-lined 22 July 1853; *On Colonialism*, p. 77.
[185] *Tribune*, article date-lined 22 July 1853; *On Colonialism*, p. 79.

there were estimated to be 1,231,284 spindles employed in Indian factories, so that Manchester was up in arms for tariff measures to throttle the young industry.[186]

Marx, in spite of his critical view of the past culture of India, believed firmly that the Indian people were endowed with sufficient capacities to create a modern society. He reserved considerable sarcasm for Sir Charles Wood, President of the Board of Control (the British Minister for India), for saying that 'In India you have a race of people, slow of change, bound up by religious prejudices and anti-quated customs. There are, in fact, all obstacles to rapid progress.'[187]

Marx did not also agree with Munro and Elphinstone in their favourable opinion of the Indian aristocracy. 'A fresh class', on the contrary, had to be created to fill administrative offices in India; and Marx quoted Campbell to say that 'from the acuteness and aptness to learn of the inferior classes, this can be done in India as it can be done in no other country'.[188] Marx drew upon Prince Saltykov who found that 'even in the most inferior classes', the Indians were 'more subtle and adroit than the Italians'.[189] And finally Campbell, again, but most relevant of all: 'the great mass of the Indian people possesses a great industrial energy, is well fitted to accumulate capital, and remarkable for a mathematical clearness of head and talent for figures and exact sciences.... Their intellects... are excellent.'[190] There should have been really no difficulty, Marx thought, in Indians 'accommodating themselves to entirely new labour and acquiring the requisite knowledge of machinery.'[191]

Indians were thus well suited to become capitalists as well as industrial workers. The Indian industrial proletariat, once it was created, would be caste-free: 'Modern industry, resulting from the

[186] R.C. Dutt, *The Economic History of India in the Victorian Age*, London, 1950, p. 411, for the number of spindles.
[187] Marx added in parentheses: 'Perhaps there is a Whig Coalition Party in India'. He also remarked that Sir Charles Wood 'seems to have the particular gift of seeing everything bright on the part of England and everything black on the side of India'. *Tribune*, 22 June 1853; *On Colonialism*, p. 27.
[188] *Tribune*, article date-lined 12 July 1853; *On Colonialism*, p. 68.
[189] *Tribune*, article date-lined 22 July 1853; *On Colonialism*, p. 80.
[190] Ibid.
[191] Ibid.

railway system, will dissolve the hereditary divisions of labour upon which rest the Indian castes, those decisive impediments to Indian progress and Indian power.'[192] This was confident prophecy; and the Indian working class has largely fulfilled it though not to the extent, perhaps, that Marx might have expected.

While the material conditions were being created for the implantation of a modern society in India under the impact of British rule, the process could not attain its fulfilment under that regime. This was because a basic conflict of interest existed between the English bourgeoisie and the Indian people: 'All the English bourgeoisie may be forced to do will neither emancipate nor materially mend the social condition of the mass of the people, depending not only on the development of their productive powers, but on their appropriation by the people.'[193]

In these circumstances the genesis of the modern elements in India under the aegis of British dominance could not create any lasting groundwork for collaboration between the new classes and the British rulers; on the contrary, the process of regeneration produced new contradictions.

As early as 1858 Marx could note a divergence of outlook between the young Indian bourgeoisie and the East India Company. When the Company floated a loan in Calcutta, it obtained poor response. 'This proves that the Indian capitalists are far from considering the prospects of British supremacy in the same sanguine spirit which distinguishes the London press.'[194]

The suppression of the 1857 rebellion shattered the sepoy army and the resistance under traditional auspices. But the conditions that generated disaffection continued. In 1871 the General Council of the International Workingmen's Association—of which Marx was the real moving spirit—received a letter from Calcutta drawing attention to the 'great discontent . . . among the people' and 'the wretched conditions of the workers' in India.[195] In a letter Marx wrote

[192] Ibid.
[193] Ibid.
[194] *Tribune*, article date-lined 22 January 1858; *On Colonialism*, p. 147. The Calcutta middle class was, however, hostile to the Mutiny.
[195] Extracts from the minutes of the Council and newspaper report of the letter are given in P.C. Joshi and K. Damodaran, *Marx Comes to India*,

in 1881, he referred to the 'bleeding process' to which India was subjected and the imminence of famine. He then went on to speak of 'an actual conspiracy going on where Hindus and Mussalmans co-operate', the true scale of which was not realized by the British government.[196] This was certainly a period of grave mass unrest, marked by the Deccan peasant riots of 1875 and the bourgeois-led agitation against removal of import duties on cotton goods in 1879. A.O. Hume derived a similar impression of conditions of widespread 'unrest' and 'danger to the government' during the very same years.[197] These conditions were the prelude to the formation of the Indian National Congress in 1885, from which event the formal history of the Indian national movement begins.

Whether the moderate beginnings of 1885 would have satisfied Marx, one cannot say. But surely what followed till the finale of 1947 contained much that should have gratified him, for it was all according to the perspective he had outlined in 1853:

> The Indians will not reap the fruits of the new elements of society scattered among them by the British bourgeoisie, till in Great Britain itself the new ruling classes shall have been supplanted by

---

Delhi, 1975, p. 2. The Council advised the correspondent in Calcutta (not identified) to start a branch of the Association with special attention to 'enrolling natives'.

[196] Letter to N.Y. Danielson, 19 February 1881; *Selected Correspondence*, pp. 340–41; *On Colonialism*, p. 304. It is possible that Marx was here relying on the memoranda submitted in 1880 by Dadabhai Naoroji to the Secretary of State for India. Naoroji drew attention to the growing unrest, and said: 'Those Englishmen who sleep such foolish sleep of security know very little of what is going on . . . Hindus, Mahommedans and Parsees are alike asking whether the English rule is to be a blessing or a curse'; *Poverty and Un-British Rule in India*, pp. 182–83. In the same letter to Danielson, Marx gives details of the drain of wealth, and these may be based on a memorandum of Naoroji (13 September 1880), where he gave a computation of the annual loss to India ($30 million); ibid., p. 176. Very possibly, the information reached Marx through H.M. Hyndman, who is mentioned by Naoroji as a friend of India (ibid., p. 184) and who was also a frequent visitor of Marx's house until the summer of 1881. *Selected Correspondence*, pp. 344, 351.

[197] Sir William Wedderbum, *Allan Octavian Hume, Father of the Indian National Congress*, 1913, pp. 50, 80–81; quoted in R.P. Dutt, *India Today*, Bombay, 1947, pp. 258–59.

the industrial proletariat, or till the Hindus themselves shall have grown strong enough to throw off the English yoke altogether.[198]

If there is one man in modern history who does not stand in need of adjectives that is Karl Marx; and what eulogy, in any case, can be adequate for this passage? In 1853 to set colonial emancipation, not just colonial reform, as an objective of the European socialist movement; and, still more, to look forward to a national liberation ('throw[ing] off the English yoke') attained through their struggle by the Indian people, as an event that might even precede the emancipation of the European working class—such insight and vision could belong to Marx alone.

[198] *Tribune*, article date-lined 22 July 1853; *On Colonialism*, p. 80. (As noted earlier, Marx often uses the word 'Hindu' as a substitute for Indian.) It is interesting to compare Engels's reflections on the same theme in his letter to Karl Kautsky, 12 September 1882; *Selected Correspondence*, pp. 352–53; *On Colonialism*, pp. 306–7.

# The Social Distribution of Landed Property in Pre-British India: A Historical Survey

[The present paper was especially written for the International Economic History Conference, Munich, August 1965, which had a separate section on the Social Distribution of Landed Property.

Since the words 'landed property' may call forth different connotations in different minds, I should perhaps make it clear that I have used it in the broadest sense, conforming in this respect to the guidance given by Professor J. Habakkuk, Chairman of the section. I take it to include all shares claimed by anyone in the produce of the soil, particularly, however, shares in the *surplus* produce (i.e. the portion of the produce beyond the minimum needed for the producer's subsistence). Any rights over the person or labour of the tiller of the soil are also considered forms of landed property. By 'distribution' is meant not only territorial distribution (e.g., sizes of land holding), but also the distribution of the shares in the surplus from the same land (e.g., shares claimed concurrently by different classes of exploiters).

The paper attempts a historical survey of the changes in the forms and distribution of landed property up to the British conquest. The aim is to sum up the results of the work already done and to indicate points of controversy and problems, provoking, as well as awaiting, discussion. It does not pretend, except at certain points in its treatment of the medieval period, to provide fresh material based on the writer's own research. In Section I (Ancient India) I have tried to follow scrupulously the interpretations of sources given in modern authorities, and have avoided taking any responsibility on my own shoulders by even citing the original sources (or their translations) where I had access to them.

Unfortunately, Professor R.S. Sharma's important book,

*Indian Feudalism: c. 300–1200* (Calcutta, 1965), which integrates many of the points he has made in earlier articles, while adding much that is new, came too late for me put it to adequate use in revising the paper.]

1. The history of landed property in India begins with the Indus civilization of the third millennium BC. But due to limitations of the archaeological evidence, and due to the fact that the small amount of epigraphic evidence is yet to be deciphered, it is difficult to say anything with confidence about the agrarian aspects of this civilization. It appears that cultivation by the Indus people was confined to the arid Indus basin, because not knowing the use of iron, or the device of shaft-hole for their axe, they could not have cleared the dense forests of the Gangetic plain. Their crops probably grew on lands irrigated by the seasonal inundations of the rivers of the Indus system; and they apparently built dams—the *vrtra* of the *Rigveda*—over the natural flood-channels thrown off by the rivers, and over seasonal streams. There is no firm evidence that they knew the use of the plough; perhaps they used only a toothed harrow to raise their principal crops, viz. wheat, barley and cotton.[1]

We must then conceive of the rural Indus population as a largely settled one, clustering along rivers and flood-channels. The rigid uniformity displayed by the two cities of Harappa and Mohenjodaro, so wide apart in space, and the mobilization of labour required for building and repairing dams suggest a considerable degree of autocratic control.[2] It has been argued that this control was reinforced by an elaborate unchanging 'magic' ritual.[3] But it is not clear whether the ruling class consisted of 'priest-kings' or the merchants (the *panis* of the *Rigveda*) or a combination of both. At the same time it is possible that the cultivating communities were of practically servile status—the *dasyus* or *dasas* of the *Rigveda*: the

---

[1] The best description of Indus agriculture is given by D.D. Kosambi, *An Introduction to the Study of Indian History*, Bombay, 1956, pp. 62–68, 70. For a view in favour of plough being known to the Indus people, see D.H. Gordon, *The Pre-Historic Background of Indian Culture*, Bombay, 1958, p. 71, cited in *Enquiry*, iv, 12. [See, however, p. 112 of this volume.]
[2] See S. Piggot, *Prehistoric India*, London, 1950, pp. 153–55.
[3] See especially Kosambi, *Introduction*, pp. 59–60.

presence of slave labour in towns has indeed been deduced from archaeological remains.[4]

2. According to the chronology now widely accepted, the Aryans are regarded as the immediate successors and possibly the wreckers of the Indus civilization: their immigration is supposed to have begun around 1750 BC, and their first sacred book, the *Rigveda*, composed *c.* 1500–1400 BC in the region between the Kabul river and the Ganga.

Philological research in the early Indo-European languages and detailed textual studies of the *Rigveda* allow us to have a glimpse of the productive system and social structure of the early Aryans. The Aryans had obtained great mobility by domesticating the horse. They were pastoralists; and cows and cattle were in their eyes the main form of wealth. They combined pastoralism with agriculture and knew the use of the plough. Yet barley and some other cereals were the only crops they grew in their early phase.[5] They did not have any towns and took pride in their god Indra's destruction of those which others had built.[6]

In such conditions the Aryans appear to have had in the initial stages a simple social structure. They were divided among tribes (*jana*), and lived in villages (*grama*). The *Rigveda* refers to three distinct classes: the *kshatriyas* or *rajanyas* (warriors, rulers), the *brahmanas* (priests) and the *vis* (masses).[7] The wealth of the first two classes is not counted (in references to gains from wars and gifts) in land but in cows, horses, and *dasa*-slaves.[8] The only payment to chiefs known was *bali*, an offering rather than a tax.[9] There does not seem to have existed any overlordship of the land, vesting in either the tribal chief, the village-chief (*gramani*), or anyone else.

---

[4] See D.R. Chanana, *Slavery in Ancient India*, Delhi, 1960, p. 17.

[5] For agriculture in the Rigvedic period, see N. Bandyopadhyaya, *Economic Life and Progress in Ancient India*, I, Calcutta, 1945, pp. 125–35.

[6] For a collection of relevant references, see S.K. Das, *Economic History of Ancient India*, I, Calcutta, 1937, pp. 26–27.

[7] Bandyopadhyaya, *Economic Life*, pp. 102–5; R.S. Sharma, *Sudras in Ancient India*, Delhi, 1958, p. 18.

[8] Bandyopadhyaya, *Economic Life*, pp. 206–7; Chanana, *Slavery in Ancient India*, p. 21; Das, *Economic History of Ancient India*, pp. 78–79.

[9] See U.N. Ghoshal, *Contributions to the History of the Hindu Revenue System*, Calcutta, 1929, pp. 3–5.

Some references have been collected from the *Rigveda* to
support the view that private land ownership in the homestead and
arable land had then existed, and that there was therefore no communal ownership.[10] But the most these passages suggest is that land
was divided among fields cultivated by individual peasants who were
regarded as the holders of the field (*kshetrapati*, etc.). Pasture lands
were apparently undivided and were open to the cattle of the whole
village. Whether the right to the field was permanent or hereditary or
subject to change by communal allotment cannot be established.
Indeed, if cultivation was not settled but migratory, as would be more
likely at a time when land was abundant, and with Aryans living so
often as semi-nomadic pastoralists, the conception of permanent
occupation, let alone ownership, of particular fields could not have
possibly developed. There is the further possibility that despite the
lack of evidence in the *Rigveda* to support it, some Aryan tribes did
in fact cultivate the land in common, as did some tribes in Punjab, the
cradle of the *Rigveda*, during the time of Alexander.[11]

The 'equalitarian' structure of the agrarian society of the
Aryans[12] must surely have been affected in course of time by their
struggles with indigenous enemies. The *dasas* were not all slaughtered; some were enslaved, so that slaves, both male (*dasa*) and female
(*dasi*), appear in the *Rigveda* as desirable articles to be obtained in
gifts.[13] There is also evidence, which Kosambi so ably presents,[14] of
the absorption of *dasas* in the Aryan fold. Since these people were
described in the *Rigveda* itself as city-dwellers, there is great likelihood of their having brought with them elements of a more developed
class structure. It is probable that out of the servile and subject population so brought under them, augmented also by such Aryans as were
subjugated or enslaved in internecine warfare,[15] arose the *sudra* class.
The *sudras* were recognized in the last portion of the *Rigveda*, in its

---

[10] Bandyopadhyaya, *Economic Life*, pp. 111–15, following Baden-Powell
and Macdonell and Keith.
[11] Kosambi, *Introduction*, pp. 91–92.
[12] See Sharma, *Sudras*, p. 26.
[13] Ibid.
[14] Kosambi, *Introduction*, pp. 92ff.
[15] Sharma, *Sudras*, pp. 30ff, urges the view that *sudras* arose out of an Aryan
tribe of this name.

only reference to them, as the fourth *varna* (caste-class), placed beneath the *vaisya*, the old *vis*. Although there is no evidence as to the actual status of the *sudras* in the early Vedic period, it is reasonable to suppose that they were not peasants, but servile field-labourers for the tribes or for their individual masters, or were possibly 'helots', as they are thought to have been in the later Vedic phase.[16]

3. The late Vedic period, when the other three Vedas, particularly the *Atharvaveda* and the early *Brahmanas* were composed, represents a phase of great expansion of the Aryans. Archaeological evidence testifies to the presence of iron in the upper Ganga basin some time before 1000 BC, or at any rate around 800 BC.[17] With iron the Aryans could penetrate the dense forests of the Ganga plains.[18] They used fire to clear the forests;[19] they had heavy ploughs drawn sometimes by six or eight or even twelve yokes of oxen,[20] and, therefore, still needed very large supply of cattle. It is probable that the settlements were not permanently fixed. The fertility of the soil would have been exhausted after some years, and a new clearing would have to be made.[21] Yet the yield must have been much greater than in the arid tracts of the west, and we know that the Aryans now had a greater variety of crops, including rice and sugarcane.[22] The surplus so gained made possible the beginnings of urban life. Names of towns,

---

[16] Kosambi, *Introduction*, pp. 94–95; Sharma, *Sudras*, pp. 46–48. Sharma, however, denies that there was a 'considerable Sudra or slave population' in the Rigvedic period and argues that their 'disabilities' arose only later (p. 41).

[17] Kosambi fixes the date 800–700 BC on the basis of literary evidence; *Journal of the Economic and Social History of the Orient (JESHO)*, VI, No. 3, p. 314. This date may be modified by archaeologists' finds. Traces of iron have been found at the level of Painted Grey Ware: middle phase, assigned by carbon-dating to *c.* 1025 BC at Atranjikhera, and at a level dated eighth century BC at Noh. I owe this information to my colleague, R.C. Gaur, who has supervised the excavations at Atranjikhera.

[18] Chanana, *Slavery in Ancient India*, pp. 23–25; Kosambi, *JESHO*, VI, No. 3, p. 314.

[19] Kosambi, *Introduction*, pp. 116–17.

[20] Bandyopadhyaya, *Economic Life*, pp. 133–34; Das, *Economic History of Ancient India*, pp. 90–91.

[21] This has happened in recent times wherever forest land has been abundant; and the practice has been followed by immigrant peasants who were previously settled cultivators.

[22] Bandyopadhyaya, *Economic Life*, pp. 131–32; Das, *Economic History of Ancient India*, pp. 93–94.

still too few, begin to appear in the literature of the period.[23]

These new developments were bound to affect the old simpler forms of landed property. Fields are for the first time counted as an index of wealth,[24] showing that large landed possessions became possible. The heavy plough may well have tended to put control over cultivation in the hands of those who possessed numerous cattle as well as slave-labourers. Keith has indeed suggested that 'for the peasant working on his own fields was being substituted the land-owner cultivating his estate by means of slaves'.[25] References to slaves being given away with ploughs, and similarly, to *sudras*, with lands, occur in the *Srautasutras*.[26] In a famous passage in the *Aitareya Brahmana* the *sudra* is described as a 'servant of another', bound to render labour whenever called upon to do so, and to be beaten at pleasure.[27] Perhaps the ranks of slaves and *sudras* were augmented by the autochthonous tribes—the *vratyas*—of the Ganga basin, who were being continuously subjugated or absorbed in the Aryan fold.[28]

The peasants, the *vis* or *vaisyas*, too became increasingly subject to the exactions and oppressions of a superior class. Thus the *vaisya* came to be described as 'tributary [paying *bali*] to another, eaten by another and oppressed at will'.[29] A kind of embryonic village (*grama*) overlord appears, who has 'creatures led by the nose', has authority over his relatives and keeps 'the folk dependent upon him'.[30]

Another superior non-peasant right on the land developed in the form of villages and fields held by the priests, the *brahmanas*, who were essentially independent of tribal affiliations.[31]

Behind this increasing class differentiation can be traced the growth in the power and pretensions of the ruler or chief (*rajan,*

---

[23] Das, *Economic History of Ancient India*, pp. 81–82.

[24] Chanana, *Slavery in Ancient India*, p. 21; Das, *Economic History of Ancient India*, p. 82.

[25] The *Cambridge History of India*, I, Delhi reprint, 1955, pp. 114–15.

[26] Sharma, *Sudras*, p. 46.

[27] Ibid., pp. 59–60.

[28] See Kosambi, *Introduction*, pp. 114ff.

[29] Sharma, *Sudras*, p. 59; Ghoshal, *History of the Hindu Revenue System*, p. 7.

[30] U.N. Ghoshal, *The Agrarian System in Ancient India*, Calcutta, 1930, p. 4.

[31] Kosambi, *Introduction*, pp. 100–1, 125–26, 131.

*kshatriya*). In the beginning his claim seems to have been over a sixteenth of the produce of the land; and he also aspired to an undefined share 'in villages, in horses, in kine'. Afterwards he levied a tax, *bali*, of an undefined nature, on the *vaisyas*, or peasants.[32] Furthermore, he began to grant authority over lands and villages to his lesser chiefs (*kshatriyas*).[33] Finally, we see him giving away lands and villages to brahmanas.[34] Such grants were apparently first made with the consent of the *vis*, or the peasant community;[35] but in course of time the grants tended to become arbitrary acts of the king, and as such appear to have aroused some protest.[36]

There were, however, also tribes, which were within the Aryan fold, but among which neither the Brahmanical caste–class differentiation nor the monarchy had developed. These tribes assumed the form of oligarchies sustained by the labour of *sudra* helots.[37] It is of course not very material for our present purpose whether these oligarchies are to be regarded as survivals of the original Aryans or, as Kosambi urges, of the semi-Aryanized 'autochthonous' tribes of the Ganga basin, whose cousins ('Nagas', 'candalas') must have still survived with their nomadic food-gathering in the forests.[38]

4. The three hundred and fifty years from *c.550* to 200 BC represent a very interesting period of change in Indian history. The rise of Buddhism spearheaded an ideological revolt against brahmanical dominance. Large kingdoms appeared and expanded, culminating in the vast Mauryan empire (322–184 BC) which embraced practically the whole of India and most of Afghanistan. Accompanying and possibly underlying these developments was a considerable advance in economic life, marked by the rise of towns, growth of commerce, and the use of ('punch-marked') coins.

The source material for the period is large and varied: the early canonical literature of the Buddhists and the *Jatakas*, the *Artha-*

[32] Ghoshal, *History of the Hindu Revenue System*, pp. 6–8.
[33] Das, *Economic History of Ancient India*, p. 85.
[34] Ibid., pp. 88–89; Kosambi, *Introduction*, p. 125.
[35] Das, *Economic History of Ancient India*, p. 86.
[36] Ghoshal, *Agrarian System*, p. 5; Sharma, *Sudras*, p. 46.
[37] Kosambi, *Introduction*, p. 141; Chanana, *Slavery in Ancient India*, pp. 43–44; Bose, *Social and Rural Economy of Northern India, 600 BC:-AD 200*, Calcutta, 1961, pp. 48–49.
[38] Kosambi, *Introduction*, pp. 121–29, 140–141, 143–44.

*sastra* (treatise on polity, statecraft and administration) of Kautilya
and early Brahmanical legal literature; the Greek accounts, largely
derived from Megasthenes; and the inscriptions of Asoka (273–36
BC), with which Indian epigraphic evidence begins. The dating of the
Indian sources (except Asoka's inscriptions) and the degree of vera-
city of the Greek accounts pose very difficult problems for the historian. But it is now generally agreed that the Indian texts contain
elements genuinely coming from this period, though as they stand
they also contain later interpolations. With some reservations, the
Greek accounts too are accepted as largely authentic.

On the basis of a critical examination of this material,
carried out by many scholars, a distinct picture of the agrarian relations of the period emerges.

There appear to have continued from the earlier times
peasant communities, in which productive effort of certain kinds was
undertaken by the peasants in common.[39] So deeply entrenched seems
to have been the institution of the village community that artisans,
like smiths, carpenters and others, also tended to settle in villages
comprising exclusively people of their own profession or caste.[40] Such
manufacturers' villages are a peculiarity of this period and may
perhaps be explained by the fact that in this earlier phase of commercial evolution it was not possible for artisans to feed themselves
without carrying on some cultivation themselves.

The growth in commerce and introduction of money probably made urban land (and, possibly, orchards) into a marketable
commodity, but it is doubtful if arable land became as freely subject
to sale.[41] The *Arthasastra* in any case allows sale of land to a limited
extent only, confining the purchasers to kinsmen and neighbours.[42]
This is understandable, since land must still have been abundant, and
not usually worth purchasing, while individual peasant-holdings
could not have been conceived of outside the limits of the village
community.

[39] Das, *Economic History of Ancient India*, pp. 188–89; Bose, *Social and Rural Economy*, p. 48.
[40] R. Fick, *The Social Organization in North-East India in Buddha's Time*, English translation, Calcutta, 1920, pp. 280–85.
[41] See Kosambi, *Introduction*, p. 145.
[42] See Bose, *Social and Rural Economy*, pp. 54, 83–85.

Alongside the peasant communities, men possessing wealth, particularly in the form of cattle or slaves, controlled large stretches of land. The *Jatakas* introduce us to veritable 'cattle magnates' owning enormous herds (e.g., 30,000 heads), with numerous slaves and hirelings (1,250 under one magnate are reported).[43] But still more frequently we meet 'big *brahmanu* landowners [who] have their fields cultivated by their slaves or day labourers'.[44] The *brahmana* occupation of land must have been substantially encouraged by the royal assignments of revenue-free lands (*brahmadeya*) to them.[45] Fick is so impressed with the constant *Jataka* references to *brahmanas* as landowners (including small and rather impecunious *brahmana* cultivators as well) that he declares it 'probable' that the land was then 'mostly in the possession of *brahmanas*'.[46] But we can be certain that the *brahmanas* alone do not by any means constitute the entire class of non-peasant landholders. There are references in the *Jatakas* themselves to *setthis* (merchants, or merchant-officers) possessing villages and fields.[47] Moreover, *kshatriya* tribal oligarchies continued to have their lands cultivated by slaves, servants or helots.[48] Kautilya designates these tribes *srenis* or *kshatriya* guilds, and considers the question whether new land should be settled by them, and not by ordinary peasants, thus implying an antithesis between the two modes of cultivation.[49]

It is probable that ordinary peasants had everywhere fallen under some kind of subjection to local superior classes, whose members were designated *gahapatis* and *kutumbikas* (who included *setthis*). They controlled villages, while they also possessed lands in their own right.[50] They engaged in usury too, which must have helped

[43] Ibid., p. 93.
[44] Fick, *Social Organization*, pp. 243–44; Bose, *Social and Rural Economy*, pp. 63–64.
[45] Fick, *Social Organization*, p. 210. Fields as large as 1,000 *karisas* in area are mentioned. *Karisa* has been held to be about eight acres; Bose, *Social and Rural Economy*, p. 64n. But one hesitates to accept such a definite statement when the imponderable factors are so many.
[46] Fick, *Social Organization*, p. 241.
[47] Chanana, *Slavery in Ancient India*, p. 42.
[48] Ibid., pp. 43–44.
[49] Kosambi, *Introduction*, pp. 203–4, 221.
[50] Fick, *Social Organization*, pp. 251–66.

to further their control over the peasants (through their obtaining a share in the crop).[51]

By the time of the Mauryas such a superior class had come to be recognized (according to Kosambi's interpretation of Kautilya) under the name *paura-janapada*, the town and country 'citizenry'. Kautilya recommended that higher administrative officers of the government should be recruited from this class; and of its two components, urban and rural, he thought the rural or the *janapadas* to be politically the more important. The *janapadas* paid the king's tax of 'one-sixth' of the produce (*sadbhaga*) along with some of the taxes under the heading of *rastra* (district). On the other hand they must have extracted a much larger part of the surplus from the peasants, sometimes possibly employing *ardha-sitikas* or share-croppers from whom they took half the crop.[52]

Superior private right over the land was accompanied by a new and important form of landed property, the king's domain. Kautilya attaches great significance, from the point of view of the king's revenues, to the *sita* or the crops brought in from the king's own lands.[53] Moreover, only the fact that the royal domains were very large could adequately explain the Greek report that in India all land belonged to the king, who took either three-fourths or one-fourth of the crop.[54] If we follow Kautilya's detailed description of the management of the *sita* lands, it would appear that these initially arose out of wasteland appropriated by the king to establish agricultural settlements. The king's lands were divided into two parts: one, cultivated by the labour of slaves, wage earners and convicts under the direction of royal officials; the other leased to sharecroppers (*ardha-sitikas*) for half the crop, and also to others—by one interpretation, to labourers who contributed nothing but labour and so surrendered three-fourths of the crop to the king; and by another, to men of 'valour', who were encouraged to settle by being allowed to pay only a quarter of the crop[55] (there were also revenue-free grants

---

[51] For *Jataka* references to rural usury, see Fick, *Social Organization*, p. 257; Bose, *Social and Rural Economy*, p. 64. See also Kosambi, *Introduction*, pp. 139–40.

[52] Kosambi, *Introduction*, pp. 212–16.

[53] Ghoshal, *Revenue System*, pp. 28–29.

[54] Ibid., pp. 167–71; Kosambi, *Introduction*, p. 219.

[55] Ghoshal, *Revenue System*, pp. 29–31, 34; Kosambi, *Introduction*, p. 215.

made to *brahmanas* out of wastelands, ostensibly as part of the policy to extend cultivation[56]). The taxes on the leased royal lands did not exhaust the royal demand. There were heavy additional charges for irrigation.[57] And thee were labour services (*visti*) taken from certain groups of subjects, composed possibly of such *sudra* labourers as did not have any land under their own occupation and so could not be asked to pay taxes.[58]

It is significant that Kautilya should stress that the settlements in royal lands ought to consist overwhelmingly of *sudra* peasants (*sudra-karshaka*) and low-class elements, whom he regards more amenable to exploitation.[59] It is obvious that settlements were often the result of large-scale deportations of whole communities;[60] and by this means what were previously labouring or non-agricultural populations were transformed into semi-servile peasants.[61] These peasants, once settled in the royal lands could not move freely; their right to the land was for life only; and they could lose their right, if they failed to cultivate the land properly.[62]

5. In recent researches it has been stressed that the Mauryan empire accelerated two processes which, when they were substantially completed in the following period, *c.* 200 BC–AD 650, resulted in the creation of the traditional Indian village, closed and self-sufficient, and based on individual peasant-farming.

Kosambi has shown how once the population of craftsmen increased and certain skills, like iron-smelting, became widely known, under the impetus of the growth of commerce and the centralized administration of the Mauryas, individual artisans could begin moving to the villages.[63] The results of this ruralization of crafts may be seen from evidence relating to the first five or six centuries after Christ. For example, we hear no more of the separate carpenters'

[56] Sharma, *Aspects of Political Ideas and Institutions of Ancient India*, Delhi, 1959, p. 220.
[57] Ghoshal, *Revenue System*, pp. 32–34.
[58] Sharma, *Sudras*, pp. 151–52.
[59] Kosambi, *Introduction*, pp. 218–19, 221; Sharma, *Sudras*, pp. 146–49.
[60] Kosambi, *Introduction*, p. 196; Romila Thapar in *Readings in Indian Economic History*, edited by B.N. Ganguli, Bombay, 1964, pp. 25–26.
[61] Sharma, *Sudras*, pp. 146–47.
[62] Kosambi, *Introduction*, p. 218; Sharma, *Sudras*, pp. 147–48.
[63] Kosambi, *Introduction*, p. 222.

settlement of the previous epoch; on the other hand, sixth-century epigraphs introduce us to the village carpenter with his own separate plot within the peasant village.[64] When each village had its own carpenter, smith and potter, it would not only make the village self-sufficient, but it also could, to borrow a phrase from Gordon Childe, 'democratize agriculture', each cultivator having access, without need of an intermediary, to his essential productive needs.

Secondly, the settlement of *sudras* as cultivators, which Kautilya regards as a deliberate measure of policy to be enforced by the king, led in this period to the transformation of a substantial part of the *sudra* population into peasants. R.S. Sharma has shown by a detailed examination of the evidence how the older conventional assumption (in the *Manusmriti, c.* 200 BC–AD 200) that the *sudras* were simply servants of the higher castes and could not be tax-payers (and so not peasants),[65] is modified in the legal literature of the subsequent centuries until by the seventh century peasants are generally assumed to be *sudras*.[66]

This consolidation of peasant cultivation is reflected in the absence of any reference after the Mauryan period to large 'farms', whether of private owners or of the king, worked by slaves and hired labour.[67] Along with the large farms, agrarian slavery, i.e. the employment of slaves in agriculture, also seems to have largely disappeared, the last traced reference to village slaves coming from the *Milindapanho* (*c.* AD 100).[68]

At the same time, a class of rural labourers continued to

[64] Ibid., p. 312.
[65] Sharma, *Sudras*, p. 178.
[66] Ibid., pp. 232–34.
[67] Ibid. p. 231; also see Sharma in *Journal of Bihar Research Society* (*JBRS*), LXIV, Nos. 3–4, 1958, p. 8. The negative evidence would appear to suffice. Epigraphic specification of areas of grants by private donors in north Bengal during the fifth and sixth centuries can hardly be regarded as relevant since we do not know what was the actual mode of cultivation (if any) carried on in these lands before and after the transfer. This is besides the fact that it is very difficult to be sure about the actual value of the measures of areas used. See S.K. Maity, *Economic Life in Northern India in the Gupta Period*, Calcutta, 1957, pp. 200–1 (for tabulated information from the inscriptions) and pp. 35–41 (for measures of area).
[68] Sharma, *Sudras*, pp.227–28, 230–31. See Maity, *Economic Life inNorthern India*, p. 145. For the *Milindapanho* reference, see Sharma, *Sudras*, p. 178.

exist. The existence of such a class would have been needed by conditions of peasant-farming[69] and it is possible that its ranks were continually reinforced, as cultivation extended, by the conversion of aboriginal and pastoral tribes[70] into menial castes under subjection to communities of caste peasants. In any case, several references to agricultural labourers have been collected from the sources of the period. Patanjali (second century BC) speaks of a landowner supervising ploughing done by five hired labourers, and the *Manusmriti* refers to servants of peasants.[71] Subsequent legal literature even lays down the rates of wages for agricultural labourers (*bhrtyas*), ranging from one-tenth of the crop to one-fifth plus food and clothing, or one-third of the crop only.[72]

Theoretically speaking, since there were still large tracts of forest and waste, both in northern India and in the Deccan and southern India (where plough cultivation began on a large scale probably at the beginning of this period),[73] it could not have been possible to establish a monopoly of the ownership of land in the hands of a small non-peasant class. The *Milindapanho* declares that 'when a man clears away the jungle and sets free the land, people say "that is his land"'.[74] This may be read with the oft-quoted dictum of the *Manusmriti* that land belongs to him who first removed the weed, and the deer to him who first wounded it. Such statements are held to show that land could be directly occupied by individual peasants at the expense of the jungle, without the intermediation of the king or a superior class. It has been argued, however, that it is inconceivable for forest-clearing to have been attempted by individual peasants except as members of larger groups or communities.[75]

Evidence like this leads Kosambi to postulate implicitly a

---

[69] See Irfan Habib, *Agrarian System of Mughal India*, Bombay, 1963, pp. 121–22.

[70] For Yuan Chwang's description (*c.* AD 640) of a large primitive pastoral community in Sindh, see Kosambi, *Introduction*, pp. 292–93.

[71] Sharma, *Sudras*, p. 178.

[72] Ibid., pp. 224–25; Maity, *Economic Life in Northern India*, pp. 74–75, 149–50.

[73] Kosambi, *Introduction*, pp. 228–29, 278–80.

[74] Bose, *Rural Economy*, p. 40.

[75] Kosambi, *Introduction*, p. 249; Maity, *Economic Life in Northern India*, p. 12, disputes the significance of Manu's dictum without much good reason.

stage around the beginning of the Christian era, when a closed peasant-village economy prevailed with practically no superior, landowning class or overlords, and with only limited authority and exactions claimed by the king. This simple structure of society was in course of time disturbed by the king's alienation of his rights to subordinate chiefs who came to have direct relations with the peasantry, a process which Kosambi terms 'feudalism from above'. He seems to think that it had reached an advanced stage of development during the period of the Guptas (fourth–fifth centuries) and of Harsha (seventh century). At a still later stage 'a class of landowners' was to develop from within the village, this later development being termed 'feudalism from below'.[76]

Interesting as this theory is, there has been no adequate discussion of it so far. The appropriateness of the terms 'feudalism from above' and 'below' has been questioned from a Marxist point of view.[77] But on the question whether a pre-'feudal' society of the type postulated by Kosambi actually ever existed, admittedly with exceptions and regional variations, which Kosambi himself would be the first to admit, little light has been shed by other scholars.

Sharma appears to reject—for he does not explicitly take issue with Kosambi on this point—the supposition that a landowning class above the peasantry did not come into existence until the later centuries of the first millennium. He cites Yajnavalkya (c. fifth century AD) for the statement that the land is to be assigned to the cultivator (karshaka) by the landowner (kshetra-svami), the king (mahapati) being only entitled to the fruits of improvements made in the land in the absence of the owner (svami). He points out that Brihaspati too provides for a svami or owner above the actual tiller. It thus appears to him that the svamis leased their lands to 'temporary cultivators'.[78]

Epigraphic evidence too attests to the existence of such a class. Kosambi himself notices (as 'unique') the purchase of a field by the Saka prince Usavadata (c. AD 120) near Nasik from a brahmana in order to provide food for monks.[79] The presence of a non-peasant

---

[76] Kosambi, Introduction, pp. 275–76.

[77] Irfan Habib in Seminar 39: Past and Present, New Delhi.

[78] Sharma in JBRS, XLIV, 3–4, p. 9; also Political Ideas and Institutions, pp. 222–23.

[79] Kosambi, Introduction, p. 257.

private right to the produce of the land is here unmistakable. This may be set alongside the evidence of two inscriptions of the third and fourth centuries AD which indicates 'the practice of letting out land to cultivators who received half the produce'.[80] We are thus offered evidence for both non-peasant landowners and their counterpart, sharecroppers.

It is not even unlikely that some of the peasants were semi-serfs and, having been denied the freedom of movement, could not occupy virgin soil even if available. Again, Kosambi himself, while noting that Fahien, *c.* AD 400, refers to the cultivators having the free choice of staying on or leaving the land, points out that the same traveller describes Buddhist abbeys as holding land 'along with the resident population and cattle', which would suggest something approaching serfdom.[81]

The king, as we have seen, appears in Kautilya as proprietor of a part of the land under his sovereignty. This division of the land between the *sita*-lands or king's domains (where the king claimed the bulk of the surplus either by organizing their cultivation or by sharing the crop with the cultivators) and the general lands (where he only took his conventional tax of one-sixth and other dues) seems to have disappeared during this period. The last possible survival of the *sita*-land may be seen in a Nasik inscription (*c.* AD 130) which refers to a 'royal field' (*rajakamkheta*) in a village.[82] The supposed sales of 'state lands' recorded in inscriptions of the fifth and sixth centuries are not really sales of lands, but sales of immunity from royal taxation.[83]

The Chinese travellers Fahien (AD 399–414) and Yuan Chwang (AD 629–45), it is true, refer, the first, to the 'king's lands' and, the other, to the 'king's tenants'. But since they speak of the tillers of these lands alone as paying him revenue in the form of a share in the crop (which Yuan Chwang puts significantly at the conventional one-sixth), it seems as if they mean by king's land simply the revenue-

---

[80] L. Gopal in *JESHO*, VI, 3, 1963, p. 306.
[81] Kosambi, *Introduction*, pp. 278–79. See L. Gopal in *JESHO*, IV, 2, pp. 306–7.
[82] Ghoshal, *Revenue System*, p. 187. Also see Bose, *Rural Economy*, p. 45.
[83] Kosambi, *Introduction*, p. 297. For the contrary assumption, See Maity, *Economic Life in Northern India*, pp. 19, 200–1.

paying land (as distinct, perhaps, from the dominions of the tributary rulers).[84] Their statements would thus in fact confirm the disappearance of the king's domain, separate from the ordinary revenue-paying land.

A significant feature of the period, initially due, as suggested by Kosambi, to the rise of the self-sufficient village, was the beginning of allotment of the king's own revenues from particular areas to his officials and vassals in lieu of salary. Kautilya had prescribed salaries in cash; but the *Manusmriti* lays down a scheme whereby officials posted over an area were to be assigned the revenues of a part of their charge (e.g., revenue of one village to the officer placed over a hundred).[85] Epigraphic evidence illustrating this practice is lacking, owing possibly to the perishable materials used for record of such allotment.[86] But from the account of Yuan Chwang it seems that it was well established by the seventh century, for he declares that all officers, high and low, were renumerated by allotments of revenues of lands.[87]

We have no direct information about the conditions on which these allotments of revenue were held. But since there is some evidence that the *bhogikas* or administrative officers were, already in the Gupta period, tending to become hereditary and to be set permanently over particular localities,[88] the revenue allotments also must have become fixed and usually not subject to resumption. It is likely, therefore, that the officers were able to extend their rights in the land to beyond the conventional claims of the king. For example, the village headman (*gramadhipati ayuktaka*) is represented in the *Kamasutra* (*c.* fourth–fifth centuries AD) as exacting unpaid labour from peasant women, compelling them, among other things, to fill his granaries and work on his fields.[89] The official thus appears as having land of his own and enjoying semi-feudal rights over the peasantry.

Epigraphic evidence for royal grants to Buddhist monks and

[84] See Ghoshal, *Revenue System*, pp. 191–92, 224–27.
[85] Kosambi, *Introduction*, pp. 241–42.
[86] See Sharma in *JESHO*, IV, 1, 1961, pp. 70–71.
[87] Ghoshal, *Revenue System*, pp. 228–29; Sharma, *Political Ideas and Institutions*, p. 207.
[88] Sharma, *Political Ideas and Institutions*, pp. 207ff.
[89] Ibid., pp. 211, 225; L. Gopal in *JESHO*, VI, 3, 1963, p. 305.

monasteries and to *brahmanas* and, later brahmanical temples, begins with the earlier part of the second century AD. The texts of the grants preserved on stone and, oftener, on copper plates, contain lists of the rights transferred and exemptions and immunities promised. It is generally agreed that what was usually granted was the king's own fiscal and semi-fiscal claims, with some administrative or semi judicial privileges or immunities.[90] The land of the grants is often described as wasteland. It has, therefore, been suggested that the *brahmanas* obtaining such grants helped to extend cultivation.[91] But it is also possible that the references to wasteland were often a mere matter of form, and lands already cultivated were also granted.[92] However, even if the priestly *brahmanas* were not always pioneer cultivators themselves, it is probable that on lands previously waste, or, by Ghoshal's interpretation of a term, under 'temporary tenants',[93] they would tend to become practically landowners. The phrase often used in the grants, that they were entitled 'to cultivate the land or get it cultivated', in fact, shows that they could either cultivate the land themselves or lease it to peasants on terms.[94] Early in the eighth century I-tsing tells us of Buddhist monasteries providing bulls and fields to cultivators (who should, therefore, be regarded as their tenants and not taxpayers) and taking one-sixth of the crop (which was the conventional royal share).[95] It appears inherently probable that the actual share of the crop in such cases was much larger than the stated conventional one.

6. There is a widespread tendency to designate the period from the seventh to the twelfth centuries as 'feudal'. Some historians, when they do so, appear to have in mind little more than the decay in monarchical power and the appearance of 'feudatories' of various grades which marked the polity of the period.[96] But suggestions have

---

[90] Ghoshal, *Revenue System*, pp. 186ff, contains a detailed analysis of the nature of the grants. See Kosambi, *Introduction*, pp. 291ff.

[91] Kosambi, *Introduction*, pp. 291ff.

[92] Sharma, *Political Ideas and Institutions*, pp. 216–20.

[93] For the interpretation of *uparikara* as 'impost levied on temporary tenants', see Ghoshal, *Revenue System*, pp. 210–13. But see Maity, *Economic Life in Northern India*, pp. 61–62.

[94] Kosambi, *Introduction*, pp. 300–1.

[95] Sharma, *Political Ideas and Institutions*, p. 222.

[96] See for example, B.P. Mazumdar, *Socio-Economic History of Northern India*, AD 1030–1194, Calcutta, 1961, pp. 1–41.

been made that in the structure of agrarian relationships too certain elements may be traced which, for want of a better term, can be called 'feudal'.

There is little evidence to suggest that the general prevalence of peasant cultivation, whose consolidation has been postulated for the previous period, was in any important respect modified. The existence of a form of serfdom, inferred from references to transfer of individual peasants and labourers as part of grants of lands, is attested by epigraphic records from Marwar, Saurashtra, Orissa and Bengal.[97] Though the epigraphic evidence is confined to a few regions only, Sharma quotes a Chinese account of AD 732 to show that the practice of donating villages together with the villagers to monasteries and temples was universal in India; and he takes it to indicate a general emergence of serfdom.[98] Passages from literature suggesting that the peasants were able to migrate in order to escape from oppression[99] are not decisive, and may only mean that on occasions the restraints on peasants could not be enforced.

The introduction of the Persian wheel (*araghata*),[100] besides helping to extend cultivation in the Indus basin and western Rajasthan, where the water-table is low, could also have had some effect on agrarian relations. An ingenious wooden machine, which was within the reach of the common peasant by the sixteenth century,[101] it was in the earlier phase apparently a possession of only the rich.[102] Inscriptions refer to a share in the barley crop claimed from peasants by potentates in Marwar on account of the Persian wheel wells, presumably owned by them.[103] There is also the possibility, inferred from a passage in a literary work, that the owner of a Persian wheel could be a

---

[97] See L. Gopal in *JESHO*, VI, 3, 1963, pp. 297ff; R.S. Sharma, *Indian Feudalism, c. 300–1200*, pp. 231–32.

[98] Sharma, *Indian Feudalism*, pp. 57–60.

[99] L. Gopal in *JESHO*, VI, 3, 1963, p. 296.

[100] L. Gopal gives reference to it from the literature and epigraphs of this period, in *University of Allahabad Studies (Ancient History Section)*, 1963–64, pp. 9–10. See also Kosambi, *Introduction*, p. liv.

[101] As shown by Babur's account of its use, *Baburnama*, II, translated by S. Beveridge, p. 486.

[102] L. Gopal, *University of Allahabad Studies*, p. 10.

[103] Ibid., pp. 83, 93; also see *JESHO*, IV, 1, 1961, p. 89.

'landlord' employing 'cultivators, workers and servants'.[104]

The principal characteristics of the agrarian system of the period, however, concern the mode of distribution of the surplus. The large amount of epigraphic evidence and some literary sources as well as Arabic and Persian accounts relating to the period enable us to have a more intimate view of this aspect than is possible for earlier times.

In essence, what happened during these five centuries may be called the ruralization of the ruling class. This appears to be linked up closely with the decline in urban life, which has been postulated for all the centuries since the Mauryas,[105] and with a marked decline in commerce, which can be the only reason for the extreme paucity of coins surviving from this period.[106] It is natural to expect in such conditions that the officials and aristocracies in the empires or kingdoms would be dispersed in the country and 'live off the land'.

The tendency can be closely traced in the polity of the period. First, there is considerable evidence of the wide prevalence of the practice, already present in the preceding period, of the assignment of revenues of particular territories to officers of the king.[107] It would appear that officers now held the revenues of the entire area placed in their administrative charge,[108] which perhaps marked a substantial change from the previous practice. This could explain a phenomenon whose existence is otherwise established, namely, the disappearance of distinction between royal officials and 'feudatories', hereditary feudatories being appointed to royal offices, and officials being granted the titles and, presumably, the privileges of feudatories.[109]

This meant really a division of the entire territories of each

---

[104] See L. Gopal in *University of Allahabad Studies*, p. 10.

[105] Kosambi, *Introduction*, pp. 282–83.

[106] L. Gopal, *University of Allahabad Studies*, pp. 75–76.

[107] The epigraphic evidence for this is set out by R.S. Sharma in *JESHO*, IV, 1, 1961, pp. 70–105, and L. Gopal, *University of Allahabad Studies*, pp. 75–103.

[108] L. Gopal, p. 101. R.S. Sharma, who appears to take the contrary view (*JESHO*, IV, 1, pp. 90–91), is probably guided by his identification of the land grants made to officers with their revenue assignments (for which see below).

[109] See Sharma in *Journal of Indian History* (*JIH*), XLI, 1, 1963, pp. 281–83; L. Gopal, *University of Allahabad Studies*, p. 83–86.

kingdom, leading inevitably to sub-division. In its extreme form the process is seen in the so-called 'clan monarchies' or the proto-Rajput kingdoms, especially under the Gurjara-Pratiharas, eighth–tenth centuries, and the dynasties succeeding them in the various regions once ruled over by them. Here the territory was parcelled out by the ruler after retaining his own share (*svabhujyamana svabhuga*) among his kinsmen and clan chiefs.[110] Each of the latter then set about dividing his territory among his own clansmen, while retaining 'his own share' (*svabhogavaptah*), until by this process of 'sub-infeudation' every village was assigned to a particular man in return for supply of troopers when needed by the assignor.[111]

It is in the same period and the same regions that new territorial units, comprising groups of villages, specified by numbers that were all multiples of 6, viz. 12, 42 and 84, were established. These units are mentioned in the records of the Pratiharas, and the succeeding dynasties of Chahamanas, Gahadvalas, Paramaras and Chalukyas; they were unheard of before, but many of the units of 84 (*chaurasis*) survive to the present day.[112] Even now they are particularly associated with the Rajput castes.[113] U.N. Ghoshal offers the only plausible explanation for their emergence, namely, that they were created for convenience of distribution of territories among the chiefs in the 'clan monarchies'.[114] Their sturdy survival down the centuries indicates the sweeping and, indeed, lasting nature of the territorial distribution that took place among the dominant clans at that time.

The most common titles of the new potentates are *samanta*,[115]

---

[110] See U.N. Ghoshal, *History of the Hindu Revenue System*, p. 236; Sharma in *JESHO*, IV, 1, pp. 87ff, 96–98; L. Gopal, *University of Allahabad Studies*, pp. 86–95.

[111] Sharma in *JESHO*, IV, 1, pp. 96–98. See Mazumdar, *Socio-Economic History*, p. 28.

[112] See Sir Henry Elliot's long note on *Chaurasi* in his *Memoirs on . . . the North-Western Provinces of India*, II, edited by Beames, London, pp. 47–78.

[113] See ibid., p. 77.

[114] Ghoshal, *Revenue System*, pp. 241, 259–60. His suggestion is reinforced by L. Gopal's examination of epigraphic evidence in *University of Allahabad Studies*, pp. 95–99.

[115] The change of meaning of *samanta* from 'king' to 'feudal baron' is dated late in the sixth century by Kosambi on the basis of epigraphic evidence, *JESHO*, II, 3, pp. 283–84.

*ranaka, rauta, thakkura* and *rajaputra*. It is not always easy to establish the place of the different titles in the hierarchy. *Rajaputra,* for example, is used for a prince under the Chahamanas,[116] but for the lowest ranking 'fief'-holder under the Chalukyas.[117] It also appears that neither this nor its abbreviated form *rauta,* nor *thakkura,* necessarily denoted a particular caste.[118] But it is possible that a new caste, ancestor of the later 'martial' caste of Rajputs, was already emerging. Sharma has shown how once a particular tribe, the Gurjaras, for example, had established its domination, a rapid process of differentiation would take place within it, with the ordinary tribesmen-cultivators, the common Gujars, joining the ranks of the ordinary exploited masses. It may be expected that simultaneously with this political and economic depreciation of the mass of the tribesmen, their betters would tend to form a separate, superior caste. It is, therefore, not without reason that the tribes of the 'clan monarchies' have been regarded in tradition as the ancestors of several clans of the Rajputs.

Formally speaking, the rights of members of the new ruling class should not have extended beyond those claimed by the king, from whom their authority nominally derived. It is difficult to establish the exact magnitude of the land revenue demand set by the rulers. References to the conventional royal 'one-sixth' or even 'one-tenth' share of the crop have been found in two or three inscriptions.[119] But it is likely that these were more formal terms like 'tithe' and did not represent the actual state of affairs.[120] In any case, inscriptions mention a host of other taxes and imposts on the peasants besides the share in the crop, which would have inflated the burden on them to an unknown extent.

It seems, moreover, that besides their territorial assignments,

---

[116] L. Gopal, *University of Allahabad Studies,* p. 93.

[117] Sharma, *JESHO,* IV, 1, pp. 96–98.

[118] Thus a *brahmana* is described as grandson of a *rauta* and great-grandson of a *ranaka,* ibid., p. 79. For *thakkura* being a title sometimes held by *brahmanas* and so having not caste but 'feudal implications' see Kosambi, *Introduction,* p. 335.

[119] P. Niyogi, *Contributions to the Economic History of Northern India, from the Tenth to the Twelfth Century AD,* Calcutta, 1962, pp. 180–81.

[120] See Moreland, *Agrarian System of Moslem India,* Allahabad reprint, n.d., p. 5.

the potentates were obtaining particular lands under hereditary right. From the ninth century we have epigraphic records of hereditary grants of revenues of land to state officers, and these greatly increase from the eleventh century.[121] These are not 'service grants', i.e. grants in lieu of cash pay or in return for service but grants simply patterned on those made so far only to *brahmanas* and religious institutions.[122] Being hereditary and unconditional, these were different from territorial assignments; and it is possible that the grantee's right tended to become almost fully proprietary. Early in the thirteenth century under the Chandellas in eastern Uttar Pradesh we find a *ranaka* accepting a village in mortgage, and another *ranaka* mortgaging his fields to two other *ranakas*.[123] We very probably have here an early indication of how the personal landholdings of rural chiefs, surviving into the fourteenth century and later times, were created.

The inscriptions of the period bear testimony to the continuous stream of grants by rulers as well as their 'feudatories' to *brahmanas*. From the sixth century we have an increasing number of grants bestowed on brahmanical temples, many of which tended to have large bodies of priests and attendants.[124] The extent of land under the control of temples during this period must have been considerable, for it is probable that revenues from them were one of the chief sources of their fabulous wealth.[125]

## II

1. The Ghorian conquests of northern India, leading to the establishment of the Delhi Sultanate (1206–1526) may be said to mark the true beginning of the medieval period in India. We now have historical works, properly so called; and a connected narrative history becomes for the first time possible. There are, however, other reasons than an improvement in the nature of the historical record that make the thirteenth century an important watershed in Indian history.

[121] Sharma, *JESHO*, IV, 1, p. 70. See also Kosambi, *JESHO*, II, 3, p. 293, for a similar case of mortgage from Rewa, AD 1212.
[122] See L. Gopal, *University of Allahabad Studies*, pp. 78–79.
[123] Sharma, *JESHO*, IV, 1, p. 81.
[124] Sharma, *Political Ideas and Institutions*, pp. 221–22.
[125] See P. Niyogi, *Contributions*, pp. 284–98, for a rather uncritical collection of information relating to the 'temple economy' of the period.

To begin with, the new conquerors and rulers, who were of a different faith (Islam) from that of their predecessors, established a regime that was in some profound respects different from the old. The Sultans achieved power that was, in terms of both territorial extent and centralization, unprecedented (except, perhaps, for the Mauryas 1,500 years earlier). Their principal achievements lay in a great systematization of agrarian exploitation and an immense concentration of the resources so obtained. This ensured that the land revenue (*kharaj/mal*) demanded on their behalf should comprehend the bulk, if not the whole, of the peasant's surplus produce; and the king's bureaucracy thereby became the principal exploiting class in society.

Immediately after the conquest the conquerors tended to enter into settlements with members of the defeated and subjugated aristocracies—the *ra'is* (=rajas), *ranas* (=ranakas) and *rawats* (=rauts).[126] *Kharaj* was then really no more than tribute fixed on the subjugated rulers, except for some small areas where direct relations between the new rulers and the peasants might have been established.[127] Nearly a century of experience and adaptation cleared the ground for the radical step taken in the first decade of the fourteenth century. Alauddin Khalji (1296–1316), the most powerful and successful of the Sultans, decreed that the land revenue was henceforth to be set at half the produce and was to be levied separately on the holding of each individual cultivator.[128] The exact magnitude of land revenue demanded under Alauddin Khalji's successors is not stated, but there is no reason to believe that the standard of one-half was ever substantially altered by them.[129]

It must, of course, be recognized that any standard of revenue demand had to be theoretical; and the actual share in the crop,

---

[126] See, for example, Minhaj Siraj, *Tabaqat-i Nasiri*, Bib. Ind. ed., p. 247; and Barani, *Tarikh-i Firuz Shahi*, Bib. Ind. ed., pp. 106, 182 (henceforth referred to as 'Barani').

[127] See Moreland, *Agrarian System*, pp. 29–30.

[128] The basic authority is Barani, p. 287. For an interpretation of the passage, see Moreland, *Agrarian System*, pp. 32–33, 224–27.

[129] Moreland, *Agrarian System*, pp. 44, 48 and n, 62. I.H. Qureshi, *The Administration of the Sultanate of Delhi*, Lahore, 1942, pp. 110–13, puts forward the view that the general standard of revenue demand both before and after Alauddin Khalji was only a fifth of the produce. But the evidence he offers and the interpretation he seeks to impose on it are both difficult to accept.

except under simple crop-sharing arrangements, must have varied from locality to locality and year to year. Thus under Alauddin Khalji the land was measured and a fixed tax in kind on each unit of area (*biswa*), presumably worked out on the basis of an approximation to the standard, was levied irrespective of the current year's harvest.[130] A further variation was possible, generally to the disadvantage of the revenue-payer, when tax in grain (or the authorities' share of the crop) was commuted into cash at market prices. Payment in cash had become quite widely prevalent by the fourteenth century, although Alauddin Khalji himself preferred collection in grain.[131] Besides the land revenue, other burdens were also imposed upon the peasants; in particular, the tax on cattle or grazing tax.[132]

The revenue resources so created were distributed among the ruling class principally through the Sultan's assigning to individuals the right to levy the revenue in particular territories. Territorial units assigned in this way were termed *iqtas*, while the territory whose revenues were directly collected for the Sultan's own treasury was designated *khalisa*. Both these terms are Arabic in origin and represent long-established institutions of the polity of Islamic countries.[133]

If appropriation of the surplus produced by the peasant above the requirements of his subsistence is taken to be the principal criterion of landed property, the *iqta* may be considered the basic unit of such property, and its holders as forming the main class of landed proprietors. It is, therefore, necessary to examine the nature of the *iqta* and the rights and position of its holders in some detail.

Broadly speaking, three stages in the history of the *iqta* under the Sultans can be distinguished.

(a) It was natural, in the earlier phase, for the Turkish Sultans to assign different regions as *iqtas* to their commanders, who were required to maintain themselves and their troops out of the revenues of the *iqtas*. The *iqta* then stood for a revenue assignment as well as

---

[130] Moreland, *Agrarian System*, pp. 33, 224, 226.

[131] Ibid., pp. 11, 114, 136–37.

[132] Barani, pp. 287–88. Shams Siraj Afif, *Tarikh-i Firuz Shahi*, Bib. Ind., p. 98, says rhetorically, that if a peasant had two milch cows, one was taken away from him.

[133] For the development of the concept and nature of *iqta*, see F. Lokkegaard, *Islamic Taxation in the Classic Period*, Copenhagen, 1950, pp. 14ff.

an administrative charge, and the *muqtis* (=*walis*) or holders of *iqtas* were also governors.

The *iqtas* were constantly transferred from one person to another—a practice which makes the conventional English rendering of *iqta* as 'fief' particularly misleading.[134]

Besides the troops maintained by the *muqtis* out of the revenue of their *iqtas*, the Sultan had his own personal troops (*qalb*). In the thirteenth century men of the royal calvary were paid by assigning them revenues of villages around the capital and in the Doab country. These assignments too were termed *iqtas*; but these tended to become semi-permanent, and even hereditary.[135]

(b) Under the Khaljis and the early Tughlaqs (1290–1351), as the administration of the Sultanate was consolidated, the earlier simple arrangements were considerably modified. The transfers of *iqtas* became even more frequent; at the same time, the *muqtis* no longer remained in absolute control of the revenues of their *iqtas*. They had to submit accounts of their collection and expenditure,[136] and to send the balances (*fawazil*) to the king's treasury.[137] An estimate of the revenue-paying capacity (*jama*) of each locality was prepared. The personal salaries of the officers were fixed in terms of cash; and the revenues of particular districts or territories, whose estimated revenue income equalled their sanctioned pay, were assigned to them.[138] The pay of the troops under them was now deemed to be a direct charge on the Sultan's treasury rather than on the commanders;[139] and a portion of the revenues of the *iqta* was set apart for the

---

[134] See Moreland in JIH, VIII, pt i, pp. 1–8; *Agrarian System*, pp. 216–23.

[135] Barani, pp. 61–64. See Moreland, *Agrarian System*, pp. 27–28.

[136] This appears from Barani, pp. 430–31, 556, and Afif, *Tarikh-i Firuz Shahi*, pp. 341, 408, 414–15. See Moreland, *Agrarian System*, pp. 43, 220–21.

[137] Barani, pp. 220–21, 468. See Moreland, *Agrarian System*, p. 220.

[138] The most direct evidence is Afif, *Tarikh-i Firuz Shahi*, p. 94, but an inference for the prevalence of this system may be drawn from Shihabuddin al-Umari, *Masalik-al-Absar*, portion on India, edited by K.A. Faruqi, Delhi, p. 26. See Moreland, *Agrarian System*, pp. 51–52, 56–57; he calls the estimate of revenue income 'valuation'.

[139] *Masalik-al-Absar*, p. 25, where the interesting observation is also made that this distinguished the Indian *iqta* system from that of Syria and Egypt. In these two countries the commanders themselves paid their troops by assigning them lands. See Moreland, *Agrarian System*, pp. 51–52.

payment of the troops of the *muqtis*.[140] Such limitations of the authority of the *muqti* necessitated the appointment of Sultan's officers within the *iqtas*, a practice which apparently had begun under Balban (1266–1286).[141] The tendency towards royal intervention reached its peak under Sultan Muhammad Tughlaq (1325–51). In several cases he handed over the collection of the revenue of the *iqtas* to either revenue farmers or his own financial officers, the commanders or *amirs* posted in the *iqtas*, presumably drawing their pay in cash from the local treasury and having nothing to do directly with revenue collection.[142]

One form of *iqta*, the assignment in lieu of salary to the cavalry troops of the king, was abolished by Alauddin Khalji and the troops under him and his successors drew their pay in cash.[143]

In general, the *khalisa*, comprising lands whose revenues were reserved for the king's treasury, appears to have expanded very greatly. Still it seems to have consisted not of shifting territories scattered throughout the empire, as was the case with the *khalisa* under the Mughals, but of a large block of territory around Delhi, principally the country of the Doab.[144]

(c) With the accession of Sultan Firuz Tughlaq in 1351, which took place after a severe political crisis created by rebellions of a large section of the ruling class, the entire trend of the preceding period was reversed, and a series of concessions were granted by the Sultan to his officers. First of all, the *jama* or estimated revenue income was fixed permanently,[145] so that the assignees obtained all benefits of increase in actual revenue collection. While *iqta* transfers were still effected,[146] they appear to have become rarer. Indeed Firuz

---

[140] Barani, pp. 430–31.

[141] Ibid., pp. 36–37.

[142] For the farming (*muqata'a*) of *iqtas*, see Barani, pp. 487–88. See Moreland, *Agrarian System*, pp. 46–48. Ibn Battuta tells us incidentally of the arrangements in the *iqta* of Amroha, where the *wali al-Kharaj* (revenue collector) and the *amir* (commander) were different officers independent of each other; *Rehla*, translated by Mahdi Husain, Baroda, 1953, pp. 144–46.

[143] Barani, pp. 323–24; Afif, *Tarikh-i Firuz Shahi*, pp. 94–96. Moreland, *Agrarian System*, p. 39, however, goes too far when he supposes that Alauddin Khalji wished to dispense with the large *iqtas* as well.

[144] See Barani, pp. 323–24.

[145] Afif, *Tarikh-i Firuz Shahi*, p. 94. See Moreland, *Agrarian System*, p. 57.

[146] Afif, *Tarikh-i Firuz Shahi*, p. 220.

Tughlaq's declared policy of bestowing administrative offices upon the sons of the previous incumbents[147] suggests strongly that *iqtas* too were similarly treated when their holders died. Finally, he instituted the practice of paying his troopers by assigning them revenues (*wajh*), thus recreating the small *iqtas* under a new name. Moreover, he made both the assignments and the posts of troopers practically hereditary.[148]

The concessions that Firuz made proved to be of long duration. Under the Lodis (1451–1526) the administrative charges and revenue assignments were assimilated, so that *sarkars* and *parganas* represented administrative divisions as well as assignments.[149] Like Firuz, Sikandar Lodi (1489–1517) too did not claim the balance if the revenue income of the assignee increased;[150] and he is also said to have confirmed the assignment, in the event of an assignee's death, upon one of the latter's sons, chosen by the Sultan himself.[151] The principal commanders raised and maintained their troops by sub-assigning parts of the territory under their charge to their subordinates, who, in turn, could pay the troops by the same means.[152] The ultimate assignee, however, levied the land revenue directly on the peasants.[153]

From this survey the principal features of the three stages in the history of the *iqta* system may be thus stated. First, during the thirteenth century there was a simple division of the empire among tribute-receiving governors. Then, in the first half of the fourteenth century there took place an enlargement of the revenue demand, and so of the income of the *iqta*, while an extreme degree of royal control was established over the *iqta*. Finally, from the middle of the fourteenth to the early years of the sixteenth century, there was a reversion

---

[147] *Futubat-i-Firuz Shahi* (Aligarh edition) 22. See Afif, *Tarikh-i Firuz Shahi*, p. 482.

[148] Afif, *Tarikh-i Firuz Shahi*, pp. 94–96, 220–21.

[149] See I.H. Siddiqi in *Medieval India Quarterly*, V, 1963, pp. 26–31.

[150] *Waqi'at-i Mushtaqi*, Br. M. MS., Add. 11, 633, f. 26a. See Moreland, *Agrarian System*, p. 72.

[151] Abbas Khan, *Tuhfa-i Akbar-Shahi*, MS. I.O., 218, f. 27a. See Moreland, *Agrarian System*, p. 68.

[152] This appears from Abbas Khan's account of the career of Farid's father, Hasan, and of Farid's own arrangements in his father's assignment in Bihar. See Moreland, *Agrarian System*, pp. 67–68.

[153] See Abbas Khan's account of Farid's proceedings as revenue collector in his father's assignment in Bihar, ff. 17b–19a.

to the simpler form of *iqta* organization, but with the difference, perhaps, that the assignees directly appropriated the bulk of the peasants' surplus for themselves.

These developments in the *iqta* system appear to be closely related to the changes in the composition of the ruling class. In the first stage the composition was relatively stable, the ruling class being largely confined to royal slaves of nomad Turkish origin and their families (in Barani's phrase, 'The Forty Slaves of Iltutmish').[154] But along with the inauguration of a regime of monarchical despotism under Alauddin Khalji, a series of veritable upheavals occurred in the composition of the ruling class. The older elements were destroyed:[155] 'upstarts', Indianized Turks, Indian slaves, and foreign immigrants now formed the bulk of the Sultan's bureaucracy. Alongside the loss of its exclusiveness, this class also lost its stability. The contemporary historian noticed three successive groups of officers, one substituted for the other, during the two decades of Alauddin Khalji's reign.[156] Even more sensational phenomena were witnessed under Muhammad Tughlaq: large-scale recruitment of foreigners,[157] still greater recruitment from the lower strata of the Indian population[158] and from Hindus;[159] and an attempted wholesale destruction of the older, chiefly military elements (represented by the cavalry officer-corps, the *amiran-i sada*).[160]

Such sweeping changes in the composition of the class that in effect held the bulk of landed property could only have been possible because of the nature of the *iqta* system. The individual members of the ruling class had no claim whatsoever to any particular parcel of land or locality and thus could be provided with, or deprived of, their income at the will of the king. It would seem that for a time the concentration of such authority in the hands of the king, implying

---

[154] Barani, pp. 25–28. See M. Habib, Introduction to Elliot and Dowson, *History of India*, II, Aligarh edition, 1952, pp. 94ff.

[155] Barani, pp. 250–51.

[156] Ibid., p. 336.

[157] Ibn Battuta, *Rehla*, pp. 4–5, 107.

[158] Barani, pp. 504–5; see K.M. Ashraf, *Life and Conditions of the People of Hindustan*, second edition, Delhi, 1959, pp. 63–64.

[159] Ibn Battuta, *Rehla*, p. 8; Isami, *Futuhu's Salatin*, edited by Usha, Madras, 1948; Barani, pp. 504–5.

[160] Barani, pp. 503–4, 516–17.

immense political and economic centralization, was necessary for the establishment of the new mechanism of exploitation. Once this had been accomplished, the sentiment in favour of permanent and semi-hereditary right in the assignments became irresistible. Firuz Tughlaq at last made a complete capitulation to this sentiment, winning in return the fulsome gratitude of the nobles and their hangers-on.[161] He publicly announced the policy of letting son succeed father to official posts;[162] and but for his large collection of slaves he scrupulously kept away all new elements, thus paying full respect to the principle of birth, which was so much lauded by the historian Barani.[163] The fullest degree of fixity of rights for its members was achieved by the nobility under the Lodis. It now consisted of Afghan tribal leaders, whose control over the revenues of their territorial charges tended to be hereditary, and derived only partly from the king's favour.[164]

On the whole, unlike in the previous period, the ruling class of the Sultanate was mainly urban in character. The *iqta*-holders, subject to periodic transfer from one locality or region to another, could not base their authority upon the control of any particular rural area. Many of them lived or served in Delhi, and presumably at other big towns, far from their current assignments. They had, therefore, a strong tendency to commute their revenues into cash. Even under Alauddin Khalji, when they were asked to collect the land revenue in kind it was laid down that the grain should be sold to merchants at fixed prices 'by the side of the field'.[165] Since the land revenue constituted the bulk of the peasants' surplus, large-scale trade between town and country must have resulted. This in turn promoted the cultivation of superior, or cash, crops. For the first time in the fourteenth century we find the substitution of high-priced crops for low-grade crops meant for local consumption being proclaimed as an object of state policy.[166]

---

[161] For samples of the praise showered on Firuz Tughlaq see Barani pp. 548, 555, and Afif, *Tarikh-i Firuz Shahi*, passim.

[162] *Futuhat-i-Firuz-Shahi*.

[163] Barani, p. 18; and his praise of Firuz for keeping his father's officers, p. 549.

[164] See R. Williams, *An Empire-builder of the Sixteenth Century*, Delhi, reprint, pp. 15–18, 159–60.

[165] Barani, pp. 304–5.

[166] Barani, p. 498. See Moreland, *Agrarian System*, p. 51.

The large export of grain and other produce from the country, caused by the exaction of the revenue, maintained a class of specialized grain merchants (*karvanis*, the later *banjaras*) which appears for the first time now in our historical record.[167] On the other hand it is said that the *multanis* (Hindu merchants) and *sahs* (money-lenders) of Delhi became enormously rich by advancing very large loans to the Turkish nobles against drafts on the revenues of their *iqtas*.[168] The *iqta* system may thus be said to have forced in some ways the pace of medieval commercial development.

The immense drain of a substantial part of rural produce to the towns in the form of revenues of the *iqta*-holders helped to create large town populations. Town crafts also grew. So great was the demand of the nobility that slaves were trained to be artisans in large numbers;[169] and the Sultans, and so presumably also the nobles, maintained large workshops (*karkhanas*) where free and servile artisans worked to meet their needs.[170]

Besides the *iqta*, there was also one other form of alienation of the king's revenue, which may be briefly mentioned. This is what Moreland terms grants. These grants were assignments of revenues of relatively small areas, given to persons for life. These were often in fact hereditary, but were subject to resumption at the Sultan's pleasure.[171] These were known generally as *milk* (pl. *amlak*), *idrarat* or *madad-i ma'ash*; and some of them as *in'am*. They were given to theologians, scholars, petty courtiers and retired officials and thus chiefly maintained the Muslim educated class. Some of the grants were in the nature of endowment (*waqf*, p;. *auqaf*) for Muslim religious shrines. The nobles made grants out of their own *iqtas*; but these were presumably for as long as they themselves had their *iqtas*. From figures given by Afif it seems that under Firuz, who bestowed the largest number of grants, the revenues so alienated amounted to less than 5.5 per cent of the whole.[172] Much of the area covered by the

[167] Barani, pp. 304, 306.
[168] Ibid., p. 120. See Irfan Habib, in *Comparative Studies in Society and History* (*CSSH*), The Hague, VI, 4, pp. 407–8.
[169] Afif, *Tarikh-i Firuz Shahi*, pp. 267–73.
[170] Ibid.
[171] See Moreland, *Agrarian System*, pp. 10, 32, 39, 58, 63.
[172] Afif, *Tarikh-i Firuz Shahi*, pp. 94, 359–60.

grants was in wastelands, which the grantees wee expected to bring under cultivation.[173]

The Turkish conquests resulted naturally in a considerable depression in the position of the previous ruling class. It was not in the main exterminated, but subjugated, its members being converted initially into tributary chiefs. In the eleventh century, we hear of the *kharaj* being collected from *thakurs* (*thakkuras*) in Ghaznavide Panjab;[174] and in the thirteenth century, similarly, from *ra'is, ranas* and *rawats*.[175] The very designations of these tributary rural chiefs proclaim them to be members or descendants of the previous aristocracy. But we know practically nothing of the social structure and property relations existing under them during this early phase.

With the increased pressure of the Sultanate ruling class, beginning with Alauddin Khalji's land-revenue measures, the modern historian can penetrate the countryside almost at the heels of the Sultan's revenue collector. The *ra'is* and *ranas* now represent the bigger chiefs. Of lower status are *chaudhuris* (Hindu headmen of groups of '100' villages),[176] *khuts* and *muqaddams* (village headmen). Persons of this second class, who might have also included men depressed from amongst the *ra'is* and *ranas*, seem to have had large landholdings of their own, which were generally not liable to land revenue. In return for this share in the agricultural surplus, these rural and village 'chiefs' collected the land revenue from the peasantry on behalf of the Sultan and his assignees.[177]

A very interesting development, to which little attention has been paid so far, appears to be the social consolidation of this superior rural class, through the absorption of its various elements, as clans or sub-castes, into the great Rajput caste over the larger part of northern India. Both the term *Rajput* (*Raja-putra*) as name for the

[173] See I.H. Qureshi, in *Proceedings of Indian Historical Records Commission*, 31st Session, 1944, p. 61.
[174] *Tarikh-i Baihaqi*, edited by Ghani and Faiyaz, Tehran, AH 1324, p. 407.
[175] See note 126 above.
[176] Ibn Battuta, *Rehla*, p. 123.
[177] This paragraph is based mainly on the following passages in our sources: Barani, pp. 287–91, 429–31; and Afif, *Tarikh-i Firuz Shahi*, pp. 36–39. See Moreland, *Agrarian System*, pp. 29–30, 33, 38–39, 41–42, 224–26. Alauddin Khalji had imposed, and Ghiyasuddin Tughlaq abolished, land revenue upon the lands of the *khuts* and *muqaddams*.

caste,[178] and the sense of the unity of its components, appear suddenly in the Persian authorities of the sixteenth century, and must, therefore, have quietly evolved in the preceding period. This caste cohesion of the rural aristocracy possibly developed out of a real class cohesion, as higher elements were pressed into the lower ranks of the rural aristocracy. The history of the term *zamindar*, denoting the superior rural class in the Mughal period (sixteenth and seventeenth centuries), indicates an evolution parallel to the term Rajput. In the latter part of the fourteenth century, when it first appears, it only indicates the big chiefs of the level of *ra'is* and *ranas*.[179] Within a century and a half *zamindar* became the standard designation for the larger class, which previously had no name because presumably it had no integral entity.

At its lower levels the rural aristocracy must have sometimes stood at the fringe of the big peasantry. The occasional vagueness of the line of distinction between the two is indicated by the contemporary use of the term *ri'aya* or *ra'iyat*, which stood sometimes for the common peasantry and sometimes for the rural revenue-payers in general, thus including the headmen and other superior elements. At the same time there seems to have been considerable stratification within the peasantry. A sharp antithesis between the two extremes among the peasants is suggested by the historian's remark that Ala-uddin Khalji imposed the same rate of land revenue upon the lands of the *khut* as well as *balahar*.[180] The *khut* signified the large village landholder, presumably the headman, seeking to keep his lands revenue-free and to shift the burden of the revenue demand upon the 'weak'; the *balahar* was the village menial (of the lowliest, untouchable caste), allotted a small plot for his bare subsistence by the village community.[181]

In so far as there was a tendency on the part of the superior elements in the countryside to escape from paying land revenue on their own lands, while collecting it from the mass of the peasants,

---

[178] See S.H. Hodivala, *Studies in Indo-Muslim History*, Bombay, 1939, p. 352.
[179] For instance, see Afif, *Tarikh-i Firuz Shahi*, p. 170. Also see Moreland, *Agrarian System*, p. 18.
[180] Barani, p. 287.
[181] See Moreland, *Agrarian System*, pp. 32n, 224–26; Irfan Habib, *Agrarian System of Mughal India*, pp. 120–21.

besides levying their own imposts on them, there was an obvious conflict of interests between the two classes. Barani's passage on Alauddin Khalji's measures suggests that the Sultan consciously utilized this contradiction by standing forth as the protector of the 'weak' against 'the strong' in the village and seeking to enlarge the state's share of the surplus produce at the expense chiefly of the rural aristocracy.[182] But when, following Ghiyasuddin Tughlaq's concessions to the *khuts* and *muqaddams*,[183] Muhammad Tughlaq increased the revenue demand again,[184] it provoked an armed uprising in the Doab (c. AD 1330), which from the historian's description of it, appears as a rebellion of peasants led by the lower rural aristocracy, viz. the *khuts* and *muqaddams*.[185] Apparently, the two rural classes united when they were alike hit by the newly imposed burden. Their uprising, by its severity, extent and duration, occupies a very significant place in the annals of India's peasant revolts.

2. The sixteenth century saw the establishment of the Mughal empire in India. This empire not only united the large part of India within its limits, but also attained a degree of centralized authority and stability far surpassing that of any of the earlier dynasties of the Sultans. Although it was founded by Babur in 1526, its classic period begins with the accession of Akbar, 1556, and ends with the death of Aurangzeb, 1707.

For the Mughal empire our records of all kinds are very extensive; and for the first time in Indian history we can claim to have direct evidence for almost all significant aspects of society. The day is still awaited when at least the major part of this evidence will have been used by students of the subject. Nevertheless, the broad features of the economy and the social and political structure appear now to be fairly clear.[186]

A study of the official Mughal area statistics and other geographical information indicates that the extent of cultivation then

[182] Barani, pp. 287–88.
[183] Ibid., pp. 429–31.
[184] Ibid., pp. 472–73. See Moreland, *Agrarian System*, p. 48.
[185] Barani, pp. 472–73, 479–80. See Ibn Battuta, *Rehla*, pp. 153–58.
[186] In this section, at many points I have drawn heavily upon my own work, *The Agrarian System of Mughal India* (henceforth referred to as I. Habib). References to sources and modern works cited there are not, as a rule, repeated in this paper.

was about half of what it was about the beginning of this century in the middle Ganga basin and the Indus basin and in central India; and from two-thirds to one-fifth in the other regions.[187] Large stretches of virgin soil were, therefore, still available for cultivation in almost all regions, except perhaps some territories such as the Doab and the region around Agra and Delhi. As far as the means of cultivation are concerned, they were practically the same as existing about the year 1900, and the only important factor missing was the extensive irrigation-canal system laid out by the British chiefly in the Indus basin and the upper Ganga region.[188] In such circumstances peasant cultivation had to be the most widely prevalent form of agricultural production. At the same time, in view of the availability of virgin soil, no intrinsic value could yet be attached to most of the land under the plough. It is significant that seventeenth-century peasants are known to have been in debt to moneylenders for their seed and cattle, and for meeting the revenue demand, but not for the land under their occupation.[189]

'Landed property', therefore, could not have consisted of any right to a particular parcel of land. In the absence of full-fledged serfdom, it had to lie principally in a share of the produce wherever the peasant might cultivate, within the village, or the district, or the whole empire. The Mughals firmly consolidated the tendency already at work under the Sultans: namely, to claim from the peasant the bulk of his surplus produce. Such a claim was now possible to enforce particularly because of the growth of commerce and the extensive cultivation for the market.[190] The rapid spread of the tobacco crop within the first fifty years of the seventeenth century throughout the length and breadth of India is an index of how quickly the peasant was now able to follow the market.[191] A cash-nexus could now be established more widely than ever before;[192] and this immensely simplified the assessment and collection of land revenue.

[187] L., Habib, pp. 1–24. Moreland offers a still lower estimate, *India at the Death of Akbar*, London, 1920, pp. 20–22.
[188] I. Habib, pp. 24–36.
[189] *CSSH*, VI, 4, p. 394.
[190] I. Habib, pp. 61–81.
[191] Ibid., pp. 45–46, 81.
[192] Ibid., pp. 236–40.

The detailed information that we possess about the methods of assessment and collection of land revenue under the Mughals enables us to form an idea of the magnitude of the revenue demand. When the demand, as under the *zabt* system, was expressed in cash, the actual part of the produce which the peasant had to part with in order to pay the revenue must have varied from harvest to harvest and locality to locality. But the rate had itself been determined on the basis of its being one-third of the estimated produce, and the demand in practice probably amounted to much more.[193] Under other systems, one-half appears often to have been the standard rate of demand. In some outlying or arid regions the standard was lower, but in certain fertile areas, such as coastal Gujarat, it reached three-quarters of the produce.[194]

When the bulk of the peasants' surplus was thus being claimed for the king, it is not surprising that contemporary European travellers should have declared, without a single voice of dissent, that the king was the owner of the soil in India.[195] Even an Indian writer of the earlier half of the eighteenth century asserted that the *kharaj* (land revenue) was due to the king because of his property right (*milkiyat*) in the land.[196] No official Indian writer, however, subscribed to this view; and an Indian jurist explicitly rejected the notion.[197] This rejection may partly have been due to the fact that the king did not claim the right to eject the peasant occupant of the land so long as he continued to cultivate it.[198] There was also the spectacle of the king buying particular plots of land from his subjects for his

---

[193] The revenue rates under the *zabt* system were not permanent and were changed from time to time. Moreover, the whole system could be replaced by another, such as assessment in kind or crop-sharing. Revenue demand could, therefore, be adjusted without much difficulty to a rise in prices. This may be the reason why the great rise in prices due to the influx of silver during the earlier part of the seventeenth century did not create any noticeable disturbance in the mechanism of rural exploitation. For this seventeenth century inflation, see I. Habib, pp. 81–89, 327, 384–94.

[194] Ibid., pp. 190–96.

[195] Ibid., p. 111.

[196] Tekchand 'Bahar', *Bahar-i-Ajam* (s.v. *kharaj*).

[197] Qazi Muhammad Ala, *Risala Ahkam al Arazi*, MS. Aligarh, Abdus Salam, Arabiya (4): 331/101, ff. 43b, 44b.

[198] Ibid. ff, 47b–48a. Since land was abundant, there was in any case no practical use in claiming this right.

own use, to inhibit any speculation about royal ownership of the entire land.[199]

Whether the right that the Mughal emperor claimed was in name proprietary or not, in terms of our discussion he must be supposed by his exaction of the land revenue to have enjoyed a major share of the fruits of proprietary possession (which did not then exist as a single integral right at all). It rested with his will to dispose of this enormous tribute. Over the larger portion of the empire he transferred his right to collect the land revenue and other taxes due to him to concern of his subjects. The areas whose revenues were thus assigned were known as *jagirs* (less often, *tuyuls*); and the assignees were termed *jagirdars*.

The *jagirdars* were officers and servants of the emperor, and their *jagirs* were normally assigned to them in lieu of their pay.[200] Each officer of the Mughal emperor was given a dual numerical rank (*mansab*), the first number representing his *zat*, and the second his *sawar* rank. The *zat* rank determined, according to the sanctioned schedule, the personal pay of the *mansab*-holder (*mansabdar*); and the *sawar* rank the size of the cavalry contingent maintained by him for the emperor's service as well as the pay he was to receive to meet his expenses for maintaining it. The total amounts sanctioned for both *zat* and *sawar* made up his pay-claim (*talab*); and this could be met either by payment in cash from the imperial treasury or by assigning to him territories in *jagir* whose revenue income as officially estimated (*jama, jama-dami*) had exactly to equal the pay due to him.[201]

Besides the ordinary *jagir*, there was a kind known as *watan jagir*. A *watan jagir* was really the territory of a subordinate chief who had been enrolled in the imperial service, and granted a *mansab*; his pay was then supposed to be met by the income of his home territory,

---

[199] I. Habib, pp. 111–12.

[200] There were extremely rare cases when a *jagir* was assigned not against a rank, but as *inam*, free bestowal, without placing the assignee under any obligation.

[201] I. Habib, pp. 257–66. Moreland was the first modern writer to appreciate the essential aspects of the *jagir* system, *Agrarian System*, passim. Similarly, in *Journal of the Royal Asiatic Society* (*JRAS*), 1936, pp. 641–65, he brought out the most significant features of the *mansab* organization of the Mughals.

which was treated as his hereditary *jagir*.[202] The relative extent of area covered by *watan jagirs* was not large. These in the main comprised many of the subjugated kingdoms of Rajputana, Saurashtra, central India and the Himalayan sub-hills.

Lands not assigned in *jagir* formed a category known as *khalisa-i sharifa*, the revenue being collected here directly for the king's treasury. The total extent of the *khalisa* varied. Akbar (1556–1605) once resumed all *jagirs* to the *khalisa* in the larger portion of his empire; later in his reign it appears to have accounted for one-fourth of the total revenues. Under Jahangir (1605–27) its *jama* (estimated revenue income) fell to less than 5 per cent of the total *jama* of the empire. Under Shahjahan it was gradually expanded, so that its *jama* rose to one-seventh, and early under Aurangzeb (1659–1707) to nearly one-fifth of that of the empire.[203] The emperor drew his cash income mainly out of the revenues of the *khalisa*. Out of this he paid some *mansabdars* in cash and maintained his own personal troops (*ahadis*), artillery and the whole palace establishment, besides meeting expenditure in the provinces.

The Mughal system of *jagirs* was essentially similar to that of the *iqta* system under the Sultans. In fact, in the Mughal period the two terms were considered to be synonymous. But in most respects the *jagir* was closer to a pure revenue assignment than the *iqta* had ever been. It was never a fixed territorial unit, and had no connection, except for convenience in assignment, with the administrative units, *sarkars* and *parganas*. These latter units had their own officers, appointed by the emperor and independent of the assignees, in whose *jagirs* the units might be placed, whether wholly in one man's *jagir* or divided up among those of several.[204] The official assumption was that the *jagirdars* or their agents could collect the land revenue only in accordance with the imperial regulations and levy only such other taxes as were authorized.[205]

The *jagir* of a person was usually transferred from one locality to another every three or four years. Each increase in *mansab* of anyone or a new posting must have disturbed the existing distribution

[202] I. Habib, pp. 184–85.
[203] Ibid., pp. 271–73.
[204] Ibid., p. 261 and n.
[205] Moreland, *Agrarian System*, pp. 98, 138; I. Habib, pp. 273ff.

of *jagirs*, initiating a chain of *jagir*-transfers. This was apart from the
fact that the Mughal court was deeply committed to the principle of
periodic *jagir*-transfers as a means of preventing its officers from developing into local autonomous rulers.[206] Though less affected by
transfers, the *khalisa* too consisted of shifting territories scattered all
over the empire.[207]

It is not possible to draw a map showing the territories of
individual *jagirs* held in the empire or in any of the provinces in any
particular year. But there is evidence available which shows that the
assignments held by the big *jagirdars* covered a very large portion of
the empire. This may be seen from the data extracted from the official
list of the higher *mansabdars*, with specifications of their *zat* and
*sawar* ranks, given for the year 1647.[208] Since the pay schedules of the
time have also survived,[209] it is possible to work out the total salary
bill of the various ranks of *mansabdars*. Only a very small number of
these *mansabdars* was paid in cash out of the revenues of *khalisa*
(whose *jama* in any case during this particular year was about 13.6
per cent of the total *jama* of the empire);[210] and so the pay statistics
would not only indicate the share of the various ranks of *mansabdars*
in the total revenues of the empire, but also roughly indicate the
relative area lying within their *jagirs*.

Our information may be tabulated as given on the facing
page.[211] The significance of this table can be judged better when it is
noted that the total number of *mansabdars* then was 8,000;[212] so that
there were about 7,555 *mansabdars* holding ranks of below 500 *zat*,
who are not listed by the official chronicler. Since the *khalisa*

---

[206] I. Habib, p. 260 and n.

[207] Ibid., pp. 270–71 and n.

[208] Lahori, *Badshahnama*, Bib. Ind. ed., ii, 717–52. There is a similar list for
1637, but other data, such as the *jama* of the empire in that year, are not
available.

[209] One such schedule is printed in the *Selected Documents of Shah Jahan's
Reign*, Hyderabad, 1950, pp. 79–84.

[210] From figures given in Lahori, *Badshahnama*, pp. 710, 712–13.

[211] I am grateful to my colleague, A.J. Qaisar, who has let me use the figures
worked out by him and submitted in a paper contributed to the Indian
History Congress, Allahabad session, 1965. He has naturally excluded all
*mansabdars* reported in the list as dead, or otherwise not holding *mansabs*
that particular year.

[212] Lahori, *Badshahnama*, p. 715.

*Income of the top 445 mansabdars in the Mughal empire*

|  | Total salary bill, for both zat and sawar ranks (millions of dams) | Percentage of estimated revenue income (jama) of the empire |
|---|---|---|
| 4 princes of imperial family with ranks above 7,000 *zat* | 724.0 | 8.2 |
| 21 *mansabdars* of 5,000 to 7,000 *zat* | 1,417.7 | 16.1 |
| 43 *mansabdars* of 3,000 to 4,000 *zat* | 1,080.2 | 12.3 |
| 151 *mansabdars* of 1,000 to 2,500 *zat* | 1,454.0 | 16.5 |
| 226 *mansabdars* of 500 to 900 *zat* | 735.0 | 8.1 |
| Total: 445 *mansabdars* of 500 and above | 5,410.9 | 61.5 |

expenditure, apart from that on paying cash salaries, has to be allowed for, it would seem that these 7,555 *mansabdars* probably accounted for barely 2.5 per cent, or at the most 30 per cent, of the total revenues of the empire. On the other hand, 445 of the higher *mansabdars* controlled over 61 per cent of the revenue income of the empire, and must have held well over half of the empire in *jagir*. At the top of the pyramid a mere 68 princes and nobles drew 36.6 per cent of the total revenue of the empire, and presumably held nearly a third of its area within their *jagirs*.

There is one consideration to be borne in mind in interpreting these figures: the high cost of maintenance of the established system. Each *mansabdar* was required to maintain from his own income a contingent whose size was determined by his *sawar* rank, it being assumed that the pay for the *sawar* rank actually accounted for the larger part of the salary-bill, as may be seen from the figures in the following table.[213] It would appear from this table that about three-quarters of the higher *mansabdars*' income was spent on keeping the soldiery. Actually, several *jagirdars* used to sub-assign parts of their *jagirs* to their troopers in lieu of their pay.[214] It is, however, quite possible that since the Mughals, unlike the Sultans, made no attempt to demarcate the portions of assignments earmarked for the pay of the assignees' troops, the *mansabdars* kept a much larger portion of the revenues of their assignments than was due on the basis of their personal or *zat* pay alone.

Even when the expenditure on the troops has been considered, the fact remains that less than 450 men disposed of over three-fifths of the revenues of the empire. When it is recalled that the revenue comprised the bulk of the peasants' surplus and the empire covered the larger part of the Indian sub-continent, it becomes possible to appreciate the extreme degree of concentration of wealth existing in Mughal India. Seldom, except perhaps for the present, has

*Proportion of pay against zat and sawar ranks in total salary of mansabdars*

| Class of mansabdars | Total salary bill (mn dams) | Pay against zat ranks (mn dams) | % of total salary bill | Pay against sawar ranks (mn dams) | % of total salary bill |
|---|---|---|---|---|---|
| Princes of above 7,000 *zat* | 724.0 | 124.0 | 17.1 | 600.0 | 82.9 |
| *Mansabdars* of 5,000–7000 *zat* | 1,417.7 | 229.7 | 16.2 | 1,188.0 | 83.8 |
| *Mansabdars* of 3,000–4,000 *zat* | 1,080.2 | 266.6 | 24.7 | 813.6 | 75.3 |
| *Mansabdars* of 1,000–2,500 *zat* | 1,454.0 | 398.8 | 27.4 | 1,055.2 | 72.6 |
| *Mansabdars* of 500–900 *zat* | 735.0 | 209.6 | 28.5 | 525.4 | 71.5 |

[213] I am, again, indebted for these figures to Qaisar who has worked them out.
[214] I. Habib, pp. 283, 285–86.

the contrast been so great in Indian history as then between 'the rich in their great superfluity and the utter subjection and poverty of the common people'.[215]

This small ruling class of the Mughal empire consisted, in theory, of men appointed to the imperial service by the emperor at his pleasure. In practice, however, considerable heed was paid to the principle of heredity and birth. Sons, indeed, did not inherit the *mansabs* and *jagirs* of their father. On the contrary, all other worldly possessions of the dead noble escheated to the crown, so that even these could not be inherited. But the emperor usually left a large portion for the heirs, generally selecting one of them for the largest share and special favour.[216] Often *mansabs* or increments in *mansabs* (if they were already in service) were granted to them, but they had generally to start from a much lower rung of the ladder. Although direct succession was thus not possible, the leading families of the Muslim nobles of the same racial groups were often related to each other, and we can trace the same families supplying some of the leading officers of successive emperors. Members of such families were known as *khanazads*. Among the Rajput officers the dynastic element was still more preponderant, the *watan jagirs* of the Rajput chiefs being hereditary, but not divisible.[217]

The Mughal ruling class was not, however, a closed body, and there was constant recruitment from amongst Central Asian and Persian immigrants of 'aristocratic' families, from Muslim 'martial' clans, from amongst the *zamindar*-chiefs (especially Rajputs), from ruling groups in the annexed kingdoms (of which the Marathas and the Dakhinis were the most significant examples), and from the small intelligentsia and the financial services.[218] Direct recruitment from the world of commerce appears to have been extremely rare.[219]

The Mughal ruling class was thus extremely heterogeneous,

[215] Ibid., p. 320, citing Pelsaert.
[216] See M. Athar Ali, *The Mughal Nobility under Aurangzeb*, Bombay, 1966, p. 64.
[217] In many Rajput dynasties the law of primogeniture prevailed, but it was by no means universal.
[218] See Athar Ali, *Mughal Nobility*, pp. 11–33.
[219] The famous Mir Jumla began his career as a merchant, but when admitted to Mughal service, he was already the most powerful noble in the Golkunda kingdom.

and contained elements from practically all regions of the empire and large numbers of outsiders. By the system of empire-wide postings of *mansabdars* and transfers of *jagirs* the local ties of the various elements, wherever they existed, tended to loosen further. While this was an important factor in maintaining the integrity of the Mughal empire, it also resulted in the *jagirdars* having no customary links with the local population, or any long-term interest in the improvement of the *jagir*. It, therefore, encouraged an excessive exploitation of the peasantry.[220]

It may, however, be supposed that the extraction of such a large portion of agrarian produce by so few might lead, through their expenditure and investment of the resources so obtained, to a certain amount of economic growth. The Mughal period, it is true, saw the rise of a number of large towns, and the relative number of urban population in Mughal India might well have been much larger than it was in 1900.[221] Yet the basis of this urban growth remained largely parasitical: provisioning of the needs of the large number of troops and attendants of the nobles, and fashioning of luxuries needed by the potentates. The Mughal nobles might have invested part of their wealth in usury and commerce, but they also often used their administrative authority to monopolize trade or even requisition the labour of artisans.[222] When quite excessive profits by these means were available to them, it is not surprising that they did not pay any attention to the improvement of the tools and organization of production, in which sphere not even a single invention or innovation under their aegis is recorded during the whole of the seventeenth century.

Like the Delhi Sultans, the Mughals emperors granted the revenues of particular areas of lands to individuals, generally for life, and always subject to resumption or reduction. These grants were known as *madad-i ma'ash, suyurghal, amlak, aimma*, etc. (and *waqf*, in case the grant was for the benefit of a shrine or school). The total amount of revenues alienated through these grants ranged from nearly 2 per cent to above 5 per cent in different provinces under Akbar. The prime object of these grants was to maintain an 'Army of Prayer',

[220] I. Habib, pp. 319–21.
[221] Ibid., pp. 75–76.
[222] See Athar Ali, *Mughal Nobility*, pp. 154–60.

namely, a class of Muslim (and sometimes non-Muslim) theologians and scholars, pensioned-off officials, and the women and the idle of respectable families. The grants were usually curtailed at the death of a grantee, the reduced area being distributed among the heirs usually, but not invariably, in accordance with Muslim law. In 1690, however, Aurangzeb declared the grants hereditary. But sale or transfer was always prohibited. It may, therefore, be assumed that the process of fragmentation of the grants was usually extremely rapid.[223]

The grantees were prohibited from interfering with the rights already existing in the area. The land of the grants, therefore, contained usually two portions: *raiyati*, peasant-held, from which the grantees merely collected the land revenue, and *khwud-kasht*, the land cultivated by the grantees themselves with the aid of servants or hired labour, or by peasant-tenants. This latter category was probably created by bringing under cultivation wasteland, which was usually explicitly included in the original area of the grants.[224]

Besides the share in landed property arising out of the appropriation of land revenue, there existed another right with a history going back to the Turkish conquests and beyond. We have seen in the previous section how during the period of the Delhi Sultanate the various strata of the subjugated rural aristocracy and other superior elements within the villages were tending to merge into a single rural exploiting class. This process was largely completed by the beginning of the Mughal period. The old terms indicating the different elements had by now disappeared and a single designation, *zamindar* (=*bumi*), had been substituted for them. A number of local names representing a variety of rights were still preserved, but they were almost invariably treated as mere synonyms of the universal term, *zamindari* (=*milkiyat*).[225] So broad seems to have been the connotation of this term that autonomous chiefs too were described as *zamindars*.[226]

With all its varieties *zamindari* may, in essence, be described as a right superior to that of the peasants, and originating, in the

---

[223] I. Habib, pp. 298–316. The *jagirdars* also conferred grants, but these could only be for the periods of their assignments, though successive *jagirdars* might tend to conform the grants of their predecessors. Ibid., pp. 315–16.

[224] Ibid., pp. 299–300, 303.

[225] Ibid., pp. 138–40.

[226] Ibid., pp. 182–83.

main, independently of the existing imperial power. It implied a claim to a share in the produce of the soil which was completely distinct from, although it might be laid side by side with, the land-revenue demand. This claim took many forms. It might consist of a cess, levied in kind or cash, on the cultivator; or it might be made up of the difference between the *zamindar's* actual collection of land revenue from the peasants, and the amount assessed by the state; or it might be compounded by the authorities for a definite share, either out of the land revenue or by allotment of revenue-free land. In the last case, the conventional share of the *zamindar* was called *malikana* and amounted to one-tenth of the revenue in northern India. In Gujarat it amounted to a fourth, the land left revenue-free to the *zamindar* being called *banth*. Besides holding this right to a share in the produce of the soil, the *zamindar* also levied a number of other cesses and exacted certain customary perquisites from the peasants under him.[227]

It is obvious that the *zamindar's* share in the surplus was subordinate to that of the king or his assignee, appropriated in the form of land revenue. This is also confirmed by the sale-prices of *zamindaris*, which, if they are capitalized values of returns expected from the respective *zamindari* holdings, show the *zamindar's* income to have been very substantially smaller than the land revenue imposed on the area of his holding.[228]

Another factor to be considered while assessing the share of the whole *zamindar* class in the rural surplus is the extent of the land subject to *zamindari* right. It is almost certain that the *zamindari* right was to be found in one form or another in every locality, or *pargana*, of the empire.[229] But whether all lands, or all villages, were covered by *zamindari* is another matter. In fact, it seems that in most regions there were villages, termed *raiyati*, or peasant-held, which were not subject in any way to a *zamindar*.[230]

On the other hand, on some lands the *zamindar's* claims appear to have been of much greater magnitude than on other lands.

---

[227] Ibid., pp. 144–50.
[228] Ibid., pp. 150–53.
[229] Ibid., pp. 137–38.
[230] Ibid., pp. 141–43. For the contrary view, see N.A. Siddiqi in *Indian Economic and Social History Review* (*IESHR*), I, 3, pp. 73–80.

Such were their *khwud-kasht* lands, presumably cultivated by their servants or hired labour. There were other lands, where the peasants appeared simply to have been their tenants-at-will.[231] Sufficient evidence is not available to enable us to say whether the *zamindars* could also restrain the peasants from abandoning their lands.[232]

The historical roots of *zamindari* were apparent in its close association with caste and clan. *Zamindari* holdings of the same clan were generally contiguous, lending support to the usual tradition that they had originated from the dominance gained over the territory by the ancestors of that particular clan. Since possession of armed retainers (and still better, a fort) was a hallmark of the right of even a small *zamindar*, this association was further reinforced when the clan supplied him his retainers.

The pattern of *zamindari* possession that had been so established was, however, subject to constant alteration under the influence of three factors. First, the application of Hindu and Muslim laws of inheritance to *zamindari* led to increasing fragmentation of *zamindari* holdings. This gave rise to the traditional mode of division of the *zamindari* right in a village, consisting of an initial division into *pattis*, and of an ultimate one in terms of *biswas* or one-twentieth of the whole.[233]

Second, the sale and purchase of *zamindari* introduced strangers and altered the sizes of holdings. During the Mughal period the *zamindari* right was fully saleable with almost no restraints. This was true of almost all parts of the empire. Purchasers are often found to be of different castes, and also faith, from those of the sellers, so that the caste monopoly of the *zamindari* of any locality was quite vulnerable to the inroads of money. It is quite possible that the marketability of *zamindari* also encouraged fragmentation, the heirs tending to break up joint-holdings to be able to sell their shares. On the other hand the surviving sale-deeds often show a single purchaser buying from a number of holders, and thus substituting one holding for several.[234]

Finally, the emperor claimed the ultimate authority to

[231] I. Habib, pp. 141, 143–44.
[232] Ibid., p. 144.
[233] Ibid., pp. 155–57; also p. 140.
[234] See the evidence set out in ibid., pp. 155–59, 162–63.

depose as well as appoint *zamindars*. This authority was exercised generally in case of non-payment of revenue or rebellion; but it seems as if sometimes the Mughal emperor might have created *zamindars* where none existed before. On the whole, imperial action must have resulted in considerable changes in *zamindari* possession.[235]

The relationship subsisting between the imperial administration and *jagirdars* on the one hand and *zamindars* on the other is of very great interest. Inasmuch as the *zamindars* formed a powerful local element, the Mughal authorities aimed at using them, as did the Sultans, for the collection of land revenue from the peasantry. Thus in several cases the land revenue, though supposedly assessed directly upon the peasants, was paid by the *zamindar* who actually collected it from them. For the 'service' the *zamindars* were allowed compensation, *nankar*, in the form either of a percentage of the revenue collected or of a portion of revenue-free lands. The semi-hereditary local official, *chaudhari*, chosen from amongst the *zamindars*, was charged with assisting the *jagirdars* and their agents with the collection of revenue, and was compensated for his pains by *nankar*. By the latter half of the seventeenth century a particular term, *ta'alluqdar*, arose to designate a *zamindar* who paid the land revenue not only on his *zamindari* but also on lands outside of it.[236]

At the same time, considerable antagonism between the imperial ruling class and the *zamindars* seems to have existed on the score of their respective shares in the surplus produce of the peasantry. With its armed retainers and its local customary ties with the peasants, the *zamindar* class appeared to the Mughal nobility a subversive element in the whole political structure. Moreover, as the pressure of the land-revenue burden increased, *zamindars* found themselves either unable to collect it or saw their own share being reduced. By the latter half of the seventeenth century the relations between them and the Mughal ruling class appear to have reached a point of crisis, which was marked by a series of rural uprisings led by *zamindars*.[237]

---

[235] Ibid., pp. 179–82. See also B.R. Grover, *IESHR*, I, 1, pp. 14–15.

[236] I. Habib, pp. 169–79. S.N. Hasan introduces a useful distinction between such a *zamindar*, whom he calls 'intermediate *zamindar*' and the ordinary or 'primary *zamindar*', *IESHR*, I, 4, pp. 114ff.

[237] I. Habib, pp. 333–51.

We may now consider the nature of the peasant right in the land. It is difficult to speak of the peasantry of Mughal India as a whole, since, as we shall note presently, a considerable degree of stratification prevailed within it. But it does appear that the peasants were in general expected to enjoy security of occupancy. The conversion of peasant-tilled (*raiyat-kasht*) land into 'self-cultivated' (*khwud-kasht*) land by officials and grantees was prohibited. That this should be so was quite natural at a time when land was abundant, and men were scarce. But as we have seen, there were certain lands which were cultivated by peasants at the pleasure of their proprietor-*zamindars*; so that tenants-at-will were not altogether unknown.[238]

While the peasant was offered a full right of occupancy, the right to abandon it was not as readily conceded to him. Officials were asked to use force in order to make peasants cultivate the land, and to restrain them from leaving their villages. From seventeenth-century Gujarat comes more specific evidence of peasants being treated as semi-serfs. We have record of a full-scale expedition being organized to bring numbers of them back when they had fled from the imperial territories proper to the domains of a chief; and we find local officials disputing with each other over the locality to which a peasant migrant was to be returned.[239]

From the relative paucity of references to such restraints it is doubtful whether one could speak of full-fledged serfdom. It would rather seem that restraint on the peasants was an ultimate right resting with the emperor and his assignees, exercised in practice only in exceptional circumstances. Whether the *zamindars* on their own possessed this right of restraint is by no means certain.

There has been much speculation about the village community. Whether we rely upon the records of the Mughal period or early British records, it seems certain, at least in northern India, that communal ownership or cultivation of land was extremely rare. At best, the community was based on a common financial pool to meet the land-revenue demand, the exactions of the officials and headmen, and certain common village expenses. It is probable that the community

---

[238] Ibid., pp. 114–15, 117–18.
[239] Ibid., pp. 115–17; B.R. Grover in *Proceedings of the Indian History Congress*, Delhi Session, 1961, pp. 152–55 (note).

invariably consisted of men of one caste, which was usually the
dominant peasant caste in the village.[240] Moreover, in a number of
villages the headmen appear to have enjoyed a very privileged position, with revenue-free lands of their own. Their office sometimes
became so profitable that, like *zamindari*, it came to be sold and
purchased.[241]

Among the peasants in general, considerable economic differentiation appears to have existed. At the one end were the headmen
and the upper peasants domineering over the rest; at the other, 'the
small peasants' (*reza riaya*) who are said to have been sunk in debt for
meeting the expenses of cultivation and for obtaining their seed and
cattle.[242] It is unlikely that this differentiation arose out of mere fragmentation of peasant-holdings. While a local scarcity of land might
have led to the formation of a category of peasants such as *paikasht*
(tilling in a village other than their own),[243] so long as land as a whole
was abundant, such cases could only have been exceptions. Indeed,
except for one semi-rhetorical reference in Khafi Khan[244] there is no
evidence that peasant-holdings had yet become saleable.

It is likely that the economic differentiation within the
peasantry was inherited partly from the past, and had been reinforced
or consolidated by the caste system. But the increased pressure of
revenue demand, by pauperizing certain weaker or more vulnerable
sections of the peasantry more than others, must have increased it
further. Cultivation for the market, which seems to have been spreading partly under the pressure of revenue collection in cash, could also
have had the same effect.

The basic line of division among the working people of the
countryside was, however, between the peasants and the landless.
This line was set socially by the caste system which prevented by compulsion the 'menial' castes (such as *chamars* or *begaris, dhanuks,
thoris* or *balahars*) from tilling the soil on their own. Besides following their prescribed professions, leatherwork, scavenging, etc., they
formed a rural reserve force for work on the fields of *zamindars* and

[240] I. Habib, pp. 122–29.
[241] Ibid., pp. 129–34.
[242] Ibid., p. 120.
[243] See B.R. Grover, *IESHR*, I, 1, p. 5.
[244] *Muntakhab-ul Lubab*, Bib. Ind. i, pp. 157–58.

peasants. There is evidence to show that peasants used hired labour at harvest times; and the existence of such a large rural proletariat was in fact one of the pillars of peasant-farming.[245]

Although the Mughal empire offered greater stability than its predecessors, there appear to have developed within it a number of contradictions arising out of its system of property relationships. The transfer of *jagirs* and the complete alienation of the *jagirdars* from all local ties encouraged an excessive exploitation of the peasantry and a mounting pressure on the *zamindars*. This led ultimately to peasant uprisings (e.g., Jats, Sikhs, Satnamis) whose leadership was assumed at one stage or another by *zamindars*; or the peasants served as cannon-fodder in revolts of *zamindars* themselves (e.g., Marathas). Naturally, other explanations have also been put forward for these revolts; but it is quite possible that, more than anything else, the social contradictions were the real source of the political crisis of the Mughal empire.[246]

The states that arose on the ruins of the Mughal empire could not create any new social structure. Wherever the *zamindar*-leaders of the Marathas or Jats were successful, they not only sought to overthrow Mughal *jagirdars*, but also replaced other *zamindars* by themselves, thus combining in one the roles of rulers and *zamindars*.[247] Elsewhere, revenue-farmers aspired to acquire a hereditary status by claiming the position of *zamindars*.[248] When the British regime began, the *zamindars*, whether new or old, appear to have been exercising greater authority than under the Mughals. But, essentially, the British found the Mughal system still surviving. The pivot of this was the large revenue demand, 'the property [vested in government by immemorial usage] of ten-elevenths of the net rental of the

---

[245] Ibid., pp. 120–22; *IESHR*, I, 3, p. 66. See Dharma Kumar in *CSSH*, IV, 3, pp. 337–63.

[246] I. Habib, pp. 316–51. The other principal explanations are the rise of Hindu reaction (put forward most cogently by J.N. Sarkar), and the rise of nationalities (which is espoused, if I am not mistaken, by some Soviet scholars). For a plea that my own views should be regarded as 'strictly tentative', see Athar Ali, *Mughal Nobility*, pp. 89–92.

[247] For Marathas seizing big as well as petty *zamindars*, see Azad Bilgrami, *Khizana-i Amira*, Kanpur, 1871, p. 47. For the expansion of the Jat *zamindari* in middle Doab, see I. Habib, p. 341.

[248] See Moreland, *Agrarian System*, pp. 172–75.

country.'[249] Initially the British government found itself in the same relationship of cooperation and antagonism with the *zamindars* as had the Mughal government. But it was immensely more powerful than its predecessor; and the change in the economic context following the 'drain of wealth' to England and then the impact of the Industrial Revolution altered the whole nature of the relationship between the British government and the *zamindars*, as well as that between the *zamindars* and the peasantry.

---

[249] Holt-Mackenzie, Minute of 1 July 1819, *Selections from the Revenue Records of the North-West Provinces, 1818–20*, Calcutta, 1869, p. 62 n.

# The Peasant in Indian History

The momentous events of this century have led to worldwide recognition that peasants, who constitute the largest single segment of mankind, may have a special part to play in shaping our destinies. In interpreting the historical qualities of the peasantry, Chayanov and Mao Tse-tung offer two widely different, even opposite, outlooks. Yet both of them have inspired renewed explorations into the past of the peasantry with a view to discovering its capacity for resistance and change.

In India, in an endeavour to reconstruct the history of the peasants as a precondition for identifying the main historical periods and processes, D.D. Kosambi and R.S. Sharma, together with Daniel Thorner, brought peasants into the study of Indian history for the first time. In what follows, the debt to these and other scholars for knowledge as well as inspiration would be obvious.

A rigorous definition of the peasant is desirable, though it is naturally elusive. I take the peasant to mean a person who undertakes agriculture on his own, working with his own implements and using the labour of his family. This definition, acceptable to Marxists as well as to Chayanov in so far as it goes, omits any consideration of the extent of use of hired labour and control over land. The moment these are considered, peasants seem to fall into different strata. Thus, for example, Marxists would distinguish the rich peasant (with extensive use of hired labour), the middle peasant (mainly using family labour) and the poor peasant (with land insufficient to absorb the whole of family labour). But this distinction is accompanied by yet another, based on property relations. We can then recognize the peasant-proprietor, the peasant with some claim to permanent or long-term occupancy, and the seasonal sharecropper, as separate categories. These do not (and need not) directly coincide with the three mentioned earlier, though in practice many poor peasants, and very few rich peasants are sharecroppers. There is then the distinction by 'wealth' alone: ownership of more expensive and productive devices, better cattle, more fertile land. This again may partly overlap the other classifications. The 'stratification' that we would be meeting with can be viewed in the context of all these three criteria, and I would be using evidence of any of the three kinds of classification to establish differentiation within the peasantry.

While landless labourers are not peasants, they form with peasants the working agricultural population, and their history too (which in many ways has been different from that of peasants) remains for me a part of peasant history.

Finally, any study of peasants must involve an enquiry into how they pay rent or surrender their surplus. This necessitates shifting the focus, from time to time, from the exploited to the exploiters. But without seeing peasants in their actual relation with the exploiting classes there can be no peasant history; the relationship is crucial.

### Origins: The Indus Basin

The stage at which peasants originate within a society must naturally arrive only after the pursuit of agriculture is established as a major provider of food. A family can then spend the larger part of its labour-time on the cultivation of plants and harvesting of seeds. In this process not only do the food-gatherers (mainly hunters) turn into producers; the monogamistic family itself evolves as a basic unit of social organization.

When plant seeds are gathered in the wild, there is of course no agriculture. Mesolithic communities like those of Chopni Mando (in the valley of the Belan, a tributary of the Son) among the Vindhyan foothills, who consumed wild rice, belong to the pre-history of agriculture. Domesticated plants came with the neolithic revolution; and two zones where crops were raised have been identified within the India of the pre-1947 frontiers. The first is in the Belan valley itself (Kodihwa and Mahagara) where grains of cultivated rice and bones of domesticated 'cattle' and 'sheep-goat' have been found for the period 6500 to 4500 BC. The second zone is that of the Kachhi plain

south of the Bolan Pass—an arid area, but experiencing seasonal
floods from hill torrents. Here at Mehrgarh (seventh to fourth millennium BC) have been found remains of barley (two-row as well as six-
row) and wheat of three varieties (corn-wheat, emmer and bread-
wheat). The lowest levels give bones of wild animals only; but the top
two metres yield those of domestic cattle, sheep and goats.[1]

The domestication of plants and, possibly later, that of cattle, marked a notable stage in human progress; but the full-blooded
agricultural revolution was yet to come. The draught potential of cattle was still unexploited, and there was no trace of the plough, which
alone could assure a substantial yield–seed ratio. Moreover, given
the paucity of the crops cultivated, there could only be one cropping
season, 'kharif' in the Belan valley and 'rabi' in the Kachhi plain. The
cultivated tracts were in any case very restricted, since there were no
means of clearing the dense forests and making land there fit for cultivation. It is difficult to conjecture what the internal structure of these
crop-raising communities was like; cultivation might still be a continuation of food-gathering with women as the 'principals', as Gordon
Childe had thought.[2] Men had to hunt, and later on, also tend cattle
for meat and milk. The 'sexual' division of labour was not sufficient
to produce a surplus which could create any class division or even
occupational stratification. In a much more advanced hoe-using neolithic community of Anatolia (sixth millennium BC) W.A. Fairservice,
Jr finds evidence of social 'equalitarianism',[3] and this should have
been even more true of the Indian communities.

In India the agricultural revolution and the first urban revolution in fact coincide in the Indus (Harappan) civilization, which cali-
brated carbon dating now places within 2600–1800 BC.[4] The fabric

---

[1] For the information used in this paragraph, I have relied on my colleague
M.D.N. Sahi's paper 'Early History of Agriculture in Pre- and Proto-
Historic India', Indian History Congress, Bodhgaya, 1981. The Belan
evidence is now held to be dubious.

[2] V. Gordon Childe, *Man Makes Himself*, London, 1948, p. 123.

[3] *The Threshold of Civilization*, New York, 1975, pp. 40ff. Not all the
evidence, specially such as inferences from art, can be beyond dispute.

[4] The simple carbon-dates (based on half-life of 5730 years) are given in
Bridget and Raymond Allchin, *The Birth of Indian Civilization*, 1968,
p. 140; and there are useful discussions in D.P. Agarwal and A. Ghosh
(eds.), *Radio-carbon and Indian Archaeology*, Bombay, 1973, pp. 205–

of Indus agriculture rested undoubtedly on plough cultivation. Since the ox had already been converted into a draught animal for pulling the bullock cart, the case for the Indus people using a plough should have been an unanswerable one in spite of Kosambi's strong objections.[5] The discovery of the furrows of a 'ploughed field' at Kalibangan has now met the doubts over the absence of any positive evidence.[6] The plough explains the really large extent of Indus agriculture, covering the north-western plains and extending into Gujarat. The Indus people raised wheat and barley (six-row), both of standard modern Indian varieties; in the Indus sites in Gujarat, rice has been found along with the bajra millet. The field pea represents pulses; and sesamum and a species of brassica, oilseeds.[7] The most remarkable of the Indus crops is cotton, the earliest of 'industrial' crops.[8] The multiplicity of crops shows that the two-harvest system was now firmly established: agriculture would henceforth be a full-time occupation;

---

10, and in *Puratattva*, No. 7 (1974), pp. 65–73. Calibration has resulted in pushing back the lower date of the Indus culture and considerably lengthening its span.

[5] For the toy clay wheeled carts and bronze oxen found at the Indus sites, see Stuart Piggott, *Pre-Historic India*, 1950, pp. 176–77. The humped ox (*zebu*) of the Indus culture was particularly suited for traction: the hump made possible such an effective harness. Kosambi's objections in *An Introduction to the Study of Indian History*, Bombay, 1956, pp. 63–67 were grounded on the lack of positive evidence for the plough, and a conjectured small size of surplus owing to the presence of only two cities in contrast to Mesopotamia. There are some comments on the negative evidence in D.H. Gordon, *The Pre-Historic Background of Indian Culture*, second edition, Bombay, 1960, pp. 70–71.

[6] *Indian Archaeology 1968–69—A Review*, New Delhi, 1971, pp. 29–30, and Plate XXXIV. The ploughed field is described as 'pre-Harappan' since it is partly covered by Harappan occupation strata.

[7] For wheat and barley, John Marshall, *Mohenjodaro and the Indus Civilization*, London, 1931, pp. 586–87. G. Watt says of the six-row barley that it is 'almost the only cultivated form [of barley] in India'. See *Economic Products of India*, IV, London, 1890, p. 275. The *hordum vulgare* and *hexatichaum* are identical varieties (but see also S. Piggott, *Pre-Historic India*, p. 153). For other information on the crops, see Piggott, *Pre-Historic India*, and Sahi, 'Early History of Agriculture'.

[8] Marshall, *Mohenjodaro and the Indus Civilization*, I, pp. 31–32. The variety of cotton was found to be 'closely related' to *gossypium arboreum* and thus confirmed a finding, already made on botanical grounds, that this variety was 'quite an ancient if not more ancient than any other cotton'. See G. Watt, *Commercial Products of India*, London, 1908, p. 577.

# The Peasant in Indian History 113

and the presence of a peasantry as a social class must therefore be inferred.

But the very moment of the emergence of a peasantry is apparently also that of the emergence of a differentiated society. There seems to be no basis for the belief that there could ever have been a pure peasant society for any period, long or short, such as Burton Stein hypothesizes for south India in another chronological epoch.[9] Full-fledged agriculture meant creation of surplus enough to feed a certain number of persons other than the food producers themselves. In the arid zone in which agriculture had to spread first, dykes and embankments to hold and divert flood waters were a prerequisite; and these demand a certain amount of social and administrative organization—the bedrock of Marx's Oriental despotism.[10] Finally, the control over bronze (alloy of copper and tin), an expensive metal, could give a small town-based class an effective sway over a mass of stone-tool-using peasantry.[11] Cementing the structure created by these material circumstances was a religion of gods, superstitions and priests, which apparently bound the rulers and the ruled alike in awesome dread of change, giving to the Indus culture its characteristic uniformity in geographical terms as well as over time.[12]

The Indus culture then not only gave India its first cities in Harappa and Mohenjodaro, but also its first peasantry. The towns were to disappear with the fall of that culture; but what of the peasants? A 'flood' theory can explain the abandonment of a town or two; it cannot surely postulate the submergence of whole agricultural communities. There has not, therefore, been any valid or persuasive alternative to the hypothesis first boldly set forth by Wheeler in 1947, which was reinforced by Kosambi in 1956 through a brilliant

[9] *Peasant State and Society in Medieval South India*, Delhi, 1980.
[10] The classical statement is in Marx, 'The British Rule in India' (1853), reprinted in Karl Marx and Frederick Engels, *On Colonialism*, Moscow, n. d., p. 33.
[11] See V. Gordon Childe, *What Happened in History*, revised edition, 1954, p. 132.
[12] D.D. Kosambi, *Introduction*, pp. 59–61. He possibly overstates the role of religion when he argues that force (through bronze weaponry) was rendered superfluous by the solidifying role of religion, p. 59.

interpretation of the Rigvedic hymns.[13] This saw the Aryans as directly succeeding the Indus culture, whose authors they destroyed or subjugated.[14]

The success of the Aryans is ascribed to the possession of the horse, and, still more, the horse-drawn chariot.[15] Since, compared with all previous armour and weaponry, the chariot was an immensely expensive machine, its possession implied a pre-existing aristocracy;[16] it is therefore difficult to envision an early egalitarian stage within Rigvedic society, as has sometimes been suggested.[17]

The state of agriculture glimpsed through the *Rigveda* shows the continuance of the ox-drawn plough (*sira*).[18] The technology was still chalcolithic and the Rigvedic *ayasa* is generally thought to mean copper, not iron. Barley (*yava*) is the chief foodgrain; but rice seems to have begun to be cultivated in the upper Indus basin ('Saptasindhavah') so that the two-crop annual cycle survived in a new form. But wheat, cotton and other crops of the Indus culture are not mentioned.[19] Moreover, the Aryans seem to have regarded with scorn the dyke-based agriculture of their enemies: Indra would force

---

[13] R.E.M. Wheeler, 'Harappa 1946, the Defences and Cemetery 38', *Ancient India*, No. 3, January 1947, pp. 78–83; D.D. Kosambi, *Introduction*, pp. 66–90.

[14] One should always use the word 'Aryan' with the reservations which Romila Thapar has so cogently urged in her Presidential Address to the Ancient India section of the Indian History Congress, *Proceedings of the Indian History Congress*, Varanasi session (1969), pp. 15–46. There can absolutely be no racial elements involved in it.

[15] On the absence of the horse in the Indus culture see Bridget and Raymond Allchin, *Birth of Indian Civilization*, p. 260. The Aryan success seems to parallel that of the Hyksos who overran Egypt with their chariots in the eighteenth century BC.

[16] See Leonard Woolley, *The Beginning of Civilization* (UNESCO History of Mankind, 161, I, part 2), London, 1965, p. 190. The point is lightly touched upon by Sarva Daman Singh, *Ancient Indian Warfare, with special reference to the Vedic period*, Leiden, 1965, p. 31, but is specially noted by Sir Mortimer Wheeler in his foreword to the book.

[17] R.S. Sharma, *Sudras in Ancient India*, Delhi, 1958, p. 26; see also his article 'Conflict, Differentiation and Distribution in Rigvedic Society', *Indian Historical Review*, IV (1), pp. 1–12.

[18] B.S.K. Das, *Economic History of Ancient India*, Calcutta, 1937, pp. 28–29.

[19] See Das, *Economic History*, p. 32; and N. Bandyopadhyaya, *Economic Life and Progress in Ancient India*, Calcutta, 1965, pp. 130–31. The word held to mean rice is *dhanah*: see however, Kosambi, *Introduction*, p. 83.

open the dams that imprisoned the water.[20] It is possible that the change in agricultural conditions was linked to the disappearance of cities with their markets, and the supplanting of one structure of control by a completely different one. Pastoralism seems to have become more important, for the Aryans coveted wealth chiefly in the form of cows, horses and camels, along with slaves.[21]

Whatever the mechanism of control, the surplus still came from peasants. These formed the mass of the community, the *vis*, since the words for 'cultivators', *kristi* and *charsani*, were often employed for the Aryan folk as a whole.[22] The peasants were masters of their own fields (*ksetrapati*).[23] But such 'free' peasants belonged to the superior tribes: a larger population would seem to have comprised the subjugated *dasyu* communities compelled to part with grain and cattle.[24] In the lowest levels were the *dasas* working like 'cattle', presumably on the field, or tending the herds, for their masters.[25] At the apex were the aristocracy (*rajanyas*) proudly driving in their chariots with Indra as their model, and the priests (*brahmanas*) who presided over animal sacrifices and a complex ritual. A celebrated hymn in Book X of the *Rigveda* offers a picture of this class-divided society whose creation the hymn seeks to ascribe to divinity. However simplified, the *varna* scheme of the hymn seems to reflect faithfully the deep division of the peasantry into its free *vis* and the servile *dasyus*, who, transmuted as *vaisyas* and *sudras*, form respectively the third and fourth *varnas*.

### The Long Transition: The Gangetic Basin

The next stage in the history of the Indian peasantry is dominated by the clearing of extensive tracts in the Gangetic basin. It was undoubtedly a long and tortuous process, with its countless unrecorded heroisms and tragedies; and it could not have taken place without substantial alterations in the mode of social organization.

[20] Kosambi, *Introduction*, pp. 70–71.
[21] Ibid., p. 83.
[22] Bandyopadhyaya, *Economic Life*, I, p. 125.
[23] Das, *Economic History*, pp. 25–26.
[24] See Dev Raj Chanana, *Slavery in Ancient India*, Delhi, 1960, p. 20.
[25] Kosambi, *Introduction*, pp. 92–93. Women slaves were particularly prized, Chanana, *Slavery*, pp. 20–21; but this does not necessarily mean that they and their children could not be put to work for their masters.

Down to 2000 BC or thereabouts, agriculture was mainly
confined to the Indus basin and its periphery, hardly ever venturing
beyond the 30-inch isohyet. The area of the heaviest concentration of
rural population in India today, the Gangetic basin, was probably then
as densely forested as was the Amazon basin not long ago. But with
the appearance of copper and the shafted axe, present in a late stratum
at Mohenjodaro,[26] the first clearings could begin. These started
naturally enough from the drier or western side. The 'Copper Hoard'
people, using ochre-coloured pottery (OCP), first established a few
scattered settlements in the Doab and Rohilkhand during the earlier
half of the second millennium.[27] The succeeding 'black and red ware'
(B&R) culture continued with the copper and stone industry; the settlements now extended, though in the same sparse fashion, up to western
Bihar. These were agricultural communities which, like the Rigvedic
Aryans, raised rice and barley, but not wheat. Two pulses, gram and
khesari, also appear, along with black gram; and an unpublished
identification would put even cotton among the OCP-level crops.[28]

These settlements could not, however, multiply until the
coming of iron, or rather, the coming of the metallurgy which could
produce iron tools with steeled edges.[29] Iron being cheaper than copper, iron tools tend to be substituted for bronze as well as stone blades.
Moreover, with iron, tools in other materials (such as bone arrowheads)
too can be made more easily. The impact of iron is therefore immediately reflected in the archaeological record.

Archaeologists have gradually been pressing back the date of
the introduction of iron; on present evidence, it is likely that its arrival

[26] Stuart Piggott, *Pre-Historic India*, p. 228. It has not so far been found
among the tools of the 'Copper Hoard' people, however.
[27] B.B. Lal, 'The Copper Hoard Culture of the Ganga Valley', *Antiquity*,
XLVI, pp. 282–87; R.C. Gaur, 'The Ochre–Coloured Pottery', *South
Asian Archaeology*, 1973, edited by van Lohuizen de Leeuw and Ulbagho
1974, pp. 53–62. The dating is on the basis of thermoluminiscence; after
the calibration of the carbon-dates of the Indus culture, the OCP culture
can no longer be regarded as contemporaneous with it, excepting its last
phase.
[28] See K.A. Chowdhury, *Ancient Agriculture and Forestry in Northern India*
(a report on plant remains at Atranjikhera), Bombay, 1977, pp. 60–63;
and Sahi, 'Early History of Agriculture.'
[29] For an illuminating survey of the pre–history of iron, see Leonard Woolley,
*The Beginnings of Civilization*, pp. 277–83.

in the upper Gangetic basin took place around 1000 BC near the beginning of the painted grey ware (PGW) culture (*c.* 800–500 BC).[30] The archaeological evidence has not been precisely reconciled with the literary evidence; but it is practically certain that the PGW represents an 'Aryan' phase, for iron already begins to be mentioned in the late Vedic texts.[31]

In its immediate impact iron seems to have caused a rapid spread of the clearings, as can be established by comparing the large number of PGW and contemporaneous B&R settlements with those of the preceding OCP and B&R cultures over a much longer time-span.[32] Conditions conducive to the raising of wheat reappear, and new pulses and lentils are added to the crop-list.[33]

Agricultural conditions in the Gangetic basin were vastly different from those of the Indus culture. Canals and dykes were of only marginal significance here. The bounty of the monsoon liberated the peasant from those narrow strips to which alone the flood gave fresh doses of moisture and silt. In the Gangetic plains the yield would improve if after some years of cultivation one shifted one's field anew to virgin land (claimed from the forest). The 'jhum' method required collective action by groups living in small migratory hamlets; and this was basis enough for the formation of tribes like the Sakyas, who were pre-eminently peasants.[34] 'Free men farmers', possibly answering

[30] Dilip Chakrabarti, 'The Beginning of Iron in India', *Antiquity*, L, (1975), pp. 118–19. His date is 800 BC for the upper Gangetic basin and 750 BC for 'Eastern India'. M.D.N. Sahi, however, argues for as early a period as the thirteenth century BC on the basis of the evidence from Eran and Ahar in central India, *Proceedings of the Indian History Congress*, Bombay (1980) session, pp. 104–11. The precise time limits of the PGW culture are difficult to set because of the varied carbon-14 dates at different sites. B.B. Lal has summed up the evidence in a cyclostyled monograph, 'The Painted Grey Ware Culture', 1981, pp. 34–37.

[31] For the references to iron in the *Atharvaveda* see Bandyopadhyaya, *Economic Life*, I, pp. 158–60. A synthesis of archaeological and literary materials is offered in R.S. Sharma, 'Class Formation and its Material Basis in the Upper Gangetic Basin', *Indian Historical Review (IHR)*, II (1), 1975, pp. 1–13.

[32] See B.B. Lal, 'Painted Grey Ware Culture', pp. 5–8. About 650 PGW sites are said to have been discovered.

[33] K.A. Chowdhury, *Ancient Agriculture*, p. 63; Sahi, 'Early History of Agriculture'.

[34] Kosambi, *Introduction*, p. 144.

to the free peasants of the *Rigveda*, are also encountered in the *Jatakas*.[35]

Conditions of forest clearance also necessitated at the same time a form of non-peasant agriculture. In the freshly cleared ground, full of roots and hard soil (now difficult even to trace owing to centuries of ploughing), a very heavy plough would be needed; it would be heavier still if it was armed with stone, instead of an iron tip. This makes intelligible the reference in the late Vedic and Brahmana literature to ploughs drawn by six, eight or even twelve oxen.[36] Such ploughs imply masters working with servile labourers. Keith, indeed, stated his impression that during this period, 'for the peasant working on his own field was being substituted the landowner cultivating his estate by means of slaves'.[37] The impression is corroborated by the testimony of the *Jatakas*, where we frequently meet 'big Brahmana landowners who have their fields cultivated by their slaves or day labourers'; also 'cattle magnates' owning enormous herds (e.g., 30,000 heads) with numerous slaves and hirelings (1,250 under one magnate).[38] The evidence closes with Kautilya's *Arthasastra*, where there are references to slaves and hired workmen of apparently large private landowners.[39] The same text introduces us even more prominently to the ruler's personal demesne, the *sita* lands, in part cultivated by slaves, wage earners and convicts, under the supervision of officials, and in part leased to sharecroppers (*ardhasitikas*) and others.[40]

The Gangetic forests also brought in a new element of population which in the Indus basin could not have been very significant—

[35] Narendra Wagle, *Society of the Time of the Buddha*, Bombay, 1966, p. 151.

[36] See references in Bandhyopadyaya, *Economic Life*, I, pp. 133–34; Das, *Economic History*, pp. 90–91.

[37] *Cambridge History of India*, I, edited by E.J. Rapson, Delhi reprint 1955, pp. 114–15. The presence of 'serfs' is doubted by R.S. Sharma, *IHR*, II (1), p. 8.

[38] R. Fick, *The Social Organization of North East India in Buddha's Time*, English translation, Calcutta, 1920, pp. 243–44; and Atindra Nath Bose, *Social and Rural Economy of Northern India, c. 600 BC–AD 200*, Calcutta, 1970, pp. 62–93.

[39] See Sibesh Bhattacharya, 'Land System as Reflected in Kautilya's *Arthasastra*', *Indian Economic and Social History Review* (*IESHR*), XVI (1), pp. 85–95.

[40] U.N. Ghoshal, *Contributions to the Hindu Revenue System*, Calcutta, 1929, pp. 29–31, 34; Kosambi, *Introduction*, p. 215.

the hunting folk. As the agricultural communities initially penetrated the Gangetic basin, the forest became accessible to the hunting tribes. Copper and, later on, iron-fashioned tools would make hunting more efficient; in the later levels at the PGW sites, iron spearheads and arrowheads become common.[41] On the other hand, the expanding population of the agricultural settlements would provide markets for animal skins, other forest produce, and even meat.[42] In return, the hunters could supplement their own forest diet with foodgrains. It is possible then to suggest that all around settled communities the food-gathering population kept on expanding, and so the Nagas, Kolis and Nisadas would flourish, and their influences would even begin to permeate the fringes of late Vedic ritual.[43] They were important enough even by the end of fourth century BC to form with the cattle-tenders the third of the seven Indian castes described by Megasthenes, the peasants comprising the second.[44]

By the middle of the first millennium BC the long period of agricultural penetration eastward had created a complex social formation marked by peasant communities created within tribes, interspersed with settlements of servile or semi-servile labourers working under landowning masters, while hunting groups enjoyed a fresh though passing economic importance. These varied social forms probably explain the rather heterogeneous nature of the emerging polities of the *mahajanapadas*, with the rulers' powers strongly circumscribed by powerful aristocracies and by the rising pretensions of the brahmana priesthood already in control over large areas of lands.[45]

---

[41] B.B. Lal, 'Painted Grey Ware Culture', pp. 22–23.

[42] Bones of wild animals (stag, nilgai and even leopard), evidently eaten, have been found at the PGW sites of Hastinapura and Atranjikhera, ibid., p. 17. One is reminded of Asoka's taste for peacocks and deer; he still ate their meat when the number of animals daily killed in his kitchen had been vastly reduced (Rock Edict I).

[43] Kosambi, *Introduction*, pp. 121–23. For the Nisadas, see Vivekanand Jha, 'From Tribe to Untouchable; the Case of Nisadas,' *Indian Society, Historical Probings*, edited by R.S. Sharma and V. Jha, New Delhi, 1974, pp. 69–75.

[44] R.C. Majumdar (ed.), *The Classical Accounts of India*, Calcutta, 1960, pp. 225, 237, 264.

[45] Fick, indeed, believed on the basis of the evidence of the *Jatakas* that the land was 'mostly in the possession of Brahmanas' (*Social Organisation*, p. 241).

The king was called 'the devourer of peasants', since it was the peasants alone, and not the great landowners or the *brahmanas*, who paid him the levy in grain.[46]

### Formation of the Caste Peasantry

The conditions I have outlined in the preceding section ultimately proved to be those of a transition—a long transition certainly, but one leading ultimately to a quite different structure of social and economic relations. It seems to me that from around 500 BC there was an immense acceleration in the process of change for almost 500 years, which universalized peasant production and also simultaneously created a caste-divided peasantry.

For the universalization of peasant farming, we can perhaps suggest two factors as of crucial importance. The first is the extending use of iron. As time passed the extraction of the metal increased in volume and the resulting cheapness diversified its use. Quantity influenced quality. In time iron tools would become directly available to the peasant, and that would be the turning point. The first recorded reference to the plough containing the 'iron point' is apparently in the *Manusmriti* (X, 84), which may be of as early a date as 200 BC, but is probably to be put a little later.[47] But iron 'ploughshares' have been found with the northern black polished ware (NBP), beginning *c.* 500 BC.[48] For the effect of this wider use of iron one may invoke Gordon Childe's perceptive observation that 'cheap iron *democratized* agriculture'. 'Any peasant' could now 'afford an iron axe to clear fresh land for himself and iron ploughshares wherewith to break stony ground'.[49]

The other factor which must have contributed to the spread of peasant agriculture was the growing multiplicity of crops. Sugar-

---

[46] See R.S. Sharma in *IHR*, II (1), pp. 8–9.

[47] *The Laws of Manu*, translated by G. Buhler, Oxford, 1886, pp. 420–21.

[48] B.B. Lal, 'Painted Grey Ware Culture', p. 13. A sickle and hoe–tip have been found at the PGW site of Jakhera (ibid., p. 13); and this suggests a slight modification of the statement that 'iron agricultural implements' begin only with the NBP, R.S. Sharma, *IHR*, II (1), p. 2. Yet the large relative increase in the number of such implements beginning with NBP remains a fact.

[49] *What Happened in History*, revised edition, 1954, p. 183. The first depiction of a peasant in India, driving a plough with a pair of oxen, is in a Kusana frieze, *c.* AD 200, reproduction in D.D. Kosambi, *Culture and Civilization of Ancient India in Historical Outline*, London, 1965, plate 15. The picture may well be of a twentieth century Indian peasant ploughing.

cane is mentioned in the *Atharvaveda*, cotton and indigo in the *Jatakas*.[50] Quite a long list could be prepared of the crops noticed in the Indian and Greek sources before the birth of Christ.[51] The growth of the urban markets resulting from the rise of towns from the sixth century BC onwards,[52] was bound to induce an extension in cultivation of market and industrial crops. There were new methods of cultivation too, notably, rice transplantation by which Kosambi explains a passage in the *Arthasastra*.[53] These developments required more intensive and skilled labour, and called for close decisions to be made on the basis of knowledge of both soil and crop. Extensive agriculture controlled by 'magnates' thus must have tended to become obsolete and competitively unrewarding, since only peasant farming could possess the capacities that were now in demand.

Once the greater efficiency of peasant agriculture was established, pressures for surplus extraction, whether in the form of tax or 'rent', would reinforce its expansion. Already, as we have seen, the peasants were the basic tax-payers; and the kingdoms of the fifth and fourth centuries BC and, finally, the Mauryan empire, probably greatly intensified the drive for tax revenue and so sought to settle more peasants. According to Megasthenes, the peasants paid to the king a 'land tribute' as well as a fourth of the crop (by another version, three-fourths).[54] Kautilya indeed stressed that settlements in the royal lands should consist overwhelmingly of *sudra karshakas* (sudra cultivators/peasants) and other lower classes, they being more amenable to

[50] Das, *Economic History*, pp. 93, 202.
[51] For such a list see N.N. Kher, *Agrarian and Fiscal Economy in the Mauryan and Post-Mauryan Age*, Delhi, 1973, pp. 379–400. Some individual items on the list, such as maize, groundnut and chilli, are however demonstrably erroneous. Kautilya (*Arthasastra*, II:24) specifies the major crops sown for the spring and autumn harvests; see *Arthasastra*, translation by Shamasastry, Mysore, 1956, pp. 127–31.
[52] For this second 'urban revolution', see A. Ghosh, *The City in Early Historical India*, Simla, 1973; and R.S. Sharma's review in *IHR*, I (1), pp. 98–103.
[53] Kosambi, *Introduction*, p. 130. One would wish for a more explicit statement of this practice in view of its importance.
[54] See accounts of Diodorus Siculus and Strabo, translations in R.C. Majumdar (ed.), *The Classical Accounts of India*, Calcutta, 1960, pp. 237, 264, 287 (note 20). It is possible that the 'land tribute' represents the king's traditional levy of one-sixth of the produce also laid down by Kautilya.

exploitation.[55] The large landholders with their own cattle and labourers as also the ruler's labour-tilled lands, significant still in the *Arthasastra*, could not easily survive the new conditions. Even where ownership continued with the 'lord' or master (*svami*), it was obviously becoming more convenient for him to lease out the land to *karshakas* rather than till it under his own direct management.[56] There would certainly remain some exceptions: even after the Mauryan period, we encounter in Patanjali (second century BC) a landholder supervising ploughing by five labourers.[57] The modest scale may be noted.

A social change accompanied this 'democratization' of agriculture. The tribes (*janapadas*) disintegrated, to be replaced by *jatis* (castes). In the Buddha's time, we begin to hear of *jatis*, 'excellent as well as low'; but the tribe and *jati* were still only loosely differentiated; the Buddha could be said to belong to the Sakya *jati* where it surely enough means the tribe.[58] Endogamy characterized tribal organization, a feature which was to be transmitted in such rigorous form to the *jatis*.[59] Megasthenes' descriptions of the seven castes, where the 'husbandmen' form a separate caste by themselves, would seem to be the outcome of a genuine confusion caused by the rise of peasant and occupational *jatis* by the side of the formal *varna* system.[60] Manu's

[55] R.S. Sharma, *Sudras*, pp. 146–49. See also Kosambi, *Introduction*, pp. 219–20. Sibesh Bhattacharya, *Indian Economic and Social History Review* (*IESHR*), XVI (1), pp. 85–96 is right in pointing out that Kautilya does not recommend peasant ownership but Sharma, whom he criticizes on this score, seems quite well aware of the distinction between peasant cultivation and peasant ownership and also of the rather vague connotation of *karshaka*, which may mean peasant as well as agricultural labourer. But the *Arthasastra* in the present case uses the term clearly enough in the sense of peasant cultivator.

[56] See Sharma, *Sudras*, pp. 230–31; also *Journal of Bihar Research Society* (*JBRS*), LXIV, III and IV, 1958, p. 8.

[57] Sharma, *Sudras*, p. 178.

[58] See Narendra Wagle, *Society of the Time of the Buddha*, pp. 122–23.

[59] Note the Buddha's story of the Sakyas who married their own sisters to avoid marrying outside the tribe; also the legend of the origin of the Lichhavis. Wagle, ibid., pp. 103–4.

[60] The Greek accounts of the Indian castes will be found in R.C. Majumdar (ed.), *Classical Accounts of India*, pp. 224–26, 260–68. The Arab geographers of the tenth century AD and even later continue with this number of seven castes, showing how an error can be perpetuated by simple auto-

codification of the occupational *jatis* as mixed castes, seems to set the lower limit to the period of the formation of the essential elements of the *jati* system.[61] Once occupational *jatis* were formed, the tribe naturally broke up into separate endogamous segments, within a larger social system.[62] Such separation of the peasants from superior elements can be inferred by analogy from later known examples. The Badgujars separated from the Gujars out of an original Gurjara tribe and the Rajgonds similarly from the Gonds: in each case the superiors claimed a *kshatriya* (Rajput) status, while the peasants were relegated to the position of a *sudra jati*.

What resulted from this breakdown of the tribal system was not a single peasant caste, but a large number of peasant *jatis*. Some perhaps simply retained, like the later Gujars and Gonds, the names of the original tribes.[63] The *vis* peasantry was now a matter of the past. Manu still repeats the formal statement that agriculture was one of the *vaisya* occupations, though it was clearly held to be the lowliest of these; and the 'labourer in tillage' was *sudra*. But Kautilya's designation of *sudra-karshakas* more properly defined the actual status of the peasants. By the seventh century AD, Yuan Chwang would classify the peasants simply as *sudras*.[64]

The emergence of a 'peasant caste' was the reflection in part of another development, namely, the further growth of the social division of labour demarcating the peasants more firmly from the artisans. Writing of the second Iron Age in Europe, Gordon Childe stressed the importance of the entry into the 'archaeological record' of 'new tools and labour-saving devices [such as] hinged tongs, shears, scythes, rotary querns'. These laid the basis for 'a number of new full-time specialists' like glass-workers, potters, etc.[65] By the first

nomous transmission in the face of every opportunity for direct observation.

61 *Manusmriti*, X, 6–57; Buhler's translation, pp. 493–515.

62 One is reminded here of Kosambi's view of the historical growth of the caste system as a process of 'tribal elements being fused into a general society', *Introduction*, p. 25.

63 *Manu*, V, 53, 79; Buhler's translation, pp. 419–20. Also see Sharma, *Sudras*, p. 232.

64 T. Watters, *On Yuang Chwan's Travels in India*, I, London, 1904, pp. 168–69. Also see Sharma, *Sudras*, pp. 232–34.

65 V. Gordon Childe, *Social Evolution*, edited by Sir Mortimer Wheeler, 1963, p. 110.

century AD, the Taxila excavations give us firm indications of the
occurrence of some of the technological devices (shears, rotary
querns) which Childe has spoken of.[66] The new full-time professions
must have led to a separation of the artisan communities from the
peasantry; the *Jatakas* introduce us to 'manufacturers' villages'
exclusively peopled by smiths or carpenters.[67] These formed the basis
of the new occupational *jatis*, the 'mixed castes' of Manu, which
include those of carpenters, charioteers and physicians.[68]

There was, finally, the subjugation of the food-gathering
population which involves the creation of the 'menial' castes. It is of
some significance that in all early texts the ancestors of the later 'untouchables' are extensively connected with hunting, fishing, working
on animal skins and dealing in bamboo.[69] In other words, their
origins lay mainly amidst the food-gathering forest folk. I have suggested that during the 'long transition' in the Gangetic basin the size
of forest populations increased considerably. At a particular point,
reached probably at different times in different localities, this co-
existence between agriculture and hunting broke down. The raising
of leguminous crops reduced the villagers' dependence on animal
meat or fish;[70] and growing use of cotton affected the demand for animal skins. The areas of forest that the hunters had to have for their
subsistence had now to go; the clash between the Sakyas and Kolis
may well illustrate the conflict between the advancing agricultural
pioneers and their opponents in the forests.[71] In the foresters' obstruc-
tion of the peasants' quest for more land, there was reason enough for

[66] See John Marshall, *Taxila*, II, Cambridge, 1951, p. 555, for scissors, a
developed form of shears; and ibid., p. 486, for rotary querns.
[67] R. Fick, *Social Organization*, pp. 280–85.
[68] *Manu*, X, 47–48; Buhler's translation, p. 413. What is difficult to explain
is why these artisans should have received a status lower than that of
*sudras* in social ranking.
[69] This can be seen from *Manu's* enumeration of the occupations of most of
the 'mixed' *jatis*: Nisadas, fishing; Medas, Andhras, Chunchus and
Madgus, 'slaughter of wild animals'; Kshattris, Ugras and Pukkasas,
'catching and killing [animals] living in holes'; Karavara, Dhigvanas,
working in leather; and Pandusopaka, dealing in cane. *Manu*, X, 39, 37,
48, 49; Buhler's translation, pp. 411, 413–14. See also Vivekanand Jha,
*IHR*, II (1), p. 19. The Chandalas and Nisadas (Nesadas) both appear as
hunters in Buddhist texts, ibid., pp. 22–23.
[70] Kosambi, *Introduction*, p. 189.
[71] Ibid., p. 122.

the peasants to entertain a bitter hostility towards the forest peoples. The animal-killing *jatis* are indeed looked down upon with as much scorn in the Buddhist texts as in the Brahmanical works of the period.[72] Manu sets down the code according to which they were to be treated once they were subjugated and reduced to mixed *jatis*. As '*Chandalas* and *Svapachas*' they were to be kept out of towns and villages and they were to perform the most menial offices only.[73] Here was the beginning of 'untouchability' and the creation of the menial castes, forming an ostracized rural proletariat that was henceforth to remain a specific feature of the Indian social order.

The five hundred years preceding the birth of Christ must have been one of the most formative periods of Indian social history. They moulded the basic contours of the caste system, with a peasantry deeply divided into endless endogamous communities and rigorously separated from the artisans as well as 'menial' labourers. This social fabric could not have come of itself; its erection needed direction and sustenance from a whole new system of ideas and beliefs.

This new system is profoundly associated with Buddhism. Kosambi saw in its attack on Brahmanical animal sacrifices, the hostility of the 'cattle-raising' *vaisya* against obsolete pastoralism.[74] This seems to reduce the social relevance of Buddhism to a very narrow sphere. With much trepidation, I would venture to suggest that the belief in the *karma* doctrine and *ahimsa*, the two basic elements of Buddhism, had a much profounder relationship with the larger social processes at work.

Gautama Buddha is not known to have preached the excellence of the caste system; and the Asokan edicts are remarkable for their exclusion of all references to any obligation imposed by *varna* and *jati*.[75] And yet the *karma* theory, which both Buddhism and

---

[72] Vivekanand Jha, *IHR*, II (1), pp. 22–23.

[73] The basic constraints are given in *Manu*, X, 40–56; Buhler's translation, pp. 414–15.

[74] Kosambi, *Introduction*, 158–59.

[75] Modern views of the Buddhist attitude to 'caste' are discussed in Debiprasad Chattopadhyaya, *Lokayata*, New Delhi, 1959, pp. 459–66. The particular negative aspect of the Asokan edicts has received surprisingly little attention, so also the humane injunction in them to treat well the slaves and wage-earners (*dasa-bhataka*) (R.E. IX, XI and XIII and P.E. VII; also R.E. V). These last may refer to domestics, but Asoka might well

Jainism vigorously propagated, proved to be the most effective
rationalization of the caste system. Whatever the Buddhist notion of
the individual soul, the Buddhist tradition saw cycles of birth and re-
birth in individual terms.[76] Once the cycle was so conceived, it justified one's present position in a low *jati* by virtue of the deeds in a previous existence, and promised a higher one if one performed the set
obligations excellently. By Manu's time, this is firmly a part of the
caste doctrine.[77]

Ahimsa, in its precise application, might have owed something to the jealousy aroused by the rich, land-controlling *brahmanas*,
who displayed the power of their ritual by large animal sacrifices. But
the prejudice against animal slaughter was likely to have derived in
much larger measure from the peasant's hatred of the hunting tribes
of the forest. The Asokan edicts contain express injunctions against
hunting and fishing.[78] This explains too the hostility in the Buddhist
texts towards the hunting peoples. Ahimsa could thus justify the subjugation and ostracism of these communities, the basis of untouchability. But the cycle went on: as the *ahimsa* doctrine came to be
accepted by Brahmanism, even the occupation of the peasant could
be termed a sinful and lowly one, for did not the plough with its iron
point injure the earth and the creatures living in it?[79] This view came
to be shared by later Buddhism as well.[80]

The new social situation, in its own turn, affected the religious world. As the tribal moorings, with their local customs and
superstitions, collapsed, and the peasant became, as member of a *jati*,

---

have in mind the village slaves and labourers. Compare the village *dasi-
dasa bhataka kammakara* in *Milindapanho*, edited by V. Trenckner, London, 1962, p. 147; translated by Rhys Davids, Vol. I, Oxford, 1890, p. 209.

[76] The *Jatakas* do this for Gautama Buddha himself. The *Milindapanho*
recalls that Nagasena and King Milinda had been born in a previous life
as a monk and novice. *Questions of King Milinda*, translated by T.W. Rhys
Davids, I, pp. 4–6.

[77] See for example, *Manu*, X, 24; Buhler's translation, p. 412.

[78] Pillar Edict V and the Qandahar inscription. See Romila Thapar, *Asoka
and the Decline of the Mauryas*, second edition, Delhi, 1973.

[79] *Manu*, X, 84; Buhler's translation, pp. 420–21.

[80] The Sage is said to have forbidden the monks from engaging in cultivation
because this involved 'destroying lives by ploughing and watering field',
I-tsing, *A Record of the Buddhist Religion as Practised in India and the
Malay Archipelago*, translated by Takakusu, Oxford, 1896, p. 62.

part of a 'general society', he equally stood in need of a general religion. For this there was no provision in the sacred ritual of the *Brahmanas* and the elitist Sangha of Buddhism. But Buddhism developed by first century AD the concept of the Bodhisattva, a power whose grace every one could invoke by direct forms of worship.[81] Almost simultaneously, if not a little earlier, came the emergence of Vaishnavism, with its concept of *bhakti*, establishing a personal rela tionship between the deity and the devotee.[82] The literal significance of the name Krisna and the anecdotes of his childhood proclaim vividly the rustic elements in the great cult.[83] This was the beginning of a kind of peasant Hinduism.

### South India

Southern India deserves separate treatment because in its early social evolution it followed an independent line of development down to the Mauryan conquests (third century BC). The plough appeared in the south in the second millennium BC with a basically neolithic culture;[84] the crops raised were the ragi millet (in two varieties), wheat, horse gram and green gram. Rice and the bajra millet began to be cultivated after the coming of iron, c. 1000 BC. Agriculture of this kind implied the existence of a peasantry from the late neolithic times. A large pastoral sector is also suggested by remains of enormous cattle-pens.[85] Almost all pre-Mauryan sites are on the Karnataka plateau, suggesting that cultivation was as yet confined to

[81] A late Kusana fourth century AD sculptured relief shows a Bodhisattva with a peasant driving a plough placed beneath him; Kosambi, *Introduction*, plate 16. A.K. Warder's essay, 'Feudalism and Mahayana Buddhism', *Indian Society: Historical Probings*, edited by R.S. Sharma and V. Jha, pp. 156–74, contains interesting suggestions, but the association with 'feudalism' is rather weakly argued.
[82] Suvira Jaiswal, *The Origin and Development of Vaisnavism*, Delhi, 1967, pp. 110–15.
[83] Ibid., pp. 151–52. There is support for this in iconography as well. Sankarsana, with whom Krisna-Vasudeva was jointly worshipped in the first century BC, 'invariably figures' holding the pestle and the plough; ibid., pp. 53–54, 56–57, 68.
[84] This is deduced from the anchylosis of the hock joints in cattle bones, indicating their use for heavy draught work. M.D.N. Sahi, 'Early Agriculture'.
[85] For the crops and cattle-pens, Bridget and Raymond Allchin, *Birth of Indian Civilization*, pp. 262–64. For iron, Dilip Chakraborti, *Antiquity*, L (1976), pp. 119–22.

the drier zone. Here too are concentrated all the eleven rock inscriptions of Asoka found in the south.[86] Apparently the eastern coastal plains, the home of the Andhras, Cholas and Pandyas mentioned in Asokan Rock Edicts II and XIII were still only very partly cleared. It was at this point that, with the Mauryan arms, the northern culture arrived.

The effects of its arrival on the south are important also for understanding what had really been happening in the north. The 'four-*varna*' system of the legal theorists failed to be implanted in the south.[87] The peasants were classed as *sudras*, not *vaisyas*, an important index of the contemporary status of the peasants in India generally. The warriors and merchants could not separate and form into distinct castes, and this perhaps suggests that social differentiation in south India had not yet reached a sufficiently high level. But *jatis* came to be as firmly established in the south as anywhere else in India, possibly by wholesale conversion of the tribes. In such conversion the *Brahmanas* apparently played a crucial role as high priests of the new order.[88] So too was brought about the harsh social division between the peasant caste (*ulavars* or *vellalar*) and the menial castes. The hierarchical distinction between the two classes is brought out in 'late classical [Tamil] works' of the fifth or sixth century AD.[89]

The absence of the second and third *varnas* does not necessarily mean that differentiation did not subsequently proceed rapidly enough. In spite of it having been vigorously asserted, it is difficult to admit, even as a hypothesis, that there was ever an 'alliance' between the *Brahmanas* and peasants and that this served as 'the keystone of local south Indian societies'.[90]

---

[86] Brahmagiri and Maski, two sites of these inscriptions, are themselves prehistoric settlements.

[87] For a somewhat different appraisal of the factors which caused this result, see R.S. Sharma, *Social Changes in Early Medieval India*, Delhi, 1969, p. 12.

[88] It is, however, open to question whether the *Brahmanas* were not preceded by the Jaina and Buddhist monks. But their social outlook in respect of *jatis* could not have been different from that of the *brahmanas*; and they shared the same culture.

[89] Burton Stein, *Peasant State and Society*, p. 71.

[90] Ibid., pp. 70–71, 83. It would have been a strange alliance, where the *brahmanas* would not even concede a *vaisya* status to their allies.

### First Millennium: Village Community and 'Feudalism'

Kosambi propounded a sombre view of the economic and cultural performance of this entire period and ascribed it to a 'complete victory of the village with consequences far deadlier than any invasion'.[91] He believed that agricultural productivity actually declined.[92] For southern India during the same millennium Burton Stein postulates the concept of a 'peasant society' with agricultural technology as a 'constant factor'.[93]

The notion of changelessness is, however, not supported by the evidence we can assemble on agricultural technology. Additions to crops continued. Bajra, the bulrush millet, which does not appear in Kautilya's *Arthasastra*, II, 24, became an important crop in the north along with the great millet, juar (*sorghum vulgare*), which seems to have arrived after the beginning of the Christian era.[94] Together they greatly reinforced 'kharif' cropping in the dry zone of the northwest. Fine varieties of cotton were developed to provide the muslin that won an important luxury market in the Roman world.[95] Kosambi himself pointed out that the first evidence for the coconut on the eastern and western coasts comes from the first century before and after Christ.[96]

The Sudarsana lake in Saurashtra, its history from the Mauryas to the Guptas illuminated by epigraphic evidence, marks the beginning of the recorded history of tank and bund irrigation.[97] The construction of irrigation tanks seems to have become well

---

[91] Kosambi, *Introduction*, p. 243.

[92] 'The average yield became less (though compensated by somewhat improved methods of cultivation) as deforestation increased'; ibid., p. 228.

[93] *Peasant State and Society*, pp. 16 ff. See p. 24 for the statement about agricultural technology. It is always dangerous to assume that a factor, just because it is unknown, must be a constant one.

[94] Bridget and Raymond Allchin, *Birth of Indian Civilization*, p. 266.

[95] E.H. Warmington, *The Commerce between the Roman Empire and India*, second edition, Delhi, 1974, pp. 210–12.

[96] Kosambi, *Introduction*, pp. 255–56.

[97] The inscriptions are those of Rudradaman (AD 150) and Skandagupta (fifth century) on the same rock on which Asokan rock edicts are inscribed (Girnar). See James Burgess, *Report on the Antiquities of Kathiawad and Kachh*, 1874–75, reprint, Varanasi, 1971, pp. 93–95, 128–38. R.N. Mehta gives a detailed report of his survey of the area with a persuasive reconstruction of the original works and the repairs, *Journal of the Oriental Institute*, XVIII, 1 and 2, 1968, pp. 20–38.

established in the south by Chola times.[98] The 'tremendous' reservoir of King Bhoja (eleventh century) in central India finds a description in Kosambi's own pages.[99] Throughout the Indian peninsula, the tanks created by bunds have utilized every convenient undulation in the ground; and their construction as it took place must have greatly extended cultivation and improved cropping.[100]

The use of cattle power for continuous rotary motion too would seem to belong to this period. This is no older in the Chinese and Mediterranean civilizations than second century BC.[101] In India, the first evidence for even the manual rotary quern and quartzite crushing mill comes from Taxila, about first century AD.[102] It is, therefore, almost certain that the use of cattle to rotate a horizontal drawbar belongs to the succeeding centuries. Once the possibility was known, its applications could be multiple; for threshing;[103] for pressing oil;[104] and for crushing sugar in both kinds of mills, viz. the mortar-and-pestle and the wooden rollers.[105] In all these operations cattle power would have replaced an enormous amount of human labour, rendered hitherto presumably by slaves or semi-servile labourers.

Agriculture, then, did not remain stable during the first thousand years after Christ; and over this long span productivity probably increased considerably. None of the improvements were, how-

---

[98] Burton Stein, *Peasant State and Society*, pp. 24–25.

[99] Kosambi, *Introduction*, p. 281.

[100] See Spate's description of the Madurai-Ramanathapuram Tank Country in O.H.K Spate and A.T.A. Learmonth, *India and Pakistan*, London, 1967, pp. 775–78.

[101] Lynn White, Jr, sees the first continuous rotary motion in the large *mola versatilis*. *Medieval Technology and Social Change*, New York, 1966, pp. 107–8; and Joseph Needham, *Science and Civilization in China*, IV (2), Cambridge, 1965, pp. 187–90, dates its first appearance in both civilizations to the first half of second century BC.

[102] John Marshall, *Taxila*, II, pp. 485–88. None of the specimens are large enough to have needed animal power. Marshall's reconstructions in Vol. III, plate 140, are inaccurate in showing vertical crank-handles.

[103] For references to threshing by circular treading of cattle, see Lallanji Gopal, 'Technique of Agriculture in early Medieval India (c. AD 700–1200)', *University of Allahabad Studies*, Ancient History section, 1963–64, p. 56.

[104] See Needham, *Science and Civilization in China*, IV (5), pp. 202–3, for a Hellenic 'analogue' of the Indian oil mill.

[105] See Irfan Habib in *IHR*, V (1–2), pp. 155–59.

ever, of a nature to subvert peasant production; on the contrary, as we have seen, some tended to make agrarian slave labour superfluous.

In terms of social relations, the period saw the completion of the great division between the peasantry and landless labour. I have argued elsewhere that the immense seasonal fluctuation in demand for labour on the field, called for a constant reserve of accessible labour supply.[106] Theoretically, this could have been created by simple free market forces; but these would have enlarged the share of wage costs in the peasant's produce and so reduced correspondingly the size of the surplus. The presence of a specially repressed proletariat was thus of advantage to almost every other class of rural society, the peasant as well as his superiors. This proletariat in India was largely created out of the food-gatherers and forest folk who had been already converted into ostracized *jatis* during the five centuries before Christ.

One would have expected that once these depressed *jatis* accommodated themselves to settled agrarian life, they might have invoked some form of 'Sanskritization' to rise in the hierarchy and turn into peasants themselves. This actually seems to have happened with the Jats whose history we can follow, though with immense gaps, from the seventh century.[107] But such cases were exceptions. Vivekanand Jha shows that during the two phases that he distinguishes, AD c. 200–600 and c. 600–1200, the number of untouchables went on increasing by the addition of new castes to the category.[108] Excluded from the village and prevented from holding land, the untouchables could never become peasants; they were thus forced to follow the prescribed menial occupations which kept them alive in the slack seasons so as to be available when needed for work in the field. The peasant, sorely exploited himself, joined in practising the severest repression of the menial labourer. This has surely been one of the fatal tragedies in Indian social history.

[106] Irfan Habib, *Agrarian System of Mughal India*, Bombay, 1963, pp. 121–22.
[107] They are found as an ostracized community at level with Chandalas in seventh and eighth century Sind; they are described as *sudras* in the tenth century, and as peasants and 'low *Vaishyas*' in the seventeenth. See Irfan Habib, in *Essays in Honour of Dr Ganda Singh*, edited by Harbans Singh and N.G. Barrier, Patiala, 1976, pp. 92–103.
[108] *IHR*, II (1), pp. 24–31; see the conclusions stated on p. 31.

There was within the peasantry itself a considerable degree of stratification: there were large numbers who were mere sharecroppers on the fields of others. When Manu says that the field belongs to one who 'first cleared away the timber',[109] he is possibly thinking of peasant cultivators possessing their own field. But he says elsewhere that the claims of 'the owner of the field' have precedence over the actual tiller ('owner of the seed');[110] and the latter can only be a sharecropper. Yajnavalkya underlines this when he says that the owner of the field (*kshetrasvami*) has the right to assign it to a cultivator of his choice.[111]

The choice to give the land out on lease is implicit in the obligation placed on the donees, in inscriptions from the fourth century AD onward, 'to cultivate the land [themselves] or *get it cultivated*'.[112] I-tsing (seventh century) shows that usually the Buddhist monasteries too leased out their lands to sharecroppers, giving them sometimes oxen, but never anything else. At Tamralipti he saw a third of the produce being brought in by the 'tenants'. It was only some 'avaricious' monasteries which 'do not divide the produce, but the priests themselves give out the works to servants, male and female, and see that the farming is properly done'; but this necessitated the priests 'urging on the hired servants by force'.[113]

Some segments of the peasantry were also subject to various constraints. On this much has been written; but the evidence unluckily is sparse and vague. Fa-hsien (fifth century) says that the Buddhist monasteries were provided by the kings, elders and lay Buddhists with land and 'with husbandmen and cattle';[114] this practically

---

[109] *Manu*, IX, 44; Buhler's translation, p. 335. The *Milindapanho*, edited by V. Trenckner, p. 219 (translated by Rhys Davids, II, p. 15) has a similar dictum: 'When a man clears away the jungle, he is called the owner of the land [*bhumisamiko*].'

[110] *Manu*, IX, 52; Buhler's translation, p. 336.

[111] See R.S. Sharma, *Aspects of Political Ideas and Institutions in Ancient India*, Delhi, 1959, pp. 22–23.

[112] Kosambi, *Introduction*, pp. 300–1; R.S. Sharma, *Indian Feudalism, c. 300–1200*, Calcutta, 1965, p. 47.

[113] I-tsing, *A Record of the Buddhist Religion*, translated by J. Takakusu, pp. 61–62. He says at one place (p. 61) that the monasteries took a sixth part of the produce, which was perhaps a theoretical amount only, after the proverbial sixth share of the king in the land's produce.

[114] *A Record of the Buddhist Countries*, translated by Li Yung-hsi, Peking, 1957, p. 35.

implies a serf-like status of the peasants donated. Other evidence suggests constraints on the peasants' movements only. R.S. Sharma presents epigraphic evidence of uneconomic constraints going back in south India to the third century and in Orissa and Gujarat to the sixth.[115] The evidence becomes a little stronger for the subsequent centuries.[116] A form of subjection is also implied in *visti* or forced labour, which was almost universally present in India; its use in regular agricultural operations seems, however, to have been limited.[117]

As against the sharecroppers and possible semi-serfs, there is evidence of the existence of an upper stratum among the peasants placed in a position to domineer over the rest. There is the cultivator (*kshetrikasya*) who appears in Manu as the employer of a hired servant or labourer (*bhritya*).[118] The *Milindapanho* (compiled, first century BC to fifth century AD) tells us of the 'husbandman' (*kussako*) who by successful work in his field becomes 'the owner of much flour and so the lord of whomsoever are poor and needy'.[119] Then there is the 'young son of a peasant' (*halottavrittiputrosya*) in the *Kamasutra* (fourth century): like the village headman (*gramadhipati*) and official (*ayukta*) he has access to village women as they render forced labour (*vistikarma*), work in his field (*kshetrakarma*) as also in his house, or taking away cotton and other fibrous material from him, bring him yarn in return.[120] This is a rare picture that we get of the actualities of the sub-exploitation of peasant by peasant in the ancient Indian countryside.

This degree of peasant stratification raises questions about the real nature of the Indian village community, which Marx and Maine both suppose to have been based on a common ownership of

---

[115] *Indian Feudalism*, pp. 53–57. B.N.S. Yadava would trace such subjection to Kusana times, 'Some Aspects of the Changing Order in India during Saka-Kusana Times', *Kusana Studies*, Allahabad, cited *IHR*, I (1), p. 19n.

[116] This is assembled and cautiously presented in B.N.S. Yadava, *Society and Culture in Northern India in Twelfth Century*, Allahabad, 1973, pp. 163–73. See also Lallanji Gopal in *Journal of the Economic and Social History of the Orient* (*JESHO*), VI, iii, 1963, pp. 297 ff.

[117] See G.K. Raj, *IHR*, III (1), 1976, pp. 16–42.

[118] *Manu*, VIII, 243; Buhler's translation, p. 297.

[119] *Milindapanho*, edited by Trenckner, p. 360; translated by Rhys Davids, II, pp. 269–70.

[120] *Kamasutra*, 5:5:5 and 6. I am indebted to S.R. Sarma for a literal rendering of this passage.

the land.[121] It is indeed possible that in conditions of abundance of land, private property in the form of saleable individual right to specific fields might not have arisen, and, as seems to be the case with non-*Brahmana* villages of early Chola time (ninth and tenth centuries), much of the land might have been held to be vested with the community.[122] But this does not necessarily imply lack of stratification. There would be peasants with seed, reserve of grain, cattle, even possibly slaves, and others bereft of these. It would be the former who would dominate.

In the earliest traceable allusion to the village community it is forcibly brought home to us that only the upper stratum mattered in the community. In a little-noticed passage in the *Milindapanho*, Nagasena tells King Menander that words do not often signify what they mean on the face of them, and he takes as an illustration the word 'villagers' (*gamika*):

> Suppose, O king, in some village the lord of the village [*gamasamiko*] were to order the crier saying: 'Go crier, bring all the villagers [*gamika*] quickly together before me' . . . Now when the lord, O king, is thus summoning all the heads of houses [*kutipurise*], he issues his order to all the villagers, but it is not they who assemble in obedience to the order; it is the heads of houses. There are many who do not come: women and men, slave girls and slaves, hired workmen, servants, peasantry [*gamika*], sick people, oxen, buffaloes, sheep and goats and dogs—but all those do not count.[123]

---

[121] 'These small and extremely ancient Indian communities based on possession in common of the land. . .' Karl Marx, *Capital*, I (1867), translated by S. Moore and E. Aveling, edited by Dona Torr, London, 1938, p. 350. Sir Henry Maine, *Village Communities in the East and West*, appeared first in 1871. His views were criticized by Baden-Powell, notably in *Indian Village Community*, London, 1896, mainly on the basis of Settlement Reports.

[122] See Noboru Karashima, 'Allur and Isanamangalam, Two South Indian Villages of the Chola Times', *Proceedings of the First International Conference Seminar of Tamil Studies*, Kuala Lumpur, 1968, pp. 426–36. Karashima admits to presence of 'agricultural labourers, who are not members of the ur (the village assembly)'.

[123] *Milindapanho*, edited by V. Trenckner, p. 147; translated by Rhys Davids, I, pp. 208–9. 'Village headmen' may possibly be a better rendering of *gamasamiko*. In the last sentence, *gamika*, which Rhys Davids renders as

It is thus the villagers of substance who alone are summoned by the headman to confabulate with him on matters of the village. Altekar notices that those who gathered at what he styles the primary village assembly were called *'mahattamas* in UP, *mahattaras* in Maharashtra, *mahajanas* in Karnataka and *perumakkal* in Tamil country, all [of which] mean the same thing, Great Men of the Village'.[124] The exclusiveness of the community was naturally still more marked in the *Brahmana* villages where all the power lay in the hands of the non-peasant landowners.[125]

Unfortunately, there is very little evidence to answer in specific terms the crucial question: why need the upper village strata have acted in unison and operated the village as a kind of corporation controlled by themselves? Part of the answer may lie in the economic autonomy of the village, which developed once agriculture had been 'democratized', above all by the iron-pointed plough. Kosambi describes the post-Mauryan villages as yielding surplus in kind to the rulers while being self-sufficient in the minimum requirements for maintaining the continuity of production, very much as Marx had conceived the position of the village in his 'Asiatic' system. Kosambi believed that these conditions first developed in northern India, and later in the Deccan.[126] Artisans had to move to the villages to meet the peasants' needs, subsisting on customary shares in grain and allot-

---

'peasantry', literally means 'villagers'; here, almost certainly, ordinary villagers.

[124] S.A. Altekar, *State and Government in Ancient India*, third edition, Delhi, 1958, p. 228. The terms occur in inscriptions of the Vakatakas, Pallavas and Gahadvalas. Eleventh-century references to *brahmana mahajans* in Karnataka are cited by Sister M. Liceria, A C, in *IHR*, I(1), pp. 32–33. The Chola inscriptions have *Peringurimakkal*, 'the great men of the assembly', Burton Stein, *Peasant State and Society*, p. 145.

[125] For the *sabhas* of the *brahmana* villages in the Chola kingdom, see Altekar, *State and Government*, pp. 231–35, and Burton Stein, *Peasant State and Society*, pp. 145ff. Kosambi in *Introduction*, pp. 301–10, has some charming pages on the *Brahmana* village communities of Goa, a combination of recorded information (traced to the fourth century) and his own recollections. See also his *Myth and Reality*, Bombay, 1962, pp. 152–71; Baden-Powell, 'The Villages of Goa in the Early Sixteenth Century', *Journal of the Royal Asiatic Society* (*JRAS*), 1900, pp. 261–91; and Monserrate's description (1579), translated by Hosten, *Journal of the (Royal) Asiatic Society of Bengal* (*JASB*), NS, XIII (1922), pp. 351–52, 365.

[126] Kosambi, *Introduction*, pp. 227, 253–54.

ments of small plots for cultivation. Epigraphic evidence attests to carpenters' plots in northern India in the fifth century,[127] and the *Lekhapaddhati* speaks of the five artisans (*pancha-karuka*), the carpenter, ironsmith, potter, barber and washerman, as entitled to receive handfuls of grain from the peasant.[128] All this is sound evidence of the artisans' fixed association with the village, which in turn strongly implies the existence of the village as a separate but collective unit.

The relationship between the peasants and artisans within the village must largely have depended upon custom; but the actual land allotments and settlements of disputes called for a controlling organ. So too the important matter of the hamlet or huts of the 'menial' castes within the village boundaries being kept under proper subjection. The further use of wasteland around the village and the terms for admission of non-resident cultivators, had also to be settled by some authority. In other words, the economic unit had to be a social unit as well; and the 'great men' of the village, by exercising authority in its name, enlarged their own income and perpetuated their own dominance by carrying out the social functions.

The benefits of the dominance came mainly through the fiscal system. A large part of the surplus had to be alienated by the village in payment of taxes.[129] The power to distribute this burden upon the individual villagers gave an immense advantage to the controlling stratum: the 'strong' in the village used to shift the burden on to the 'weak', as it would be said for the early fourteenth century.[130] This fiscal differentiation within the peasantry is seen by some authorities in the distinction between *udranga* and *uparikara* already present in fifth-century inscriptions.[131] It may well be that it

---

[127] Ibid., p. 312.

[128] See B.N.S. Yadava, *Society and Culture*, p. 267.

[129] See Karashima, *Proceedings of the First International Conference Seminar of Tamil Studies*, p. 429, on the responsibility of the *ur* (assembly in non-*brahmana* villages) to pay tax (*irai*) on the village land.

[130] Zia Barani, *Tarikh-i Firuz-Shahi*, edited by Sayyid Ahmed Khan, W.N. Lees and Kabiruddin, Calcutta, 1860–62, p. 287 (henceforth referred to as 'Barani').

[131] U.N. Ghoshal, *Contributions to the History of the Hindu Revenue System*, second edition, Calcutta, 1972, pp. 275–77, 280, 283–86, 299, 307, 319. See however, D.N. Jha, *Revenue System of Post-Maurya and Gupta Times*, Calcutta, 1967, pp. 53–56.

was ultimately its tax-gathering functions that gave the village community at once its firmest basis and oligarchic character.

We may here leave the stratified peasantry and our speculations about the village community to consider the pressures to which the taxation subjected the peasantry as a whole. The view offered often in textbooks and elsewhere that this amounted normally to one-sixth of the produce has little reality behind it.[132] This was prescribed as the maximum for *bali* in the *Smritis*;[133] but the *Arthasastra* has *bali* and *sadbhaga* (one-sixth) as separate taxes.[134] The Rummindei Pillar inscription of Asoka confirms the existence of this double tax. He remitted the *bali* for the holy village, and continued the other tax at the reduced rate, *athbahaga* (one-eighth). The Greek accounts derived from Megasthenes also speak of two taxes, a 'rental' or 'land tribute' and a land tax of one-fourth of the produce.[135] The two taxes occur in Rudradaman's Girnar inscription (AD 150),[136] whereafter there is an increasing multiplicity of taxes.

The fact that *sadbhaga* (even *dharmasadbhaga*) continues to appear among these taxes, hardly justified the view that agrarian taxation was 'at lower rates in Gupta times than in the Mauryan days'.[137] Indeed, the term *bhaga-bhoga* has been held to represent two taxes, the older *sadbhaga* and an additional levy (*bhoga*).[138] R.S. Sharma states his impression that the increasing number of taxes appearing in later inscriptions indicates a real increase in the fiscal burden on the peasants.[139] A passage ascribed to Varahamihira (sixth

[132] See W.H. Moreland, *Agrarian System of Moslem India*, Cambridge, 1929, pp. 5–6.

[133] U.N. Ghoshal, *Hindu Revenue System*, p. 71.

[134] *Arthasastra*, 11:15, translated by Shamasastry, Mysore, 1967, p. 99.

[135] Translations of the passages in Diodorus Siculus and Strabo are in R.C. Majumdar (ed.), *Classical Accounts of India*, pp. 237, 264. There is some doubt as to whether Strabo means that the peasants paid or received one-fourth of the produce. Diodorus is apparently unambiguous here, ibid, p. 287, n 20; but see U.N. Ghoshal, *Hindu Revenue System*, pp. 224–29.

[136] See U.N. Ghoshal, *Hindu Revenue System*, p. 252; D.N. Jha, *Revenue System*, pp. 43–45.

[137] D.N. Jha in *Land Revenue in India—Historical Studies*, edited by R.S. Sharma, Delhi, 1971, p. 5.

[138] D.N. Jha, *Revenue System*, p. 43.

[139] *Indian Feudalism*, p. 265. For these taxes see Lallanji Gopal, *Economic Life of Northern India*, 700–1200, Delhi, 1965, pp. 32–70.

century) describes the sight of desolate villages abandoned by peasants owing to the oppression of the *bhogapati*, or tax collector.[140]

While tax extraction had an immediate terror for the peasantry, its mode of distribution also affected it in the long term. In its
two main versions, Kosambi's and R.S. Sharma's, the theory of
Indian feudalism rests essentially on the mode of alienation of the tax
resources by the rulers.[141] Sharma holds the land grants made to the
*Brahmanas*, for which epigraphic evidence begins from the first century, to be the forerunner of secular feudalism; but there are difficulties in accepting this, especially owing to a time gap of some eight
hundred years or more before hereditary land grants to the ruler's
kinsmen, vassals and officials begin in northern India (mainly from
AD 1000).[142]

A more important source of 'feudalism' was the decay of
commerce and decline of towns, which seems to have continued
down to the eleventh century.[143] This synchronized with a ruralization
of the ruling class, a tendency towards its dispersal at each level, and
so the creation of hereditary tax-collecting potentates (*samantas*,
*thakkuras*, *ranakas*, *rautas* [*rajaputras*], etc.) placed one over the
other in some hierarchical order.[144]

Cavalry supported such dispersed political power. Chariots
were obsolete in India by the seventh century.[145] On the other hand,

---

[140] *Subhasitaratnakosa* of Vidyakara, cited by Kosambi, *Introduction*, p.
268, and Sharma, *Indian Feudalism*, p. 267.

[141] Kosambi sets out his theory in *Introduction*, pp. 274ff, in two chapters;
the description of 'Indian Feudalism' as compared with European is given
on pp. 326–28. Alienation of tax rights by rulers led to 'feudalism from
above', while in 'feudalism from below' a class of 'landowners developed
within the village, between the state and the peasantry, to wield armed
power' over the population, ibid., p. 275. Sharma in his seminal work,
*Indian Feudalism*, does not seem to consider the latter process as contri-
buting to feudalism. Sharma summarizes his conclusions on pp. 263–72.

[142] Sharma's own date (*Indian Feudalism*, p. 283). See Rushton Coulborn's
perceptive remarks (in spite of his excessively narrow view of feudalism)
on the role of *Brahmanas* in *Comparative Studies in Society and History*
(*CSSH*), X (3), 1968, pp. 57–59, especially the note on p. 358.

[143] R.S. Sharma, *IHR*, I (1), p. 5; B.N.S. Yadava, *IHR*, III(1), p. 44. The
paucity of coins, as index of the decline, is also commented upon by
Lallanji Gopal, *Economic Life*, pp. 215–21.

[144] See R.S. Sharma, *Indian Feudalism*, pp. 156–209; B.N.S. Yadava, *Society
and Culture*, pp. 136–63.

[145] V.R.R. Dikshitar, *War in Ancient India*, Madras, 1944, pp. 165–66.

the effectiveness of the horse-rider was immensely improved with the arrival of the saddle some time in the early centuries of the Christian era, and of the (non-metallic) true stirrup by the tenth century.[146] When the Arabs faced Dahar in battle in 712–713, the ruler of Sind was accompanied by '*sons of kings* numbering 5,000 horsemen'.[147] Clearly, the sons of kings represent, through a practically literal translation, the *rajaputras* (*rautas*, ancestors of the modern Rajputs). These horsemen were the knights of 'Indian feudalism'.[148] By the tenth century they formed the warrior class in most of northern India and a large part of the Deccan, even if their coalescence into a single caste was a later phenomenon.[149]

The horseman represented an effective single unit of armed force; the warrior clans could lay claim to separate groups of villages (traditionally numbered in multiples of six), their members dispersed among the villages to extract taxes and keep the peasants subjugated.[150] The lower ranks of the warriors would turn into village despots: the village headmen (*khots* and *muqaddams*) who rode horses, wore fine clothes and chewed betel-leaf in the Doab in the early fourteenth century could well have been such proto-Rajputs.[151] The local power and rights that these 'feudal' potentates and warriors carved out for themselves long survived the polities within which they had origi-nated. It was largely out of these deeply entrenched elements that the

---

[146] On the ineffectiveness of cavalry without saddle and stirrup, see Sarva Daman Singh, *Ancient Indian Warfare*, pp. 69–71. The arrival of the saddle in the West is dated first century AD, but its spread was slow; Lynn White, Jr, *Medieval Technology*, pp. 7–8. A saddle is probably shown in a Khajuraho sculpture of the tenth century; Vidya Prakash, *Khajuraho*, Bombay, 1967, p. 38 and plate 47. On the stirrup, see Irfan Habib, 'Changes in Technology in Medieval India', *Studies in History*, II (1), 1980, pp. 25–26.

[147] *Chachanama*, edited by Umar Daudpota, Delhi, 1939, p. 169.

[148] The historical implications of the emergence of the Rajput horseman are missing in most discussions of the period; but Coulborn, almost by chance, draws a parallel between the *rajaputra* and the 'knight', *CSSH*, X (3), 1968, p. 369n.

[149] On the emergence of the Rajputs, see B.D. Chattopadhyaya, 'Origins of the Rajputs', *IHR*, III (1), pp. 59–82.

[150] On the groups of villages, many of which survive as traditional territorial division under different Rajput clans, see Irfan Habib, 'Distribution of Landed Property in Pre-British India', *Enquiry*, NS, II (3), 1965, p. 42, where other references will be found; pp. 59–108 of this volume.

[151] Barani, pp. 287–88, 291.

*zamindar* class of medieval India, continuing into modern times, was created.[152]

Our evidence tends to show the peasant as no more than a pliant victim while his superiors fought it out for the control of the surplus he produced. This may however well be due to limitations of our evidence. The epigraphic *prasastis* of rulers were not likely to dwell on agrarian revolts. We owe to R.S. Sharma the identification of one peasant uprising in the eleventh century. The Kaivartas, traditionally a low 'mixed' *jati* of boatmen,[153] held plots of land on some service tenure in north Bengal. A literary account (*Ramacharita*) says that upon being subjected to heavy taxation they revolted, fighting naked with bows and arrows and riding on buffaloes. They defeated and killed one Pala ruler and forced another to mobilize all his vassals, before they could be subdued (*c.* 1075).[154] The revolt was thus also a caste revolt: the Kaivartas might have been trying to throw off their social disabilities as well. A later Sena ruler of Bengal (Ballalasena, *c.* 1159–85) is indeed said to have made a 'clean caste of the lowly Kaivartas'.[155]

### The Medieval Peasantry

The degree of changelessness in the conditions of the peasantry can always be overstressed. One should, on the other hand, also be wary of assuming change just because of an alteration in the quality of record, as happens when we move into the thirteenth century. It is, therefore, perhaps best to reserve judgement on the issue of periodization in the history of the peasantry until certain basic matters are first clarified.

---

[152] I have tried to trace this transformation (thirteenth–fourteenth centuries) in *The Cambridge Economic History of India*, Vol. I, edited by T. Raychaudhuri and Irfan Habib, Cambridge, 1982, pp. 54–60. The predominance of the Rajputs among the *zamindar* clans recorded against individual *parganas* in Akbar's empire with numbers of retainers (horse and foot) (*Ain-i Akbari*: Account of the Twelve *Subas*) is proof enough of the·'Indian-feudal' roots of that class.

[153] *Manu*, X, 34; Buhler's translation, p. 410.

[154] R.S. Sharma, *Indian Feudalism*, p. 298. Also see R.D. Banerji, *The Palas of Bengal*, reprint, Varanasi, 1973, pp. 44–51.

[155] H.C. Ray, *The Dynastic History of Northern India*, I, Calcutta, 1931, p. 364.

The first question to be elucidated is whether there developed any internal factors for change in the mode of peasant production and structure of the village community. Among such possible factors, agricultural technology deserves prime consideration. Undoubtedly the intrusion of Islam into Indian history opened the gates a little wider for the admission of techniques received from external sources.[156] There were accordingly certain improvements in agricultural tools and methods, which can be ascribed to the medieval centuries.

A notable advance seems to have been made with the provision of right-angled gearing to the Indian 'saqiya' or *araghatta* (water-wheel with potgarland), the fully developed device being described as in use in the Punjab and cis-Sutlej territory by early sixteenth century. It is almost certain that the geared wheel had been diffused within the previous two or three centuries.[157] Its diffusion should have contributed considerably to irrigation in the Indus basin and Rajasthan. The lime and bitumen mortar which arrived with the Muslims should have made indigo extraction easier by providing water-proof walls for indigo vats.[158] Liquor distillation established by the end of the thirteenth century added a new and admittedly widespread agricultural industry.[159] The introduction of sericulture by the fifteenth century made Bengal one of the great silk-producing regions of the world in the seventeenth.[160] After the discovery of the new world, India received important new crops, such as maize and tobacco whose

[156] See Kosambi's general observation about 'Islamic raiders . . . breaking down hidebound custom in the adoption and transmission of new techniques', in *Introduction*, p. 370.

[157] The evidence is presented in my address, 'Technology and Society in the Thirteenth and Fourteenth Centuries', *Proceedings of the Indian History Congress*, Varanasi, 1969, pp. 149–53, 161, to be read with the additions and revision made by me in 'Changes in Technology in Medieval India', *Studies in History*, II (1) (1980), pp. 18–20. In the latter paper (p. 19), I noted evidence for the potgarland in India from the sixth and seventh centuries. Lallanji Gopal brings together many passages bearing on the *araghatta* in his *Aspects of History of Agriculture in Ancient India*, Varanasi, 1980, pp. 114–68; but his insistence that gearing is pre-medieval seems excessive pleading.

[158] *Studies in History*, II(1), p. 22.

[159] Ibid., pp. 23–24.

[160] Ibid., pp. 28–29. Silks other than mulberry, such as tasar and eri, have probably a much older history in India.

cultivation belongs to the seventeenth century.[161] Grafting practices spread too in the same century, resulting in the improvement of some fruits, notably oranges.[162]

These developments are sufficient to shake any assumptions about static agriculture; but taken in the aggregate they would not amount even remotely to a technological revolution. In general, they contributed to the extension and reinforcement of peasant agriculture, not to its subversion or transformation.

Nor did the fundamental social relationships within the village undergo any visible change. Islam made almost no impression on the caste system. Indeed, except for a very low-keyed disapproval by the scientific-minded Alberuni, medieval Islam produced no critique or condemnation of the system.[163] Caste thus remained as prominent an element of village life as in any previous period.[164] Upon their conversion Muslim peasant communities also tended to practise endogamy, though a greater degree of occupational and status mobility seems to have been tolerated among Muslims in general.[165]

The relations of the peasants with other elements of the rural population also remained basically unaltered. This was especially

---

[161] Irfan Habib, 'Technology and Economy of Mughal India', *IESHR*, XVII (1), p. 4.

[162] Ibid., pp. 4–6.

[163] After a fairly sympathetic speculation on the caste system (even pointing to an Iranian parallel), Alberuni remarks: 'We Muslims, of course, stand entirely on the other side of the question, considering all men as equal, except in piety'; *Alberuni's India*, translated by Edward C. Sachau, I, London, 1910, p. 100. Such counterposition of the theoretical equality in Islam and the caste system stands unique in medieval literature, and clearly Alberuni was by no means representing the general trend. To most Muslim writers (of whom Barani, author of the *Tarikh-i Firuz-Shahi*, 1357, is the outstanding spokesman), a stable hierarchy was a most praiseworthy social idea.

[164] 'In our countries the people who are nomads of the steppes are distinguished by names of different tribes; but here [in Hindustan] people settled in the country and villages are distinguished by names of tribes.' Babur, *Baburnama*, Br. Mus. MS, Or 714 f 410a; see A.S. Beveridge's translation, II, p. 518. Kosambi would have appreciated this analogy with tribes.

[165] See D. Ibbetson's remarks on the conditions in western Punjab, 'where Islam has largely superseded Brahminism', *Punjab Castes*, Lahore, 1916, pp. 10–11.

true in respect of the menial castes. No sympathy is wasted on them in Indo-Islamic texts. The Arab conqueror of Sind, Muhammad bin Qasim approved the humiliating restraints that had been placed by the previous regime upon the Jats, very similar to those imposed upon the Chandalas by the *Manusmriti*.[166] The subjection of the menial proletariat to the caste peasantry thus continued practically unabated throughout medieval times. The occupation set for castes like Chamars, Dhanuks and Dhirs at the end of Mughal rule was quite firmly that of 'working in the fields of *zamindars* and peasants'.[167] It was owing to this continuity from earlier times that the menial and depressed castes formed about a quarter or a fifth of the rural population when censuses and surveys began to make a count of them and describe their conditions in the nineteenth century.[168]

Strong survivals attest with similar force to the continuance through medieval times of the fixed positions of village artisans and servants. This is corroborated by documentary evidence. The *balahar* (low-caste village porter) represented the lowliest tax-paying land-holder in the village in the eyes of Zia Barani (fourteenth century);[169] he must have held a small plot in recompense of his services. There were also the twelve *balutas* in Maharashtra villages, whose custom-ary landholdings and other rights are the subject of a valuable study by Fukazawa, based on pre-British eighteenth-century evidence.[170] In

---

[166] *Chachanama*, edited by U. Daudpota, pp. 214–16; these pages and also pp. 47–48 for the earlier disabilities. A later Arab Governor reechoed *Manu* in insisting that the *jatis* should be accompanied by dogs; Balazuri, *Futuh al-Buldan*, in Elliot and Dowson, *History of India as Told by its Own Historians*, I, London, 1867, p. 129. See also *Manu*, X, 51; Buhler's translation, p. 416.

[167] Col. James Skinner, *Tashrih-ul Aqwam* (AD 1825), MS Br. Mus. Add, 27, 255, ff, 187a 188a. This work describes very accurately the castes and their traditions in the Haryana region at the time.

[168] See an important paper by Dharma Kumar, 'Caste and Landlessness in South India', *CSSH*, IV (3) (1962), pp. 338–63; also her book, *Land and Caste in South India*, Cambridge, 1965, especially p. 161.

[169] *Tarikh-i Firuz-Shahi*, p. 287. On balahar, see H.M. Elliot, *Memoirs of the History, Folklore and Distribution of Races in the North-Western Provinces*, II, edited by John Beames, London, 1869, p. 249; and Irfan Habib, *Agrarian System of Mughal India*, pp 120–21.

[170] Hiroshi Fukazawa, 'Rural Servants i      Eighteenth Century Maharashtrian Village—Demiurgic or Jajmani System?', *Hitotsubashi Journal of Economics* (*HJE*), XII (2), 1972, pp 14–40.

fact the system was universal.[171] It can, therefore, hardly be disputed that the caste structure of the village and its attending elements as formed in ancient India continued to function without recognizable change till the eighteenth century. Apparently, then, there were no internal processes at work to disturb the social structure of the village. But the surroundings in which the structure stood, were altered in certain crucial respects. It is this alteration, in the nature of the ruling class and the pattern of distribution of the surplus, which, by its effects on the conditions of life of the peasantry, provides the justification for demarcating the medieval from the ancient.

The urban orientation of Islam, practically from its inception, was undoubtedly an important factor in furthering a consciously town-centred culture.[172] Whether or not this provided the primary impulse, there did occur during the early centuries of Islam a considerable growth of commerce and craft production all over western and central Asia.[173] This was accompanied by the formation of large polities each unified under a strong despotism (under the Caliph, then under the Sultan).

The Ghorian invaders brought these cultural and political traditions to India. The invaders and their successors owed their supremacy to the effective combination of their mounted archers in contrast to the dispersed strength of the Rajput soldiery.[174] In one

---

[171] It is practically found almost wherever one looks. When the English temporarily took possession of Broach (Gujarat) in 1776, the Collector reported: 'That a certain proportion of the land of each village is requisite to be set apart for the maintenance of such artificers and labourers as are absolutely necessary for the common services of the village is according to the custom of the country true.' *Selections from the Letters. . .*, *in the Bombay Secretariat*, Home Series, edited by G.W. Forrest, II, Bombay, 1887, p. 184.

[172] In the confrontation of town and bedouin in Arabia, Islam was hostile to the bedouin. See the *Quran*, IX, 97, 98. See also Lokkegaard, *Islamic Taxation in the Classic Period*, Copenhagen, 1950, p. 32.

[173] E. Ashtor, *A Social and Economic History of the Near East in the Middle Ages*, Berkeley, 1976, is a competent survey with useful references. A useful guide to conditions in the Islamic East is G. Le Strange's classic work, *Lands of the Eastern Caliphate*, Cambridge, 1905 (reprinted, 1930).

[174] That the essential difference between the invader and defender was one between mounted archer and swordsman or lancer was first pointed out by Simon Digby, *Horse and Elephant in the Delhi Sultanate*, Oxford, 1971, pp. 15ff. See also Irfan Habib, *Studies in History*, II (1), pp. 25–27.

sense, it was a triumph of centralized polity.[175] The tendency towards centralization was reinforced by the coming of gunpowder and artillery, whose first dramatic result was Babur's victory at Panipat (1526).[176]

The centralization expressed itself pre-eminently in the organization of transferable territorial revenue assignments (*iqtas* in the Sultanate, *jagirs* in the Mughal empire), a system borrowed entirely in its fundamentals from the Islamic world.[177] As a result, members of the ruling class (formally officers or nobles of the king) were prevented from growing into permanent hereditary local potentates so long as the central organization, based on the king's court, functioned normally. This system too implied the concentration of the nobles and their troops in the towns from where they exercised control over rural territory, with which they themselves possessed no independent or customary ties.

In an important contribution, Mohammad Habib described the change which took place upon the establishment of the Sultanate as an 'urban revolution', followed subsequently by a 'rural revolution'.[178] One may differ with him, as I venture to do, on the extent of liberation of artisans that the first process implied; and, indeed, on the designation of the two processes.[179] But the interconnection that he saw between the conquests, centralization, urban growth and changes in the sharing of the agrarian surplus, must still stand.

The shift of balance in favour of the town as against country is an important element of medieval Indian economic history. The

---

[175] Behind this need lay the hesitation of the Sultans in paying their own cavalry troopers by assignments of villages instead of in cash. See Barani, pp. 163–64, 220–21, 303, 324, 553; Afif, *Tarikh-i Firuz-Shahi*, Bib Ind, Calcutta, 1850, pp. 94–96.

[176] See V. Barthold, *Iran*, translated by G.K. Nariman, edited by I.H. Jhabavala, in *Posthumous Works of G.K. Nariman*, Bombay, 1935, pp. 142–43.

[177] This immensely fruitful insight belongs to W.H. Moreland. See his *Agrarian System of Moslem India*, especially pages 289–92. The system as it worked in the Delhi Sultanate is also discussed in *Cambridge Economic History of India* (*CEHI*), I, pp. 68–75. For the Mughal empire, see my *Agrarian System*, pp. 257–97, and M. Athar Ali, *The Mughal Nobility under Aurangzeb*, Bombay, 1966, p. 95.

[178] Introduction to a new edition of Elliot and Dowson, *History of India as Told by its Own Historians*, II, Aligarh, 1952, pp. 36–82.

[179] My own views are set out in 'Economic History of the Delhi Sultanate— An Interpretation', *IHR*, IV (2), pp. 287–88.

evidence for the Delhi Sultanate, literary as well as numismatic, suggests a fairly noticeable upsurge in urban life.[180] It is likely that in the Mughal empire the urban population amounted to as much as 15 per cent of the total, a distinctly higher proportion than at the end of the nineteenth century.[181] This urban growth chiefly rested on the surplus extracted by the ruling class in the form of the land tax, which was mainly distributed among its members and their dependents and retainers living within the towns.[182]

The medieval land tax, *kharaj* or *mal*, came into its own with Alauddin Khalji (1296–1316). Until then, except in some localities, the Sultans or their assignees had taken the *kharaj* as a kind of tribute extorted from the chiefs of the defeated regimes. It was now set at half the produce, taken by application of an estimated crop rate on measured land.[183] In terminology as well as in its character, the tax is essentially similar to the single heavy *kharaj*[184] of the Islamic countries. Once instituted in the Sultanate,[185] it continued in the Mughal empire at about the same magnitude, approaching the limits of 'economic rent'.[186] The difference between this tax and the pre-

---

[180] I have presented the evidence in *IHR*, IV (2), pp. 289ff. It is possible that there was a modest revival of commerce and towns before the Ghorian conquests to which Sharma draws attention, *Indian Feudalism*, pp. 242–62. B.D. Chattopadhyaya, 'Trade and Urban Centres in Early Medieval India', *IHR*, I (2), pp. 203–19, even contests Sharma's thesis of the earlier urban decline; but it is difficult to evaluate the evidence he adduces, since it is not Sharma's position that the towns completely disappeared after the Guptas or that no new towns were founded at all. These questions may ultimately be resolved more precisely by archaeology; it would seem, however, that the thirteenth century does mark an immense extension of urban sites whose remains have survived.

[181] *CEHI*, I, pp. 167–71.

[182] On this relationship, my own argument is presented in 'Potentialities of Capitalist Development in the Economy of Mughal India', *Enquiry*, NS, III (3), pp. 1–56 (pp. 180–232 of this volume), especially pp. 22–36.

[183] For Alauddin Khalji's measures, the basic source is Barani, pp. 287–88.

[184] Moreland, *Agrarian System of Moslem India*, pp. 16–18, held that in its approximation to 'economic rent', the tax was essentially Islamic in origin, while in its being fixed at a uniform share irrespective of crop, it had Hindu antecedents.

[185] For a clear-headed account of agrarian taxation under the Sultanate, see Moreland, *Agrarian System of Moslem India*, pp. 21–65; I offer a description in *CEHI*, I, pp. 60–68.

[186] See Irfan Habib, *Agrarian System*, pp. 190–96, and the references given

medieval assemblage of a 'formidable number of taxes and cesses' lay in the tax being a *single* claim on the bulk of the surplus; there was probably little change in the size of the total burden that the peasant had borne previously.[187] This is besides the fact that those who appropriated the surplus through the land tax represented an economic and social element of a different character from the previous appropriators.

The imposition of the land tax (usually called *mul* in Mughal times) remoulded the relations of the peasant with his superiors. Since the tax claimed the bulk of the surplus for the king (and his assignees), the fiscal claims of the previous aristocracy could not be permitted. Thus the prohibition of the *khot's* cesses (*huquq-i khoti, qismat*) by the Sultans,[188] and of the various cesses of *zamindars* by the Mughals.[189]

The land tax was no longer seen in the nature of tribute but as a levy directly assessable upon each cultivator, whether he was a *khot* or *balahar*.[190] In the Mughal Empire the insistence that the tax be assessed on each cultivator name-by-name (*asamiwar*) pervades revenue literature.[191] From this the next step was also sometimes taken: a claim on the peasant's person. True, says a fourteenth-century document, the peasants are 'free-born' (*hurr-asl*), but their obligation to pay tax requires that they be bound to the villages where they have been cultivating the soil.[192] This right of the authorities to force the peasants to cultivate the land, restrain them from leaving it, and bring them back if they did so, is also asserted on various occasions during the Mughal period.[193] Finally, if the peasants failed to pay the tax, they would become subject to raids and enslavement by the king's troops. Evidence for these measures begins right from the

---

there. There has been much work since then on revenue administration, but it has tended uniformly to confirm this finding.

[187] Harbans Mukhia seems to me to miss this point when he says that the Sultans in imposing their heavy land tax were merely following earlier precedents, *Journal of Peasant Studies* (*JPS*), VIII (3), 1981, p. 292.

[188] Barani, pp. 287, 288, 291–420.

[189] Irfan Habib, *Agrarian System*, p. 150 and n.

[190] Barani, p. 287.

[191] See Irfan Habib, *Agrarian System*, pp. 230–33.

[192] *Insha-i Mahru*, edited by S.A. Rashid, Lahore, 1965, pp. 61–63.

[193] Irfan Habib, *Agrarian System*, pp. 115–16. See also the seventeenth-century documents from Gujarat discussed by B.R. Grover in *Proceedings of the Indian History Congress*, Delhi session, 1961, pp. 152–55.

thirteenth century;[194] the same measures were almost *routine* in the Mughal empire.[195]

Clearly, the medieval land tax generated its own pressure upon all the rural classes. But in the interest of surplus appropriation itself it was expedient to maintain the inherited structure of rural society and utilize it for collecting the land tax. Alauddin Khalji would tax the *khots* and *muqaddams* (village headmen) and also force them to collect the land tax.[196] Ghiyasuddin Tughlaq (1320–25), however, found this impracticable, and exempted the two worthies from the tax on their lands to compensate them for their services.[197]

Here we see how the exigencies of the situation were bound to lead to a 'historical compromise'. The hereditary magnates of the days of Indian 'feudalism' would be recognized as holders of certain rights over the territory controlled by them, and be allowed to have armed retainers. In return, they were obliged to render certain services to the authorities, notably that of collecting the tax. After an inevitable process of conflict, confusion of rights and nomenclature, the class obtained the universal designation of *zamindar* in the Mughal empire.[198] The terms of the 'compromise' varied from region to region, but everywhere the *zamindars* and other superior right-holders would receive a minor share in the revenue collected from the territory placed under their rights (10 per cent of the land revenue in northern India, 25 per cent in Gujarat), and they were in practice permitted some other levies on the peasants, and other rights of pecuniary benefit.[199]

A triangular relationship thus came to exist between the peasantry, the *zamindars* and the ruling class. During the first half of

[194] See *CEHI*, I, p. 90.

[195] Irfan Habib, *Agrarian System*, pp. 322–23.

[196] Barani, pp. 287–88, 291. On the *khot*, see *IESHR*, IV (3), pp. 212–13.

[197] Ibid., p. 430.

[198] I omit giving detailed references here, because I have little substantial information to add to my description of *zamindars* in *Agrarian System*, pp. 136–89. See also an important paper by S. Nurul Hasan, 'Zamindars under the Mughals' in *Land Control and Social Structure in Indian History*, edited by L.E. Frykenburg, London, 1969.

[199] A discussion of the *zamindars'* share in the surplus occurs in my *Agrarian System*, pp. 144–54. S. Moosvi argues in favour of a higher share of the *zamindar*; *IESHR*, XI (3), pp. 359–74.

the eighteenth century Qazi Muhammad Ala wrote a tract on land rights in India. His work has not received much attention so far, although he is practically unique among Muslim jurists in taking into account the realities of agrarian relations in India.

According to him, before 'the conquests of Islam', the *rajas*, 'whose descendants are called Rajputs', used to realize *kharaj* (land tax) from the peasants. The latter, out of respect and devotion to the *rajas*, used to acknowledge them as 'proprietors of all land' and regarded themselves as their 'cultivators' only. Although with the Islamic conquests the *rajas* lost their sovereignty, the Sultans let them remain as chiefs (*rausa*) over the peasants; 'they are now called *zamindars*'. (In this the Qazi is historically correct.[200]) The *zamindars* have been given the task (merely) of collecting the tax from the peasants. Yet because the ancestors of the peasants had recognized the pre-Islamic potentates (*rausa*) as proprietors, they continue to recognize their descendants, the *zamindars*, as proprietors as well. In fact, they permit the *zamindars* to evict at will any of the peasants (*riaya*) and lease out the land to someone else. The Qazi objects to these pretensions of the *zamindars* because, he says, the land tax (*mahsul-i arazi*) is levied not on the *zamindars*, but on the peasants. But since the peasants (*harisan*) have never claimed to be 'proprietors' they too cannot be so recognized. Indeed, since the land tax, though set at half the produce, often exceeds that limit, it is not the *kharaj* of Islamic law, but rent (*ujarat*). This applies equally to fields cultivated by the *zamindars* themselves. The ownership of land belongs, therefore, to the treasury. In other words, he pronounces in conclusion what was regarded by European travellers of the sixteenth and seventeenth centuries as an undisputed principle, viz. the entire land in India 'is in the possession [*tasarruf*] of the king'. It was true, said the Qazi, that the *zamindars* bought and sold 'villages, including

---

[200] He is correct even in saying that the pre-Islamic potentates were recognized as landowners. *Rautas* are found selling or mortgaging their lands in two thirteenth-century inscriptions from UP. The Jaunpur brick inscription of 1217 has been published by V.S. Agrawala in *Journal of UP Historical Society (JUPHS)*, XVIII (1 and 2), 1945, pp. 196–201; the Kasrak inscription of 1227 is being published by my colleague Dr Pushpa Prasad, to whom I am indebted for the information.

cultivated lands', on which they claimed ownership rights; but his opinion is that this practice was based on 'false' claims.[201]

The Qazi's own opinions are less important than his depiction of the actualities in which he is quite acute. The peasants admitted themselves to be tenants-at-will of *zamindars* who were 'proprietors', but not the rent appropriators; the nearest equivalent of rent was, on the other hand, claimed through the king's tax. Such complexities would defy any legal theory; they could be explained only as the outcome of six centuries of history.

There is also possibly one piece of over-simplification in Qazi Muhammad Ala's description. The *zamindars* were not universal intermediaries. The existence of peasant-held (*raiyati*) areas was a very important aspect of the agrarian system.[202] This seems to be the main reason why Mughal revenue documents so often omit any reference to *zamindars* where we would otherwise expect them.[203] These peasant-held areas might have originated simply because the older potentates were destroyed or were unable to transform themselves into *zamindars*, or because, as is more likely, even in the 'feudal' centuries there were areas which were not held in hereditary right by any potentate. The areas could also include new villages established by older village communities or their splinters. But if there were no *zamindars* in this apparently large though fragmented zone, there was also a high degree of peasant stratification here.

In our discussion of the earlier period we have seen that peasant production almost invariably implies stratification inasmuch as it requires not only the peasant's own labour, but also demands, as a fourteenth-century divine put it, 'capital' (*maya*) in the form of seed, a pair of oxen, tools and implements.[204] In multi-caste villages,

[201] *Risala Ahkam-i Arazi*, Aligarh MSS, Abdus Salam Arabiya 331–10, ff 43v–62a; Lytton Arabiya Mazhab (2), 62 ff, 53v–62. For his biography (such as is known) see Abdul Hai Hasani, *Nazhatu-l Khawatir*, VI, Hyderabad (Dn), 1376/1907, p. 278.

[202] Irfan Habib, *Agrarian System*, pp. 118, 141–44.

[203] As a result, Moreland (*Agrarian System of Moslem India*, pp. 122–23) was inclined to equate the Mughal *zamindar* with vassal chief only. See also P. Saran, *The Provincial Governments of the Mughals* (1526–1658), Allahabad, 1941, p. III and n., for a similar view.

[204] Shaik Nasiruddin in his conversations, *Khairu-l Majalis*, recorded (*c.* 1354) by Hamid Qalandar, edited by K.A. Nizami, Aligarh, pp. 140, 272. Land, being abundant, is not considered a requirement (*CEHI*, I, p. 48).

caste would reinforce stratification, particularly when the higher castes obtained concessions in revenue rates.[205] The land revenue being a regressive tax would in any case have fallen more heavily on the smaller peasant. But this burden would be further exacerbated when, in effect contracting for the whole village, 'the great men' (*kalantaran*) and *muqaddums* (headmen) shifted the revenue due on their own lands to the shoulders of the small peasants (*reza riaya*).[206] These complaints, voiced in official documents of the Mughal empire, remind us of the fourteenth-century chronicler's reference to 'the burden of the strong falling on the weak',[207] just as the word *kalantaran* takes us back to the 'great men' of the ancient Indian village communities. Differentiation of this kind was inherent in the taxation system; but it would be intensified the heavier the land tax.

Until now we have mainly studied the impact of tax collection on the agrarian economy. The fact that in medieval India, the surplus was extracted mainly for consumption in the town by the king and his revenue assignees, meant that there was but rarely any direct consumption of agricultural produce by the tax appropriators. Already by Alauddin Khalji's time (early in the fourteenth century) the cash-nexus appears to have been fairly well established, so that the Sultan's order that tax was to be collected in kind in certain areas is specifically recorded.[208] In the Mughal empire the cash-nexus was almost universal; even when the tax was fixed in kind (under the crop-sharing

[205] Evidence of such concessional rates from eastern Rajasthan is presented in Dilbagh Singh, 'Caste and the Structure of Village in Eastern Rajasthan during the Eighteenth Century', *IHR*, II (2), pp. 299–311; by S.P. Gupta for the late seventeenth century in *Proceedings of Indian History Congress*, Aligarh session, 1975, pp. 235–37; and by R.P. Rana, *IESHR*, XVIII (3 and 4), pp. 291, 326. The *miras* tenures of Maharashtra are of a similar character, and such privileged strata would be found practically everywhere. In northern India they are often called '*khwud-kasht*' peasants.

[206] Original text of Todar Mal's memorandum, *Akbarnama*, Br. Mus. Add 27, 247, f 333b, where the great men are denounced as 'bastards and the headstrong'; Abul Fazl, *Ain-i Akbari*, I, edited by Blochmann, Bib Ind, p. 286; and Aurangzeb's *farman* to Rasikdas, Art VI, *JASB*, II, 1906, pp. 223–55.

[207] Barani, p. 287.

[208] Barani, pp. 305–6. See also Moreland, *Agrarian System of Moslem India*, pp. 37–38. Elsewhere, Barani himself says that the peasants under the same Sultan sold grain to merchants at fixed prices in order to pay the revenue, which must then have been paid in cash (pp. 304–5, 307).

system), it was most often commuted into money pay-ments.[209] The circulation cycle was completed when the merchant, purchasing agricultural produce from the villages, sold it in the towns into the hands of those who were direct and indirect recipients of the tax money. This portion of agricultural produce would naturally have a much higher composition of high-value crops (e.g., wheat, sugarcane) and raw materials or industrial crops (e.g., cotton, indigo) than the portion left unsold in the villages.[210] By one estimate, cotton and sugarcane which occupied only 8 per cent of the sown area in 'kharif' in *pargana* Malarna (eastern Rajasthan) paid 32 per cent of the revenue.[211] In other words, the crops that sold best were the high-grade crops paying correspondingly high revenue rates and requiring more water and labour and even some installations (indigo-vats, sugar mills, etc.). Clearly only the richer peasants could possibly have the resources to raise such crops, and the profits accordingly would also be theirs. On the other hand, the poorer peasants would not be able to raise the market crops, and would find it more difficult to meet the revenue demand. Inevitably, they would have to take recourse to the usurer, and, given the high rates, would inevitably be pauperized.[212] Aurangzeb in a *farman* exempted from the *jiziya* 'the small peasants [*reza riaya*] who engage in cultivation but depend wholly on debt for their subsistence, seed and cattle'.[213]

The control of the village tended to vest as before with the higher strata. A late Persian manual on Mughal land-revenue administration describes the situation in the village in these terms:

> In every village there are some *muqaddams* [headmen] who are the proprietors of the village and hundreds of persons called *asami* peasants, that is cultivators; the *asami*, with the approval of the revenue collector and the permission of those *muqaddams*, prepare

---

[209] Irfan Habib, *Agrarian System*, pp. 236–40.

[210] The detailed argument for this is advanced by me in *Enquiry*, NS, III (3), pp. 32–36.

[211] S.N. Hasan, K.N. Hasan and S.P. Gupta, *Proceedings of the Indian History Congress*, Mysore session, 1966, pp. 249, 263, Tables I and V.

[212] See the data on agrarian usury in my article 'Usury in Medieval India', *CSSH*, VI (4), pp. 394–98.

[213] Malikzada, *Nigma-i Munshi* (compiled 1684), Lucknow, 1884, p. 139.

their fields, delimit them and cultivate the land, and pay the revenue, as fixed at the beginning of the season, to the Government through the *muqaddams.* . . .

Most of the *muqaddams,* who organize their own [*khwud-kasht*] cultivation, engage wage labourers as servants, and set them to agricultural work. Obliging them to do the ploughing, sowing, reaping, and watering [of the field] from the well, they pay their fixed wages, either in cash or in kind. The crop of the field belongs to them, so that they are both *muqaddams* and *asamis* [in respect of their *khwud-kasht*]. . . .[214]

Here we have a three-tier structure: the 'headmen' cultivating with hired labour; the mass of ordinary cultivators; and the wage labourers. This accords with much of what we know of the villages of this period. A *khasra* document of 1796 from eastern Rajasthan shows two *patels* (village headmen), each cultivating a larger acreage than the bottom 10 of the 38 village peasants, all put together: one *patel* raised seven crops, while each of the 10 peasants grew only one coarse food crop during that season (*kharif*).[215] The landless labourers do not naturally enter this record.

We can see here how the stratification, intensified as it was by commodity production, still remained deeply imbedded in the village as a unit. The fiscal and economic entity of the village was shown by the financial pool (*fota*) out of which revenue payments and 'village expenses' were met.[216] Cultivators coming from other villages were always strangers, and, classed separately as *paikasht*, were obliged to settle terms with the village headmen.[217] The village, with its customary mechanism of fiscal and social management, to which we apply the term 'community', came under only a still more rigorous control of the upper strata as a result of the increased differentiation we have been describing. The customary social integument

---

[214] Chhatar Mal, *Diwan-pasand*, Br. Mus. Or, 2011, ff 7b–8a. The work was compiled some time before 1824, in the Doab area.

[215] *Khasra* document discussed by S.P. Gupta, *Medieval India—A Miscellany*, IV, Bombay, pp. 168–78.

[216] Evidence of Mughal documents on this is set out in *Agrarian System*, pp. 125–27.

[217] See Satish Chandra, 'Some Aspects of Indian Village Society in Northern India during the Eighteenth Century', *IHR*, I (1), pp. 51–64.

continued to support a sub-exploitation, which had probably originally itself served as its basis.[218]

Once the position of the 'headmen' became visibly profitable,
it could become saleable in the same way as *zamindari* right. In time,
the *muqaddami* right could silently grow into *zamindari*.[219] Both
these phenomena are illustrated by the documents of the Bilgram–
Shamsabad area (fifteenth and sixteenth centuries) which I was able
to study.[220] The converse of the process would be the sale of a village
by its peasants to a *zamindar*, of which too there is an example in the
same set of documents.[221] In either case, there is an extension of
*zamindari* right over the *raiyati* zone. Undoubtedly then there must
have been a considerable mixing on the periphery of the lower *zamindars* and the upper peasants.

The medieval peasantry was thus beset by a dual exploita-
tion, of the ruling class (king and *muqtis/jagirdars*) and the *zamindars*,
and by an intensified pace of internal differentiation from fiscal and
market factors. From what we can establish, the source of these twin
developments was essentially external, namely, the flow of the surplus to the towns forced by the medieval land tax.

For most peasants, life was a battle for bare survival. The
seventeenth century, for which we happen to have more detailed
information than for any earlier century, witnessed recurring cycles
of famine with immense mortalities.[222] Nature's calamities underlined man's oppression. To the peasant, the heaviest burden that he
had to bear was the land tax, an arbitrary confiscation of such a large
part of his produce. It was, therefore, natural that payment of the land
tax should be at the root of all major social conflicts involving the
peasantry. It is a remarkable but understandable fact that references

---

[218] I am conscious that I see the effects of commodity production on the village
community rather differently from how these had seemed to me in
*Agrarian System*, pp. 128–29. This is, perhaps, partly because my
conception of the community has also changed since then.

[219] See *Agrarian System*, pp. 133–34.

[220] They are analysed and calendared in *IESHR*, IV (3), pp. 205–32; see especially pp. 211–17.

[221] Ibid., pp. 215–16. The Kachhis and Chamars are termed the 'ancient
*maliks*' of the village in the document (No. 16 of AD 1611). Presumably,
they were simply its inhabitants, forced to 'sell' their village upon an
inability to pay the revenue.

[222] See *Agrarian System*, pp. 100–10.

to armed conflicts on any large scale between the *zamindars* and the peasants, let alone between the upper and the ordinary peasants, are very rare. The land tax represented the principal contradiction; all other conflicts of interest seemed secondary.

### Peasant Revolts

Peasant uprisings span medieval India; their immediate provocation seems uniformly to have been the demand for payment of land revenue.

A widespread rebellion occurred in the Doab about 1330. Muhammad Tughlaq (1325–51) increased the revenue demand, as a result of which 'the weak and resourceless peasants were made completely prostrate, while the rich peasants who had some resources and means turned rebels'.[223] When the Sultan sought to punish the *khots* and *muqaddams*, by killing or blinding them, those who were left 'gathered bands and fled into the jungles'. The Sultan's troops 'surrounded the jungles and killed everyone whom they found'.[224]

This describes the cause and course of the characteristic medieval uprising. In 1622, for example, Jahangir 'received a report that the villagers [*ganwaran*] and cultivators [*muzarian*] of the other [eastern] side of the river Jamuna constantly engage in thievery and, sheltered behind dense jungles and fastnesses, difficult of access, pass their days in rebellion and defiance, not paying the land revenue to the *jagirdars*'. An army was thereupon despatched to suppress the revolt 'with slaughter, enslavement and rapine'.[225]

At some stage, or from the beginning, the peasant defiance tended to merge with the *zamindars'* conflict with the ruling class over their share of the surplus. Already in the fourteenth century an official was clubbing together 'the peasants [literally villagers, *dahaqin*] and the *zamindars* who 'pay revenue only when faced with the terror of the army and the thrust of the dagger'.[226] In the Doab rebellion of 1330, the *khots* and *muqaddams* led 'the bands', as we have seen, and some of these could well have been proto-*zamindars*.

[223] Barani, pp. 472–73.
[224] Ibid., pp. 479–80.
[225] *Tuzuk-i Jahangiri*, edited by Saiyid Ahmad, Ghazipur and Aligarh, 1863–64, pp. 375–76.
[226] *Insha-i Mahru*, p. 75.

In the revolts that occurred during the seventeenth century
the *zamindars'* uprisings tended to feed on peasant unrest or merge
with peasant revolts in many areas.[227] The Doab with the trans-
Jamuna area, again, serves for an example. The peasant uprisings of
the earlier times form a prelude to the revolt of the Jat peasant under
the leadership of a succession of *zamindars*.[228] The Jat uprising was
in formal terms a successful one, ending in the establishment of the
Bharatpur state. It resulted in a very great expansion of Jat *zamindari*
in the Doab at the expense of other *zamindar* clans, and it is therefore
possible that a number of upper Jat peasants moved into the ranks of
*zamindars*. It had no other sequel as far as the ordinary peasants were
concerned. As for the menial castes, the attitude was the traditional
one: Surajmal 'seized a number of Chamars [tanners], who are called
the menials of the Hindus, from different villages', and set them to
guard the ditch at Bharatpur.[229] They were obviously considered
mere chattel.

It is to be considered how far the Maratha power in its
formation in the seventeenth century fed on peasant unrest. The
Maratha chiefs were clearly of *zamindar* origins.[230] Yet their armed
strength was based on a constant accession to them of peasant soldiers, the *bargis*, who left their villages to escape oppression and
devastation from the Mughals as well as the Marathas.

> It came to be represented [to Aurangzeb] that the Marathas
> obtained collaboration from the peasants [*muzarian*] of the Impe-
> rial dominions. It was therefore ordered that the horses and
> weapons found in every village should be confiscated. When this

---

[227] See *Agrarian System*, pp. 333–51.
[228] Ibid., pp. 339–42. The *zamindar* aspect of the Jat revolt is stressed by R.P.
Rana in a very detailed and informative article based on the Amber records
(now at the Rajasthan Archives, Bikaner): 'Agrarian Revolts in Northern
India during the Late Seventeenth and Early Eighteenth Century',
*IESHR*, XVIII (3 and 6), pp. 287–326.
[229] Saiyid Ghulam Ali Khan, *Imadus Su'adat*, Naval Kishore, 1897, p. 55.
[230] See Satish Chandra, 'Social Background to the Rise of the Maratha
Movement during the Seventeenth Century', *IESHR*, X (3) 197 (3), pp.
209–17, and P.V. Ranade, 'Feudal Content of Maharashtra Dharma',
*IHR*, I (I), pp. 44–50. See also *Agrarian System*, pp. 349–50.

happened in army villages, the peasants providing themselves with horses and arms joined the Marathas.[231]

A later writer (*c.* 1761) accordingly asserted that the army of the Marathas 'consists mostly of low-born people, like peasants, shepherds, carpenters and cobblers, while the army of the Muslims comprises mostly nobles and gentlemen'; and he ascribed the Maratha successes to this cause.[232]

The conditions of the peasants did not improve upon the success of the Maratha chiefs; but it is possible that here too certain warriors of peasant origin joined the privileged rural strata, and the *miras* tenures in Maharashtra were considerably enlarged.[233] The position of the *kunbis*, the inferior peasants, seems to have largely remained as miserable as before.

There are two other uprisings which deserve particular notice, because here peasant revolts combined with religious movements. The movements are those emanating from the great monotheistic preaching of the sixteenth century, associated with Kabir, Nanak, Raidas and other teachers. These teachers employed the language of the people chiefly to propagate submission to God; but their teaching tended towards social egalitarianism, since they condemned ritual and caste observance. Most of the teachers belonged to the low *jatis*—Namdev, a calico-printer; Kabir, a weaver; Raidas, a scavenger; Sain, a barber; Dadu, a cotton-carder; Dhanna, a Jat peasant.[234] In the verses of Kabir and Arjun God's faithful worshipper appears as a peasant as well as a village headman.[235] The movement undoubtedly represented the urge of a number of low-ranking classes to rise in the social scale. Its openness to the menial castes is its outstanding achievement, practically unprecedented in our history.

---

[231] Bhimsen, *Nuskha-i Dilkusha*, Br. Mus. Or 23, f 139 p–b.

[232] Mir Ghulam Ali Azad Bilgrami, *Khizana-i Amira*, Kanpur, 1871, p. 49.

[233] I form this impression from H. Fukazawa, 'Land and Peasants in the Eighteenth Century Maratha Kingdom', *HJE*, VI(1), June 1965.

[234] The bold assertion that access to God could be acquired by men of such low birth is made in beautiful verses composed in Braj by Guru Arjun in the name of Dhanna Jat, where the names and occupations of some of the great preachers are given. *Guru Granth Sahib*, I, Devanagari text, Amritsar, 1951, pp. 487–88; see also p. 109.

[235] I have examined these verses in 'Evidence for Sixteenth Century Agrarian Conditions in the *Guru Granth Sahib*', *IESHR*, I, 1964.

The Satnamis were a sect belonging to this movement, as their scripture makes clear. Their revolt in 1672 in the Narnaul region shook the Mughal empire. A contemporary Hindi poem represented them as comprising 'a crore of *ganwars* [villagers]',[236] and the quasi-official chronicler, Saqi Musta'idd Khan concedes that in battle they repeated the scenes of the *Mahabharata*.[237]

The composition of the sect is of much interest. Mamuri says they were peasants and also carried out 'trade in the manner of *baq-qals* [*banyas*] of small capital'.[238] There was, therefore, the possibility of some peasants seeking to enter the trading profession, and acquiring the status of *banyas*. Saqi Musta'idd Khan says that their ranks included menials of all description, 'goldsmiths [?], carpenters, sweepers, and tanners',[239] and Isardas Nagar seems to confirm this when he speaks at some length of the filthiness and impurity of the community's customs, their eating pork and familiarity with the dog.[240] Here, then, we possibly see 'menial' elements aspiring to be recognized as peasants under the protection of a casteless community.

The Satnamis were defeated and crushed. But the Sikhs were successful, and they offer us the other uprising where peasants appear as rebels under the monotheistic leadership. It was recognized by an intelligent observer of the mid-seventeenth century that the Jats had acquired a predominant position in the Sikh community—and 'Jat', he adds, means 'a villager, a rustic' in the dialect of the Punjab.[241] Besides its undisputed peasant composition, the community admitted men of the low and menial castes as well; Banda would give high authority to 'the lowliest sweeper and tanner, filthier than whom there is no race in Hindustan'.[242] A later writer speaks of many of the great Sikh chiefs being 'of low birth such as carpenters, shoe-makers and Jats'.[243] As among the Satnamis, we see here a perceptible urge

---

[236] Verses reproduced in Muzaffar Husain, *Nama-i Muzaffari*, I, Lucknow, 1917, p. 255.

[237] *Ma'asir-i Alamgiri*, Calcutta, 1870–73, pp. 115–16.

[238] Abul Fazl Mamuri, *History of Aurangzeb's Reign*, Br. Mus. Or 161, f 148b.

[239] *Ma'asir-i Alamgiri*, pp. 114–15.

[240] *Futuhat-i Alamgiri*, Br. Mus. Add 23, 884, f 61b.

[241] *Dabistan-i Mazahib*, edited by Nazar Ashraf, Calcutta, 1809, p. 285.

[242] Muhammad Shafi Warid, *Miratu-l Waridat*, Br. Mus. Add 6579, f 117b.

[243] *Imadus Satadat*, p. 71.

on the part of the lower classes to achieve social elevation through a casteless alternative to 'sanskritization'.

This is an important social achievement; but while it lifted sections of the community from a lowly status it did not yet change the major elements of the social order. Even in Guru Gobind Singh's long Persian poem composed in criticism of Aurangzeb, there is no reference to the oppression of the peasants.[244] There was little in the agrarian structure of the Sikh regimes of the eighteenth and nineteenth centuries to distinguish them from their predecessors.[245]

The Mughal empire owed its collapse very largely to the agrarian crisis which engulfed it, and of which the uprisings with their varied record of failure and success were the consequence. Peasants, as we have seen, were deeply involved in these uprisings. Yet the goals of the uprising in each case were not those of the peasants; and for them the fundamental conditions remained unaltered.

That peasant revolts before modern times have not generally succeeded is a matter that hardly needs to be debated. The specific features of Indian peasant uprisings however deserve careful consideration. The basic one, it seems to me, is their comparatively backward level of class consciousness. In China peasant revolts with specific demands for tax reductions have caused dynastic changes. In the English rising of 1381 and the Peasant Wars in Germany in the sixteenth century, the peasants came forward with the objective of securing specific changes in their legal and economic status. In other words, the peasantry, in its own consciousness, stood forth as a class. It is here pre-eminently that the Indian peasant revolts exhibit a remarkable deficiency. The peasants might fuel a *zamindar's* revolt (Marathas), they might rise in a locality (the Doab), or as a caste (Jats), or as a sect (Satnamis, Sikhs), but they fail to attain a recognition of any common objectives transcending parochial limits.

Much of what I have said aims at attempting at least a provisional (and partial) explanation of this historical failure. The caste divisions in our society, the immense gulf between the peasantry and the 'menial' proletariat, and the deeply rooted authority of the *zamindars* all probably have had a part in determining this result. Still, it has to be admitted that no last word can be said on so complex a matter as the role of the peasants in a civilization.

The history of the Indian peasantry did not end with the seventeenth or eighteenth century with which I have closed. The peasantry's first steps towards the attainment of its self-awareness is an achievement of the national movement, for whose success the peasants were so largely responsible. It is apparent, however, that many of the burdensome vestiges of the past, the divisions and superstitions, still hinder the cementing of those bonds among the peasants and the rural poor which are so essential for the advance towards a just society in India.

# Caste in Indian History

Caste is the most characteristic—and, many would say, unique—social institution of India. No interpretation of our history and culture can demand a hearing unless it encompasses the caste system. One of the abiding achievements of D.D. Kosambi's scholarship was his ability to unite a lively spirit of anthropological investigation with a critical analysis of historical evolution. I hope that by choosing the role of caste in Indian history as the theme of this lecture, I may be able to touch on some of Kosambi's most valuable insights.

Any such endeavour must, first, come to grips with the problem of definition. It is not surprising that this should be difficult, but perhaps a working definition could still be attempted to serve us as a point of departure. Caste, we may say, is a fairly well-marked, separate community, whose individual members are bound to each other through endogamy (and hypergamy), and very often also by a common hereditary profession or duty, actual or supposed. Many sociologists, however, appear to regard this definition as quite insufficient. They would add that we must also stipulate the existence of a perception of the rank of one caste in relation to other castes, a ranking which finds expression in the degree of 'purity' and 'impurity' of the other castes in relation to one's own, and in specific rites and practices followed by, or assigned to, each caste.[1] Louis Dumont, in his *Homo Hierarchicus*[2] considers, as the very title of the work shows,

---

[1] See J.H. Hutton, *Caste in India*, fourth edition, Bombay, 1969 (reprint) p. 71 and passim.

[2] All my references are to the Paladin edition, London, 1972.

the hierarchical principle to be the very core and heart of the caste system; without it, there would be no caste.

Whether we should follow the very simple definition we have suggested, or the kind of definition that Dumont would approve of is not a mere matter of semantics: it is of crucial importance for understanding the history of the caste system as well as the history of our civilization. I, therefore, crave the reader's indulgence for examining Dumont's views in some detail.

To Dumont the caste system must be understood in terms of its essentially religious ('Hindu') ideology, which pervades all the immense variety that it displays. It is reflected in the endless, complex, even conflicting, arrangements of ranks, the highest belonging always to the *Brahmanas*, who are the 'purest' and command much of its ritual.[3] The ranking does not originate in, or correspond to, the actual distribution of power or wealth, but arises, so to speak, out of the elaboration of the basic principle of purity or pollution. Thus neither are castes 'an extreme' form of classes,[4] nor is the caste system a system of social stratification: it need not, and does not, correspond to the distribution of wealth or power.[5] Dumont insists that caste must be understood as 'part of the whole' (a favourite phrase of his), which means that the entire society must be divided up among castes, and there must be no significant residue. Thus, in effect, caste must exist as the sole or dominant form of social organization, or not exist at all.[6]

If all this is to be accepted, if, that is, caste arose out of an ideology of 'purity' unfolding as an elaboration of hierarchy on the basis of relative 'purity', without any reference to economic phenomena, then the economic impulse within Indian society must surely have been very weak. Further, if the caste system has given India an unchanging hierarchy, India can have had no history that one may recognize as such. Both these positions Dumont readily espouses.

'I would like to raise', he says, 'the very question of the applicability to traditional India of the very category of economics.' He

---

[3] *Homo Hierarchicus*, p. 300. ('Hierarchy culminates in the Brahman.')
[4] Ibid., pp. 288ff.
[5] Ibid., p. 300.
[6] Ibid., pp. 262, 274. Accordingly, to Dumont, 'Hindus and Muslims form two distinct societies' (p. 257).

points, in justification, to the 'elementary' fact that 'even in our own
[western] society it was only at the end of the eighteenth century that
economics appeared as a distinct category, independent of politics'.[7]
The argument is so illogical that one hesitates over whether one has
understood Dumont aright. The fact that there was at one time no
science of sociology does not mean that there have been no societies
before the arrival of that science; similarly, because economics did
not exist as a science before the eighteenth century, one is not excluded from speaking of the economic factors behind the English Civil
War, or any other earlier historical process or event.

So too is India to be deprived of history:

> The indifference to time, to happening, to history, in Indian
> literature and civilization in general, makes the historian's task very
> hard—But under these conditions, is there a history of India in a
> sense comparable to that in which there is a history of Christian
> civilization or even [!] China?[8]

In other words, shall we say, no biography can be written of anyone
who has not authored an autobiography!

Dumont offers here and there examples of how one can interpret India's 'non-history'. The most impressive example is his exposition of the rise and fall of Buddhism. The ideology of the caste system,
he says, requires individuals' renunciation of society.[9] Some of 'the
renouncers' begin competing with *Brahmanas*. Out of such competition, the Buddhists and the Jainas expounded the doctrine of *ahimsa*
and condemned animal slaughter and meat-eating as polluting acts.
This led the *Brahmanas* to give up animal sacrifice and stress vegetarianism to a greater or more systematic degree than even their chal-
lengers.[10] The Buddhists were thus thwarted, vegetarianism became
yet another symbol of purity, and the *Brahmanas* slept more easily
until the next round of renouncers (e.g., the Lingaits) came round with
some other eccentric competing propositions. Kosambi may point to
the shift from pastoralism to agriculture, R.S. Sharma to the rise of
towns and growth of commerce, in order to explain the success of

[7] Ibid., p. 209.
[8] Ibid., p. 242.
[9] Ibid., pp. 230–31.
[10] Ibid., pp. 192–95.

early Buddhism; but their attempts are vain. The only factor behind it was a more successful appeal to the 'idiom of purity'; and what made such an appeal at all possible was, again, the phenomenon of 'renunciation'.

If such is to be the history of India, to fit a contemporary western sociologist's image of the caste system, is it not more likely that there is something wrong with this image rather than with Indian history? It may, in fact, well be that there is a good historical explanation for Dumont's excessively narrow view of caste. During the last hundred years and more, the hereditary division of labour has been greatly shaken, if not shattered.[11] As a result, this aspect has increasingly receded into the background within the surviving domain of caste.[12] The purely religious and personal aspects have, however, been less affected. (One can see that this is by no means specific to India: religious ideology survives long after the society for which the particular religion had served as a rationalization has disappeared.) It is obviously tempting to take the caste system's surviving elements (mainly religious) as the sole or crucial elements, and the declining aspects (economic) as secondary and even superfluous. Dumont not only falls to the temptation, he builds a whole theoretical structure on a false premise to explain what India is. But then what he postulates about the hierarchical man in India is, perhaps, as difficult to accept as his other belief that western society today is 'egalitarian'.

## II

If then, *Homo Hierarchicus* fails to convert us, from where are we to begin? I think it is important to use the approach that Kosambi explicitly and consistently followed, the one that was introduced by Karl Marx. Caste should be viewed primarily in its role in different social formations that have arisen in a chain of sequence. A social formation, in so far as it is based on the form of the 'labour process', arises after the producers in society are able to provide a 'surplus'. It is vain to expect a social institution like caste to exist

---

[11] Dumont shows an almost total lack of awareness of this development in his remarks on the unchanging caste framework. Ibid., pp. 265–66.

[12] So Dumont can now say: 'In the caste system the politico-economic aspects are relatively secondary and isolated'. Ibid., p. 283.

before this stage has arrived. Indeed, Dumont himself recognizes this, for he admits that the emergence of castes presupposes division of labour which cannot be found in primitive societies.[13] The *purusasukta* in the *Rigveda*, the original statement for the four *varnas*, is more a description of social classes than of castes: the *rajanyas*, aristocracy, the *brahmanas*, priests, the *vis*, people at large (mainly peasants), and the *sudras*, springing from the *dasyus*, servile communities. There is no hint yet in Vedic times of either a hereditary division of labour or any form of endogamy. The *varnas* thus initially presaged very little of the caste system that was to grow later.

Kosambi, in *An Introduction to the Study of Indian History*, offers the view that castes did not arise out of any internal division of the *varnas* in the original Vedic society, but from an external process altogether: 'The entire course of Indian history shows tribal elements being fused into a general society. This phenomenon . . . lies at the very foundation of the most striking Indian social feature, namely, caste.'[14] For this insight one can adduce confirmation from the use of the word *jati*. When the Buddha is spoken of as belonging to the Sakya *jati* the word obviously means a tribe. When, in the same literature, we also read of 'excellent as well as low' *jatis*, castes are clearly implied.[15] Tribes are often rigorously endogamous: thus the Buddha's story of the Sakya brothers who married their own sisters in order to avoid marrying outside the tribe.[16] Can we suppose that as the tribes entered the 'general society', they carried their endogamous customs into that society? If the tribe was already an agricultural community, it would simply turn into the peasant caste of its territory.

However, the tribes 'entering the general society' would include a large number of primitive hunting or food-gathering tribes living in forests, who would be subjugated by the advancing peasant communities. This may be illustrated by the struggle between the

[13] Ibid., pp. 260, 331–32. Compare Kosambi's dictum that 'caste is class on a primitive level of production'. *Culture and Civilization of Ancient India in Historical Outline*, London, 1965, p. 50.
[14] D.D. Kosambim *An Introduction to the Study of Indian History*, Bombay, 1956, p. 25.
[15] Narendra Wagle, *Society of the Time of the Buddha*, Bombay, 1966, pp. 122–23.
[16] Ibid., pp. 103–4.

Sakyas and Kolis.[17] Kosambi has a long passage on the Nagas, the forest folk, who retreat before the Aryan advance, but leave their traces behind in brahmanical lore and later Vedic ritual.[18] As the food-gatherers were subjugated they were reduced to the lowest *jatis*, so low as to be outside the four *varnas* altogether.[19] The enumeration of the 'mixed *jatis*' in the *Manusmriti* shows a preponderance of such communities: the Sair Andhra ensnare animals, the Kawarta are boatmen; the Nisadas pursue fishing; the Medas, Andhras, Chunchus and Madgus live off the 'slaughter of wild animals'; the Kshattris, Ugras and Pukkasas by 'catching and killing [animals] living in holes'; the Karavara and Dhigvanas by working in leather; and the Pandusopaka by dealing in cane (*Manu*, X, 32, 34, 36–37, 48–49). The Chandalas and Nisadas both appear as hunters in Buddhist texts. These were the original 'untouchable' castes.[20] Since they were excluded from taking to agriculture, and their own original or altered occupations were of minor or seasonal importance, they became a large reservoir of unfree, servile landless labour available for work at the lowest cost to peasants as well as superior landholders. It is difficult to avoid the view that the bitter hostility which the rest of the population has displayed for these menial *jatis* has derived from this fundamental conflict of interest. Concepts of 'purity' and 'pollution' were a rationalization of this basic economic fact.

The separation of the peasant and menial *jatis* represents a division of labour in a very generalized form. But R.S. Sharma has called attention to a second urban revolution (the first being represented by the Harappan culture) which took place on the eve of the rise of Buddhism.[21] This implies that a multiplicity of productive skills must have developed. Gordon Childe has stressed the importance of 'new tools and labour-saving devices, such as hinged tongs, shears, scythes, rotary querns' for the emergence of 'a number of new

---

[17] Kosambi, *Introduction*, p. 122.

[18] Ibid., pp. 121–23.

[19] See Kosambi, *Culture and Civilization of Ancient India*, p. 15.

[20] See Vivekanand Jha in *Indian Historical Review* (*IHR*), II(1), pp. 22–23.

[21] R.S. Sharma's review of A. Ghosh, *The City in Early Historical India* (Simla, 1973), in *IHR*, I (1), pp. 98–103.

full-time specialists'.[22] Some of these tools (shears, rotary querns) appear by the first century AD at Taxila.[23] The *Jatakas* introduce us to 'manufacturers' villages', peopled by smiths and carpenters.[24] It is possible that tribes brought wholesale into the general society began to throw off splinters under the pressure of the emerging division of labour. Different craftsmen isolated from the original tribe were formed into specific *jatis*. Thus *Manu* (X, 47–48) includes among the 'mixed *jatis*' those of carpenters, charioteers and physicians. A similar process of differentiation, based on the growth of commerce, led to the mercantile castes, which are quite prominent in the *Jatakas*. In time, they would make the *vaisya varna* exclusively their own.

The position of the *brahmanas* in the caste framework derived naturally enough from their priestly functions, and their guardianship of the *dharma* protecting the caste system. Kosambi suggests that part of their position also derived from their grasp of the calendar, which was so essential for regulating agricultural operations.[25]

The one segment of the caste structure most vulnerable to change was that of the ruling and warrior class, the *kshatriyas* (*rajanyas*). Invasions and rebellions made a hereditary monopoly of armed power extremely difficult, as the Puranas so amply bear witness to. Thus where, logically, the caste system should have been strongest, in actual terms, it was the weakest—namely, in the stability of the ruling community. The entire caste structure has thus supposed a system of exploitation whose major beneficiaries, by its own terms, have so often been usurpers or outsiders.

### III

Almost everyone seems agreed that in universalizing the caste system within India, *Brahmanas* have played a key role, and that by integrating the caste doctrine into the *dharma*, *brahmanas* made the caste system and brahmanism inseparable. One result of these

[22] V. Gordon Childe, *Social Evolution*, edited by Sir Mortimer Wheeler, 1963, p. 110.

[23] See Sir John Marshall, *Taxila*, II, Cambridge, 1952, pp. 486 (rotary querns) and 555 (scissors).

[24] R. Fick, *The Social Organization of North East India in Buddha's Time*, English translation, Calcutta, 1920, pp. 280–85.

[25] Kosambi, Introduction, pp. 236–37.

assumptions has been that the role of Buddhism in the process of caste formation has often escaped notice.

To anyone who reads Kautilya's *Arthasastra* with its heavy stress on the *varna* system, and then turns to Asoka's edicts, the contrast is a striking one. The word *varna* (or *jati*) never appears in Asoka's texts; obedience to the *varna* rules does not form even implicitly a part of the *dharma* that Asoka propagated and whose principles he inscribed on rocks and pillars. In so far as Buddhism rejected the religious supremacy of the *brahmanas*, it necessarily questioned the legitimacy of the *varna* division inherited from the Vedas.

And yet it may be asked whether Buddhism did not have its own contribution to make to the development of the caste system. The *karma* doctrine or the belief in the transmigration of souls which formed the bedrock of Buddhist philosophy, was an ideal rationalization of the caste system, creating a belief in its equity even among those who were its greatest victims. In the *Manusmriti* (XI, 24–26) it already appears as a firm part of the caste doctrine.

Second, there was the stress on *ahimsa*. Kosambi attributed the stress on avoidance of animal-killing in Buddhism to the irrationality of large-scale slaughter of livestock for sacrifice by *Brahmanas*, once settled agriculture had replaced pastoralism.[26] Kosambi did not, of course, intend to disparage the sincerity of the Buddha's disapproval of violence or cruelty (and, after all, Asoka condemned the massacres by his army in Kalinga).[27] What he implied was that any criticism of the large-scale animal sacrifices would be popular among the 'cattle-raising *vaisya*'. But I would like respectfully to suggest what seems to me to be a more plausible reason why *ahimsa* should have become a popular doctrine. It provided reason for the subjugation and humiliation of the food-gathering communities. The Asokan edicts contain injunctions against hunting and fishing,[28] and the Buddhist texts look down on 'animal-killing *jatis*' as much as the brahmanical texts do.

Indeed, here Buddhism also contributed to the ultimate denigration of the peasantry in the *varna* structure. R.S. Sharma's exposition of how the *sudra* and not the *vaisya varna* came to be regarded

[26] Ibid., pp. 158–59.
[27] Recorded on Rock Edict XIII.
[28] Especially P.E.V and the bilingual Qandahar inscription.

as the category to which peasants must belong is practically definitive.[29] In this denigration the *ahimsa* doctrine too was made to play a part. *Manu* (X, 84) condemns the use of the plough for the injury that its iron point causes to living creatures. This is echoed in later Buddhism; I-tsing says that the Buddha forbade monks from engaging in cultivation because this involved 'destroying lives by ploughing and watering field'.[30]

It would, therefore, be wrong to suppose that the caste ideology has been exclusively brahmanical in its development.

### IV

The period from the rise of Buddhism (*c.* 500 BC) to the Gupta age (fourth and fifth centuries AD) may, then, be supposed to be the period of the formation of the Indian caste system and its supporting 'ideology'. It is significant that outsiders were struck not by the 'hierarchy' of the system, but by its hereditary occupations. Megasthenes (*c.* 300 BC), with his listing of the seven castes, and Yuan Chwang, both make unqualified statements in this respect, as do later foreign observers like Babur and Bernier.[31]

Being a relatively rigid form of division of labour, the caste system formed part of the relations of production. But the caste system operated in two different worlds of labour, and these two must be distinguished in order to better understand both the caste system and the social formation of which it was a part. Marx derived a very important insight from Richard Jones, when he distinguished the artisan maintained by the village and the artisan of the town, wholly dependent on the vagaries of the market. In one case the caste labour belonged to a natural economy, in the other to a commodity or monetized sector.[32]

[29] R.S. Sharma, *Sudras in Ancient India*, Delhi, 1958, especially pp. 232–34.

[30] *A Recrod of the Buddhist Religion as Practised in India and the Malay Archipelago*, translated by J. Takakusu, Oxford, 1986, p. 62.

[31] For Megasthenes see R.C. Majumdar, *The Classical Accounts of India*, Calcutta, 1960, pp. 224–26, 263–68; Yuan Chwang, *Buddhist Records of the Western World*, I, translated by S. Beal, London, 1884, p. 82; Babur, *Baburnama*, trnaslated by A.S. Beveridge, London, 1921, p. 520; Francois Bernier, *Travels in the Mogul Empire, 1655–68*, translated by A. Constable, edited by V.A. Smith, Oxford, 1916, p. 259.

[32] Karl Marx, *Theories of Surplus Value*, Vol. III, English translation, Moscow, 1971, p. 435.

Those who are familiar with Marx's writings on the Indian village community may remember that he locates the base of its economy on two opposite elements existing side by side: 'the domestic union of agricultural and manufacturing pursuits', limiting thereby the domain of exchange within the village; and 'an unalterable division of labour', with the artisans and menials belonging to particular castes as servants of the village as a whole, maintained through customary payments in kind or land allotments, dispensing, again, with commodity exchange.[33] Max Weber gave to this kind of caste-determined labour the name of demiurgical labour.

Modern sociologists since W.H. Wiser have been sprinkling cold water on this view. To them, the actual system was not of demiurgical labour, but the *jajmani* system, that is, a system of the artisans serving only particular families. For Louis Dumont, as one would expect, it becomes immediately a matter of a ritualistic relationship between certain upper-caste families and the 'purity' specialists, viz. the *brahmana* and the barber, which was then extended to relationships with other artisans and labouring castes. So, we are told: 'In the last analysis, the division of labour shows not a more or less gratuitous juxtaposition of religious and non-religious or "economic" tasks, but both the religious basis and the religious expression of interdependence. Further it deduces interdependence from religion.'[34] Dumont has apparently let his edition run on without paying much attention to current historical work. In 1972 Hiroshi Fukazawa published the results of his investigations in the eighteenth-century records, in which Maharashtra is so rich. His definite conclusion, closely based on documentary evidence, was that the *jajmani* theory was applicable only to the family priesthood; the traditional twelve *balutas* (carpenter, smith, potter, leather-worker, barber, etc.) were basically village servants, paid through land allotments (*watan*) and out of peasant crops. So strong is Fukazawa's evidence[35] that he is led to the perceptive comment that if modern village artisans appear to

---

[33] *Capital*, I, edited by Dona Torr, translated by Moore and Aveling, London, 1938, p. 351.
[34] Dumont, *Homo Hierarchicus*, p. 150.
[35] H. Fukazawa, 'Rural Servants in the Eighteenth Century Maharashtrian Village—Demiurgic or Jajmani System', *Hitotsubashi Journal of Economics (HJE)*, XII(2), 1972, pp. 14–40.

be servants of certain families alone, this is due to the decay of the old system under modern conditions.

Historical evidence for the village servants in fact goes back to a fairly early period. Kosambi cites epigraphic evidence attesting to carpenters' plots in north Indian villages going back to the fifth century.[36] Similarly, B.N.S. Yadava draws attention to the *Lekha-paddati* documents (Gujarat, *c.* 1000), which speak of the five village artisans (*pancha karuka*), viz. the carpenter, ironsmith, potter, barber and washerman, entitled to receive handfuls of grains from the peasant.[37] The *balahar*, or the village menial, appears as the lowliest landholder in Barani's account of Alauddin Khalji's taxation measures (early fourteenth century).[38]

The hereditary artisan and servant, thus, was of crucial importance in sustaining the self-sufficiency as well as the internal natural economy of the village. Such self-sufficiency not only isolated the village, but enlarged its capacity to deliver a larger part of the surplus to the ruling class, since it did not need much extra produce to exchange for its own imports.

As the surplus was taken out of the village, it entered the realm of commodity exchange, as Marx particularly noted in his classic passage (already cited) on the Indian village community in *Capital*, Volume I. Outside the village the artisan appears as an individual selling his wares on the market. The hereditary occupation by caste was necessary to enable 'special skill' to be 'accumulated from generation to generation'.[39] The hereditary transmission sustained skill while excluding even horizontal mobility. In addition, the caste system possibly created another element of advantage for the ruling class, by giving a lowly status to many artisan castes. Artisan castes already appear among the mixed *jatis* in *Manu*; and in the eleventh

[36] Kosambi, *Introduction*, p. 312.
[37] B.N.S. Yadava, *Society and Culture in Northern India in the Twelfth Century*, Allahabad, 1973, p. 267.
[38] Ziauddin Barani, *Tarikh-i Firuz-Shahi*, edited by S.A. Khan, W.N. Lees and Kabiruddin, Bib. Ind., Calcutta, 1860–62, p. 287. On *balahar*, see H.M. Elliot, *Memoirs of the History, Folklore and Distribution of Races in the North-Western Provinces*, II, edited by John Beames, London, 1869, p. 249; and Irfan Habib, *Agrarian System of Mughal India*, pp. 120–21.
[39] Marx, *Capital*, I, pp. 331–32.

century Alberuni classes eight professions, including those of weavers and shoemakers, among the outcaste *antyajas*.[40] Their depressed status and lack of mobility must surely have helped to curtail the powers of resistance of the artisans and so to keep wage costs low.

The caste system, in its classic form, could therefore function with as much ease in a natural economy as in a market-oriented one. In either case it helped essentially to maintain not a fabric of imagined purity (if it did, this was incidental), but a system of class exploitation as rigorous as any other.

## V

In many ways the beginning of the thirteenth century marks a 'break' in Indian history. This break arises not only from the intrusion of Islam: we begin to see a social formation which is at last close to Marx's 'Oriental despotism' as against the preceding age of 'Indian feudalism' delineated by Kosambi and R.S. Sharma. We must, however, allow for a much larger extent of commodity production and urbanization than Marx seems to have visualized for pre-colonial India.

The caste structure in both villages and towns continued essentially to be the same as in the earlier period. As will be seen from what we have said in the foregoing section, the evidence for hereditary caste labour in villages and towns is practically continuous from ancient India to the eighteenth century. It is true that Islam in its law recognizes differences based only upon free man and slave (and man and woman); caste, therefore, is alien to its legal system. Nevertheless, the attitude of the Muslims towards the caste system was by no means one of disapprobation. When in 711–14, the Arabs conquered Sind, their commander Muhammad Ibn Qasim readily approved all the constraints placed upon the Jatts under the previous regime, very similar to those prescribed for the Chandalas by the *Manusmriti*.[41] Muslim censures of Hinduism throughout the medieval period centre

---

[40] Edward C. Sachau, *Alberuni's India*, I, London, 1910, p. 101.

[41] Anonymous, *Chachanama*, Persian version of the thirteenth century, edited by U-Daudpota, Hyderabad-Dn., 1939, pp. 214–16 (also see pp. 47–48). A later Arab Governor insisted that the Jatts should, as mark of identification, be always accompanied by dogs. See Elliot and Dowson, *History of India as told by its own Historians*, I, London, 1867, p. 129.

round its alleged polytheism and idol worship, and never touch the question of the inequity of caste. The only person who makes a mild criticism of it is the scientist (and not theologian) Alberuni (*c.* 1030) who said: 'We Muslims, of course, stand entirely on the other side of the question, considering all men as equal, except in piety.'[42] But such an egalitarian statement is almost unique; the fourteenth-century historian Barani in his *Tarikh-i iruz-Shahi* fervently craved for a hierarchical order based on birth, although he was thinking in terms of class, rather than of castes, and does not appeal to the Hindu system as a suitable example.

In so far as the caste system helped, as we have seen, to generate larger revenues from the village and lower the wage costs in the cities, the Indo-Muslim regimes had every reason to protect it, however indifferent, if not hostile, they might have been to *Brahmanas* as the chief idol-worshippers. (Does not this also mean that the supremacy of the *Brahmanas* was by no means essential for the continuance of the caste system?) Nevertheless, the caste system had to undergo certain adjustments and changes, which must be recognized as important, not as a result of the policy of the Sultans, but of the new circumstances.

In the first place, the new ruling classes and their dependents brought not only demand for new products and new kinds of services, from their central and west Asian backgrounds, but also a fairly wide range of new craft technology. Kosambi, with his usual perceptiveness, spoke of the 'Islamic raiders—breaking hidebound custom in the adoption and transmission of new techniques'.[43] Among the technological devices which came early (thirteenth and fourteenth centuries) were right-angled gearing (for the final form of the Persian wheel), the spinning wheel, paper manufacture, vault construction, use of bitumen and lime-cement, iron horse-shoe, and so on.[44] These necessitated, in some cases, the creation of new professions (e.g., paper-makers, lime-mixers) and, in others, the learning of new devices; in general, one can postulate the need for a considerable expansion of the artisan population, to accompany what, in fact, may be

[42] *Alberuni's India*, I, p. 100.
[43] Kosambi, *Introduction*, p. 370.
[44] See Irfan Habib, 'Changes in Technology in Medieval India', *Studies in History*, II, NO. I (1980), pp. 15–39.

designated the third 'urban revolution' in India history.

The pressure of the new circumstances led initially to large-scale slave-trading and the emergence of slave labour as a significant component of urban labour during the thirteenth and fourteenth centuries. The numbers of slaves in the Sultan's establishments were very high (50,000 under Alauddin Khalji, and 1,80,000 under Firuz Tughluq). Barani judges the level of prices by referring to slave prices, and the presence of slaves was almost all-pervasive. Slaves were, in effect, deprived of caste and, converted to Islam, could be put to almost any task or learn any trade. Manumitted in course of time, they probably created, along with artisan immigrants, the core of many Muslim artisan and labouring communities. There was also in time a conversion of free elements, possibly in many cases sections of castes splitting off from their parent bodies in search of higher status or willing to take to occupations or practices not permitted to them previously. There thus arose, in course of time, a substantial Muslim population.[45]

Caste undoubtedly continued to exercise its influence on these communities. To judge from their practices as reported since the nineteenth century, weavers, butchers, barbers and others had strong tendencies to be endogamous. The menial castes duplicated themselves as *kamin* communities among Muslims, not untouchable but still kept separate and held in contempt. Nonetheless, it would still be correct to say that sectors of Muslim populations remained outside the caste framework even in its most rudimentary form; and in any case, the framework remained weak, since both shifts of occupation and deviations from endogamy could occur.[46] In other words, there was always a much greater degree of mobility.

It is questionable whether the presence of such relatively caste-free populations at all undermined the caste system. Such populations might indeed have reinforced it by providing reserve labour for new professions or occupations without causing any disruption to the structure of existing castes. But it is also doubtful whether the caste

---

[45] This paragraph is based on evidence already presented by me in *Cambridge Economic History of India*, Vol. I, Cambridge, 1982, pp. 89–93, where detailed references to sources will be found.

[46] See D. Ibberson's remarks on conditions in western Punjab 'where Islam has largely superseded Brahminism', *Punjab Castes*, Lahore, 1916, pp. 10–11.

system was so completely devoid of capacity for mobility as has been assumed by Max Weber. Morris D. Morris in a notable paper argues that in actual practice the caste system has been vastly different from how one thinks it should have operated on the basis of the law books —or of what Dumont calls its 'ideology'.[47] Castes divided to enable one section to take to new professions; Fukazawa draws attention to a well-documented case from eighteenth-century Maharashtra, where a section of tailors took to dyeing and yet another to indigo-dyeing and set up as endogamous sub-castes.[48] A historically singular case is that of the Jatts, a pastoral Chandala-like tribe in eighth-century Sind, who attained *sudra* status by the eleventh century (Alberuni), and had become peasants par excellence (of *vaisya* status) by the seventeenth century (*Dabistani-i Mazahib*).[49] The shift to peasant agriculture was probably accompanied by a process of 'sanskritization', a process which continued, when, with the Jat rebellion of the seventeenth century, a section of the Jats began to aspire to the position of *zamindars* and the status of Rajputs.

Moreover, where sanskritization failed or was too slow a process, hearing began to be given to monotheistic movements, which condemned the 'ideology' of the caste system. It may be that the monotheistic belief of Islam and the legal equality of the Muslim community exercised a certain influence on these movements. But their stress on equality and condemnation of caste and ritual observance was certainly much greater than is to be found in any contemporary Islamic preaching. Most of its great teachers belonged to the low *jatis*: Namdev, a calico-printer; Kabir, a weaver; Raidas, a scavenger; Sain, a barber; Dadu, a cotton-carder; Dhanna, a Jat peasant. In beautiful verse, composed in the name of Dhanna Jat, the fifth Guru of the Sikhs (Arjun) insists on God's special grace for such lowly worshippers.

In these communities (*panths*) the doors were open to people

---

[47] Morris D. Morris, 'Values as an Obstacle to Economic Growth in South Asia,' *Journal of Economic History (JEH)*, XXVII, pp. 588–607.

[48] *HJE*, IX(1), (1968), pp. 39ff.

[49] This evidence is examined in my paper 'Jatts of Punjab and Sind', *Punjab Past and Present: Essays in Honour of Dr Ganda Singh*, edited by Harbans Singh and N.G. Barrier, Patiala, 1976, pp. 92–103.

of all castes. The Satnami sect (which arose in the seventeenth century, with some allegiance to Kabir), contained goldsmiths, carpenters, sweepers and tanners, according to one account,[50] and peasants and traders of small capital, according to another.[51] The Sikh community in the seventeenth century consisted in bulk of Jat peasantry; early in the next century, the complaint was being made that authority could be given among them to 'the lowliest sweeper and tanner, filthier than whom there is no race in Hindustan'.[52] The practices of these *panths* forbade caste distinctions within the community, and, there was a tendency in the communities, as with the Satnamis, amongst whom this was prescribed by scripture, to become endogamous.[53] The net result was the creation of religious communities which drew their following from the caste framework but which ultimately returned to that framework though usually at a higher 'rank' than at the time of their departure from it. This had happened before, as in the case of the Lingayats in Karnataka; and these movements of the sixteenth and seventeenth centuries similarly made necessary adjustments in the caste system, without however subverting it.

The caste system, therefore, remained an important pillar of the system of class exploitation in medieval India. As we have said before, its chief beneficiaries could only be the ruling classes; in the medieval case, these were, first, the nobility and, second, the rural superior class, the *zamindars*. To the extent that the political structure was sustained by the *zamindars*, caste again was important, since the *zamindars*, by and large, belonged to the 'dominant castes' which maintained their position by force. It is worth remembering that when Abu-l Fazl in his detailed statistical tables of the Mughal empire in the *A'in-i Akbari* (1595–96) gives the castes of *zamindars* of each locality, this information is followed not by the area of land they held

[50] Saqi Musta'idd Khan, *Ma'asir-i Alamgiri*, edited by Agha Ahmad Ali, Calcutta, 1870–73, pp. 14–15.

[51] Khafi Khan, *Muntakhabu'l Lubab*, edited by Kabiruddin Ahmad, Calcutta, 1860–70, Vol. II, p. 252.

[52] Muhammad Shafi Warid, *Miratu'l Waridat*, British Library (London) MS., Add. 6579, f. 117b.

[53] The Satnami scripture, containing these injunctions, is titled *Pothi Gyan Bani Sadh Satnami*, and is preserved in Royal Asiatic Library, London, MS. Hind. No copy is known.

but by the numbers of their retainers, horse and foot.[54] There was, therefore, an undoubted connection between caste dominance and military power.

Barrington Moore Jr expresses some surprise that in his detailed descriptions of the Mughal Indian economy. W.H. Moreland should have had so little to say on caste.[55] This applies to some of my own work as well. The reason, perhaps, is that when one looks at the specific relations, such as those of the peasant and the tax-appropriator, or the petty producer and the merchant, caste is not immediately visible. What it did mainly was to provide a large part of the setting for these relations. It divided the agrarian classes into two antagonistic camps, the caste peasants and the menial labourers; and it stabilized the division of labour in petty production. But it is questionable if these functions were crucial enough for us to propound that caste defined the form of the labour process in medieval India (*c.* 1200–1750). The factors of mobility and competition were present to a certain degree, as we have seen. Iran was very similar to India in its economic and political organization in medieval times, but without the benefit of the caste system. Can we nevertheless say that Mughal India and Safavid Iran belonged to two separate social formations, just because one had caste and the other lacked it? Any comment on the matter can at present be only tentative, and one may look forward hopefully to more discussion on the subject.

But one final word, before we leave the question of caste in medieval India. Any class formation like medieval Indian society was bound to generate internal tensions, finding expression notably in the struggles of the oppressed. India has a history of peasant uprisings, going back to the revolt of the buffalo-riding Kaivartas of Bengal in the eleventh century.[56] But it is from the seventeenth century that we get perhaps the richest evidence of peasant uprisings. One great weakness of these uprisings, when compared with those of Europe or China, is the rebels' extremely backward class consciousness. Peasant rebels appear as *zamindars'* followers (Marathas), or members of religious

---

[54] This point is lost in Jarrett's translation of the *A'in-i Akbari*, since the translator has altered the arrangement of the columns. See my *Agrarian System of Mughal India*, Bombay, 1963, p. 139.

[55] *Social Origins of Dictatorship and Democracy*, 1977, pp. 317–18 n.

[56] R.S. Sharma, *Indian Feudalism*, second edition, Delhi, 1980, p. 220.

communities (Sikhs, Satnamis) or of castes or tribes (Jats, Afghans); they fail to see themselves as peasants or to raise economic or social demands for any section of the peasants. It seems to me that caste provides part of the reason for this failure. It prevented peasants of one caste from finding common ground with those of another, and so all the time undermined the growth of self awareness of the peasantry as a class.

## VI

The history of caste in the foregoing pages has been brought close enough to modern times. I do not intend to pursue it further, but a few concluding remarks may still be offered.

In 1853, discussing the results of British rule, Marx predicted that 'modern industry, resulting from the railway system will dissolve the hereditary divisions of labour upon which rest the Indian castes, those decisive impediments to Indian progress and Indian power.' It has become customary to deride this statement (vide Louis Dumont) as having been too optimistic.[37] But it will be futile to deny that modern conditions have gravely shaken the economic basis of the caste system. This is not only because workers of several castes come together on the factory bench; and once this happens the traditional division of labour begins to collapse. Even more important has been the fact that industrial production has destroyed the crafts of a whole series of professional or artisanal castes. This process began with the import of Lancashire cloth, even before Marx was writing. The basis of the caste division of labour has weakened due to one further factor. As Surendra J. Patel has pointed out, commercialization of agriculture has converted large numbers of peasants into landless labourers, so that no longer does landlessness remain a monopoly of the 'menial' castes, though they still form in most areas its largest contingent.[38]

But if the economic base of the caste system has been shaken, can the same be said of its ideology? Endogamy continues to reinforce caste; and there has been a process of territorial enlargement of castes through mutual identification and absorption. 'Sanskritization', which modernization at one level strongly fosters, converts the erst-

---

[37] *Homo Hierarchicus*, p. 265.
[38] Surendra J. Patel, *Agricultural Labourers in India and Pakistan*, Bombay, 1952, especially pp. 9–20, 63–65.

while victims of the system into its votaries. So long as the conflict of interest between landless labour and landholding classes remains, there is an incentive for all castes to combine against the untouchables, whom we euphemistically call the scheduled castes. Caste still remains perhaps the single most important divisive factor in our country.

For all those who wish to see the Indian people united in a struggle for their material and spiritual liberation, it is of utmost importance that there be a renewed effort to eradicate the sway that caste continues to hold over the minds of our people. What Marx called the decisive impediment to Indian progress could only then be removed, and caste at last relegated to history, to which it properly belongs.

# Potentialities of Capitalistic Development in the Economy of Mughal India

When we ask ourselves the question why India failed to industrialize (and develop a capitalistic economy) either before or after the British conquest, we touch the core of an old and hallowed controversy in which the partisans and opponents of British imperialism had once confronted each other. To admirers of British rule, generally, it seemed that the fault lay with certain inherent weaknesses in Indian society. The influence of an 'enervating climate', the heritage of 'Oriental despotism' and recurring cycles of anarchy (inhibiting the accumulation and investment of capital), primitive techniques and ignorance, the rigidities of the caste system, the prevailing spirit of resignation as opposed to enterprise, all created conditions in which nothing but a subsistence economy could function. From such wretched beginnings, the British could not, whatever they did, lift the Indian economy to European levels. The critics of imperialism saw things in a different light. They insisted that the primitive nature of the Indian economy before the British conquest ought not to be overstressed, and they ascribed India's backwardness chiefly to the strangulating effects of British rule, to 'the drain of wealth', the destruction of handicrafts, heavy taxation, and discrimination against Indian industry and capital. It will thus be seen that though the controversy involved a number of important aspects of modern Indian economic history, in part at least it centred on the potentialities of development in the Indian economy prior to the British conquest.[1]

---

[1] Instructive for an appreciation of the main points of the old controversy is the recent debate provoked by a restatement of the imperialist case by Morris D. Morris, 'Towards a Reinterpretation of Nineteenth Century

For a long time there was little information at hand on this particular subject; a great advance was accomplished when, under the impetus of the wider controversy, scholars like W.H. Moreland and Brij Narain attempted to study the economy of Mughal India on the basis mainly of contemporary evidence.[2] A number of simple generalizations that had till then held sway were now relegated largely to the pages of the propagandists, though they still reappear from time to time in the writings of the learned. Since then, again, there have been considerable additions to our knowledge. Unfortunately, large gaps in our information still remain, and on many crucial aspects our data are pitifully scarce. But, while we must bear the limitations of our evidence in mind, it is yet possible to generalize. Though many such generalizations may still be in the nature of tentative conclusions, or even speculations, these may at least possess the merit of indicating the problems that historians of the Mughal Indian economy are seeking to resolve.

In the present paper we are, formally speaking, concerned not with the potentialities of growth, but specifically with the potentialities of capitalistic development. It is a reasonable assumption, however, that for all societies other than those of our own day, the only possible road to modern industry (as the principal lever of growth) lay through capitalism, and it may therefore be taken for granted that the proximity to or distance from true capitalistic relations that a given pre-modern or modern society maintained offers a valid criterion for judging its capacities of growth, so that, in essence, the two questions may be treated as identical. A rather more difficult question is one of definition. What do capitalistic relations consist of? For the sake of consistency and clarity, the Marxist definitions of the terms capital and capitalism, and also of certain other terms, have been followed in this paper. Capitalistic relations are, therefore, considered by us as not

Indian Economic History,' *Journal of Economic History (JEH)*, XXIII, No. 4 (1963), pp. 606–18; for the critical comments upon it by Toru Matsui, Bipan Chandra, and T. Raychaudhuri, see *Indian Economic and Social History Review (IESHR)*, V, 1 (1968), pp. 1–100, in which Morris' paper is also reprinted.

[2] W.H. Moreland, *India at the Death of Akbar*, London, 1920, and *Akbar to Aurangzeb*, 1923; Brij Narain, *Indian Economic Life, Past and Present*, Lahore, 1929.

mere money or market relations, but relations based on a particular mode of production, in which the producer is separated from his tools, so that while he himself is a wage labourer, the implements of production, together with the raw materials and the finished product, are owned by his employer, the capitalist. This definition, in effect, restricts capitalism properly to the economic organization that became dominant with the coming of the Industrial Revolution. This may be objected to by those who regard the essence of capitalism as consisting in the prevalence of a market economy, and so would date the rise of capitalism in Europe to a period much before the eighteenth and nineteenth centuries.[3] However, without anticipating our own arguments about the Mughal Indian economy, it may be suggested as a possibility that a society may have a well-developed money economy without evolving machine industry, and it would therefore be better to have a definition of capitalism which is narrow, if not also more precise. At the same time, the importance of a market economy as a precondition (though not necessarily the fountainhead) of capitalistic development has to be given due recognition;[4] and therefore we shall be concerning ourselves also with the scale and nature of money relations and commodity production in the various sectors of the economy of Mughal India.

## I

Capitalism means the sway of capital, and the latter implies accumulation, which again must directly or ultimately arise out of production, or rather out of the surplus product (the total net product minus the cost of subsistence of the producer). It may be argued that the emergence of capitalism becomes possible only when the surplus products attain a certain minimum magnitude, enabling 'primary accumulation' to take place. If per capita production is very low, the surplus might not reach that minimum, and accumulation might not

---

[3] See Maurice Dobb, *Studies in the Development of Capitalism*, London, 1946, pp. 5–7, for a discussion of such views.

[4] 'The wealth of those societies in which the capitalist mode of production prevails presents itself as an "immence accumulation of commodities"'— the opening words of Marx, *Capital*, Vol. I, translated by Moore and Aveling, edited by Dona Torr, London, 1946, p. 1. All references to *Capital*, I, are to this edition.

occur. Since it has been said that the Indian economy was precisely in such a situation before the British conquest,[5] we may be justified in giving some space to this matter.

For all practical purposes, in the case of Mughal India, this is a question of the level of agricultural production. Though we should like to know a great deal more about Indian agriculture during the seventeenth century, some essential facts are fairly well established. First of all, there was great abundance of land. A study of the official Mughal area statistics and other geographical information indicates that the extent of cultivation then was about half of what it was about the beginning of the twentieth century, in the middle Gangetic basic and central India, and from two-thirds to one-fifth in other regions.[6] From this it may be reasonably inferred, compared to the conditions around the year 1900, that cultivation was confined to the more fertile lands in 1600; that owing to larger wastes and pastures more cattle could be kept (indicating not only a larger output of pastoral products per capita, but also a greater use of cattle power in agriculture); that each household farm should have approximated more closely to the optimum size; and, finally, that a greater amount of double-cropping could have been undertaken by the peasants. At the same time, the agricultural technology in 1600 differed in no significant respects from what it was in 1900. A new important factor in 1900, undoubtedly, was the large-scale canal irrigation network laid out by the British in the Indus basin and the upper Gangetic region. It may also be urged that the railways facilitated the raising of crops for which particular lands or localities were most suited; and there were some new crops, the cultivation of which expanded substantially during the nineteenth century, namely, maize and the plantation crops, tea and coffee. On weighing all these factors, it would hardly be possible to consider per capita agricultural output as being lower in 1600 than in 1900.[7] It is also very likely that in per capita agricultural productivity Mughal India was not in any way backward when compared with other

[5] Morris, *IESHR*, V (1), pp. 3–7.
[6] Irfan Habib, *Agrarian System of Mughal India*, Bombay, 1963, pp. 1–24. Hereinafter referred to as I. Habib.
[7] Moreland, *India at the Death of Akbar*, pp. 100–24; I. Habib, pp. 36–57. Moreland's arguments are a little different from those presented in the text above.

contemporary societies, including those of western Europe.[8]

However, it is not simply the output that is to be considered in estimating the scale of the surplus. Of direct significance for accumulation is not so much the amount of output as the size of the surplus. It is, therefore, important to consider what the cost of subsistence was. Not much argument is needed to demonstrate that the mere cost of survival in a tropical or semi-tropical climate is less than in a colder one. Within India the cost of subsistence was not uniform and in fact would seem to have varied more often in an inverse ratio to the productivity of the soil. It struck a seventeenth-century observer from the north, for example, that southern India had large and massive temples because, while the land was so immensely productive, the subsistence needs of the population (in comparison presumably with those of the northern regions) were extremely few, so that the surplus available was very large.[9] There is little doubt, then, that the absence of capitalistic development in India cannot be attributed very simply to a low level of agricultural production.

Given the minimum size of the agricultural surplus, it is probably the mode of its appropriation, and ultimate distribution, which may (but may not) contain the seeds of capitalism.

The agricultural surplus may be appropriated and shared in various ways that are reducible, theoretically speaking, to two basic forms: (A) a demand from outside imposed on the producer (e.g., rent); (B) a gain accruing as a result of the appropriator's undertaking or organizing the productive process himself (e.g., peasant's savings, profits of the capitalist-farmer). Since this division is merely theoretical, not historical, there is no chronological sequence involved in it; each

---

[8] It is not clear to me why Morris, *IESHR*, V(1), pp. 3–7, insists on the 'low yields' of traditional Indian agriculture. In some of his arguments there is a failure to distinguish between output per acre and output per head in conditions of a favourable man/land ratio, as when he speaks of 'very short growing seasons' (owing to there being two harvests in the year). He also seems to overlook the likelihood that the yield to seed ratio in such crops as wheat was generally higher in India than in western Europe before the nineteenth century.

[9] Bhimsen, *Nuskha-i Dilkusha*, passage translated in M. Athar Ali, 'Karnatik at the End of the Seventeenth Century,' *Proceedings of the Indian History Congress* (Mysore), 1966, p. 238. For a survey of the actual conditions of the life of the peasantry in Mughal India, see I. Habib, pp. 90–99.

embraces numerous types of relations, found at various stages of economic development. Thus, though capitalistic farming proper belongs to Form B, farming carried on through slave labour is also a category of Form B. On the other hand, rent in kind and rent in cash are both covered by Form A, but the latter type of rent has been held to be of considerable significance in encouraging commodity production, and thereby preparing the ground for the rise of capitalism. Form A might also be superimposed on Form B—for example, the landlord's rent obtained from the capitalist farmer—and thus does not of itself imply any particular mode of production serving for its basis.

In Mughal India, the dominant form of surplus appropriation was what we have styled Form A. Its two distinct elements were peasant agriculture (as the mode of production) and land revenue (representing the bulk of surplus appropriated). Our pursuit of possible capitalistic elements in the agricultural sector must therefore begin with a closer study of the interaction of these two elements.

Our information on the point is sufficient for us to say with confidence that but for rare possible exceptions Indian peasant farming was organized on individualistic lines. Each peasant had his own separate holding. Owing to land abundance, land in most areas had little or no price, but seed and cattle were important forms of peasant property, and individual ownership must necessarily have given rise to stratification within the peasantry, even if other causative factors are ignored.[10] At the same time, the Indian village presented the appearance of a closed, custom-based social and economic unit. The close settlement of peasant households and the need for peasant migrants to move in a body, for better protection, furnished the basis for a collective organization of peasants, within the framework of clan and caste, the Indian village community. With this community were associated hereditary artisans and village servants, who provided the peasants with goods and services needed by them. They were paid by the peasants, as a body (for the community had a financial pool), and as individuals, according to customary rates, usually in kind, or through allotments of land.[11] To a certain degree the Indian village

---

[10] I. Habib, p. 119 and n.
[11] I. Habib, pp. 118–29. It is not clear to me why the Soviet writers Alaev and Pavlov should attach so much importance to the existence outside the

was a stable economic unit, essentially self-sufficient in respect to its own consumption needs. It is, therefore, difficult to see how an inner village market, or capitalistic elements, could have arisen from any internal development in the Indian village community in its classic form, despite the individualistic organization of production and the economic stratification that must have existed among the peasantry.

Nor would a simple appropriation of the surplus produce by any local potentate introduce any change, if what was appropriated was in kind and was consumed either directly in the magnate's household, or distributed among his servants.[12] This would be true very largely of the appropriations by the *zamindars*, hereditary possessors of a right to a share in the peasant's produce. In the only instance we have (from Awadh) of the 'customary' rate of the *zamindar's* claim upon the peasant, the collection in kind (10 *sers* of the crop per *bigha*) dwarfs completely that in cash (1 copper coin per *bigha*.)[13]

However, the *zamindar's* share of the 'rent' was, in Mughal India, definitely subordinate one. It amounted, nominally, to 10 per cent of the land revenue in northern India and 25 per cent in Gujarat.[14] In other words, it was the land revenue that represented the bulk of the rent,[15] and it is, therefore, important to study its nature and magnitude, and to consider what consequences it was likely to have for the rural economy.

*Mal*, which we render as land revenue, was not, formally speaking, rent from the land, but a tax on the crop. It was basically

---

village of weavers (and, we may add, cotton carders and oil men) and ascribe to this phenomenon a significant role in the 'break-up' of the Indian village community; see V. I. Pavlov, *Indian Capitalist Class: a Historical Study*, English translation, Delhi, 1964, pp. 12–13. So long as the relations of such artisans with villagers continued to be determined by custom, there would have been little cause for the village community to be subverted.

[12] See Karl Marx, *Capital*, I, p. 610.

[13] I. Habib, p. 145 and n: the interpretation of this document given in the footnote, however, seems to me now to need emendation at one or two points. The *ser* is a unit of weight and *bigha* a unit of area.

[14] I. Habib, pp. 145–50.

[15] It is for this reason principally that contemporary European travellers uniformly declared the Mughal emperor (and also other Indian rulers within their kingdoms) to be the sole owner of the soil, though no such claim was made by official writers. Irfan Habib, *Enquiry*, NS, II (3), p. 59.

a share of the crop; and the most simple form in which it was collected was through an actual division of the harvest (*batai*). But in actual practice more complex (and, administratively less strenuous) forms were followed. The revenue, for example, was imposed in kind, but the demand[16] was fixed by means of surveys of the crop land, and the application of an estimated crop rate upon the area so determined, so as to give the estimate of the total crop (*kankut*). The revenue being a given share of the produce, the total revenue demand could now be stated in kind, but might subsequently be commuted into cash at market (or arbitrary) prices. In the most developed form, and in some provinces the most prevalent, a standard cash rate was levied per unit of area, varying according to the crop (*zabt*). Here too, for purposes of drawing up the schedules, the revenue had to be assumed as fixed portion of the crop, more so since any particular piece of land, under this system of assessment, could be placed under either of the other systems mentioned, and vice-versa. By and large, it seems that the share of the produce taken as revenue ranged from one-third to half in most parts of northern India and the Deccan, but was less in certain arid areas, and substantially more in certain fertile tracts.[17]

The revenue demand was, theoretically, assessed separately, on each individual peasant, according to his holding and the crops raised by him; but, in fact, the whole village body was usually made into a single assessee, and collectively called upon to pay the revenue levied.[18]

Finally, despite the fact that it was basically a share of the produce, land revenue was realized most often in cash, not only under *zabt*, but also under other systems through commutation of the demand into demand in cash. Often when fixed on a village it takes the form of an amount of money, quite arbitrarily determined. Cash-nexus appears as an established institution in the Delhi region as

[16] It is best, perhaps, to explain that 'demand' and 'revenue demand,' terms familiar in British-Indian land-revenue administration, represent the Persian term *jama*, and mean the amount at which the revenue was assessed or fixed.
[17] I. Habib, pp. 190–230.
[18] Ibid., pp. 230–36.

early as the beginning of the fourteenth century.[19] In Mughal India
our evidence indicates quite plainly that collection of revenue in
cash was far more prevalent than collection in kind, throughout the
empire, although there were local exceptions, and also periods in
certain regions when there might have been a shift from one mode to
the other.[20] Even when the revenue was collected in kind, the authorities resorted to such a course in order to obtain the produce, not, quite
often, for purposes of consumption directly, or for storage, but for
sale.[21]

These characteristics of land revenue were historically inter-
woven with the emergence of a ruling class among whose members it
was distributed. The revenue was collected from the peasant directly
in the name of the king, either by his own officials for the royal treasury, or by his assignees for themselves. The area from where the revenue went to the treasury were known as *khalisa*. The *khalisa* consisted of areas scattered throughout the empire, and its total size varied.
In 1647 the estimated revenue of the *khalisa* amounted to about 13.6
per cent of the total.[22] The remaining portion consisted of *jagirs*, or
territories whose revenues were assigned by the king to his *mansabdars* (officers or nobles) in lieu of their personal pay, and allowances
for the maintenance of their military contingents. Such assignment
holders were known as *jagirdars*. But some *mansabdars* also drew
their pay (wholly or in part) in cash from the royal treasury. For all
practical purposes these *mansabdars*, especially those holding higher
rank, might be considered as forming the ruling class of the Mughal
empire.

This class was largely urbanized and contained a considerable
foreign element.[23] It was largely without local roots, and was prevented from forming such roots by a system of transfers of posts as well as
*jagirs*. On an average, the period for which an area was held in *jagir*

---

[19] See W.H. Moreland, *Agrarian System of Moslem India*, Allahabad,
reprint of 1929 edition, n.d., pp. 11, 114, 136–37.
[20] I. Habib, pp. 236–39.
[21] Ibid., p. 237.
[22] Ibid., p. 272 and n.
[23] See Moreland, *India at the Death of Akbar*, pp. 69–70. There is a detailed
analysis of the racial composition of the Mughal nobility in M. Athar Ali,
*The Mughal Nobility under Aurangzeb*, Bombay, 1966, pp. 11–13.

by any assignee was less then three years.[24] Neither the rank in service, nor the *jagir* (except in the case of certain chiefs) was hereditary. It was surely this highly disciplined class, completely subordinate to a centralized royal despotism, that could make possible the realization of the massive claim on the entire rural surplus of the country that the land revenue represented.

Owing to the system of transfers, the noble's household and contingents could not naturally be established permanently on a *jagir* so as directly to live off the land. In general, the larger the *jagir*, the greater the distance of the headquarters of the *jagirdar's* establishment from the villages; and this was apart from the fact that, being highly urbanized, the Mughal nobles in any case disdained rural life. It is, therefore, no wonder that *jagirdars* preferred to collect revenue in cash, or to commute collections in kind immediately into cash. Since the royal treasury too had to pay out salaries (to the *mansabdars* and others) in cash, the tendency in the *khalisa* too must have been overwhelmingly toward collections in cash.

The major aspects of the land-revenue system that we have earlier described are thus explained by the power, organization and composition of the ruling class. In this is also to be seen the source of a historical phenomenon which is tolerably well documented, namely, the tendency toward a steadily intensified pressure upon the peasants and other revenue payers. The source of this tendency, as seventeenth-century writers observed so frequently, was the system of transfer of *jagirs*, which meant that individual revenue assignees could have no interest in the long-term maintenance or growth in the revenue-paying capacity of any particular area.[25] The excessive pressure for greater revenue was ultimately self-defeating, since for immediate gain it sacrificed future possibilities; but the Mughal system did not contain any effective mechanism whereby restraints could have been put against such a fatal course.[26]

---

[24] Moreland, *Agrarian System*, passim; I. Habib, pp. 257–97.

[25] Bernier made this a basic element in his famous analysis of the defects of Mughal policy; see *Travels in the Mughal Empire*, 1656–68, translated by A. Constable, edited by V.A. Smith, London, 1916, p. 227. See also I. Habib, pp. 320–211.

[26] For such administrative restraints as existed, see I. Habib, pp. 273–97, and for their ineffectiveness, p. 321ff.

The collection of land revenue would have had two important consequences for the rural economy. In the first place there was an
enormous drain of wealth away from the rural sector. Part of the land
revenue undoubtedly stuck to the hands of certain rural elements,
through shortfalls in collection, remissions, concessions and com-
missions to certain local magnates (*chaudhuris, qanungos*) and the
village headmen (*muqaddams*), salaries and perquisites of local
revenue staff, etc. Some of the *jagirdars* sub-assigned their *jagirs* to
their soldiers, who lived in the villages.[27] Besides these, there was a
whole class of revenue grantees (comprising the intelligentsia and
idlers), the revenue alienated through the imperial revenue grants
(*madad-i-ma'ash*) alone accounting for 4 to 6 per cent of the total
estimated revenue.[28] But after making allowances for all these leakages, it must be assumed that the total net value of produce annually
lost by the countryside, without any return, must have amounted to
a very large portion of the total—at least a fourth of it, if not a third
or a half.

Second, the mechanism by which the bulk of the rural surplus
was removed created the conditions for the establishment of the rural
market. When the land revenue was collected in cash, the revenue
payer was compelled to sell his produce in order to get money to pay
for it, but when it was collected in kind, then too, as we have noted,
the revenue authorities preferred to sell it. In either case most of the
surplus was put on the market, and therefore, a very large portion of
agricultural production would not have been directly 'for use', but
would have been commodity production, properly speaking.[29] The
market mechanism once established must have reacted on the mode
of agricultural production. It not merely introduced money relations
into a system of 'natural economy', but also engendered a shift to
high-grade crops and cash crops (e.g., from coarser grains to wheat,

---

[27] I. Habib, pp. 285–86.

[28] Ibid., pp. 298–316.

[29] So far as I know, attention to this major economic implication, or even
consequence, of the Mughal revenue system was drawn first by W.C.
Smith in *Islamic Culture*, 1944, pp. 358–59; and, subsequently, by K.
Antanova (1957) cited by V.I. Pavlov, *The Indian Capitalist Class: A
Historical Study*, Delhi, 1964, p. 10.

and to cotton, sugarcane, indigo, poppy, tobacco, etc.).[30]

This two-fold impact of the Mughal revenue system[31] must have led to a considerable subversion of the 'pure' peasant economy, and an alteration in the nature of the other methods of exploitation (belonging to our Form A).

The land revenue represented, we have seen, an enormous drain on the countryside. Moreover, the built-in tendency in the Mughal system was toward an increase in pressure upon the revenue payers. If the estimated revenue statistics do not show any real increase in the totals (i.e. in terms of prices), this provides no ground for supposing that the degree of exploitation (in terms of real share in the produce) remained stable. Excesses in the latter were bound to reduce the total produce and so adversely affect actual revenue collection in the long run.[32] Nor would the cash-nexus provide any lasting relief to the peasantry in case of an increase in prices, as one might expect from one's reading of European economic history. Unlike the lord's 'rents', the land-revenue rate was firmly based on the conception of its being a set proportion of the produce, and was accordingly variable when stated in cash. As a result, though agricultural prices appear to have risen during the seventeenth century,[33] the revenue demand did not fall in real terms.[34]

Now, within the peasantry, the land revenue, being in essence a regressive tax, fell more heavily upon the poorer than upon

[30] This progress in cropping was summed up during the fourteenth century in a simple formula by Muhammad Tughlaq, who enjoined his revenue officials to encourage peasants to improve their cropping by shifting from barley to wheat, from wheat to sugarcane, and from sugarcane to grapes. See Moreland, *Agrarian System*, p. 57.

[31] The wording of this clause needs two qualifications. The Mughal revenue system was not unique; the characteristics it possessed were really implanted during the earlier part of the fourteenth century, in the Delhi Sultanat. See Irfan Habib, *Enquiry*, NS, II (3), pp. 45–46. Secondly, cause and effect are difficult to distinguish, and some allowance should be made for the argument that the Sultanat–Mughal revenue system became possible owing to certain developments in Indian rural economy (e.g., growth of trade and commodity production), which we are here viewing virtually as consequences of these revenue systems.

[32] See I. Habib, pp. 326–28.

[33] Ibid., pp. 81–89.

[34] Ibid., pp. 190–96.

the richer strata. When it represented a set proportion of the produce, it is obvious that the peasant who produced less would have a smaller amount left to him than the one who produced more. It is also possible to argue that when each individual peasant was assessed separately, the village community was naturally bypassed, and the individual was alone made to face all the risks as a revenue payer. This too should have led to economic differentiation. In practice, however, as we have noticed, the village was the usual unit of assessment, and we have evidence that the village community had a distinct role to play in the payment of revenue by means of a financial pool into which all the peasants paid, and out of which the revenue demand, the other fiscal burdens, and the expenses of the village establishment were met.[35] Significantly, for this shows at once the degree of monetization and the degree of flexibility of the village community as an economic organization, the accounts were kept in terms of cash. However, the danger in this arrangement was that the stronger (and richer) peasant would dominate the community and distribute the revenue demand at will among their brethren to the great detriment of the poorer peasantry (*reza riaya*). Individual assessment was indeed often seen by the officials as a device to prevent such unjust distribution.[36] Sometimes, too, the whole village could be so heavily assessed that the peasant population was threatened with slaughter and enslavement, in case the revenue demand was not met.[37] We may say, then, that in its initial impact the tendency generated by land revenue was toward increasing stratification and pauperization of the poorer strata, though in the long run it pressed upon the whole peasantry as a class.

Monetization could also directly or indirectly lead to pauperization. Prices could fluctuate to the great detriment of peasants as commodity producers.[38] Moreover, most of the cash crops involved

[35] Ibid., pp. 124–27.

[36] I. Habib, pp. 128–29 and n. As T. Raychaudhuri, *Enquiry*, NS, II (1), pp. 96–97, points out, the status and economic position of peasants did not always correspond; for example, the technically lower peasants (*paikasht*) might be better off (in some cases) than the headmen. But it would be unlikely if such differences were anything more than exceptions, and were not 'corrected' over a long period, only to arise, of course, in some other localities in the meantime.

[37] I. Habib, pp. 322–23.

[38] Ibid., p. 249.

larger investments in cattle (owing to the necessity of more frequent ploughing and watering) and in installations (such as the sugarcane press and boilers, indigo vats, etc.), and heavier risks, in respect of harvest and prices. It was unlikely that the poorer peasants could compete with their richer brethren in the raising of such crops.

In such circumstances, it was inevitable that the peasant should contract debts in order to pay the land revenue or to obtain his 'subsistence, food and cattle', as a *farman* of Aurangzeb put it. Once the rural market had developed to a certain degree, moneylending could have extended rapidly. It is, indeed, likely that peasant indebtedness in Mughal India was more widespread than has hitherto been supposed.[39] The ultimate effect of usury, particularly since the interest rates were extremely high,[40] must have been to add to the burden borne by the peasantry. Usury, whatever its actual forms, thus really represented exploitation of our Form A type. The beneficiaries were not only *zamindars* (especially *chaudhuris*) and headmen, who thus added to their customary exactions,[41] not only professional usurers, who thereby augmented their usurious capital, but also merchants (who often gave advances to the peasants to establish claims on their produce) and, quite generally, merchant-moneylenders.[42] In the last case, usury could have fed merchant capital, and so led to an expansion of trade.

While land revenue and monetization thus added—or at any rate increased—another means of exploitation of the peasantry in the shape of usury, they also created the conditions for increased pressure upon the peasantry from yet another source, namely, the *zamindar* class. The pressure came, first, through an alteration in the substance

[39] *Comparative Studies in Society and History (CSSH)*, VI(4) pp. 394–95, 397. I have, however, slightly corrected my own previous rendering of the clause from Aurangzeb's *farman*.

[40] In eighteenth-century Bengal, 150 per cent per annum at the simple rate was usual, but the loan was usually advanced to the peasants for two or three months, at the end of which interest was added to the principal. Ibid., p. 395. In Maharashtra villages, the interest on cash loans was generally 24 per cent per annum, but on smaller loans it worked out at 40 per cent; see Thomas Coats in *Transactions of the Literary Society of Bombay*, III, London, 1823, pp. 212–13.

[41] *CSSH*, VI(4), p. 397 and n.

[42] Ibid., pp. 394–95.

of the *zamindar's* economic right, and second, through an expansion of the area under that right.

The land revenue, as the principal claim upon the surplus, appears to have pressed upon the *zamindar's* fiscal claims, which were of independent origin, so much so as to annex them to itself; these claims then reappeared as claims on the land revenue collected (as a share thereof, whether as *malikana* or *nankar*, or both), and the *zamindar* was transformed into an intermediary (e.g., *talluqdar*) responsible for the collection of the revenue and its payment to the authorities.[43] As a result, the *zamindari* right became a saleable right, allowing some *zamindars* to sell out under fiscal pressure. Generally speaking, however, the *zamindars* found themselves pressed, or tempted, to recompense themselves at the expense of the peasantry. It is possible that the rights of the *zamindars* to distribute vacant lands among the peasants, or even to evict a peasant in order to install another on the land,[44] were assumed in order to increase their authority over the individual peasants, although in conditions of land abundance the economic significance of such rights must have been limited.

There is, simultaneously, evidence for extension of *zamindari* right over areas which were previously *raiyati*, i.e. purely peasant-held without any superior right.[45] This expansion had, it would seem, two major sources.

First, owing to monetization, the *zamindari* right became a fully saleable commodity, at least from the sixteenth century onward.[46] This meant that new elements, including a small section of the nobles and officials, and cavalry troopers and revenue grantees, or, in other words, persons who obtained their wealth initially out of the distribution of land revenue, could purchase *zamindaris*.[47] Urban merchants did

---

[43] I. Habib, pp. 169–79.

[44] Ibid., pp. 143–44. See also Qazi A'la, *Risala Ahkam al-Arazi*, MS. Aligarh, Abdus Salam, Arabiya (4): 331/101, f. 44a. This work was written during the earlier part of the eighteenth century.

[45] I. Habib, pp. 141–43.

[46] Ibid., pp. 157–58; *IESHR*, IV(3), p. 216.

[47] See S. Nurul Hasan in *IESHR*, I(4), p. 9. For documentary evidence of such transactions, see Munshi Muzaffar Hussain, *Nama-i Muzaffari* (Urdu) I, p. 315 and II, p. 163; Shamsabad Docs. 7 photograph in the Library of Department of History, Aligarh; I. Habib, p. 309 and n; *IESHR*, IV(3), p. 217.

not yet seem to have found in *zamindari* purchase suitable avenue for investment of their superfluous capital;[48] but rural usurers sometimes converted their capital into *zamindari* rights.[49] Such a market in land rights not only contributed to the increasing heterogeneity of the *zamindar* class (hitherto comprising in the main distinct castes and clans), but also placed larger 'capital' at the disposal of that class as a whole.[50] This should have enabled the *zamindars* either to expand the area under them by organizing new peasant settlements or to buy out established peasant rights and convert them into *zamindari*.[51]

Second, the increasing economic differentiation and social stratification within the peasantry could lead to the emergence of a dominant section (*muqaddams*, headmen, etc.) whose claims might in time grow into *zamindari* rights.[52]

There is thus the greatest likelihood that the exploitation of the kinds we have grouped under Form A steadily intensified during the Mughal period, causing a crisis in peasant agriculture. We know that the peasants' flight from the land was a common phenomenon of the seventeenth century, and it is indeed possible that there was a net decline in cultivation over part of the period.[53]

In itself, the subversion of peasant agriculture might or might not pave the way for capitalistic or semi-capitalistic farming. Some Soviet writers appear to assume that the *zamindari* right already contained within itself the seeds of 'capitalist private property'.[54] The question should perhaps be more specifically posed. Was the subversion of peasant agriculture leading not simply to a decline in the rural economy, but also to a shift from Form A to Form B of agrarian exploitation? For it is only out of such a shift that capitalistic relations in

---

[48] See English factors' report from Surat, 1669, in *English Factories in India 1668–69*, edited by W. Foster, p. 184.

[49] *IESHR*, IV(3) pp. 216–17; *CSSH*, VI(4), p. 398.

[50] *IESHR*, IV(3), p. 215.

[51] Ibid., pp. 215–16.

[52] I. Habib, pp. 133–34.

[53] Ibid., pp. 324–29.

[54] Pavlov, *Indian Capitalist Class*, pp. 4–9. This is also apparently the view of K.F. Ashrafyan, *The Agrarian System of North India in the Thirteenth-Mid-Eighteenth Centuries*, Moscow, 1965. Unfortunately, not knowing Russian, I am unable to follow the details of the argument developed in this well-documented work.

agricultural production, and therefore 'capitalist property' could conceivably evolve.[55]

There are two principal categories classifiable under Form B that appear to have been the most widespread, namely, (a) orchards, and (b) direct cultivation of agricultural land by the superior classes themselves (*khwud-kasht*).

Orchards were laid out by members of almost all the higher classes of society, by the emperor himself, by the princes and nobles, by revenue grantees, by the *zamindars*, and by village headmen and even (the richer?) peasants.[56] 'Capital' invested in horticulture thus not only came from rural sources but also from outside. The scale and economic significance of the latter should not be underrated. The king and the nobles laid out orchards not only to secure fruit for their table but also (and mainly) to sell on the market, either doing it directly themselves, or leasing the season's crop to professional contractors.[57] Their investments and the yields of their orchards were both considerable since they planted fruits brought from various regions, imported seeds as well as gardeners, laid out expensive systems of irrigation, and improved certain varieties of fruit (especially mangoes and oranges) by propagating grafting techniques.[58] The pull of the urban market, together with revenue concessions,[59] should also have encouraged the rural classes, principally the revenue grantees and *zamindars*, in taking to horticulture. The rapid acclimatization of some new fruits introduced from the New World (e.g., pineapple)[60] might also have contributed to the expansion of fruit-growing in some areas.

But, however extensive might have been the expansion of horticulture, it cannot be regarded as having been at any time an alternative to peasant agriculture, and while its expansion sheds much light on the growth of market relations and commodity production in the countryside, it has little bearing on the possibilities of the genesis of capitalistic agriculture. In this respect, it is the other category under

---

[55] This argument may not necessarily be acceptable to non-Marxists, but Soviet scholars ought to see the justice of it more readily.

[56] I. Habib, pp. 48–49, 303; *IESHR*, IV(3), p. 215.

[57] I. Habib, p. 49.

[58] Ibid., pp. 50–51.

[59] Ibid., pp. 244–45.

[60] Ibid., p. 50.

Form B, that we have mentioned, namely, the *khwud-kasht* mode of cultivation, which is of much greater importance.

The term *khwud-kasht* literally means 'self-cultivated' but it has a distinct technical meaning attached to it.[61] Headmen 'who organize *khwud-kasht*', it is stated in a reliable account, 'employ labourers as their servants and put them to the tasks of agriculture; and making them plough, sow, reap and draw water out of the well, they pay them their fixed wages, whether in cash or grain, while appropriating to themselves the gross produce of cultivation.'[62]

The most interesting feature of *khwud-kasht* is the use of hired labour. Although slavery existed in Mughal India, it was almost universally domestic slavery; semi-servile relations in agriculture existed sometimes but in certain regions only, like parts of Bihar; and labour services for agricultural or semi-agricultural purposes were not exacted (except perhaps in Kashmir), being confined mainly to the transport of baggage and other non-economic operations.[63] The relative absence of the use of unfree labour in production is, perhaps, to be explained by the presence of a very large class of landless labourers, who could be called upon to work in the fields in return for the provision of their barest needs of subsistence. The existence of this large class in conditions of land abundance did not derive initially or in the main from any incapacity of peasant cultivation but from a social structure maintained by custom and force. The landless belonged to the menial castes, compelled to serve the interests alike of peasants and of superior cultivators, and forming therefore a vast rural semi-proletariat, maintained entirely through non-economic compulsions.[64] In time, however, their numbers could have been added to

---

[61] Ibid., pp. 114–15, 175, 300, 303 and n. for the use of this term in the Mughal period.

[62] *Diwan-pasand*, MS, Br Mus. Or. 2011, f. 8a. This Persian work written during the first decade of the nineteenth century, describes the agricultural conditions and revenue practices in the Doab practically at the same time as the British occupation of the area. Many of its statements are in line with those made by the authorities of the Mughal period.

[63] I. Habib, p. 239; Grover in *IESHR*, I9(1), p. 15. For evidence relating to agricultural debt-bondage in Bihar, see *Journal of Bihar Research Society (JBRS)*. XLIV (1958) (I & II), pp. 50–51.

[64] I. Habib, pp. 120–22; T. Raychaudhuri, *Enquiry*, NS, II(1), pp. 97-98.

by caste peasants who, unable to pay the revenue, abandoned cultivation on their own fields.

This rural proletariat was not a creation of the Mughal
period, but was the legacy of centuries. Cultivation by superiors
could also have come down from earlier times, during which we
actually catch glimpses of it here and there.[65] It could have easily
prevailed in a natural economy, or in one where production was
directly for use. But there are reasons to believe that in Mughal India
much of such superior or *khwud-kasht* cultivation was being linked
to the market, and that in this way it was incorporating into itself
another essential element of capitalistic farming (besides the use of
wage labour), namely, commodity production.

We have already noted how the cultivation of cash crops
generally required a larger investment than an ordinary peasant
could afford; so that these were precisely the crops in the production
of which farming on a larger scale could have economic superiority
over small peasant farming. Similarly, the bigger men could also have
easier access to credit[66] and to the market.[67] The extreme limit of
commercialization of superior agriculture was reached when at
Bayana, the great centre of indigo trade, 'rich and substantial merchants' turned into farmers, producing the commodity in which they
dealt.[68] It may also be mentioned that cash wages, which the description of *khwud-kasht* quoted above refers to, could not have been
paid unless the employers sold at least a portion of the produce on the
market.

The classes that carried on *khwud-kasht* were principally
the *zamindars*, and village headmen, and also revenue grantees and
revenue officials.[69] It is noticeable that the nobility, whose members

---

[65] See I. Habib, *Enquiry*, NS (II(3), pp. 38–39, 40, 54–56.

[66] For the close relations between *zamindars* and usurers, see *CSSH*, VI (4), p. 398.

[67] In 1630 the headman (*patel*) of a village near Broach negotiated with the English the sale of 1000 Gujarat *maunds* (=33, 190 lb avdp.) of wheat to be supplied at Surat. Of this, half belonged to the *patel* himself and the remainder to the other villagers. *English Factories in India, 1630–33*, p. 91.

[68] Pelsaert, 'Remonstrantie,' translated in Moreland and Geyl, *Jahangir's India*, Cambridge, 1925, p. 17.

[69] I. Habib, pp. 114–5, 141, 175, 300, 303 and n. The peasants who cultivated lands in their own village were (in post-Mughal times, so far

showed such interest in horticulture, almost never undertook the establishment of agricultural farms. Their lack of interest in agriculture is also reflected in contemporary Persian works on horticulture and agriculture, where the larger space is given to the former and relatively little is said about the latter.[70] The merchant farmers, such as those at Bayana, were also exceptions, and as a general rule, mercantile classes do not appear to have assumed the role of agriculturists. We may, therefore, suppose that by and large, the capital for *khwud-kasht* came out of the accumulations of the rural superior classes themselves.

Unfortunately, we have no statistical information about the area under *khwud-kasht* or its expansion. That it did, in fact, expand, and in the course of such expansion press upon peasant cultivation, is suggested by official bans upon the conversion of peasant-cultivated lands (*raiyat kashta*) into their *khwud-kasht* by revenue-grantees and revenue officials.[71]

In so far as *khwud-kasht*, organized for commodity production, comes closest to capitalistic farming, its expansion at the expense of peasant agriculture would have great significance for us. But there seem to be certain strong reasons why such an expansion on a very large scale cannot be easily postulated.

For one thing, other conditions (such as imposition of land revenue) remaining the same, it is difficult to believe that in crops other than cash crops, the *khwud-kasht* could have compared with peasant cultivation in productivity per acre. Moreover, whether under cash crops or under ordinary crops, personal supervision in *khwud-kasht* would become less and less effective as its area expanded. Accordingly, the expansion of an individual unit of *khwud-kasht* beyond a certain size would have become uneconomical. Finally,

---

as our present evidence goes) termed *khwud-kasht* peasants, as against those who cultivated outside their village and were called *pai kasht*. See Grover in *IESHR* I(1), pp. 4–5. This usage has, of course, nothing to do with the *khwud-kasht* that we are here considering.

[70] See, e.g., *Nuskha dar fan-i Falahat*, MS. 1.0.4702; and Aligarh Lytton Farsiya 'ulum, 51. This work was written during the earlier half of the seventeenth century by an important noble, Amanullah Husaini Khanazad Khan.

[71] I. Habib, pp. 114–15.

since the entire 'capital' for *khwud-kasht* came from the rural classes alone, it could not show such improvements in production as horticulture under royal and aristocratic auspices did, owing largely to heavier investment.

It does not, therefore, seem possible to argue that the increasingly heavy pressure of direct appropriation (Form A) upon the peasant in conditions of extensive commodity production led to a substantial or critical increase of appropriation through control over production (Form B). In other words, the subversion of peasant agriculture did not lead directly to a semi-capitalistic form of agriculture. What seems to have happened instead is that the economic crisis transformed itself into a political crisis, marked by agrarian uprisings often under *zamindar* leadership, bringing about in the end the collapse of the Mughal empire and, with it, the weakening of several aspects of the economic and social structure that it had sustained.[72] It would be interesting to seek parallels in Chinese history, where too the repeated agrarian crises resulted in cycles of massive peasant revolts that overthrew dynasties but did not lead to the rise of capitalism.[73]

## II

From the agrarian economy, we may now transfer our attention to the non-agricultural sector. Since capitalism alters fundamentally the relationship between these two sectors, increasing phenomenally the non-agricultural (industrial) production, it is natural to look for the signs of the beginnings (or, at any rate, the seeds) of capitalism in conditions that obtained in the non-agricultural sector of the economy.

One of the many difficulties that face the student of the economic history of Mughal India is the lack of quantitative information, especially the lack of census data such as enumeration of inhabitants in general or enumeration by profession, by income, or by property. It is therefore not surprising that we should not be able to establish directly from our evidence the relative size of the population dependent

---

[72] For the detailed argument on these lines, see ibid., pp. 317–51.
[73] Mao Tse-tung, *Selected Works*, English edition, Vol III, London, 1954, pp. 75–76.

on the non-agricultural sector, the proportion of such population that lived in the towns or was engaged in craft industries. One must draw such inferences as one can from other, largely indirect, evidence.

The surplus taken away from the peasant in the form of land revenue, other dues and claims by superiors came to about a half of the produce in most areas. Superficially, this fact may be taken to suggest that as many mouths could be fed outside the agricultural sector as within it; or, in other words, that the population in the non-agricultural sector amounted to a half of the total. But one would be assuming, then, that the physical composition of the surplus was the same as that of the producer's portion retained for subsistence (of the same as that of the producer's portion retained for subsistence (of the peasant and agricultural labourer). In actual fact, it is possible that a much larger proportion of the surplus produce alienated by the peasant consisted of superior food crops (e.g., wheat, high-quality rice), products of luxury consumption (e.g., sugar, opium, high-quality tobacco), and raw materials (e.g., cotton, indigo, sesame). It is to be borne in mind that owing to the high prices fetched by the cash crops, the cash return from an acre sown with them would have been much greater than that of an acre under ordinary foodgrain crops. This may be seen from the following table, which compares cash return on various crops in the same locality in the years 1595 and 1922.[74]

**Cash return on selected crops**

| | Foodgrains | | | Cash Crops | |
|---|---|---|---|---|---|
| | 1595 | 1922 | | 1595 | 1922 |
| Wheat | 100.0 | 100.0 | Wheat | 100.0 | 100.0 |
| Rice | 82.5 | 66.6 to 77.7 | Cotton | 153.0 | 66.6 to 77.7 |
| Barley | 65.3 | 55.5 | Sesame | 76.9 | 44.4 |
| Bajra | 38.4 | 44.4 | Sugarcane (ordinary) | 211.5 | n.a. |

[74] I. Habib, p. 432. The *Ain-i Akbari* gives cash revenue rates for different crops sanctioned for each locality. The rates given here for 1595 and 1922 pertain to the district of Meerut (UP). The general picture is practically the same in other localities. See also Moreland, *India at the Death of Akbar*, pp. 103–4, and *Journal of the Royal Asiatic Society (JRAS)*, 1918, pp. 375–85.

The table shows that in 1595 not only was the value of the return on the cash crops per acre much higher than on wheat, and on wheat much higher than on the other food crops, but also that the relative value of the return on the cash crops was much higher in 1595 than during this century.[75] This would imply that a relatively small acreage under cash crops would have yielded in value a far larger proportion of the total produce. Thus, for example, while the area under cash crops (sugarcane and cotton) is estimated at 8.0 per cent of the total area sown for the autumn harvest in a *pargana* in eastern Rajasthan in 1690, as against 72.9 per cent under foodgrains, the percentages in terms of the value of the total produce work out at 32.6 per cent and 60.0 per cent, respectively.[76]

A change in the physical composition of the surplus, especially if it involved a reduction in the foodgrain component, would have considerable effect on the size and composition of the non-agricultural population. If the foodgrain component was practically the same in the surplus as in the portion of the produce retained for subsistence, then it follows: (a) The population in the non-agricultural sector would bear roughly the same proportion to the agricultural population as the surplus bore to the remainder of the produce; and its consumption approximated to subsistence-level. (b) The portion of the population engaged in industrial or craft production would be very small, since about the same amount of raw materials would be retained for meeting the needs of the peasants as for meeting those of the population fed out of the surplus. (c) The overwhelmingly larger portion of the population in the non-agricultural sector would, therefore, have been engaged in unproductive labour or personal service. It was therefore likely to have been heavily dispersed and ruralized. Such conditions we may for convenience designate Phase I. If, on the other hand, the surplus contained a higher proportion of the yield of cash crops—and as we have seen,

---

[75] Except in the case of sugarcane, and the relative value of the output of this has apparently remained stable. Moreland, *India at the Death of Akbar*, pp. 103–4.

[76] S.N. Hasan, (the late Mrs.) K.N. Hasan, and S.P. Gupta, 'The Pattern of Agricultural Production in the Territories of Amber, *c.* 1650–1750,' *Proceedings of the Indian History Congress*, Mysore session, 1966, pp. 249, 263, Tables ! & V. The figures used here are those for *pargana* Malarna.

yield accounting for a very high proportion of value could have come from a very small acreage—(a) the size of the non-agricultural sector, in terms of population, would have been much smaller than the relative size of the appropriated agricultural surplus; (b) within this population a much larger section would be engaged in productive labour (crafts); and (c) the non-agricultural population would probably tend to be concentrated in cities, so that there would be an urban population of considerable size. This we would call Phase II.

Obviously, from the point of view of the emergence of capitalism, Phase I may be regarded as representing the more backward stage; and a high development of non-agricultural production would not be possible unless Phase II arrived. Capitalism can hardly be conceived of unless a minimum concentration of non-agricultural labour (in cities) has been achieved, and, therefore, a labour market created.

To determine the phase with which the Mughal Indian economy had greater affinities, it would naturally be best if we could study the actual physical composition of the agricultural surplus (as distinguished from the total produce). Since, however, we cannot establish what it was in quantitative terms (and it is difficult even to suggest how it can be done from our documents),[77] the only possible alternative before us is to trace the directions in which the surplus (or claims to the surplus in the form of money) was channelled, and the ways in which it was consumed. From information on these matters, we may then be able to decide whether the non-agricultural sector fitted more with Phase I or Phase II, both of which are theoretically possible for Mughal India.

First of all, as we have seen, a certain portion of the surplus was left in the countryside, in the shape of the fiscal dues, allowances, perquisites, etc., of the *zamindars* and village headmen, the claims on

---

[77] It is obvious that revenue accounts will not give us this information when the cash-nexus prevailed. Even where crop-sharing took place, it is not possible to assume that the produce collected was actually consumed in the non-agricultural sector. Produce of one kind might have been sold in the rural market by the revenue authorities and so channeled for ultimate consumption by the peasants, while the money obtained in return was later on spent on the purchase of a quite different set of agricultural commodities.

revenue collection by officials and men of the revenue establishment of the *khalisa* and *jagirs*, the income of the revenue grantees, the profits of usurers, etc. Among all these local or rural claimants to shares in the surplus, the *zamindars* were, in quantitative terms, the most important. We know little, it is true, of the expenditure pattern of the *zamindars*. What we know for certain is that, either for maintaining their authority or for achieving status, they zealously pursued the ideal of possessing the largest possible number of servants and retainers. According to a detailed official census, *c.* 1595, the *zamindars* maintained within the Mughal empire (northern India) nearly 4.7 million retainers (4.3 million 'infantry', and 0.3 million horsemen). There is no reason to doubt these totals which are based on figures meticulously obtained from each locality.[78] They suggest an almost staggeringly large number of persons, namely, about 21 million (assuming an average family to be of 4.5 persons), dependent upon the service of the *zamindars*. It is possible that many such retainers were part retainers, part peasants; but even when this qualification has been made, the number remains impressive. Whatever might have been the total population of the Mughal empire at the time,[79] this would still have comprised a high proportion of it.

Using the argument we have advanced previously, we may take this large number as indicative of the fact that the expenditure of the income of the *zamindars* went largely to subsistence-level consumption and could not have generated a very large demand (per head in the non-agricultural rural sector) for the products of craft industries. This ought not to be taken to mean, though, that they did not generate any additional demand whatsoever for such goods. The same 1595 statistics show that the *zamindars* of Bengal were possessed of 4,260 pieces of cannon and 4,400 boats,[80] and these at least were products fashioned by smiths and carpenters. But we may suppose, on the whole, that the share in the surplus exacted by the *zamindars* accorded

---

[78] I. Habib, pp. 163–64.

[79] Moreland estimated the population of the whole of India at 100 million, but he based this very largely on his own estimate of the total area under cultivation, and that is probably too low. See *India at the Death of Akbar*, pp. 9–22.

[80] I. Habib, p. 164 and n.

largely with the conditions of what we have designated Phase I.

However, *zamindars* only commanded a part of the surplus. We have seen in the previous section that after allowing for all 'leakages' the net revenue collection taken completely outside the sphere of rural economy probably amounted in value to a fourth or a third if not a half of the total agricultural produce. This naturally dwarfed all other claims on the agricultural surplus, and from our present point of view it is distribution and ultimate disbursement that would be of the most crucial significance.

The land revenue (together with income from other taxes) was distributed directly (either by way of revenue assignments, *jagirs*, or through cash salaries paid out of the imperial treasury which itself received the revenues from a portion of the empire, the *khalisa*) among members of a small ruling class. This class consisted, beside the emperor himself, of about 8,000 *mansabdars*, according to an official estimate of 1647. Among these again, there was an enormous concentration of resources. The income of 445 *mansabdars* amounted to 61.5 per cent of the total revenues of empire; and of these again a mere 73 (or 0.9 per cent of the total) claimed for their share 37.6 per cent of the total revenues.[81] The concentration would appear to be substantially greater still if the income assigned to the emperor's own establishment (i.e. total *khalisa* revenues less salaries paid out to *mansabdars*) is also taken into consideration.[82]

The actual consumption of the enormous portion of the produce appropriated as land revenue thus depended mainly upon the manner in which this small ruling class spent its income.

The first claim upon their income was that of the army. Among the top 445 *mansabdars*, the total pay against their *sawar* ranks—the amount from which they were expected by the emperor to maintain cavalry contingents on his behalf—came to 77.2 per cent of their total pay, and we may well infer that while for all the 8,000

---

[81] A. Jan Qaisar, 'Distribution of the Revenue Resources of the Mughal Empire among Nobility,' *Proceedings of the Indian History Congress,* Allahabad Session, 1965, pp. 239–40.

[82] The net expenditure on the royal establishment amounted, according to the *Ain-i Akbari's* figures, to about 6 per cent of the total estimated revenue (1594–95). *Ain,* I, edited by Blochmann, p. 9.

*mansabdars* the percentage might have been lower than this, it could not have been much lower.[83] It may be conceded that the actual expenditure on these troops probably seldom accorded with the official expectation; the suspicion existed that the nobles really spent much less.[84] The nobles, on the other hand, usually pleaded that while their obligation to pay the salaries of their troopers was fixed, their income fluctuated and was sometimes even uncertain, owing to the transfer of *jagirs*.[85] It is, therefore, difficult to fix the relation of the actual expenditure on the army to the total income of the nobility; it may, however, be safe to say that it was probably around two-thirds.

Such a large diversion of resources to the maintenance of armed men is to be expected in a system where exploitation was principally of our Form A, being superimposed, that is to say, on the productive system, and so requiring for its enforcement constant use of menace of armed power. To some extent, therefore, the crowds of armed retainers of the *zamindars* and the enormous expenditure on the army by the Mughal ruling class were based on the same economic reality.

But here the similarity ceased. Though the military expenditure, in absolute figures, of the Mughal ruling class was much greater than that of the *zamindars*, the number of men among whom it was directly distributed was much smaller. The most complete official figures are available for 1647. There were then 7,000 cavalrymen and mounted matchlock bearers in the emperor's own establishment, and an estimated 185,000 horsemen maintained by the *mansabdars* against their *sawar* ranks. In addition there was 40,000 infantry, consisting of 'matchlockmen, gunners, cannoniers and rocketeers', 10,000 of them posted at the capital and the remainder in the provinces and forts.[86]

The cavalry probably accounted for the overwhelmingly

---

[83] A.J. Qaisar, 'Distribution', pp. 240–42.
[84] Pelsaert, *Jahangir's India*, translated by Moreland and Geyl, p. 54.
[85] See *Riyazu-l Wudad*, Br. Mus. Or. 1725, f. 18b; *Waqa'i Ajmer*, transcript, p. 413.
[86] Lahori, *Padshahnama*, II, Bib. Ind., 715. Lahori's figure for 200,000 cavalry is arrived at by counting the 8,000 *mansabdars* as cavalrymen as well.

larger portion of the military expenditure. The cavalryman of the Mughal armies was really a professional gentleman trooper. In most cases he had more than one horse.[87] The horses were required to be of standard breeds. Since Indian breeds were notoriously indifferent, good horses were expensive, fetching during the eighteenth century four times the price in England,[88] and had to be constantly imported from Persia and central Aisa.[89] The import of horses could naturally have created a counter-demand for Indian goods. Besides this indirect support to the market for craft products, the troopers created it more directly by their demand for armour and weapons and for certain comforts and luxuries for themselves and their families. Yet they also maintained a relatively large human establishment, comprising servants and slaves, it being stated that 'however badly off a [cavalry] soldier is, he must have three or four servants'.[90] So that part, at least, of what they received went ultimately into subsistence-level consumption. Taking account also of shopkeepers and artisans directly serving the troops in camp, Manucci estimates that 8,000 cavalry implied the presence of 30,000 persons. We may then estimate the population dependent upon Mughal cavalry (including their own families) at over three million.

Besides cavalry, there was artillery. It is not possible to estimate the amount of metal used in the artillery of the Mughal army, or the amount of gunpowder it consumed. But in view of the numbers employed in the artillery (over 40,000 men), it is certain that at any time some tens of thousands of matchlocks (surely not less than 25,000, on these numbers) must have been in use; and we know that excessively heavy cannon were much favoured in India.[91] It is, therefore, likely that the increasing employment of artillery helped extensively to develop the saltpeter industry and the metallurgical and associated crafts. When Indian copper mines proved insufficient, there were

[87] See Moreland, 'Rank (*Mansab*) in the Mughal State Service,' *JRAS*, 1936.
[88] Orme, quoted in W. Irvine, *The Army of the Indian Mughals*, p. 47.
[89] See Irvin, *The Army*, pp. 51–52.
[90] Manucci, II, 75 n. See Fryer's description of the 'Adilshahi horseman on the march,' *A New Account of East India and Persia, being Nine Years' Travels, 1672–81*, Vol. I, London, 1909, p. 341.
[91] Irvine, *The Army*, pp. 118–28.

heavy copper imports,[92] which could only have been met by corresponding exports of Indian commodities.

The emperor and his nobles were generous patrons of the professions and arts—through pensions or gifts, they maintained scholars, poets, theologians, physicians, painters, musicians and dancers.[93] Among the ranks of this professional 'middle class' may also be counted the accountants and officials who were employed in large numbers in the nobles' establishments, ten being employed says Pelsaert, where one would have sufficed.[94] This was also true of the vast bureaucratic apparatus of the imperial administration and the royal establishment. Many members of this middle class reproduced or tried to imitate on a smaller scale the mode of living of the nobility.[95] But the total income and the pattern of expenditure of this class are both difficult to work out, owing to the very heterogeneous character of the class.

If we assign two-thirds of the nobles' income to the maintenance of cavalry and artillery and about one-tenth to the support of the professional classes (probably a generous estimate), they should still have had about a fourth of their income to spend on themselves. Much of this went undoubtedly to maintain their notoriously huge establishments, for the nobles loved to spend 'great sums on an extravagant display of elephants, horses, and servants'.[96] The imperial household similarly had an enormous entourage of slaves and servants serving

---

[92] See Moreland, *Akbar to Aurangzeb*, pp. 183–85; K. Glamann, *Dutch-Asiatic Trade*, 176–77, and 'The Dutch Eat India Company's Trade in Japanese Copper,' *Scandinavian Economic History Review*, I(1), 1953, pp. 50ff.

[93] Athar Ali, *Mughal Nobility*, p. 167 and n. See the account of the leading men of letters, poets, singers, musicians, dancing girls, etc., of Delhi, from the pen of a Mughal aristocrat, 1738–39, in Dargah Quli Khan, *Muraqqa'-i Dihli*, edited by Sayyid Muzaffar Husain, Hyderabad-Deccan.

[94] Pelsaert, *Jahangir's India*, p. 55.

[95] On the good life led by the low-ranking bureaucrats during the early years of Aurangzeb's reign, see Bhimsen, *Nuskha-i Dilkusha*, Br. Mus. Or. 23, ff. 20b–21a. See also Dargah Quli Khan.

[96] Pelsaert, *Jahangir's India*, p. 54. Bernier remarked that the Indian nobles are not ruined 'by the extravagance of their table like the nobles of other countries, but by costly gifts made to the Emperor and by their large establishments of wives, servants, camels and horses.' See Athar Ali, *Mughal Nobility*, pp. 167–68.

the harem and the stables.[97] We should thus expect to find a very large number of people engaged in purely unproductive services and drawing from the nobles just the minimum provision for subsistence.[98]

If contemporaries marked anything else besides the nobles' love for a large train of servants and slaves, it was their love of hoarding coin and treasure. The 'escheat' system of the Mughal empire has long been misunderstood, and it has been urged that since the emperor took way the nobles' property at their death, they should have tended to be spendthrifts.[99] The question has now been more or less satisfactorily elucidated, and it has been found that in fact the emperor's claims upon the property of a dead noble followed certain norms beyond his simple first right as a creditor.[100] In any case, the nobles left behind vast treasure-hoards. The official history refers to the emperor's acquisition of 6 million rupees in cash, from the property of a very high noble, upon his death (1645);[101] another noble, higher still in rank, left behind 'in cash and good' 10 million rupees, at the official valuation (1657).[102] The imperial treasure-hoard was, in comparison, enormous. Rather exaggerated accounts circulated of what Akbar had left at his death;[103] but we know from an official source that his treasure contained 70 million rupees in cash.[104] Hoarding of treasure, especially gold and silver, created no direct demand for craft products and might be regarded as so much wastage of capital; but in so far as imports of gold and silver, like horses and copper, had to be counterbalanced by exports, such hoarding could lead indirectly to the expansion of demand for craft goods.

---

[97] Moreland, *India at the Death of Akbar*, pp. 87–89.

[98] See the very low wages or maintenance costs in the *Ain-i Akbar* sanctioned for ordinary servants and slaves in the various departments of the imperial establishment.

[99] Moreland, *India at the Death of Akbar*, pp. 262–63. Pelsaert, however, was puzzled why this did not happen in practice, and why the nobles yet accumulated treasure. *Jahangir's India*, pp. 55–56.

[100] Athar Ali, *Mughal Nobility*, pp. 63–68.

[101] Lahori, *Padshahnama*, II, 472–78. Each rupee weighed 178 grains and was of practically pure silver.

[102] *Amal-i Salih*, Bid. Ind., III, 248.

[103] V.A. Smith, 'The Treasure of Akbar,' *JRAS* (1915), pp. 231–43, cited in Abdul Aziz, *Imperial Treasury of the Indian Mughals*, Lahore, 1942, pp. 28–29.

[104] Amin Qazwini, *Padshahnama*, Br. Mus. MS. Or. 173, f. 221a-b.

As for the direct demand for goods of consumption by the nobility, a quantitative statement is not possible. But inferences may be drawn from some general evidence.

The Mughal nobles were, like their emperors, great builders and their palatial houses, for their scale and comforts, even passed the standard of the severest European critic of the time.[105] They built, besides, tombs, mosques, *sarais* (inns), paved tanks and bridges,[106] which have survived the ravages of time better than their houses.

The nobles' expenditure on articles of furniture and decoration as well as of personal use must have been truly great. Amidst the vast variety that was in demand, the emphasis was on the more expensive material and finer workmanship. Thus the articles ranged from the most precious jewels to the finest muslin.[107] Many of the articles the nobles needed came from their own workshops (*karkhanas*). The imperial *karkhanas* have been better described; but they were the same in nature. A *karkhana* seems usually to have been a sort of hall, and there was different one for each craft. Here the artisans were set to work, under close supervision, on material provided by the noble. Almost every kind of article was turned out in these *karkhanas*, the products made being either for use of the master or for gifts.[108] But it is certain that the nobles also bought finished goods on the market. Indeed, it is unlikely that the smaller nobles could have supplied themselves adequately from their own establishments. There were shops which sold the most expensive articles for aristocratic customers.[109] Indeed, Bernier, while disparaging the appearance of the Delhi shops, speaks of an infinite quantity of the richest commodities being there.[110]

---

[105] Bernier, *Travels*, pp. 246–48.

[106] See Athar Ali, *Mughal Nobility*, pp. 165–66.

[107] An interesting work giving all the various articles needed in an aristocratic household is *Bayaz-i Khushbu'i*, I.O. MS. 828. It was written during the reign of Shahjahan (1628–58).

[108] Athar Ali, *Mughal Nobility*, pp. 157–58. Moreland is obviously wrong in supposing that the *karkhanas* were maintained by the emperor alone. *India at the Death of Akbar*, p. 186.

[109] See Dargah Quil Khan's enthusiastic description of the famous Chandni Chauk at Delhi, *Muraqqa'-i Dihli*, pp. 17–19. A young noble could not here purchase more than the 'bare necessities' amongst the articles he fancied, though furnished with a sum of 100,000 rupees.

[110] Bernier, *Travels*, p. 248. He remarks that the 'costly merchandise' was actually kept in warehouses and not in the shops themselves, as in Paris.

Many of the goods that the nobles wanted came from abroad, particularly, Persia and central Asia; the demand for European goods was more limited and less certain.[111] This too, as we have argued above, was an indirect way of supporting craft production through stimulating exports.

From all these general facts, can we conjure up a definite picture of the pattern of distribution of the land-revenue resources, showing at least the portion that went to maintain and reproduce unproductive labour, and the portion that supported craft production? With the existing evidence, definiteness can hardly be thought of. But we are probably entitled to infer that the pattern of distribution accorded with both Phase I and Phase II of our definition; that is to say, there were, on the one hand, large numbers dependent on the service of individual nobles and their troopers and hangers-on, thus giving even a city like Delhi the appearance of a camp.[112] On the other hand, there was a substantial population of artisans and unskilled labourers employed in handicraft production and in trade and transport in order to meet the requirements of the aristocrats.[113] In actual fact, the proportion of the artisan population should have been much higher than this number would indicate. This was because the satisfaction of the bare subsistence needs (especially for clothing) of the labouring population, including those unproductively and productively employed, would call into being a large class of artisans and unskilled labourers employed in production and transport. The multiplier effect must have been high, for if the manufactures needed for subsistence per head were only of small value, the productivity per capita was also very low. It is possible then that elements of Phase II were quite strongly established in Indian economy, though they coexisted to a certain degree with those of Phase I. We should therefore expect to have had an urban population of a considerable size, but probably amounting to less than

---

[111] Moreland, *India at the Death of Akbar*, p. 227; K.N. Chaudhuri, *The East India Company, 1600–1640*, London, 1965, pp. 117–21.

[112] See Bernier's reference to the small mud and thatched roofed houses, 'in which lodge the common troopers, and all that vast multitude of servants and camp-fellows who follow the court and the army.' *Travels*, p. 246.

[113] Thus Babur's enthusiastic comment: 'Another good thing in Hindustan is that it has unnumbered and endless workmen of every kind.' *Baburnama*, II, translated by Beveridge, p. 520.

a sixth of the total population.[114] This is largely corroborated by our information about the size of Indian towns. Toward the beginning of the seventeenth century, the largest towns of Mughal India appear to have been much larger in population than the largest European towns; but during the course of that century, as the urban population in Europe grew, the largest towns in both seemed to be of equal size to contemporary European visitors.[115] Their population estimates for some of the towns (not reliable, but quoted here for all they are worth) are as follows:[116]

*Population of selected towns*

| Town | Year | Population |
|------|------|------------|
| Agra | 1609 | 500,000 |
| (reputedly the largest city) | 1629–43 | 660,000 |
| Patna | 1671 | 200,000 |
| Masulipatam | 1672 | 200,000 |
|  | 1663 | 100,000 |
| Surat | 1700 | 200,00 |

We may conclude, then, that based on the collection of enormous revenues from the agricultural sector and their concentration in the hands of a small ruling class, the Indian economy had achieved a considerable expansion of its urban sector during the Mughal period. Not only was a high proportion of the urban population employed in

[114] This is based on the simple inference that the non-agricultural population maintained on the net revenue collection would have amounted to a fourth or a third of the whole, if there had been no difference in the physical composition of the surplus taken as revenue and of the remainder. But since craft production accounted for a significant portion of consumption in the non-agricultural sector, the foodgrain component in the surplus must have been much smaller than in the remainder of the agricultural produce. The non-agricultural population should therefore have been much smaller as well, though it should have been more highly urbanized.

[115] See the statements comparing Lahore with Constantinople, Ahmedabad with London, and Delhi with Paris: Moreland, *India at the Death of Akbar*, pp. 12–13; I. Habib, pp. 75–76 and n.

[116] All figures, with sources, are mentioned in I. Habib, p. 76n., except for the estimates about Surat, which came from Manuel Godinho, translated by G.M. Moraes, *Journal of the Bombay Branch of the (Royal) Asiatic Society (JBBRAS)*, NS, XXVII, pp. ii, 124–25; and Hamilton, *A New Account of the East Indies*, edited by W. Foster, I, p. 89.

industrial crafts, but it would appear that in actual volume of output per head the period could invite comparison with the early decades of this (20th) century.[117]

### III

Little detailed work has been done so far on the techniques employed to obtain this large volume of production. This is from our point of view an extremely important matter, for it is of course through an increasing sophistication of tools that the machine can develop in time.

A common feature in the tools of Indian crafts has been the extremely sparing use of metal, wood often serving where iron might be expected. European travellers of the seventeenth century, therefore, found Indian implements of production rather simple and crude: Bernier speaks of the Delhi artisan as 'destitute of tools'. The development of tools seemed to be in an inverse ratio to the skill of the artisans, for in spite of indifferent tools they yet managed to produce works of the highest quality.[118] The development of skill involved extreme specialization. Pelsaert speaks of a hundred crafts in Agra— 'for a job which one man would do in Holland, here passes through four men's hands before it is finished'.[119] As a result, Indian craftsmen were thought to be good at imitation, but not at designing anything themselves.[120] However, the manufacture of certain mechanical devices, such as clocks, was not attempted, even in imitation.[121] There was

---

[117] For the most detailed comparison yet attempted, see Moreland, *India at the Death of Akbar*, pp. 143–84, 286–94. It must be remembered that although Moreland did not deliberately underestimate Indian production during the seventeenth century, he tended to make several assumptions about the economic and political environment which were bound to colour his judgement. It is therefore all the more noteworthy that his ultimate conclusions should be so little in favour of the per capita volume of production in his own time.

[118] Bernier, *Travels*, p. 254.

[119] Pelsaert, *Jehangir's India*, p. 60.

[120] Ibid., p. 9. See also J. Ovington, *A Voyage to Surat in the Year 1689*, London, 1929, p. 166.

[121] Ovington, *Voyage*, pp. 166–67. He contrasts the Indians with the Chinese, who, he says, had taken European clocks to pieces and then reassembled them. He attributes the Indian lack of interest in making clocks to the difficulties caused by dust, which clogged the wheels.

another great deficiency, the true significance of which we can see now: namely, the lack of development of mining engineering. Iron ore was collected through surface excavations, and coal was not mined at all.[122] In general, there are no deep mines. The salt mines of the Salt Range excited wonder, although actually the shafts there were horizontal, going into the sides of the hills, and each shaft was excavated by an individual miner.[123]

From such facts, it would doubtless be tempting to take the view that development in production in India was more a matter of improving human dexterity than the quality of tools.[124] However, such a view would appear to be rather naive in that while the roles of skill and tools in the productive process might vary in different societies and under different circumstances, no amount of human dexterity could substitute for certain basic tools if particular products were desired. Thus, for lifting water from depth for irrigation, it was essential to have the Persian wheel, which contained a gearing mechanism, and a bucket chain. In Mughal India it was made of wood, rope, and earthen pots.[125] The all-metal machine did not come into use until the latter half of the nineteenth century. The substitution of iron for the earlier machine became possible only when the additional cost of the metal became less than the cost of the greater application of cattle power and labour time needed to provide the same amount of irrigation from the less efficient wooden machines. There was little question of any basic improvement in the technical principles of the mechanism. Similarly, the ordinary spinning wheel included in it two important mechanical devices, namely belt transmission of power and flywheel, though it was entirely made of wood.[126] In other Indian crafts, the wheel was used for boring and for cutting and polishing metals and precious stones.[127] Thus, while it is true that extensive development in

[122] Moreland, *India at the Death of Akbar*, pp. 146–48.
[123] See the passage in the *Ain-i Akbari*, account of the *suba* of Lahore; and Sujan Rai, *Khulasatu-t Tawarikh*, edited by Zafar Hasan, Delhi, 1918, p. 75.
[124] Morris seems to come very near to this view. See *IESHR*, V(I), p. 6.
[125] See Babur's description in *Baburnama*, II, translated by A.S. Beveridge, p. 486. See also I. Habib, p. 26–27 and n.
[126] See Lynn White, *Medieval Technology and Social Change*, p. 119.
[127] See the eighteenth-century dictionary, *Babar-i' Ajam*, s.v. *Charkh*.

technology can only occur when metal, particularly iron, replaces other materials, this change may be delayed in a particular situation for no other reason than that a tool of lower efficiency can be used to manufacture the same commodity by employment of cheap skilled labour. Thus Pelsaert attributes the relatively high degree of skill specialization itself to the low wages prevailing in India.[128]

The crucial question would then be whether in cases where it was not possible to substitute skilled labour for improved tools and devices, the latter were yet rejected. In this respect, a study of the manufacture of artillery, the real 'heavy industry' of the time both in Europe and in Asia, is likely to be the most instructive. The requirements of this industry led to the manufacture of cast iron in Europe. In India, while heavy brass guns were cast, all iron guns, together with many brass guns were not cast but were made of welded bars hooped round.[129] Yet in Orissa, where iron was reported to be plentiful, 'they cast anchors [or iron] for ships in moulds', though the quality was stated to be not so good as that of cast iron made in Europe.[130] It is also noteworthy that during the seventeenth century there was little dissatisfaction with the quality and efficiency of the artillery pieces manufactured in India. Bernier, for example, praises Indian muskets and fowling pieces for their excellence.[131] The appearance of the screw as a fixing device in seventeenth century is also not without significance. In Europe the use of screw for this purpose is no older than the sixteenth century.[132] The Indian screw in the seventeenth century was however made by soldering wire and not by casting and cutting.[133] The example thus illustrates quite well how the acceptance of a new technological principle was not ruled out, though its full and proper application would be limited by general backwardness in practical technology. There is also evidence of a conscious effort at mechanical innovation

---

[128] Palsaert, *Jahangir's India*, p. 60.
[129] W. Irvin, *The Army of the Indian Mughal*, pp. 113–28.
[130] A. Hamilton, *A New Account of the East Indies*, I, edited by W. Foster, p. 217.
[131] Bernier, *Travels*, p. 254.
[132] Singer (ed.), *History of Technology*, III, pp. 628–29.
[133] Thevenot (1666), *Indian Travels of Thevenot and Careri*, translated and edited by S.N. Sen, p. 66.

in the curious devices of Akbar's minister, Fathullah Shirazi, though there was in them little of economic significance.[134]

There was, therefore, in India, no rigid barrier to technological innovation or adaptation. If during the seventeenth century it had begun visibly to fall behind Europe in its level of industrial development, the cause of this must be sought for in factors other than a mystic predilection for manual skill. One possible explanation has been found by some in the social institution that sustained craft specialization in India, namely, the caste system.[135] It has been held, and the opinion has been powerfully reinforced by Weber, that the caste system put a severe brake on economic development, through separating education from craft, segregating skills, preventing intercraft mobility, and killing or restricting individual ambition in the artisan.[136]

There are good grounds, however, for throwing doubt on this entire theory, for it depends so largely on one's assumptions of how a caste system, perfectly based on the law books, should have operated.[137] Three or four points ought to be borne in mind. First, the mass of ordinary or unskilled people formed a reserve, from which new classes of skilled professions could be created when the need arose. Thus diamond miners in the Karnatak must have come from the ranks of the peasantry or agricultural labourers, for when some mines were abandoned the miners went 'back to tillage'.[138] Secondly, in any region there was often more than one caste following the same profession, so that where the demand for products of a craft expanded, new caste artisans could normally be drawn to that place.[139] More

[134] See M.A. Alavi and A. Rahman, *Fathullah Shriazi, a Sixteenth-Century Indian Scientist*, New Delhi, 1968.

[135] See Karl Marx, *Capital*, I, pp. 330–32, for the connection between craft-specialization and caste.

[136] On the last point, Palsaert, *Jahangir's India*, p. 60, and Bernier, *Travels*, p. 260. See also B.B. Misra, *Indian Middle Classes*, London, 1961, pp. 37–39.

[137] See the stimulating article by M.D. Morris, 'Values as an Obstacle to Economic Growth in South Asia,' *Journal of Economic History (JEH)*, XXVII (De. 1967), pp. 588–607.

[138] Tavernier, *Travels in India*, translated by V. Ball, edited by Crooke, London, 1925, I, p. 230.

[139] See the report of the Madras factors, 1662: it was possible to bring weavers and merchants from Qasimbazar to Hugli, though not possible to bring

important still, castes were not eternally fixed in their attachment to single professions or skills. Over a long period, economic compulsions could bring about a radical transformation in the occupational basis of a caste. A well-documented case is that of the caste of tailors in Maharashtra, a section of which took to dyeing and another to indigo-dyeing, early in the eighteenth century.[140] Finally, there is evidence that sometimes at least administrative action was in favour of keeping the gates to the professions open. Aurangzeb ordered that at Ahmedabad all persons who so wished should be allowed to learn the crafts of weaving, needle-making and embroidery.[141] It seems that castes were sometimes not even as strong as guilds, for owing to their comparatively loose organization they had often to depend upon the support of the administration or to suffer its interference in their internal affairs.[142]

We may infer, therefore, that caste did not represent an insurmountable obstacle to the mobility of craft labour. It is significant that while European merchants and travellers repeatedly speak of the hereditary nature of skilled occupations in India, they do not ascribe to this cause the shortage of labour in any branch of production. On the other hand, they usually refer to the large numbers and low wages of the

---

them to Madras 'for their caste or lineage is such that they shall loose their birthright if they come upon salt water.' *English Factories, 1661–64*, p. 65. The factors seem unaware of the fact that Madras was as far from Bengal as Spain from England.

[140] H.F. Fukazawa, 'State and Caste System (Jati) in the Eighteenth Century Maratha Kingdom,' *Hitotsubashi Journal of Economics (HJE)*, IX(1), pp. 39–44.

[141] Ali Muhammad Khan, *Mirat-i Ahmadi*, edited by Nawab Ali, Baroda, I, p. 260., See also Aurangzeb's order refusing to recognize the monopoly of the Srimal caste in the work of smelting and drawing wire at the Ahmedabad mint, on the explixit ground that such restrictions were against the law, ibid., pp. 292–93. Of Ahmedabad, it was said earlier, in 1629, that 'any merchant, or artisan is free to settle here, and live by his craft, or his business without molestation or interference by anyone.' Geleynssen, translated by Moreland, *Journal of Indian History (JIH)*, IV, p. 75.

[142] See *Ain's* injunction to the head of the city police (*kotwal*) that he should appoint the head and broker of each professional group in the town. *Ain-i Akbari*, I, edited by Blochmann, p. 284. See on this, Pavlov, *Indian Capitalist Class*, p. 24. Fukazawa, 'State and Caste System,' pp. 32–44, assembles considerable evidence to show how the Maratha state authorities served as arbiters, and even legislators, in caste matters.

artisans.[143] A much greater impediment to the free supply of craft labour appears to have been the nobles' extortion of forced labour from the artisans and other forcible restraints placed upon them.[144]

Having established, then, that there was a large urban market for non-agricultural goods, and a division of labour based on skilled specialization, coupled with certain technological advances, and the superfluity rather than scarcity of skilled labour, it is desirable to enquire how far in these conditions the organization of production had progressed toward capitalistic or semi-capitalistic forms.

We may exclude from our consideration such artisan production as was directed to supplying the needs of peasants and village communities. Some of these artisans lived in the village and offered set products and services in return for set remuneration; others went from village to village to buy materials and sell their wares, with the prices possibly fixed in kind. In neither of these forms would real commodity production have taken place.

It was otherwise with the urban artisan. We find him usually a commodity producer, placed in either of two different situations. In the first, he is the master of his product until he sells it on the market; in the second, the material may remain in his hands until the productive process is completed, but all this time it is not his, but someone else's.

Of the first situation, we may cite for an example, the English factor's report from Patna in 1620:

> . . . the usual custom of buying the amberty calicoes at Lackhoure (which is the pente [*penthe*] or fair for that commodity, and is a town 14 course [*kos*] from this place) is as follows: they are daily brought from the neighbouring gonges [*ganj*] by the weavers, from whom they are bought raw [i.e., without being 'whited' and

---

[143] *Relations of Golconda in the Early Seventeenth Century*, edited and translated by Moreland, London, 1931, p. 27; Pelsaert, *Jahangir's India*, p. 60.

[144] Pelsaert, *Jahangir's India*; Bernier, *Travels*, pp. 228–29. See also *Mirat-i Ahmadi*, I, p. 260. For the conduct of the governors of Broach and Baroda, Gujarat, see *English Factories, 1662–63*, p. 97 and *1634–36*, p. 290; *English Factories*, NS, III, pp. 352–53.

starched] of length 13 coveds Jehangerye.[145] . . . and the abatements and disturyes[146] in buying them raw from the weavers [is] 4/16 per rupee or 25 per cent. In this manner, by report daily may there be bought 50, 60 and some days 100 pieces. Almost in the like nature are they sold here in Patna being likewise brought thence by the weavers, but ready whited and cured. . .[147]

Here we find the weavers producing the calicoes on their own account in anticipation of the demand. What is still more interesting is that they sometimes enlarged their 'investment' by having their product 'cured' by washers, a process taking, according to the same report, three months, and costing three rupees for twenty pieces. Weavers who arranged for such processing themselves must have been able to sell their wares dearer on the larger market.

Enrichment through such ventures might in time have enabled some weavers to expand their production by no longer confining it to the household but engaging apprentices and servants. This would have been an important development, possibly repre-senting a step in the evolution of capitalism 'from below'—the 'really revolutionary way', according to Marx.[148] But of such development there is little evidence in Mughal India. Possibly trade in the precious metals yielded a sufficiently large margin of profit to goldsmiths for them to set up *karkhanas* or workshops.[149] But in general in the various crafts there were only very few independent master craftsmen of any substance.[150]

In the second situation the artisans did not undertake production on their own but did so on behalf of merchants and others. When the merchants wished to have supplies of particular commodities according to their specifications at fixed rates and at stipulated

[145] *Gaz-i Jahangiri*, 40 and 40.5 inches.

[146] *Dasturi*, commission.

[147] *English Factories, 1618–21*, pp. 192–93. The spellings have been modernized.

[148] *Capital*, I, English edition, Moscow, 1959, pp. 329–30. A fruitful discussion of the meaning of Marx's original passage, and its elaboration in the light of existing evidence, will be found in *The Transition from Feudalism to Capitalism*, containing chiefly the contributions of Paul M. Sweezy, M. Dobb, and H.K. Takahashi, London, n.d.

[149] See the reference to *karkhana-i zargaran* in *Bahar-i Ajam*, s.v. *Khak-bez*.

[150] See Bernier, *Travels*, pp. 228–29.

times, they advanced money to artisans who bound themselves to fulfil these conditions. This system of advances appears to have prevailed all over India, though it was probably more extensive in commodities required for long-distance trade than in others.[151]

Under this system the artisan was left to buy the material himself. But such processes as washing and dyeing naturally required that the material after being sold to the merchants should again be given out.[152] From this the next step would have been for the merchant to provide yarn to the weavers, as well, and it is possible that the practice was actually adopted by the English factors in Gujarat.[153] In Bengal, the English found it cheaper to discontinue cash advances to weavers, and preferred instead to buy the silk raw and then give it out to the weavers. The reason for this was said to be that the latter, out of poverty, could not buy raw silk of the requisite quality even when granted advances.[154]

It can be seen, therefore, that the putting-out system was widely in use; and that both cash advances and the giving-out of the raw material were established practices.

Beside the forms corresponding to the putting-out system, there existed forms of productive organization corresponding to the manufactory. It goes without saying that the large architectural monuments and other buildings of the Mughal period could not have been built without large numbers of craftsmen and ordinary labourers being assembled together and made to work under unified supervision. Yet this assemblage must generally have remained accidental, breaking up when the work of construction was over. The same could also have been the case with shipbuilding. Though some of the heaviest seagoing

---

[151] Some of passages in the English records on which this paragraph is based are *English Factories, 1624–29*, p. 149; *1637–41*, p. 137; *1646–50*, p. 159; *1661–64*, pp. 111–12; *Hobson-Jobson*, s.v. DADNY, quotations for 1678 and 1683. On one occasion the Surat artisans also demanded payment of the cost of alterations in their looms for meeting the specific dimensions of cloth required by the English. *English Factories, 1661–64*, pp. 208–9.

[152] See, for example, *English Factories, 1618–21*, pp. 192–93; *1624–29*, p. 149.

[153] Fryer, *Account of East India*, I, p. 221.

[154] *English Factories, 1655–60*, p. 296.

ships were built in India, it is possible that the organization brought into being to build a particular ship did not survive its construction.[155]

More significant for potential capitalistic development was the assembling of numbers of artisans and labourers for continuous production. Tavernier's detailed description of diamond mines in the Deccan shows that the fields were divided up among plots leased by individual merchants, who then employed labourers, of which the number on a plot might be as high as 300. In all, 60,000 labourers are said to have been employed.[156] A similar form of organization prevailed in the saltpeter industry.[157] These do not yet bring us to manufactories proper, for though merchants are here seen as large-scale producers, the productive process involved neither specialized skill nor complex tools.

The real counterpart of the manufactories was the *karkhana*. The royal *karkhanas* at Delhi are thus described by Bernier:

> Large halls are seen in many places, called Kar-kanyas or workshops for the artisans. In one hall embroiders are busily employed, superintended by a master. In another, you see the goldsmiths; in a third, painters; in a fourth, varnishers, in lacquer work; in a fifth, joiners, turners, tailors, and shoe-makers; in a sixth, manufactures of silk, brocade, and those fine muslins.... The artisans repair every morning to their respective Kar-kanyas where they remain employed the whole day; and in the evening return to their homes. In this quiet and regular manner their time glides away...[158]

The *karkhanas* thus reflected the specialized skills developed outside but they converted the artisan, previously an independent or contract producer, into a wage labourer.[159] It is likely that he still retained ownership of his tools or some of them; and it is not certain that there was any such further detailed division of skilled labour as

---

155 Moreland, *India at the Death of Akbar*, pp. 185–86. For shipbuilding, see also A.J. Qaisar, 'Shipbuilding in the Mughal Empire', *IESHR*, V(2), pp. 149–70.
156 Travernier's information is summarized in Moreland, pp. 151–52.
157 See Pelsaert, *Jahangir's India*, p. 46.
158 Bernier, *Travels*, pp. 258–59.
159 For the association of wages with *karkhana*, see the couplet from Saib, quoted in *Bahar-i' Ajam*, s.v. *Karkhana*.

developed within the European manufactory.[160]

And we have noted, the *karkhanas* of the emperor and the nobles did not undertake commodity production, but production of luxury articles directly for use. This naturally set limits to their economic significance. But at least one royal establishment was different, namely, the mint. Mughal coinage was 'free'; that is, it was open to anyone to take silver bullion and get it coined into rupees, which were of practically pure silver, on payment of seignorage and mint charges. The output of these mints was considerable. The Surat mint, for example, once turned out 30,000 rupees a day for the English alone.[161] We must therefore imagine the mints to have been very large establishments where men of different skills had to work together under the closest supervision.

The very fact that contemporary observers were so greatly impressed by the royal and aristocratic *karkhanas* while they had nothing or little to say about similar establishments maintained by the merchants suggests that the latter were far smaller in size. Bernier's reference to 'rich merchants and tradesmen, who pay the workmen rather higher wages'[162] probably applies to such private 'manufactories'. In certain trades, such as the silk trade in Bengal and Bihar, it appears to have been more economical for the bigger merchants to undertake the processes of winding, dyeing, and cleaning the raw silk in their own premises. A 'Cor Conna' employing nearly a hundred workmen to wind silk was established by two visiting English factors at Patna in 1620, quite obviously following the practice of other merchants.[163] But on the whole it would seem that despite the development of manufactories in the non-mercantile sector, the characteristic form of advanced commodity production had not yet proceeded beyond the putting-out system.

[160] Cf. Marx, *Capital*, I, pp. 330–32.

[161] This happened in 1672. The source is the Surat Factory Outward Letter Book, Vol. II, 1663–71/72, p. 187, in the Department of Archives and Archaeology, Bombay; I owe the reference to Miss Aziza Hasan. In certain documents, also of Aurangzeb's reign, recently acquired by the Department of History, Aligarh, we find individual merchants being granted permission to get up to Rs 4,000 worth of gold and silver coined each day at the Surat mint. A rupee, in Aurangzeb's reign, weighed 180 grains.

[162] Bernier, *Travels*, pp. 228–29.

[163] *English Factories, 1618–21*, pp. 197–98. See also ibid, 1655–60, p. 296.

The advance from the putting-out system to the commodity-producing manufactory would undoubtedly have represented an important stage in the progressive control of labour by capital. That it did not really occur in Mughal India, except sporadically, is perhaps largely to be attributed to the better adaptability of domestic industry to excessive exploitation of labour. The paid labour of the domestic artisan included the labour of his wife and children, an advantage that would be lost in the merchant's manufactory. The merchants would not, therefore, have found it profitable to establish *karkhanas* unless the material used was too valuable to be risked by being given out to the artisans, or was too heavy, or the process of production was too short to justify the distribution of the material.

Mughal India, then, had extensive commodity production, without showing much trace of the emergence of industrial capital. Since to a number of scholars, the distinction between merchant capital and industrial capital is one of degree, and not of essence, it is necessary to enquire whether the absence of industrial capital did not stem from a lack of development of merchant capital.

A strong body of scholarly opinion has held that merchants in Mughal India could not obtain sufficient or secure profits and accumulate wealth, owing to various political and administrative causes: insecurity of roads; the insecurity of merchants' property, it being threatened constantly by the avarice of the emperor and his nobles; high taxes; and, finally, interference with the conduct of free trade by the Mughal officials, who established their monopoly in various lines of trade within the area under their jurisdiction.[164]

It will not be of much use to go into the details of the evidence that can be cited to urge the acceptance of this view. What is in dispute is really not whether the factors mentioned operated at all, but the extent to which they did so.[165]

---

[164] Moreland, *India at the Death of Akbar*, especially pp. 35–52; B.B. Misra, *The Indian Middle Classes*, pp. 22–35; M.D. Morris in *IESHR*, V(1), p. 6. For the opposite view, see Brij Narain, *Indian Economic Life, Past and Present*; P. Saran, *Provincial Government of the Mughals (1526–1658)*, Allahabad, 1941, pp. 399–403.

[165] See my own remarks on security of trade and on taxes, I. Habib, pp. 65–69; and some perceptive remarks by T. Raychaudhuri, *IESHR*, V(1), pp. 88–90.

For example, security of roads can hardly be considered as non-existent if an individual traveller met with robbers. The best indicator of the degree of security should be the inland insurance rates. The few rates available are quoted below.[166] The distance between the points here given is not road distance, but 'as the crow flies'.

*Inland insurance rates*

| Year | Goods insured | Route | Approximate distance (miles) | Insurance charges (%) |
|------|---------------|-------|------------------------------|------------------------|
| 1646 | Treasure | Daman-Surat | 60 | 1.0 |
| 1647 | Commercial goods | Ahmedabad-Thatta | 315 | 0.5 |
| 1655 | Cochineal | Surat-Agra | 550 | 2.5 |
| 1655 | Cash | Masulipatam-Surat | 675 | 1.0 |

Surely, these rates do not suggest any stifling of commerce through 'political instability'. In the present state of our knowledge we cannot provide similar quantitative tests for the other propositions, but this particular case may be taken as a warning against the dangers of generalizing from a few bits out of a very large mass of evidence.

What we know, in positive terms, is that merchant capital was considerable in size and that an efficient system of credit not only enlarged it but also gave it mobility.

The vast system of agrarian exploitation that the Mughal empire represented was based, as we have seen, on the large drain of foodgrains and other agricultural produce from the countryside to the towns. The supplies were largely marketed, and in some cases the peasants themselves brought the supplies to the local market.[167] But whether the peasant sold the grain in his village or at the nearest fair or in the urban market, the merchant usually took over. The

---

[166] From the table in my article, 'Banking in Mughal India,' *Contributions to Indian Economic History*, edited by T. Raychaudhuri, p. 16.
[167] I. Habib, pp. 78–79.

importance of the grain trade in Indian commerce may be judged from the simple fact that the term *baqqal*, 'grain merchant', was employed in Indo-Persian as the name for the *banya* (the traditional Indian merchant).[168] For the long-distance carrying trade, there had developed the famous nomadic class of *banjaras*, who first appear in our records during the fourteenth century. During the seventeenth century they probably carried many hundreds of thousands of tons of agricultural produce across most regions of the country.[169] The total capital involved in the trade in agricultural produce cannot be computed but must surely have been enormous.

In urban commodity production, many artisans must have been selling directly to the consumers. Some worked for the nobles, producing goods directly for use. This would have restricted the limits of the operations of merchants, but not perhaps to a very great extent. In any case, in the trade of all valuable commodities, especially those for the long-distance market, we find merchants buying up large quantities from the artisans.

For the size of the capital involved in these dealings we may cite the information we have about the merchants of Surat from European sources. It was stated in 1663 that the Surat merchants were 'very rich', some of them worth more than 5 or 6 million (of rupees). They had fifty ships trading with various countries.[170] Virji Vora, reputedly the richest Surat merchant at that time, was said to have an 'estate' of 8 million rupees.[171] Subsequently another merchant, Abdul Ghafur, was said to be worth the same sum, and it was reported that he possessed twenty ships, of between 300 and 800 tons each. He alone conducted trade equal to that of the whole English East India Company.[172] It is not to be supposed that Surat was exceptional in respect of its merchants' wealth. A well-travelled European visitor said that of the three great surprises at Agra, one was 'the immense wealth or fortune

---

[168] *Comparative Studies in Society and History (CSSH)*, VI(4), p. 412n.

[169] I. Habib, pp. 61–63.

[170] Godinho, translated by Moraes, *JBBRAS*, NS, XXVII (part ii), p. 127. I owe some of the references in this and the following two footnotes to A.J. Qaisar.

[171] *English Factories, 1661–64*, p. 308; *Indian Travels of Thevenot and Careri*, New Delhi, 1949, p. 22.

[172] H. Das, *Norris' Embassy to Aurangzeb (1669–1702)*, condensed and edited by S.C. Sarkar, Calcutta, 1959, p. 224n; Hamilton, I, p. 89.

of the merchants'; and the writer claimed that he saw such vast sums of money piled up in some houses that they looked like grain heaps.[173] There is little doubt then that in spite of certain unfavourable factors the wealth accumulated by Indian merchants was considerable.[174]

Besides the wealth of merchants, we may also count the sums invested in commerce by nobles. The outstanding example was Mir Jumla, one of the greatest merchants of the time and also one of the premier nobles of the Mughal empire.[175] The nobles had little hesitation in turning money to profit if the opportunity arose, and they even speculated in the financing of ship cargoes.[176] But in many cases when their investment was combined with monopoly imposed by coercion the investment can hardly be regarded as an addition to the fund of commercial capital.[177] On the whole it would appear that compared to their enormous resources the Mughal nobles made very few investments in commerce.

A patriotic Indian during the seventeenth century could justly take pride in the system of credit and banking that prevailed in India.[178] Tavernier remarks that 'in India a village must be very small indeed, if it has not a money-changer, called shroff [*sarraf*], who acts as banker to make remittances of money and issue letters of exchange'.[179] The *sarrafs* not only transmitted money through their own *hundis* (bills), but by discounting the merchants' *hundis*, they financed commerce, particularly long-distance and international trade, to a very large extent. So brisk was the use of these bills that in the Ahmedabad market merchants made their payments, or adjusted their obligations, almost entirely through transfer of paper.[180] The

---

[173] Manrique, *Travels*, translated by C.E. Luard, II, p. 156. The other two surprises, significantly, were the vast imperial treasure and the large income of the nobles.

[174] Interesting information on the actual accumulation of Indian merchant capital is brought together in V.I. Pavlov, *Indian Capitalist Class*, pp. 76ff.

[175] See J.N. Sarkar, *Life of Mir Jumla*, Calcutta, 1951, for the large amount of information available on Mir Jumla's mercantile activities which often guided him in his political actions.

[176] Tavernier, *Travels in India*, I, p. 31.

[177] Athar Ali, *Mughal Nobility*, pp. 154–60.

[178] Sujan Rai, *Khulasatut Tawarikh*, edited by Zafar Hasan, p. 25.

[179] Tavernier, *Travels in India*, I, p. 24.

[180] *Mirat-i Ahmadi*, I, pp. 410–11.

prevalence of the system is shown also by the fact that almost any order of payment by anyone (such as a noble's order of payment of salaries to his troops) could become commercial paper, discounted by the *sarrafs*.[181]

The discount on *hundis* included the cost of insurance, since if the goods against which it was drawn were lost, the *hundi* could not be presented for payment. Insurance (*bima*), a business also carried on by the *sarrafs*, was fairly well developed. *Hundis*, goods in transit, and cargo could all be insured.[182]

Since the *sarrafs* accepted deposits while they also advanced loans directly, they acted practically as deposit bankers.[183] Thus they appear to have acquired even sums intended for the imperial treasury as deposits on loan. It is true that they too lent large sums to 'men of quality' and others at high rates, and thus converted part of their deposits into purely usurious capital. Yet it is possible, owing to their ability to advance large loans to merchants, that some of the capital mopped up through deposits with the *sarrafs* did turn into merchant capital.

From the point of view of the development of merchant capital, the Indian economy appears to have reached a fairly advanced stage. It is noticeable that seventeenth-century European merchants and factors make no serious criticism of the Indian credit system, and there is little inclination to compare it unfavourable with the European, although most of its particularities, or differences, are noted.

But despite all this, the Indian credit system seems practically to have been formed for the requirements of commerce alone. Thus there was no provision for long-term investment. Rates of interest were calculated by the month.[184] A loan was not expected to be carried beyond a year, since by customary practice the creditor could double the rate of interest on the completion of a year.[185]

---

[181] See Manucci, *Storia do Mogor*, II, translated by W. Irvine, p. 379.
[182] See I. Habib, *Contributions to Indian Economic History*, I, pp. 13, 15–17, for a more detailed treatment.
[183] Ibid., pp. 17–19.
[184] *CSSH*, VI(4), pp. 401–2.
[185] English factors at Ahmedabad report to Surat, 17 May 1647: 'Surat Factory: Inward Letter Book, 1646–47', p. 130, Department of Archives and Archaeology, Bombay. I am indebted for this reference to Miss A. Hasan.

Another feature which is difficult to explain, is the consistently high rates of interest prevalent in India. The rates of interest current at Surat, Ahmedabad, and Agra and in the Deccan show uniformly a sharp fall, which by comparison with other information may be assigned to the early 1640s.[186] In northern India there was a fall from about 1 per cent and 1½ per cent per month to ¾ per cent or ⁵/₈ per cent or even ½ per cent; in the Deccan, from above 2 per cent per month to 1½ per cent and below. The reasons for this fall remain obscure, unless it was linked up in some ways with the influx of bullion from the west. In any case, even afterwards interest rates in India remained much higher than in England, and the difference was so great that it was suggested that the English East India Company might send treasure to India solely for the purpose of being lent out at interest.[187]

The high interest rates do not by themselves suggest an intrinsically capital-starved economy. They may, on the other hand, have been due to the steady expansion of mercantile activity, following upon the wider and wider imposition of the cash-nexus, from Akbar's reign onward. It is also possible that tradition gave the merchant a larger margin of profit on commodities than in Europe, so that the higher interest rates represented a higher return on commercial investment, which was not greatly affected by competition. But on all these matters we have practically no detailed information, and it will avail little merely to speculate.

What we know of the Mughal Indian economy largely tends to confirm Marx's judgement that merchant capital, through its own development, cannot lead to industrial capital:

---

[186] See the tables in *CSSH*, VI(4), p. 402–4. The rate of interest shown under Agra against the year 1628 should read 2 per cent and not ¾ per cent. In this article, I suggested that the rates reported fell as the accounting control in the East India Company improved. This suggestion I should now like to withdraw, though there is little doubt that in the earlier years the English factors must have concealed the true rates.

[187] Ibid., pp. 404–5. Higher interest rates naturally meant higher discount rates on bills, a phenomenon to which Tavernier, in *Travels in India*, I, p. 31, refers, although he himself considers this due, in part at least, to the insurance costs that the discount included.

The independent and predominant development of capital as merchant capital is tantamount to the non-subjection of production to capital, and hence to capital developing on the basis of an alien social mode of production which is also independent of it. The independent development of merchant's capital, therefore, stands in inverse proportion to the general economic development of society.[188]

Finally, we may consider the impact on the Indian economy of the great changes in the pattern of international trade during the sixteenth and seventeenth centuries, following the discovery of the new world and the rounding of the Cape of Good Hope. In Europe expansion of the oversea trade and the price revolution which accompanied it and which was intensified if not entirely caused by it, helped to create considerable shifts in the distribution of income and wealth in different countries of Europe. This had a lasting effect on the economic life of Europe, and it is possible to trace the strands of capitalism back to the changes which these developments made possible.

Largely because information on the history of prices in the Mughal period has been so insufficient, a suggestion found in James Grant long remained practically unnoticed. This was that the large influx of bullion, especially silver, from the new world through Europe was bound to raise prices in India.[189] Recent research has suggested that the increase in prices during the first half of the seventeenth century was so considerable as to deserve, in patches at least, the designation of inflation. In the course of the century prices appear to have almost doubled. This is suggested by our information on the silver values of gold and copper and on the prices of major agricultural commodities.[190] It is also confirmed by the extraordinary approximation, with just the time gaps we would expect, that an attempted Mughal mint-output curve (based on the number of catalogued coins of each year) bears to the curve suggested by Hamilton's histogram for the

---

[188] Marx, *Capital*, III, English edition, Moscow, 1959, p. 322.
[189] James Grant in *Fifth Report*, edited by Firminger, II, p. 483.
[190] I. Habib, pp. 81–89, 384–94, and the table on p. 327. Moreland in his *Akbar to Aurangzeb*, London, 1923, pp. 160–64, 183–85, also examines some price-evidence, but concludes, largely on the basis of the prices fetched by the Sarkhej indigo, that the price level did not move up during the earlier half of the seventeenth century.

influx of American treasure into Spain.[191] It is, therefore, certain that the price revolution steadily affected India, as bullion flowed through the Middle East and round the Cape of Good Hope.

But, to us, as important as the outcries heard in Europe against the export of bullion eastward must be the silence of Indian writers in respect to the seventeenth-century 'inflation'. We know of the process from the prices they quote, but they themselves are un-aware of it. It is possible that the general trend was concealed from men's eyes by the wide price fluctuations caused by the harvests each year.[192] But this very fact suggests that the larger trend caused less economic disturbance than the annual fluctuations. It is probable that this was because neither the revenue rates nor wages were fixed in cash by custom or tradition. As we have noticed above, the Mughal authorities not only modified the cash revenue schedules when prices showed long-range changes, but could also shift from basic assess-ment in cash to assessment in kind (with subsequent commutation into cash at market prices). Similarly, if wages were already at sub-sistence level and were therefore governed directly by grain prices they would have risen as prices rose. Here, for example, are three quota-tions of the monthly wages of the lowest paid 'peons' or unskilled servants at Surat.[193]

*Monthly wages of peons, Surat*

| Year | Wages (Rs) | Index |
|---------|---------|---------|
| 1616 | 2.40 | 100 |
| 1623 | 3.00 | 125 |
| 1690–93 | 4.00 | 166 |

[191] Aziz Hasan, 'Currency Output of the Mughal Empire, and Prices in India during the Sixteenth and Seventeenth Centuries,' *IESHR*, IV, I, March 1969, pp. 84–116.

[192] See Pelsaert, *Jahangir's India*, p. 44, for the effect of the harvests on general demand for commodities.

[193] Foster, *Supplementary Calender*, p. 66; Pietro Dalla Valle, *Travels in India*, translated by E. Grey, I, p. 62; Ovington, *Voyage to Surat*, edited by Rawlinson, p. 229.

Unfortunately, detailed statistics of wages and prices in the same localities have yet to be collected. It is not yet clear how the real wages of skilled labourers behaved. But we must remember that most of them, even under the system of advances, sold their wares, and the prices paid to them should have broadly followed the trends of market prices. It is therefore unlikely on the whole that the merchants reaped long-term extra profits from the seventeenth-century inflation.

In other words, in so far as we can judge in the present state of our knowledge, the structure of the Mughal Indian economy weathered the effects of the worldwide price revolution without much difficulty.

Our principal conclusion with regard to the extend of capitalistic development within Mughal India may now be summarized. We find that in both agricultural and non-agricultural production, production for the market formed a very large sector. In agriculture, there existed *khwud-kasht* cultivation, based on hired labour, representing an advance, in form, toward capitalist farming. In handicrafts, merchant capital had developed considerably and had brought artisans under control through forms of the putting-out system. But the manufactory as an established form was yet largely outside of the sphere of commodity production. In other words, capital was by and large merchant capital, and though the economy was fairly highly monetized, domestic industry still predominated.

Any number of reasons may be offered why a society exhibiting such features should or should not have developed into full-blown capitalism in due course. By and large, our enquiry has disclosed that while some factors, such as political environment and caste, were not as effective in checking commercial expansion as has sometimes been thought, certain elements capable of actively generating capitalism are also not met with.

Here it must be considered whether the entire commercial structure of the Mughal Indian economy was not largely parasitical, depending upon a system of direct agrarian exploitation by a small ruling class. It is not to be forgotten that practically no rural market existed for urban crafts; rural monetization was thus almost entirely the result of the need to transfer surplus agricultural produce to the towns.

Accordingly, when a crisis developed within the agrarian

system, it was bound to extend to the entire structure of Indian economy. In so far as capital, confined practically to the sphere of commerce, had failed to develop any independent basis for itself, its fortunes would lie with the Mughal ruling class, and, after its collapse, with such other classes as imitated or inherited the methods and institutions of that class. Denied, during the eighteenth century, the large market that it had been provided with by the Mughal empire, merchant capital had not choice but to atrophy. With this also receded into the background those prominent economic landmarks, which in the better days of the Mughal empire might have been mistaken for capitalistic features.

# Forms of Class Struggle
# in Mughal India

The modern working class in colonial countries has had
allies, as well as precursors, in the other oppressed classes, notably the
peasantry. The revolutionary cause of the working class, accordingly,
finds its 'pre-history' in the struggles of all exploited classes in earlier
societies. These struggles arose out of contradictions existing within
each society, and the forms they took were largely determined by the
design of the social structure, of whose strains and stresses they were
the product.

Our discussion of the nature of resistance of peasants,
artisans and other elements in the Mughal empire (sixteenth and
seventeenth centuries) must, therefore, begin with an analysis of the
major contradictions in its social system. In attempting such analysis,
one has perforce to take issue with Marx himself, for Marx believed
that the Mughal empire, or rather Indian society before the British
conquest, was bereft of any fundamental, antagonistic contradictions. He held that society in India consisted of a basic layer of 'village
communities', fixed in their internal composition (peasants, artisans,
village servants) by the caste system. The tribute extracted in kind
from these communities maintained a ruling class, at the head of
which was an absolutely despotic king. The 'village community' thus
supported an 'Oriental despotism'. Marx fully approved of Francois
Bernier's view that there was no private property in land in India.[1]

---

[1] Bernier had come to India in the seventeenth century. The standard
English translation of Bernier's work is that of Archibald Constable,
*Travels in the Mogul Empire* AD *1656–1668*, second edition, revised by
V.A. Smith, London, 1916. Bernier's actual contention was that the king
was the owner of the soil in the entire East, pp. 5, 204, 226, 238.

The economic basis for the social order was the unity between agriculture and handicrafts within the village, supplemented by artisan production for direct use by the 'potentates' (i.e. not induced through the market). He saw thus an utterly passive society ('unresisting and unchanging'). The only historical events occurred when invasions changed the personnel of the ruling class, or some religious belief gained currency.[2] There was little or no room, apparently, for any noticeable class struggles, which in 1848 Marx and Engels had declared to be the very stuff of history. But, then, according to Marx, Indian society had 'no real history of its own' at all.[3]

This is not the place to enter into a debate on the theory of the Asiatic mode of production, whether in the form it was presented by Marx, or in the forms it has been sought to be preserved or revived recently. The relevant question here is whether Marx's description of pre-colonial Indian society conforms at all to the information we have about the Mughal empire. The moment one goes to the actual evidence, it becomes apparent that Marx's description contains grave errors of fact—such as his assumption that the cash nexus did not exist, or that there was no or little artisan production for the market. Even given Bernier as his source, his inferences and deductions happen to be demonstrably one-sided.

Marx's portrayal of the village community, which he derived from certain official reports, was a highly idealized one in that it implied that the peasants formed a single undifferentiated mass within each village. But it is clear from the evidence of the Mughal period as well as early British rule, that the rural population, including the peasantry, was heavily differentiated, *both* through horizontal and

---

[2] This summary of Marx's views is based on his articles on 'British Rule in India' and 'The Future of British Rule in India' in *New York Tribune*, 1853; *Capital*, I, translated by Moore and Aveling, edited by Dona Torr, London, 1938, pp. 350–52, 610; Karl Marx and Frederick Engels, *Correspondence, 1846–1895, A Selection with Commentary and Notes*, edited by Dona Torr, Calcutta, 1945, pp. 57–60 (letters of 1853).

[3] Article in *Tribune* on 'British Rule in India'. There is therefore, some basis in Marx's own writings for Karl Wittfogel's taunt that 'class struggle far from being a disease of all mankind is the luxury of multi-centred and open [i.e. west European] societies'; *Oriental Despotism, A Comparative Study in Total Power*, 1957, p. 71.

vertical division by caste and through operation of land revenue and commodity production.[4]

At the bottom there was the landless proletariat, created in Mughal India not by capitalism but by the age-old operation of the caste system for the benefit of peasant agriculture. Although the proportion of the menial ('untouchable') castes varied from region to region, it is certain that they constituted from about a sixth to a fifth of the rural population; and they were prevented from holding land or setting themselves up as cultivating peasants. Living at the brink of starvation all the time, they formed a reserve, cheaply available to the peasants when they needed labour at the time of sowing and harvesting. There are, perhaps, few parallels in the world when the oppressors and the oppressed majority in society have joined together to keep a minority in such utter degradation.[5]

The Indian peasant was an independent producer, his plough and his cattle were his own; unlike the Russian commune, there was no periodic allotment of land in the Indian village. Such records as we have hardly suggest an egalitarian community. The following is an illustration from a record of area and crops of the autumn harvest cultivated in 1796 in a village in eastern Rajasthan. Out of 38 peasants, 2 peasants designated *patels* (headmen) each cultivated more area and grew larger quantities of produce than 10 small peasants together at the bottom. Moreover, one of the *patels* cultivated seven and the other six crops (including cotton) in the same harvest, whereas each of the 10 peasants raised one coarse food crop only.[6] The differences among peasants are indicated by references to kulak-type peasants on the one hand, and completely indigent cultivators on the other. It was said of the leading peasants (*muqaddams*) who 'organize *khwud-kasht* (cultivation under their own management)', that 'they employ labourers as their servants and put them to the tasks of agriculture; and making them plough, sow, reap and draw water out of

---

[4] The description which immediately follows is largely based on my *Agrarian System of Mughal India (1556–1707)*, Bombay, 1963, where authorities are cited.

[5] Ibid., pp. 119–22.

[6] The *khasra* document giving these details is introduced and analysed by S.P. Gupta in *Medieval India—A Miscellany*, IV, Aligarh/Bombay, 1977, pp. 168–78.

the well, they pay them their fixed wages, whether in cash or grain, while appropriating to themselves the gross produce of cultivation.'[7] As for the indigent small peasants (*reza riaya*), many of them, according to a *farman* of Emperor Aurangzeb, 'were wholly in debt for their subsistence as well as for seed and cattle'.[8]

This high degree of differentiation arose out of the prevalence of commodity production as well as the highly regressive nature of the Mughal land tax ('land revenue').[9] Castes (especially superior castes) enjoyed tax concessions and leading positions in the village as tax-gatherers. Indeed, the 'village community' often operated as a mere body of these leading men, who collectively made themselves responsible for payment of tax and shifted the burden onto the common peasants. Thus even the Mughal administration repeatedly noticed how 'the big men', 'the dominant ones', repressed the 'small peasantry' (*reza riaya*), by making use of their power to distribute the assessments.[10]

Above the village peasantry, stood a class of hereditary right-holders known locally by various names, but given the universal designation of *zamindar* by the clerks of the Mughal administration. The *zamindari* right could possibly have originated partly as the surviving fragment of the fiscal and other rights enjoyed by rulers and chiefs subjugated by the Sultans; partly, as rights obtained by chieftains and members of warrior (such as Rajput) castes over peasants; partly again, as enlargement of rights of headmen, etc. Whatever the historical process, and whatever variety the rights exhibited, certain

[7] *Diwan Pasand*, Br. Mus. MS. Or. 2011, f. 8a. This work was written during the first decade of the nineteenth century, and describes agricultural conditions and revenue practices on the eve of the British conquest of the Doab.

[8] The *farman* was issued some time after 1679; its text is in Malikzada, *Nigarnama-i Munshi*, Lucknow, 1882, p. 139.

[9] See Irfan Habib, 'Potentialities of Capitalistic Development in the Indian Economy', *Enquiry*, NS, III, 3 (1971), pp. 13–14; pp. 180–232 of this volume.

[10] *Agrarian System of Mughal India*, pp. 128–29 and n. I now believe I was then in error in thinking that such domination of the 'big men' subverted the village community, for that implied that the 'village community' normally comprised all peasants. Pavlov uses the term 'community elite' for the uppermost peasants: V.I. Pavlov, *Historical Premises for India's Transition to Capitalism*, Moscow, 1978, p. 41.

features marked out the *zamindar* class: its rights were hereditary and saleable; the right did not amount to the landlord's right, i.e. claim to rent, but only to a minor part of the rent or surplus, officially regarded as an allowance out of the land revenue together with certain customary cesses and perquisites. The *zamindars* of the same localities often belonged to the same castes and exercised considerable armed power through retainers (horsemen and foot) and even possessed forts.[11]

It can be seen that the peasants and *zamindars* could have conflicts of interest over the part of the surplus that the latter claimed. It is, however, remarkable that the contradiction does not seem to have fully developed in the Mughal empire. On the contrary, the official view was that the *zamindars* generally managed to keep the peasants conciliated.[12] Caste might, perhaps, have been one factor in preserving or furthering bonds, wherever, at least, the big peasants and the *zamindars* belonged to the same caste. A jurist writing during the earlier part of the eighteenth century, claimed that the peasants regarded themselves as 'the *zamindars*' cultivators, and farmers', and even conceded to the *zamindars* the right to evict them from their lands, though the jurist himself protested that the *zamindars* were not entitled to such pretensions.[13]

The great dividing line in the Mughal empire seems, in fact, to have been drawn by the land tax, the real Indian counterpart of 'rent'. The land revenue or land tax (*mal, kharaj*) was assumed to comprise the bulk of the peasant's surplus: it could range, depending upon crop and region, from the equivalent of a third to three-quarters of the produce.[14] It was collected in the name of the king; and it was, therefore, natural that European observers, equating it with rent,

[11] *Agrarian System of Mughal India*, pp. 136–89. An important essay on the *zamindars* by S. Nurul Hasan was published in *Land Control and Social Structure in Indian History*, edited by R.E. Frykenberg, Madison, 1969, pp. 17–31.

[12] Muhammad Kazim, *Alamgirnama*, edited by Khadim Husain and Abdu-l Hai, Bib. Ind., Calcutta, 1865–73, p. 781.

[13] Qazi Muhammad A'la, *Risala Ahkam-i Arazi*, Maulana Azad Library, Aligarh, MS., Subhanullah Coll., 331/101, f. 44a.

[14] *Agrarian System of Mughal India*, pp. 190–256. The evidence for Akbar's reign has been studied afresh by S. Moosvi in *Medieval India—A Miscellany*, IV, Aligarh, 1977, pp. 91–107, and *Indian Historical Review*, IV, 2 (1978), pp. 304–25.

should consider the king to be the absolute proprietor of the land.[15]

The land revenue (together with other taxes) for particular territories was assigned by the Mughal emperor, by way of *jagir* (temporary transferable assignments) in lieu of salary to his military commanders and bureaucrats, who belonged to a single corps of *mansabdars* (holders of *mansabs* or numerical ranks determining status, salary and size of military contingent).[16] This corps, together with the Mughal emperor, formed the ruling class of the Mughal empire.

The resources this class deposed were enormous. The collection of land revenue largely in cash meant that the transfer of grain, raw materials and other produce of the country to the towns took place through private commerce and within a market environment.[17] The supplies so brought to towns maintained a large artisan population and service sector dependent directly or indirectly upon the expenditure of the ruling class, which had large households and hordes of retainers, servants and slaves to look after them.[18]

The town artisans produced, by and large, for the market.[19] Except for the nobles' *karkhanas*, which employed a very small portion of the artisans, production directly for use was extremely rare. The Mughal taxation system did not exempt artisans, and there were attempts by nobles to force them to work for them at low rates.[20] There was, therefore, some reason for the artisan's resentment against Mughal administration. On the other hand, his commitment to commodity production made him heavily dependent on the merchant-usurer. And yet, surprisingly, his view of the usurer seems to have been one of awe rather than bitterness.[21]

---

[15] See, for example, Bernier's views in *Travels*.

[16] *Agrarian System of Mughal India*, pp. 257–97; M. Athar Ali, *The Mughal Nobility under Aurangzeb*, Bombay, 1966, pp. 74–94.

[17] The extent to which land revenue was collected in cash is discussed in *Agrarian System of Mughal India*, pp. 236–42. For the prevalence of market conditions, see Satish Chandra, 'Money Economy in India during the Seventeenth Century', *Studies in Asian History*, New Delhi, 1969, pp. 368–77. For certain reservations, V.I. Pavlov, *Historical Premises for India's Transition to Capitalism*, Moscow, 1978, pp. 46ff.

[18] Athar Ali, *Mughal Nobility*, pp. 161–70.

[19] 'Potentialities of Capitalistic Development', *Enquiry*, NS, III, 3, pp. 41–44.

[20] Athar Ali, *Mughal Nobility*, pp. 157–59.

[21] I have examined the recurring comparison of God with the merchant-

The relationship of merchants and bankers with the Mughal empire was a complex one. Basically, commerce and credit flourished in large part because of the great drain of agricultural produce to the towns through the levy of the heavy land tax. Merchants and bankers had little scope for entry into the ruling class itself;[22] and conflicts with the Mughal administration or its local officials were possible. But it is difficult to cite any persuasive reason for believing that an estrangement between the empire and the mercantile classes began to develop in its later phases.[23]

## II

I have tried to delineate the different kinds of social contradictions that existed in the Mughal empire. The delineation has been based on our information about the economy and social structure, and some direct statements by contemporaries. We may now pass on to consider our evidence for the actual forms of resistance, ranging from passive to armed defiance, that these contradictions generated.

The basic contradiction in Mughal society revolved around land revenue; this, therefore, led to the most widespread conflicts between the peasants and the revenue-appropriating ruling class. Naturally, any system of exploitation, once established, has its own momentum, and there is inertia among the exploited bred by the acceptance of what is regarded as customary. The utmost privation and misery could be tolerated. Pelsaert (Agra, 1626), who spoke of the utter subjection and poverty of the common people, was surprised that 'the people endure patiently, professing that they do not deserve anything better'.[24]

Yet of the same 'common people' around the Mughal capital

---

usurer and of the artisan with man in the verses of the popular religious teachers of the sixteenth century in my paper on 'Usury in Medieval India', *Comparative Studies in Society and History* (*CSSH*), VI, 4 (1964), pp. 418–19.

[22] See A.J. Qaisar, 'Recruitment of Merchants in the Mughal Feudal Bureaucracy', Indian History Congress, Jadavpur, 1974 (cyclostyled).

[23] An extreme case for collaboration and alienation is argued by Karen Leonard, 'The "Great Firm" Theory of the Decline of the Mughal Empire', *CSSH*, XXI, 2, 1979, pp. 151–67.

[24] Francisco Pelsaert, 'Remonstrantie', translated by W.H. Moreland and P. Geyl, in *Jahangir's India*, Cambridge, 1925, p. 60.

of Agra, Emperor Akbar's minister Abu'l Fazl had written hardly thirty years earlier in the following terms: 'Owing to the peculiarities of environment [lit., climate], the masses of peasantry [*umum-i riaya*] of that region are notorious throughout the vast area of Hindustan for their contumacy, bravery and valour.'[25] Clearly, the acceptance of established conditions was not universal.

It is possible that what the peasants regarded as normal, however onerous the burden might be, was ordinarily accepted by them. But what they regarded as an excess or innovation might provoke them to defiance.

When, in 1633, Emperor Shahjahan granted the monopoly of the indigo trade throughout the empire to a merchant, Manohardas Danda, thereby causing a depression in indigo prices in the Agra region, 'the cultivators (being in general a resolute harebrained folk) . . . rooted up their plants'.[26] Their action apparently contributed to the revocation of the monopoly. It may be borne in mind that peasants who could grow indigo for the long-distance market, probably belonged to the upper strata.

The critical point, however, was reached for peasants in general, when the land revenue imposed on them attained an intolerably heavy magnitude. The first to be hurt by such an increase in land revenue were the small peasants, the *reza riaya*, onto whose shoulders the upper peasants tended to transfer their own burdens.[27]

Individuals affected in this manner had little option but to flee. B.R. Grover has introduced us to official documents from mid-seventeenth century Gujarat, in which individual 'tenants' are shown migrating from village to village in different localities, cultivating small areas of land. The official view was that it was incumbent on every such peasant to return and settle in his original village.[28]

[25] Abu'l Fazl, *Akbarnama*, III, Bib. Ind., Calcutta, 1873–87, p. 231.

[26] Report from Agra in the *English Factories in India 1630–33*, edited by W. Foster, Oxford, 1906–27, p. 325.

[27] As Akbar's minister Todar Mal put it in his own uninhibited language, 'the bastards and the head-strong [of the village] keep their own share, transferring [the revenue demand due from them] to the *reza riaya*'. *Akbarnama*, MS. of early version, Br. Mus. Add. 27, 247, f. 332 b.

[28] *Proceedings of the Indian History Congress*, Delhi session, 1961, Calcutta, 1963, p. 152. Unluckily Grover omits to give the original word that he has rendered as 'tenant'.

Indeed, flight was an unlawful act, and, of the peasants of Gujarat again, it was said by a Dutch observer that there was 'little difference between them and serfs such as are found in Poland, for here the peasants must all sow'.[29]

But flight, from being the response of an individual peasant, could also become that of an entire village, or, at any rate, of large bodies of peasants. This could happen particularly if there were accessible areas held by autonomous chiefs or recalcitrant *zamindars,* where the peasants might hope to obtain better terms. A manual of Mughal administration recognizes this to be a plain fact of life, an inevitable result of any excess in imposition of revenue demand.[30] Bernier too noted that peasants 'driven to despair by so execrable a tyranny...sometimes fly to the territories of a Raja because they find less oppression and are allowed a greater degree of comfort'.[31] For the Mughal authorities the flight of the peasants to the lands of the chiefs was sufficient justification for military expeditions being sent against them, the peasants being brought back by force.[32]

Where flight was not possible, or not likely to be rewarding, the peasants had no choice but to stay in their villages and try to delay or refuse payment. The ultimate punishment for such refusal was extremely severe. Since land was abundant, taking away land and evicting the peasants—the last resort of the twentieth-century Indian landlord—was only partly open to the Mughal authorities.[33] What could be done for the best effect was to slaughter or enslave the peasants, together with their women and children.[34] This was the

[29] Wellebrand Geleynssen de Jongh, 'Verclaringe ende Bevinding, etc.', extracts translated by W.H. Moreland, *Journal of Indian History*, XVI (1937), p. 78.

[30] Hidayatullah Bihari, *Hidayatu'l Qawa'id*, AD 1710, India Office MS., I.O. 1286, f. 65a.

[31] *Travels*, p. 205.

[32] *Agrarian System of Mughal India*, p. 116.

[33] Fruit-bearing trees, as Khafi Khan (1720–21) tells us, could always be seized besides 'proprietary' rights in land. *Muntakhabu'l Lubab*, I, edited by K.D. Ahmad and Haig, Bib. Ind., Calcutta, pp. 157–58.

[34] See statements to this effect in Pelsaert, *Jahangir's India*, p. 47; Fr. Sebastian Manrique, *Travels, 1629–43*, II, translated by C.E. Luard, assisted by Hosten, London, p. 272; Bernier, *Travels*, p. 205; Nicalae Mannucci, *Storia de Mogor*, II, translated by W. Irvine, Indian Texts Series, Government of India, London, 1907–08, p. 451.

standard punishment meted out to the defaulting peasants, a punishment whose threat often forced them, of their own, to sell their women and children in order to pay the revenue demand.[35]

Faced with prospects of slaughter or captivity some peasants might finally take to armed resistance. Manucci could speak of it as a routine matter that some villagers, in the Allahabad region as in Agra, 'objected to pay their revenue without at least one flight'.[36] The villagers retreated to jungles and ravines, and resisted the authorities. The use of such natural defences by peasants ('people of *parganas*') who refused to pay land revenue, had been noted as a general phenomenon by Babur.[37]

An illustration of such large-scale defiance by peasants in the Agra region (1622) is provided in the following description by Emperor Jahangir:

> At this time I received a report that the villagers [*ganwaran*] and peasants [*muzari'an*] of the other [eastern] side of the Jamuna river [near Mathura] constantly engage in thievery and robbing travellers [*rahzani*], and, sheltered behind dense jungles and fastnesses difficult of access, pass their days in rebellion and defiance, not paying the authorized land revenue to the *jagirdars*. I ordered Khan-i Jahan to take a number of high *mansabdars* with him and do his best to mete out stern punishment and chastisement, and, going on with slaughter, enslavement and rapine, raze their fastnesses and forts to the ground, and root out this thorn-field of mischief and villainy. The army crossed the river and attacked hot and proper the next day. Since they [the villagers] had no time to flee, they were compelled to commit the folly of a frontal battle. Large numbers of them were put to slaughter, their women and children enslaved, and large booty secured for the victorious troops.[38]

---

[35] Abdu'l Qadir Badauni, *Muntakhabu't Tawarikh*, II, edited by Ali, Ahmad and Lees, Bib. Ind., Calcutta, 1864–69, p. 189; Yusuf Mirak, *Mazhar-i Shahjahani*, II, Karachi, 1961, p. 451.

[36] Manucci, *Storia de Mogor*, II, p. 83.

[37] Babur, *Baburnama*, translated by Abdur Rahim Khan Khanan, Br. Mus. MS., Or. 3714, f. 378 b; II, English translation by A.S. Beveridge, London, 1921, p. 487.

[38] *Tuzuk-i Jahangiri*, edited by Saiyid Ahmad, Ghazipur and Aligarh 1863–64, pp. 375–76.

Almost an identical description of such action against 'the rebels', twelve years later, in the area around Delhi, occurs in the chronicles of Shah Jahan's reign (1634). The accusation again is that the rebels plundered the routes on both sides of the Jamuna river. In the expeditions undertaken large numbers of them were slaughtered, and their women and children and cattle, 'beyond computation', seized.[39]

It is not stated how well these rural rebels were armed. But it seems that by the seventeenth century at least some of the upper peasants had begun to carry muskets. Of the Bhadauryas (a Rajput caste in localities near Agra) it was said in 1650:

> They are a numerous industrious and brave race. Every village has a small fort. They never pay revenue to the *hakim* [*jagirdar*] without a fight. The peasants [*riaya*] who drive the plough keep a musket [*banduq*] slung over the neck, and a powder-pouch at the waist. The relief-loan [*taqavi*] they get from the *hakim* is in the form of lead [and] gun-powder.[40]

On his way from Agra to Allahabad in 1632, Mundy also saw in some villages, 'Labourers with their guns, swords, and bucklers lyeing by them whilest they ploughed the ground.'[41]

It is difficult to distinguish the categories of peasants who went into rebellion, or resorted to armed resistance. One can assume that those who had muskets probably belonged to the higher strata of the peasantry; even swords suggest a certain amount of substance. Pavlov, therefore, may be right in insisting that in most cases, 'the elite of the village community acted as the spearhead of armed resistance'.[42] But it is likely that the 'elite' were often followed by the ordinary peasants or *reza riaya*, especially if caste-ties united the latter (or large sections of them) with the former.

---

[39] Abdu'l Hamid Lahori, *Padshahnama*, I, i, Bib. Ind., Calcutta, 1866–72, pp. 71–2, 76. Qazwini, the earlier historian, puts the number of the 'rebels' slaughtered at 10,000; *Padshahnama*, Br. Mus. MS. Add. 29734, p. 679.

[40] Shaikh Farid Bhakkari, *Zakhiratu'l Khawanin*, Maulana Azad Library, Habibganj Collection MS. no. 32/74, f. 108a.

[41] Peter Mundy, *Travels*, II (*Travels in Asia, 1630–34*), edited by Sir R.C. Temple, London, 1914, p. 90.

[42] V.I. Pavlov, *Historical Premises for India's Transition to Capitalism*, pp. 40–41.

Unfortunately, our knowledge of the episodes in which peasants resorted to armed resistance of the simple kind so far discussed comes almost entirely from the pens of hostile officials or indifferent observers. The horizons of the thoughts and the nature of the aspirations of the rebelling peasants remain concealed from us, and can only be dimly guessed at. We do not even know if the point was at all reached when the rebel ceased to view himself as fighting for the cause of just a village or a caste, and saw himself as a member of the vast mass of oppressed peasantry.

### III

One opening, at least, for a wider sympathy seems to have been provided by religious preachings of a particular kind. Of this, the Satnami movement, breaking out into a revolt in 1672, offers the classic example. The term 'Satnami' (worshipper of the True Name or God) is applied to a number of sects, but the sect we are here concerned with was founded in 1657 by a native of Narnaul, who proclaimed himself to be of the tradition of the great monotheist Kabir, the weaver (early sixteenth century). The Satnami scripture has survived and contains harshly worded rules disdaining caste and calling upon the believers to reject any dependence upon charity—so that earning one's livelihood was compulsory. Contact with any *raja* (chief; the big *zamindars* also probably fell into this category in the eyes of the peasants) is condemned; and a puritanical austerity in life is insisted upon.[43]

The Satnamis came to comprise 4,000–5,000 householders in the localities of Narnaul and Mewat; they are said to have engaged 'in agriculture and trade in the manner of grain-merchants of small

[43] The scripture, *Pothi Gyan Bani Sadh Satnami,* is preserved in texts of both Devnagari and Arabic characters in an MS. in the Library of the Royal Asiatic Society, London (No. Hind. 1). The injunctions mentioned are interspersed in the text; the reference to Kabir comes at the end (text in Arabic character, f. 49b). That the Satnami preachings were successful to some degree is shown by the certificate given to the community by a contemporary historian who says that the Satnamis 'in earning their income never make use of unlawful appropriation, confining themselves to the legitimate means only'. Abu'l Fazl Ma'muri, untitled History of Aurangzeb, Br. Mus. Or. 161, f. 148b; copied in Khafi Khan, *Muntakhabu'l Lubab,* II, p. 252.

capital'.[44] The words suggest that in the Satnami fold peasants mixed with petty rural traders, which again strongly suggests that some of the members of the community belonged to the upper strata of peasants having accumulated enough capital to set up as rivals to the traditional caste of rural merchants and usurers, the *banyas*.

Yet another description links the Satnami peasants with the lowest-ranking artisans and village 'menials'. The Satnamis when they went into rebellion are said to have comprised a 'murderous, rebellious, statusless gang of cultivators, carpenters, sweepers and tanners and other mean and ignoble men [*arazil-uajlaf*] of artisan castes'.[45] Carpenters are regarded as a rather lowly caste of village artisans. But the sweepers (Hindi, *bhangis*, etc.) and tanners (*chamars*) constitute the bulk of the menial landless proletariat in northern India. It seems, then, that the Satnamis were able to draw to their banner the landless menial castes along with peasants. It was obviously owing to this contamination from contact with the 'untouchables' that the sect became particularly hateful in the eyes of the orthodox. A loyal Hindu official of the Mughal government accordingly describes the Satnamis as follows:

> That community, because of its extreme dirtiness, is rendered foul, filthy and impure. Thus in their religion they do not differentiate between Hindus and Muslims. They eat pork and other disgusting things. If a dog has eaten from their bowl, they do not abstain [from eating from it] or show any revulsion.[46]

The references to pork (widely eaten by the 'menial' castes) and to the readiness to eat 'contaminated' food (again, ascribed to menial castes, who would accept even dog-touched leavings) show

---

[44] Abu'l Fazl Ma'muri, op. cit., Khafi Khan, op. cit. The word 'grain-merchants' is a literal rendering of *baqqalan* used by Abu'l Fazl Ma'muri. The term was often employed in India as a designation for the *banya*, the grain-merchant and usurer par excellence. Khafi Khan reads simply *tijarat-peshagan*, 'merchants', instead.

[45] Saqi Musta'idd Khan, *Ma'asir-i 'Alamgiri*, Bib. Ind., Calcutta, 1870–73, pp. 14–15. The text reads *zargar* (goldsmith), which I consider to be a misreading (through the simple omission of a dot) of *barzgar*, cultivators. The goldsmiths could hardly have been placed among the 'statusless' or menial castes so as to be classed with carpenters, sweepers and tanners.

[46] Mehta Isardas Nagar, *Futuhat-i 'Alamgiri*, Br. Mus. Add. 23, 884, f. 61b.

that it was not physical filth, but the presence (with their habits) of the lowest, 'unclean' people among the Satnamis that raised Isardas's ire.

The Satnamis, however small a sect, are surely of extraordinary interest in that they seem to have broken the great division of the rural oppressed in India. It is conceivable that just as the position of *banyas* was challenged by lowlier men from the ranks of the peasants, by joining a strong proselytizing casteless sect, so could the landless menial castes have been using the same instrument for entering the ranks of the peasantry.

The Satnami revolt was provoked reputedly by an incident, which again brings out its essentially peasant character. A Satnami 'engaged in cultivation in the neighbourhood of the township of Narnaul had harsh words with a [revenue collector's] foot-soldier guarding a grain heap. The foot-soldier broke the Satnami's head with a blow from his club.'[47] The Satnamis thereupon collected together, and the revolt began. It soon spread over a very large area.

The sight of the plebeian mass—'an army of a crore of villagers [*ganwars*]'[48]—taking on the armed might of the Mughal empire, excited the wonder of the quasi-official historian, Saqi Musta'idd Khan. Yet, though the Satnamis were defeated by the Mughal army—amidst enormous slaughter—the determination with which the village-folk fought won the admiration of their enemy:

> In spite of the lack of provision of materials of war, they, by their prowess, made a reality of the great deeds of valour that have been recorded in the ancient books of the Infidels [Hindus]. In the language of the people of India, the Mahabharata, which means the killing of elephants [i.e. huge slaughter] in the battle-field, was now witnessed in this testing battle.[49]

The links between peasant resistance and the Satnami rebellion find a parallel, perhaps no less visible and dramatic, in Sikhism, the great religion of the Punjab. Sikhism had a similar outlook:

---

[47] Abu'l Fazl Ma'muri, f. 148b; Khafi Khan, *Muntakhabu'l Lubab*, II, 252–53.

[48] From contemporary Hindi verses quoted in Muzaffar Husain, *Nama-i Muzaffari* (Urdu), I, Lucknow, 1917, p. 252.

[49] *Ma'asir-i 'Alamgiri*, pp. 115–16.

monotheistic, casteless, oriented towards austerity; and it too had its affinities with the popular monotheistic movement of Kabir, shown, among other things by the inclusion of large numbers of verses of the latter (along with other teachers of similar traditions) in the *Guru Granth Sahib*, the scripture of the Sikhs. Like the Satnamis, early Sikhism seemed to have made an appeal to both agricultural and mer cantile elements. The Gurus (the chief preceptors) belonged to the Khatri or mercantile caste of the Punjab;[50] the bulk of the followers came from the great peasant caste, the Jats. 'Jatt in the language of the Punjab', says an important seventeenth-century account of Sikhism, 'means a villager, a rustic'.[51] Gradually, the Jats became more and more important in the *panth* or the community organization of the Sikhs. By the mid-seventeenth century, the Gurus are said to have 'made the Khatris subservient to the Jatts, who are the lowest caste, among the *Vaishyas*. Thus most of the great *masnads* ['nobles', or agents of the Guru for collecting gifts in different localities] are Jatts'.[52]

For reasons which were partly political, the Sikh Gurus became involved in a conflict with the Mughal empire after the death of Guru Arjan Mal in 1606. Guru Hargobind (d. 1645) first began to have armed retainers; and the armed conflict with Mughals assumed a noticeable scale under the last Guru, Gobind Singh (1676–1708). So far as one can judge, the grievances against the Mughals which the Gurus gave expression to, remained religious and political. In the long versified manifesto that Guru Gobind Singh composed against Aurangzeb, there is no reference anywhere to the oppression suffered by peasants.[53] Thus, in spite of the peasant character of its leadership, 'peasant liberation' in any sense, or to any degree, does not seem to

---

[50] References to mercantile life in the Sikh religion are examined by W.H. McLeod in *Punjab Past and Present, Essays in Honour of Dr Ganda Singh*, Patiala, 1976, pp. 81-91.

[51] *Dabistan-i Mazahib*, p. 285.

[52] Ibid., p. 286. See also the report of a hostile observer: 'Most of the followers of the Guru of that perdition-bound sect belonged to the castes of Jats and Khatris of the Punjab and other lowly castes of the Infidels [Hindus]'. Khafi Khan, *Muntakhabu'l Lubab*, II, p. 656. See my comments in *Essays in Honour of Dr Ganda Singh*, p. 98.

[53] *Zafarnama*, composed AD 1706 (?), edited by Nanak Chand 'Naz', Jalandhar, 1959.

have been part of the objectives which the Sikh leaders were conscious of, or proclaimed. This is important for any understanding of the subsequent evolution of the Sikh polity.

But simply because the Sikhs' armed confrontation with the Mughal empire provided an opportunity to peasants and others to take up arms, and, through their membership of the *Khalsa* (Sikh community), improve their position, the Sikh revolt fed directly upon peasant unrest.

It also, perhaps, drew upon the unrest of still lower classes. Whereas Khafi Khan contents himself by saying that 'the masses of the lowly of the Hindus' joined the Sikh banner after 1709,[54] another contemporary historian, Warid, offers a livelier description of the plebeian nature of the Sikh revolt:

> After the slaying of Wazir Khan, he [Banda, the chief of the Sikhs] had established the rule that whoever from amongst the Hindus and Muslims became Sikhs, should all eat together; and all differences between the menial and respectable having disappeared, they united together as one. The lowliest sweeper and the *raja* of high status sharing water and food, did not harbour any hostility to each other. . . . More wonderful still, the courage and daring of the inhabitants of those regions was so much lost owing to God's decree: the lowliest sweeper or tanner—filthier than whom there is no race in Hindustan—betaking himself to attend upon that accursed one [Banda], was appointed [by him] to the government of his own city, and when returning after obtaining his deed of appointment, he reached the locality, or city or village, that moment all the respectable and leading men went to receive him, and, after his alighting, stood with folded hands before him.[55]

The Sikh movement in its historical consequences proved to be an instrument through which groups of lower classes—whether from amongst Jat peasants, or, more remarkably, from amongst the menial labourers—rose in status. Early in the nineteenth century, it was observed that 'their [the Sikhs'] great chiefs [*sardars*] are, most of them, of low birth [*razil*], such as carpenters, shoemakers and

---

54 Khafi Khan, *Muntakhabu'l Lubab*, II, p. 672.
55 Muhammad Shafi Warid, *Miratu'l Warida*, Br. Mus. MS., Add. 6579, f. 117 b.

Jats'.[56] The basic elements of the agrarian system remained unaltered; but certain lower groups forced their way up, and some from them stepped into the shoes of the Mughal *jagirdars*, as well as such *zamindars* as offered unsuccessful resistance against their pretensions.[57] In spite of the fact that peasant struggles found a reflection in Sikhism, the ultimate result, after almost a century of turmoil (the whole of the eighteenth century), was the continuance, or even reappearance, of a system of class relationships practically identical with those that had existed under Mughal rule.[58]

### IV

If the intervention of religion enlarged the scale but weakened the class nature of peasant rebellions, a similar effect was obtained by the intervention of the *zamindar* class.

There were perhaps two processes whereby the *zamindars* and peasants might come together. First, in spite of the *zamindars'* position as co-sharers in the peasants' surplus, their interests might begin to coincide with those of the peasantry, if the Mughal revenue assignees (*jagirdars*) raised the land revenue to a higher and higher pitch. An administrative manual of the early eighteenth century, already referred to, tells us that if the revenue demand on peasants was raised to an excessive level, they were forced to flee to the lands controlled by the rebellious (*zor-talab*) *zamindars*. Such *zamindars* thereby became prosperous, whereas 'the pliant revenue-paying *zamindars* [*zamindaran-i raiyati*] through losing their peasants, become poor and take to false-reporting; and there is little credibility left in

---

[56] Sayyid Ghulam Ali Khan, *Imadu's Sa'adat*, Litho, Kanpur, 1897, p. 71.

[57] Muzaffar Alam in a cyclostyled paper 'Sikh Uprisings under Banda Bahadur, 1708–1715', presented at the Indian History Congress, Waltair, 1979, contests the suggestion that Jat *zamindari* might have expanded with the rise of Sikh power. He assures the reader without any support from his evidence that 'the *zamindar* column in the *Ain* noted the intermediaries (*khidmatguzar*) and the big *zamindars* alone' (p. 7). An innocent reader might think that Abu'l Fazl uses the term *khidmatguzar* in his column heading; no, it is Muzaffar Alam translating his own English into Farsi for a hypothetical Iranian reader; and mistranslating at that, since 'intermediary' does not mean *khidmatguzar*.

[58] That this was essentially the case emerges from even such a sympathetic description of the Sikh agrarian regime as Indu Banga's *Agrarian System of the Sikhs*, New Delhi, 1978.

the profession of *zamindars*'.[59] The *zamindars,* so pressed, had little option but to escape total ruin by joining the *zor-talab* or rebellious *zamindars.* Thus the pressure of increased taxation not only fanned peasant resistance, but also compelled a large number of *zamindars* to turn to rebellion.

Second, the *zamindars* often commanded traditional loyalty from some of their peasants. It should be remembered that the *A'in-i Akbari* in its detailed census of *zamindars'* retainers counts 0.38 million cavalry and 4.28 million infantry—some 4.66 million men in all.[60] At 4.5 persons per family, the total population of the *zamindars'* armed retainers and their dependents would have been nearly 21 million. The large number suggests that many, if not most, of the retainers were really armed peasants. These served the *zamindars* either because of tax concessions or caste affinities, or (since the former often followed the latter) both. Peasants could then be drawn into adventures that a *zamindar* might undertake in pursuit of his own feuds or ambitions.

In the first of the above two forms in which the *zamindars* and peasants joined each other in rebellion, peasant distress owing to the land revenue pressure was the basic factor of the peasants' support of the *zamindar;* in the second, the struggle is essentially that of the *zamindars,* in which the peasants are primarily involved owing to customary allegiance. It is not always easy to distinguish these two forms in practice, especially since once a rebellion under a *zamindar* began even if as a reaction to the pressure of the revenue system, the *zamindar's* own ambitions (plunder and dispossession of other *zamindars*) might completely divest the uprising of its original impulse.

A study of the Jat rebellion of the Braj country (contiguous parts of western Uttar Pradesh and eastern Rajasthan) during Aurangzeb's reign (1659–1707) brings out this duality fairly clearly.

The Jats form a peasant caste of the area par excellence.[61] In the eighteenth century Shah Waliullah noted that 'the cultivators of the villages between Delhi and Agra [Akbarabad] were of the Jat

---

[59] *Hidayatu'l Qawa'id,* Maulana Azad Library (Aligarh) MS., f. 65a.

[60] *Agrarian System of Mughal India,* pp. 163–64.

[61] See James Skinner, *Tashrihu-l Aguam,* Hansi, AD 1825, Br. Mus. Add. 27, 255, f. 155a. 'These [Jats] are the real *kisans* or cultivators.'

caste'.[62] Manucci, while speaking of the Jat rebels, calls them 'villagers';[63] he also refers to them as 'peasants who rose and refused to pay their revenue'.[64]

Yet there were Jat *zamindars* already when the *A'in-i Akbari's* great statistical tables were compiled (*c.* 1595), though their number in the region of the rebellion was not large: 6 out of 32 *parganas* in *sarkar* Agra have Jats entered as *zamindars*, 1 out of 21 in Kol, 1 out of 41 in Alwar, 2 out of 16 in Narnaul, but 5 out of 6 in Sahar.[65] The number was larger in the Delhi province (which, however, remained largely unaffected by the rebellion). The principal successive leaders of the Jat rebellion were incontestably *zamindars*. The first, Gokula Jat, was a *zamindar* of Talpat, who had 'raised a rebellion by bringing together a large body of Jats and other villagers'.[66] Chauraman (d. 1721) was the son of a '*zamindar-malik*' of 11 villages, with an assessed revenue of Rs 8,000.[67] Of Suraj Mal (d. 1762), under whom the Jat kingdom reached its greatest extent, it is said that 'in spite of speaking Braj and wearing the costume of a *zamindar*, he [Suraj Mal] was possessed of an intelligence, which made him a Plato among his people.'[68]

The caste basis and the *zamindar* leadership left their firm imprints on the rebellion. The village menials, for one, remained outside the pale and subject to any arbitrary action. Thus Chauraman 'built a mud-fort surrounded by a ditch. . . . He named it Bharatpur. He seized a number of *Chamars* [tanners], who are called the menials of the Hindus, from different villages, and entrusted [the up-keep of] the ditch to them.'[69] The implication that the *chamars* were a servile community, who could be forcibly made to do anything for the *zamindar,* is here unmistakable.

The notable consequence of the Jat rebellion seems to have been a significant expansion in Jat *zamindari*. We have seen that in

[62] Shah Waliullah, Letters, selected and edited with Urdu translation by K.A. Nizami: *Shah Waliullah ke Siyasi Maktubat,* Aligarh, 1950.

[63] *Storia de Mogor,* I, pp. 132–34; II, p. 319.

[64] Ibid., II, p. 223.

[65] See the table on pp. 100–1 of *Essays in Honour of Dr Ganda Singh.*

[66] Isardas, *Futuhat-i Alamgiri,* f. 53a.

[67] *Imadu's Sa'adat,* pp. 54–55.

[68] Ibid., p. 55.

[69] *Imadu's Sa'adat,* p. 55.

the Agra province the extent of areas under Jat *zamindars* was quite
limited at the end of the sixteenth century. About the mid-eighteenth
century, a Muslim divine gave testimony to its great enlargement.
'The lands that the Jats have brought into their possession are not
their own, but have been usurped from others. The [rightful] proprietors [*malikan*] can still be found.'[70] Maps of castes holding
'*zamindari* possession' drawn by Henry M. Elliot for the time of the
*A'in-i Akbari* (*c.* 1595) and for 1844 show how significant indeed had
been the growth of the area under Jat *zamindars* in the middle Doab
during the intervening period.[71] In this process many upper peasants
probably turned *zamindars,* and those who were petty *zamindars*
extended their rights over larger areas.

Here, perhaps, we can claim to have a detailed illustration
of the historical tendency ascribed to peasant resistance in Mughal
India, the tendency towards the merger of the rising of the oppressed
with the struggle between two oppressing classes, namely, the *zamindars* and the Mughal revenue appropriators.[72]

But the Jat revolt does not by any means provide the only
illustration of such transformation of peasant resistance. The great
political and military power that shook the Mughal empire and
hastened its collapse was that of the Marathas. In modern writings on
the rise of Maratha power, there has long been a tendency to attribute
to the Marathas a nationalistic fervour, and, as the cause of nationalism was often linked with economic welfare, to project Shivaji as
a great protector of the peasants, and as one who suppressed 'feudal'
potentates.[73] This view has now been subjected to fundamental criticism, and it has been shown that the Maratha leaders were greatly
motivated by *zamindari* traditions, their ambitions being largely
circumscribed accordingly.[74]

[70] Shah Waliullah, *Letters*, pp. 50–51.

[71] H.M. Elliot, *Races of the North Western Provinces of India*, edited by
John Beames, London.

[72] *Agrarian System of Mughal India*, p. 333.

[73] M.G. Ranade's *Rise of the Maratha Power*, Bombay, 1900, offers an early
interpretation of Shivaji on these lines; for Shivaji's opposition to 'feudal
landlords', see ibid., pp. 129–30.

[74] Satish Chandra, 'Social Background to the Rise of the Maratha Movement
during the Seventeenth Century', *Indian Economic and Social History
Review*, Delhi, X, 3 (1973) pp. 209–17; P.V. Ranade, 'Feudal Content of

But what is of singular interest from our point of view is the fact that the Maratha armies were of a different kind from the armies of the Mughal empire or the Deccan Sultanate. This difference lay in the *bargi,* the ill-clad, ill-armed marauding Maratha soldier, his advantage lying solely in numbers and the ability for dispersed warfare.

In 1575–76 Fryer gave a comparative description of the troops of the Bijapur Sultanate and those of Shivaji: those of Bijapur, with equipage, servants and fine horses; those of Shivaji, 'all Naked Starved Rascals', but 'fitter for any Martial Exploit, having been accustomed to Fare Hard, Journey Fast and take little Pleasure'.[75] Manucci remembered that the early Maratha troops had 'only lances and long swords two inches wide'.[76] Such equipment did not require large resources. The *bargis* were essentially lance-weilding peasants riding on country ponies.

> It came to be represented [to the Emperor Aurangzeb, 1659–1707] that the Marathas obtained collaboration from the peasants [*muzari'an*] of the Imperial dominions. It was thereupon ordered that the horses and weapons found in every village should be confiscated. When this happened in many villages, the peasants, providing themselves with horses and arms, joined the Marathas.[77]

Writing in 1762–63, another historian put the contrast in the composition of the Maratha and the Mughal armies in resonantly clear class terms:

> The army of the enemy [Marathas] consists mostly of low-born people like peasants, shepherds, carpenters and cobblers, while the army of the Muslims comprises mostly nobles and gentlemen. The success of the enemy is due to this that the enemy troops, being able to withstand great exertion, practise guerrilla warfare [*jang-i qaz-zaqi*] and at the time of war cut off the supplies of grain and fodder of their opponent, reducing him to impotence, . . . although there

Maharashtra Dharma', *Indian Historical Review,* I (1974), Delhi, pp. 44–50. Also see *Agrarian System of Mughal India,* pp. 349–50.
[75] John Fryer, *A New Account of East India and Persia being Nine Years' Travels, 1672–81,* II, edited by W. Grooke, London, 1912, pp. 66–68.
[76] Manucci, *Storia de Mogor,* III, p. 505.
[77] Bhimsen, *Nuskha-i Dilkusha,* Br. Mus. Or. 23, f. 139a–b.

is no question of the low-born's possessing the courage and dignity
that is ingrained in the nature of the noble-born.[78]

The Marathas thus had *zamindar* leaders, and peasant armies. Their strength derived from the degree to which pressure of
circumstance—initially the land revenue demand—drove the peasant
to change his sedentary life for at least that of a seasonal soldier,
where there was no pay, only the risk of death and the prospects of
plunder.[79] Under the Marathas peasant resistance is therefore completely submerged: the potential peasant rebel becomes a *bargi*
trooper of the Maratha *sardars*.

Once the war began between the Marathas and the Mughals,
the conditions of the peasantry could only worsen further. The conduct of the Mughal army in the Maratha territories is thus described
by a contemporary observer (1675):

> laying waste all in their road, both villages, fodder, and corn; and
> for their cattle they drive them along with them, and take them,
> their wives and children for slaves; so that none escape except those
> that can fly fastest, or hide themselves in the woods, which they also
> set on fire, to leave them destitute of those recesses.[80]

In the Mughal-held territories, conditions of peasants became
equally intolerable because the Marathas levied their tribute in addition to the Mughal land revenue demand. Further, 'the troops of the
Marathas who come in for the sake of plundering the country, extort
money from every *pargana*, in accordance with their desire and let
[their horses] graze on and trample upon the cultivated fields.'[81]

Shivaji was not a liberator of the peasants, his administration
was no less repressive than that of the Mughals: he 'left the Tiller
hardly so much as will keep Life and Soul together', in the heartland
of his own kingdom.[82] Indeed, unbearable conditions within his

---

[78] Mir Ghulam Ali Azad Husaini, Bilgrami, *Khizana-i Amira*, litho, Kanpur,
1871, p. 49.
[79] Fryer, *A New Account*, I, p. 341. This applied, of course, only to the *bargis*.
Shivaji and his successors also maintained conventionally paid, better
equipped cavalry and artillery.
[80] Fryer, *A New Account*, I, p. 310.
[81] Bhimsen, *Nuskha-i Dilkusha*, f. 139b.
[82] Fryer, *A New Account*, I, pp. 311–12; also p. 66.

kingdom could hardly do him much harm, for these would, if anything, compel a larger number of peasants to turn to him and serve
him as *bargis*. Inevitably, then, as the circle of oppression and depre-
dations on both sides grew, the Marathas went on gaining with their
numbers swelling, and the cause of the Mughals was more and more
irretrievably lost. And yet while the Mughal empire found, at last, its
nemesis, the peasantry found no saviour.

**V**

When we pass from the rural scene to the urban, the great
social tensions seem to be left behind. It was not that the towns lacked
misery. Pelsaert has helpfully left behind a description of the diet and
living conditions of 'workmen' at Agra about 1616,[83] and this leaves
little doubt of the prevalence of poverty in its extreme form.

If the town artisan and labourer are yet seldom seen in conflict with the Mughal ruling classes, the explanation perhaps partly
lies in the fact that unlike the peasants, they did not see taxation as
directly consuming a major portion of their product. The duties and
tolls were a burden, undoubtedly, and Kabir the weaver-saint, be-
wails the oppressiveness of the *jagatis,* the collectors of tolls[84]—but
these exactions were not of the same magnitude as the land tax.

The artisan's grievances against the Mughal administration
thus were usually of a transitory character, when harassed by actions
such as the imposition of a monopoly or demand for low-paid, forced
labour, or, again, a new tax or exaction. As with the peasant, the
artisan's major passive weapon was flight.

In 1622, the Governor of Cambay having imposed a tax on
brokerage, the merchants and brokers refused to conduct business.
The result was that the 'poor weavers cannot worke, beinge they
cannott vend whatt they make. Foure days since they hoping to have
redress by complayninge to the Governor: instead of justice which
hee should give, unjustly whipt and imprysoned since [some?] and the
rest run awaye.'[85] It is a pity that we are not told whether the weavers
here acted in unison spontaneously, or possessed some primitive caste

[83] *Jahangir's India,* pp. 60–61.
[84] Verses in *Guru Granth Sahib*, II, Devanagari edition, Amritsar, 1951–
52, pp. 1194–95.
[85] *English Factories in India, 1622–23,* pp. 169–70.

or community organization controlling their response to the particular situation.

To such artisans as sold their wares in shops (e.g., goldsmiths, silversmiths, etc.), the traditional Indian method of *hartal* was also available. The Hindi term (*hat-tal*) is actually given in the eighteenth-century dictionary *Bahar-i Ajam*[86] as signifying a closure of shops. When a prominent *banya* merchant was ill-treated by the Customer of Surat in 1616, 'the whole multitude assembled, shutt up their shopps, and (as their custome), after a generall complaynt to the Governour left the cittie pretending to goe to the courte for justice; but with much faire usage and fairer promises were fetcht back by Abram Chan [the Governor].'[87]

In the same city, in 1669, there was a similar closure of shops in protest against the oppressive conduct of a *qazi* (Muslim judge):

> The people in Surat suffered great want, for, the Bannians having bound themselves under severe penalties not to open any of their shops without order from their Mahager [*mahajan*] or Generall Councill, there was not any provisions to bee gott; the tanksall [mint] and custom house shut; no mony to be procured. . . .[88]

Here the reference to the *mahajan* establishes the existence of a caste council which had decreed the closure. It was apparently a stable body, since in 1672 we find it negotiating for better privileges for the 'Banians' at Bombay.[89]

For the *banyas* a closure of shops was a very effective weapon because they formed such a large portion of shopkeepers. But artisans who worked at home and sold their wares mainly to merchants, could hardly resort to this form of agitation. Nor could the large number

---

[86] Tek Chand 'Bahar', *Bahar-i Ajam* (many editions), s.v. *dar bandan*.

[87] W. Foster, *A Supplementary Calendar of Documents in the India Office relating to India or to the Home Affairs of the East India Company, 1600–1640*, London, 1928, p. 68. Another description of a general shop-closure by shopkeepers of Jodhpur in 1681 is in the official monthly reports from Ajmer, *Waqai Ajmer*, I, transcript in Department of History Library, Aligarh, I, p. 199.

[88] *English Factories in India, 1668–69*, p. 192.

[89] *Selections from the Letters, Despatches and other State Papers preserved in the Bombay Secretariat*, I, Home Series, edited by G.W. Forrest, Bombay, 1887, pp. 46–47.

of labourers and servants of all kinds who constituted the larger portion of the town population.

In taking a general view of the class conflicts that were generated in Mughal society, we may say, then, that the violent forms were practically confined to the villages. Every revenue-collection operation was a minor military expedition even in the usual routine of Mughal administration; at any time the countryside might seethe with discontent and rebellion as the pressure of demand became too heavy. I have argued previously that the pressure increased in course of time, and that an 'agrarian crisis' developed in the Mughal empire during the reign of Aurangzeb.[90] Since any increase in revenue pressure would intensify peasant resistance, it would not be wrong to look for peasant revolts of the kind that Mao Tse-tung proudly owned for China,[91] the 1381 revolt in England, and the Peasant War in Germany of the sixteenth century.

The agrarian rebellions we have analysed are thus the counterparts of these celebrated uprisings of two other civilizations. But an important deficiency in the Indian revolts immediately presents itself: the low development of self-recognition by the peasantry as a class. There is little in India to compare with the repeated demands for reduction of the land tax in China, or the rhymes of the Kentish peasants of 1381:

> When Adam delved and Eve span
> Who was then the Gentleman?

Or, the Twelve Articles of the German peasants of 1525. There is indeed little explicit in Indian agrarian revolts about the brotherhood of the peasants or about tangible concessions to be secured for the advantage of the peasantry.

The apparent limitation needs explanation. It may be that the slogans raised by the illiterate peasants were totally lost, left unrecorded by the hostile scribes of the ruling class. It is more likely, perhaps, that the limitation is real, not only apparent. The slogans we hope to find might never have been raised. Could it be that the peasantry was so intensely divided on caste lines, and so heavily

---

[90] *The Agrarian System of Mughal India*, pp. 315–51.
[91] Mao Tse-tung, *Selected Works of Mao Tse-tung*, III, English translation, London, 1954, pp. 75–76.

differentiated, that the idea of equality at any plane—essential for any recognizable level of class consciousness—could not flourish? Only in the religious communities of the Satnamis and the Sikhs, can we discern a little of the glimmering caused by its germination. Another possible factor obscuring peasant consciousness was the intervention of the *zamindar* class. In so far as their own contradictions with the Mughal ruling class coalesced with the unrest of the peasants, the pretensions and prejudices of the *zamindars* might well have dominated and even determined the peasants' appraisal of the cause for which they had risen.

An aura of tragedy surrounds all lower-class uprisings before modern times; those in India are, naturally, no exception. That a recognition of what they were fighting for could not reach their ordinary starving partisans, as they fell or were defrauded, only adds to the extent of tragedy; it can never exclude these lowly men from a lasting place in the history of the Indian people.

# Processes of Accumulation
# in Pre-Colonial and Colonial India

### Forms of Pre-Colonial Accumulation

It hardly needs repeating that Karl Marx greatly enriched the concept of 'accumulation' just as he so crucially defined the meaning of capital. The accumulation of capital takes place within capitalist production, as the result of a continuously extending scale of production. Yet an extending scale of production in other social formations did not imply accumulation of capital.

> In the economic forms of society of the most different kinds, there occurs not simple reproduction, but, in varying degrees, reproduction on a progressively increasing scale.... This process, however, does not present itself as accumulation of capital, nor as the function of a capitalist so long as the labourer's means of production, and with them, his product and means of subsistence do not confront him in the shape of capital.[1]

This passage, however, ought not to be construed to mean that though there was an expansion of production, there was no accumulation of productive resources at all before the appearance of capital. In the economy of antiquity, the accumulation would be of slaves. Raiding barbarian communities to obtain slaves was often a characteristic form of such accumulation: witness Julius Caesar's invasion of Britain. The enlargement of the demesne and the progressive conversion of peasants into serfs could be the specific feudal form of accumulation. Indeed, one may argue that in defining an economic formation, the forms of accumulation are no less important than the forms

[1] Karl Marx, *Capital*, I, edited by Dona Torr, London, 1938, pp. 609–10.

of labour process (e.g., serf, slave, wage labour), though both are intimately connected. Capital accumulation, then, is only one of many possible modes of accumulation.

It is of some theoretical interest that the illustration that Marx cited, of a 'reproduction on a progressively increasing scale' achieved without any capital accumulation, comes from India; it was borrowed by him from Richard Jones:

> The non-agricultural labourers in those provinces where the English rule has least disturbed the old system, are directly employed by the magnates, to whom a portion of the agricultural surplus product is rendered in the shape of tribute or rent. One portion of this product is consumed by the magnates in kind, another is converted, for their use, by the labourers into articles of luxury and such-like things; while the rest forms the wages of the labourers, who own their implements of labour. Here, production and reproduction on a progressively increasing scale, go on their way without any intervention from that queer saint, that knight of woeful countenance, the capitalist 'abstainer'.[2]

Clearly, reproduction on a progressively increasing scale could take place here only if the absolute size of surplus product that was partly converted into craft products and partly consumed as wages by the labourers, increased constantly. This increase—unless the magnates constantly reduced the share of the surplus product directly consumed by themselves—could come only out of constantly increasing the revenues of the magnate. This, in turn, implied either an increase of the proportion of total agricultural product taken as 'tribute or rent' or an increase in the total number of peasants and the area of land cultivated by them (or an improvement in cropping), leading, in both cases, to an increase in the absolute size of tribute/ rent. Land revenue or rent enhancement would thus be the basic form of accumulation here, with no intervention of capital.

There would still be no intervention of capital in the main relationship, even if commodity relations were to replace the 'natural' relations implicit in Marx's illustration. The peasants would now pay the rent not in kind but in money; and the 'magnate' would accord-

---

[2] Ibid., p. 610.

ingly accumulate wealth in the form of money, by which he would buy craft products or employ artisans on money wages and buy materials for their work in the market.[3] Yet the engine of reproduction on a progressive scale, i.e. accumulation, would still be the expansion of land tax or rent and not the cyclical investment of capitalist profits.

While these two forms of rent/tax accumulation, one in kind, the other in commodities, are both pre-capitalistic, they are by no means identical. It is surely erroneous to lump these and other intermediate forms under a single 'tributary mode of production' (a name coined by Samir Amin);[4] Wolf goes so far as to include feudalism under such a mode;[5] and Chris Wickham would chop each of the above two cases into two, according as the accumulation was of net rent (i.e. rent less land tax), when it would be 'feudal', or of land tax, when it would belong to the 'tributary mode'.[6] In neither case is the intervention of commodity relations deemed to be of basic significance. And yet this was of crucial importance in the eyes of Marx himself. He believed, on the one hand, that grain rent 'furnished the basis for stationary social conditions, as we see, e.g., in Asia';[7] and, on the other, that, with money rent, 'the character of the entire mode of production is ... more or less changed'.[8] Clearly, in terms of Marx's own appraisal, the two forms of rent/tax accumulation that we have described cannot be said to represent a single mode of production. The acceptance of Marx's view on this matter does not follow any compulsive allegiance to his judgement, but rests on the specific consequences of both kinds of rent that he so persuasively sets out in his chapters on the genesis of ground rent in *Capital*, Volume III.

[3] Intervention of commodity relations of an intermediate kind in India was recognized by Marx himself when he wrote that in pre-colonial India 'it is the surplus alone that becomes a commodity and a portion of even that not until it has reached the hands of the state into whose hands from time immemorial a certain quantity of these products has found its way in the shape of rent in kind.' Ibid., p. 351.

[4] *Unequal Development*, translated by B. Pearce, Delhi, 1979, pp. 13–16.

[5] Eric R. Wolf, *Europe and the People without History*, Berkeley, 1982, pp. 79–88.

[6] *Journal of Peasant Studies*, 8 (3), April 1981, pp. 166ff.

[7] *Capital*, III, English translation, Moscow, 1959, p. 776. Also see Marx, *Capital*, I, edited by Dona Torr, p. 118.

[8] Ibid., p. 777.

Our present concern is with the slot into which we would put accumulation based on tax rent in Mughal India, which we may suppose to represent the last of the pre-colonial economies in India.

It is now the standard view of historians that the cash-nexus was quite general in pre-colonial India, where the tax formed a large part of the peasant's surplus produce. Moreland firmly stated in 1929 that 'the view that it [the cash-nexus] is a modern phenomenon must be rejected as unhistorical', and he pointed out that Barani's statements about Alauddin Khalji's revenue measures implied that the peasants around Delhi paid their land tax in money as early as the thirteenth century.[9] W.C. Smith in 1944 emphasized the importance of the cash-nexus in the Mughal system, and K. Antonova did so in 1957.[10] I have collected evidence on the medium of payment of land revenue in the various regions of the Mughal empire, and the conclusion is that while payment in kind often occurred, money payments generally predominated.[11] Detailed documentary evidence from seventeenth- and eighteenth-century Rajasthan tends to rein-force this conclusion, for even where the tax was theoretically assessed in kind, the ultimate realization was in money.[12] In his famous Minute of 18 June 1789, Sir John Shore noted that the *ryots* in Bengal normally paid their rents in cash;[13] and it was as yet too early for the English to have altered the basic agrarian relationships.

Despite its seeming predominance, however, money rent did not entirely detach itself from grain rent in Mughal India. Land tax (*mal*) was deemed to be a share of the produce and to be imposed on the crop rather than the land.[14] This meant that land revenue could

[9] W.H. Moreland, *Agrarian System of Moslem India*, Cambridge, 1929, p. 11.

[10] W.C. Smith in *Islamic Culture*, 1944, pp. 358–59; K. Antonova, as cited by V. Pavlov, *The Indian Capitalist Class: A Historical Study*, English edition, Delhi, 1964, p. 10.

[11] Irfan Habib, *Agrarian System of Mughal India*, Bombay, 1963, pp. 236–40.

[12] Satya Prakash Gupta, *Agrarian System of Eastern Rajasthan c. 1650–1750*, Delhi, 1986, pp. 100–2.

[13] 'In general throughout Bengal, the rents are paid by the ryots in money.' *Fifth Report from the Select Committee on the Affairs of the East India Company*, Appendix I, paragraph 226, p. 192 of the original printing.

[14] See Irfan Habib, 'Potentialities of Capitalistic Development in the Economy of Mughal India', *Enquiry*, NS, III (3), pp. 8–9; pp. 180–232 of this volume.

be raised if prices increased in the long run, and there could be shifts to grain-sharing.[15] And yet the tax in cash was fixed for sufficiently long periods for 'low prices' to take their due place alongside 'fall in produce, drought and blight', in an imperial list of agricultural calamities.[16] Obviously, a fall in prices prevented peasants from meeting their money assessments as much as crop-failures did.

It should be inferred, then, that a large part of the surplus payable as tax was drawn out of the peasant economy in the form of commodities. Once this happened, it was bound to affect certain subordinate modes of accumulation existing side by side with the dominant mode based on rent extraction.

The first point at which subordinate accumulation occurred was at the level of peasant production. We have been introduced to a *khasra* document of a village in eastern Rajasthan, for the autumn harvest of 1796. Here the area is given for *zabti* crops and the total yield for the other (*jinsi*) crops. Out of 38 peasants (*asami*), 2 *patels* (headmen) raised respectively six and seven crops in that harvest (both raising cotton), while at the other end were 10 peasants growing a single inferior grain with their total production less than that of either of the 2 *patels*.[17] One must assume, almost as a matter of course, that the *patels* employed servants or wage labourers.

A description of such 'superior' peasant cultivation comes from an early nineteenth-century Persian text, written in the Agra province and largely reflecting conditions prevailing before the English annexation (1803):

> Most of the *muqaddams*, who organize their cultivation [*khwud-kasht*], engage wage labourers as servants, and set them to agricultural work. Making them do the ploughing, sowing, reaping, and watering of [the field] from the well, they pay their fixed wages either in cash or in kind. The crop of the field belongs to them, so that they are *muqaddams* as well as *asamis* [ordinary peasants].[18]

---

[15] Irfan Habib, *Agrarian System of Mughal India*, pp. 236–39.

[16] Aurangzeb's *farman* to Rasikdas, Preamble. For the various copies of this *farman*, see Irfan Habib, *Agrarian System of Mughal India*, p. 415.

[17] See S.P. Gupta, 'Khasra Documents in Rajasthan', *Medieval India—A Miscellany*, IV, 1977, pp. 171–76.

[18] Chhatar Mal, *Diwan Pasand*, British Library MS., Or. 2011, ff. 7b–8a. The work has documents dated 1213 to 1216 Fasli, or AD 1804–8.

Payment of 'wages either in cash or in kind' reminds us that the peasant-employers were commodity producers and thus enabled to pay their labourers in money. Cultivation with the aid of hired labour as a consequence of money rent was visualized by Marx himself, for he wrote that 'the custom necessarily develops among the more prosperous peasants, subject to [money] rent payments, of exploiting agricultural wage labourers for their own account'. This, in turn, naturally presupposes 'the formation of a class of propertyless day labourers who hire themselves out for money'.[19]

An interesting aspect of Indian agrarian history is that a class of wage labourers would seem to have been created by the Indian caste system in antiquity out of the 'food-gathering' folk originally subdued by agricultural communities, long before money rent could have developed.[20] The use of hired labour for field work appears in Manu, the *Kamasutra* and I-tsing's description of cultivation by Indian Buddhist monasteries.[21] The existence of a large class of landless labourers consisting mainly of the menial or untouchable castes, is borne out by Mughal-period documents, and richly corroborated by British revenue and census evidence of the nineteenth century.[22] The class of rural labourers in India did not thus 'appear . . . sporadically' with money rent (Marx) but was already in full formation, since its original creation and continuance was due not to the operation of market ('economic') forces but to social or caste ('non-economic') compulsion. Conversely, the rich peasant accumulation even when it obtained a money/commodity form, rested on dominance over a subject (not 'free') proletariat. But money relations must have strongly reinforced this originally 'non-economic' dominance, through intensifying differentiation among the peasantry.

At the same time, since the land tax levied on the peasant in pre-colonial India seldom assumed for long periods the shape of a constant contractual obligation, rich peasant accumulation was almost always vulnerable to fiscal pressure. In so far as increase in non-

---

[19] *Capital*, III, p. 779.
[20] This is the argument advanced in my address 'The Peasant in Indian History', Indian History Congress, Kurukshetra session, 1982, pp. 15–17. See pp. 109–60 of this volume.
[21] Ibid., pp. 22–23.
[22] Irfan Habib, *Agrarian System of Mughal India*, pp. 120–22.

agricultural production was based on the expansion of tax-rent resources, the differentiation intensified by money rent went on side by side with the levelling and pauperization caused by increased revenue demand.[23]

The second point at which subordinate accumulation could occur was when the tax-rent was appropriated, in part, by the *zamindars* (a convenient term which the Mughal administration employed, from the later years of Akbar, for various categories of persons possessing some claim to hereditary perquisites and shares in the land revenue on condition of collecting it or assisting in its collection). It would seem that, according to a standard recognized by the administration, the *zamindar* claimed an income outside the land revenue which amounted to one-tenth of the land revenue.[24] In addition, he claimed another one-tenth of land revenue as *nankar*, or allowance for collecting revenue. In other words, his formal share of the total surplus ('rental') was about 18.2 per cent. The actual share was likely to be considerably higher. In this respect my earlier, rather lower, estimate of the formally recognized share of the *zamindar* needs to be corrected.[25] In Gujarat it could in some tracts amount to a fourth of the land revenue.[26]

It may be supposed that being local men, the *zamindars* would derive their income mainly in kind. Quite possibly, this was sometimes the case: thus they collected a grain levy and a copper coin

---

[23] Irfan Habib in *Enquiry*, NS, III(3), pp. 13–14. Harbans Mukhia protests against this dialectical duality in *Feudalism and Non-European Societies*, edited by T. J. Byres and Harbans Mukhia, London, 1985, p. 241. A further word of explanation on my part, therefore, seems called for. Regressive land tax would intensify differentiation, as I had argued (*Enquiry*), but if the absolute size of the tax went on increasing it would begin to destroy superior cultivation as well, because the cost of superior cultivation per acre would always be higher than that of small-peasant cultivation.

[24] This was what was designated *malikana*. Since it was outside of the land revenue proper, the early English officials were correct in formally regarding the *zamindar's* own, proper hereditary share to be no more than one-eleventh of the total rental.

[25] *Agrarian System of Mughal India*, pp. 144–54. S. Moosvi, 'Zamindars' Share in the Peasant Surplus', *Indian Economic and Social History Review* (*IESHR*), XV(3), pp. 360–61, 371–72, argues for a large income of the *zamindars* (a third of the land revenue) on the basis of ratio of sale prices to land revenue and the *zamindars'* expenditure on their armed retainers.

[26] *Agrarian System of Mughal India*, pp. 141–43, 147–49.

from every *bigha* of land in a locality of Awadh.[27] And they paid their retainers in a locality of the Doab 'by grant of land or in cash'.[28] Yet over most of northern India, *zamindari* rights were being freely sold for money.[29] That there should be sufficient amount of money in the hands of prospective buyers of *zamindari* rights suggests the presence of commodity resources in the hands of such buyers, who themselves were usually *zamindars*. The prices, wherever they can be related to annual land revenue, were rather modest, not rising above two-and-a-half times the revenue.[30] This obviously represented the 'capitalized' value of the *zamindar's* income which then must have been distinctly lower in comparison with the land revenue.

It has not been established so far that the *zamindars* used their money income to invest substantially in agriculture under their own auspices. They probably advanced *taqavi* (taccavi) loans to peasants.[31] This was supposed to help accumulation by way of tax-rent, since the loans enabled the peasant to raise his crop and pay the tax; but often enough the rates of repayment concealed usurious interest.[32] Such usury simply paralleled rent accumulation and had no other result than depressing peasant agriculture further. This would essentially be the case, too, when the usurers lending to peasants were persons other than *zamindars*.[33] Here, where the usurers were grain merchants, we might have had what Amit Bhaduri has called 'forced commerce', which he believes sprang, first, from an excessive tax/tribute demand, and then flourished side by side with, and even at the cost of, tribute extraction.[34]

The *zamindars* themselves borrowed from the merchant-usurers (the *mahajan, banya* or *baqqal*), and *zamindari* rights could

---

[27] Ibid., p. 145.

[28] Ibid., p. 167.

[29] Ibid., pp. 157–59.

[30] *Cambridge Economic History of India*, I, p. 245 and n 154.

[31] See document described in Irfan Habib, *Agrarian System of Mughal India*, p. 133 (though the person advancing the *taqavi* loan here is a *muqaddam*).

[32] Yasin's glossary of revenue terms (latter half of eighteenth century), Br.Mus.Add. 6603, f. 54a. Also see Irfan Habib, 'Usury in Medieval India', *Comparative Studies in Society and History (CSSH)*, IV(4), p. 39.

[33] Ibid., pp. 394–95.

[34] Amit Bhaduri, *The Economic Structure of Backward Agriculture*, London, 1983, pp. 9–11.

be mortgaged.[35] However, to judge from the *A'in's* list of the *zamindar* castes in various localities, the actual acquisition of *zamindaris* by members of the *banya* caste, c. 1595, was very limited—far less than that of the secretarial caste of Kayasths.[36] This probably shows that though money gained from commerce could be lent to *zamindars*, the moneylenders did not necessarily themselves become *zamindars:* they could sell the foreclosed *zamindaris* to others.[37] Whether such operations added in the net to merchant capital, by transfer of usurious gains to the *banyas'* trading operations, is by no means certain, for the net transfer could be in the reverse direction as well. If trading gains, in the net, went into usury, this would ultimately strengthen rent accumulation as either the *zamindars* were better enabled to transmit land revenue to the state or the usurers themselves would become *zamindars* so that the state's claims would continue to be met.

The transmission of the revenue to the hands of the state, or, specifically, the king in the *khalisa*, and the individual nobles in their *jagirs*, created the basis for extensive circulation of commodities, which, as we have seen, Marx implicitly recognized in his passage on the village community in *Capital*, Volume I. The agricultural surplus, in a large part, obtained a money form in the hands of the ruling class. This meant that the surplus product would be sold to merchants in the villages and conveyed by them to towns, where it would find a market by the expenditure of their money income by the potentates. This circuit involved not only sale of agricultural production, but an extensive craft production for the urban market, with the merchants as intermediaries. It necessarily presupposed an enormous amount of merchant capital, involved in internal trade alone.[38]

Since the artisan may be as much capable of turning out surplus product (that is, product whose value is higher than the value

[35] *CSSH*, IV (4), pp. 397–98; *IESHR*, IV(3), pp. 216–17.

[36] The *baqqals* (*banyas*) appear as *zamindars* in one *pargana* of *sarkar* Alwar (Agra), one of *sarkar* Chanderi (Malwa) and two of Bari Doab (Lahore); this completes the list.

[37] As was possibly the case recorded in the document of 1611 calendared in *IESHR*, IV(3), p. 231.

[38] I do not go into details here, because I have already attempted a description of conditions of craft production and size of merchant capital in *Enquiry*, NS, III(3), pp. 22–53. See also Tapan Raychaudhuri's chapter on 'Inland Trade' in *Cambridge Economic History of India*, I, pp. 324–59.

of goods needed for the subsistence of the artisan and his family) as the peasant, the form of accumulation of resources out of the artisan's surplus product must be investigated. Where, as in Marx's simplified illustration, the 'magnate' himself furnished the raw materials and grain wages to the artisan,[39] he acquired by this simple means the artisan's surplus product as well. It is to be observed that this was, indeed, the case in the *karkhanas* of the kings and nobles, where the artisans came and worked on materials supplied to them, the products belonging to their masters, and consumed by them and their dependants without appearing on the market.[40] Here the product went into consumption, as embodiment of use value; but there was no exchange, and therefore no creation of that surplus value, out of which capitalist profit is realized. Thus though these workshops may suggest analogies with Marx's 'manufactory', they were in reality the very antithesis of a capitalist enterprise, since they generated surplus product but no surplus value.

The aristocratic *karkhanas* must have furnished, however, only a part of the needs of the court and aristocracy. They and their dependants largely bought on the market. Here the surplus was already embodied in the value at which the commodity was sold. The surplus product could not here be obtained by members of the ruling class, who outside the *karkhanas*, only appeared as consumers and buyers.[41]

The conditions of urban artisan production approximated heavily to the 'petty mode of production' that Marx outlines as the predecessor of the capitalist mode:

> The private property of the labourer in his means of production is the foundation of petty industry, whether agricultural, manufacturing or both.... Of course, this petty mode of production exists also under slavery, serfdom and other states of dependence. But it

---

[39] *Capital*, I, p. 610.

[40] *Enquiry*, NS, III(3), pp. 44–45.

[41] I ignore here the income that the ruling class obtained by taxing the artisans. Such taxation, though undoubtedly irksome, was light when compared with the land tax. For a description of their irksomeness, based on documents from Rajasthan, see Harbans Mukhia, 'Illegal Extortions from Peasants, Artisans and Menials in Eighteenth Century Rajasthan', *IESHR*, XIV(2), pp. 237–39.

flourishes, it lets loose its whole energy, it attains its adequate classical form, only where the labourer is the private owner of his own means of labour set in action by himself: the peasant of the land which he cultivates, the artisan of the tool which he handles as a virtuoso.[42]

Marx's words exclude slavery and serfdom from the 'petty mode', which became universal only when those and other relations of dependence for the individual ceased. It is a matter for consideration whether, when the peasant was subjected to a tax-rent and certain personal constraints, as in Mughal India, he could still be said to belong to the rank of petty producers in Marx's classical sense. But surely the artisans of Mughal Indian towns, untainted by slavery or any visible forms of dependence, should qualify.

If we take weavers as representatives of the class of artisans, we find that large numbers of them took their cloth to the local market (*ganj*); others, perhaps the more prosperous, would even have the cloth washed and 'whited', to take to the principal mart.[43] The purchasers could be the consumers directly; but for all goods made for distant markets, merchants were the principal buyers. The second form occurred when the merchants, in order to ensure supply, advanced loans to weavers to enable them to buy yarn. This, known as the *dadani* system in Bengal, was universal throughout India.[44] A putting-out system proper, with yarn or silk supplied, instead of money advances, seems to have arisen naturally from this system of advances.[45]

It need not be assumed that in the first of these two forms the weaver obtained the true value of his product. This was partly because of the merchant's dominance of the market and partly because of the weaver's own dependence on the usurer. As the weaver-saint Kabir sang:

[42] *Capital*, I, p. 787.
[43] This is what happened in respect of 'amberti' (*amriti*) calicoes, brought to Lakhawar, the local *ganj*, by ordinary weavers, but taken by the more enterprising weavers to Patna. *English Factories in India,1618–21*, edited by W. Foster, pp. 192–93.
[44] For a sample of references, see *Enquiry*, NS, III(3), p. 43, n. 32.
[45] Ibid., pp. 43–44.

Kabir, the capital belongs to the *Sah* (Usurer, God); and you waste it all.

There will be great difficulty for you at the time of rendering of accounts.[46]

The gains of the usurer eating into the surplus value would have been still more considerable where the merchant turned usurer by advancing money, and by setting prices beforehand at which the cloth would be bought.

Much of the artisan's surplus product thus passed in the form of 'surplus value' into the hands of the merchants and merchant moneylenders.[47] It constituted the basic form of accumulation of merchant capital involved in commerce outside agricultural trade. The enormous extent of merchant capital in India, with fairly sophisticated forms of commercial credit, deposit-banking and insurance,[48] rested on this commercial and usurious exploitation of artisan labour. Such a form of accumulation was the antithesis of true capitalistic accumulation; its success, as Marx pointed out, inevitably precluded the development of capitalism, i.e. the direct control of production by capital.[49]

The correctness of this judgement is shown by the rarity of forms approximating to capitalist enterprise: we find these in mines and ship-building, though sub-contracting and sub-renting must have modified wage-labour relationships considerably; and there were *karkhanas* of merchants or goldsmiths where the material worked was too expensive for artisans to work with at home.[50]

---

[46] *Kabir Granthavali*, edited by Shyamsundardas, Kashi, Vik. S. 2008, p. 42.

[47] Marx allows the existence of pre-capitalist 'surplus value' once commodity production developed under the impetus of commerce: thus 'in the ancient world', he says, the slave system came to be 'devoted to the production of the surplus-value'. *Capital*, III, pp. 326–27.

[48] I have examined these in 'Banking in Mughal India', *Contributions to Indian Economic History*, I, Calcutta, 1960; 'Usury in Mughal India', *CSSH*, VI(4); and 'The System of Bills of Exchange (*Hundis*) in the Mughal Empire', *Proceedings of the Indian History Congress*, Muzaffarpur Session (1972).

[49] 'The independent and predominant developement of capital as merchant's capital is tantamount to the non-subjection of production to capital, and hence to capital developing on the basis of an alien social mode of production, which is also independent of it'. *Capital*, III, p. 322.

[50] These forms are discussed by me in *Enquiry*, NS, III(3), pp. 44–45, and

One need not stress repeatedly that an expansion of commodity production, naturally implying a considerable accumulation of merchant capital, cannot by itself lead to capitalism. In pre-colonial India, moreover, this entire commercial fabric rested on the tax-rent circuit. Were this circuit to be disturbed, as it was, first by agrarian revolts, but mainly and finally, by the English appropriation of the tribute, the days of prosperity of Indian merchant capital would be over.

### Primitive Accumulation: The Tribute
### *1757–1813*

A new orthodoxy is now taking shape: it tells us that the colonial regime was essentially 'a continuation of prior indigenous regimes of the subcontinent'. This view is ascribed by Burton Stein to C.A. Bayly, D.A. Washbrook and F. Perlin.[51] It has found an echo in India too, for Harbans Mukhia tells us approvingly that 'the view that colonial society in India was the creation of the colonial state is also being slowly questioned'.[52] One can almost hear it being said that colonial India 'developed' out of the contradictions of pre-colonial India; and then, why not, that Spanish colonialism in America evolved out of the contradictions of Inca and Aztec societies!

What the continuity proponents overlook, first of all, is the whole matter of the tribute, the classic colonial form of what Marx called 'primitive accumulation of capital'.[53] They also overlook the fact that while colonialism created the groundwork for the emergence

---

V.I. Pavlov in *Historical Premises for India's Transition to Capitalism,* Moscow, 1979, pp. 155–58. One might say that 'ship-building' in pre-modern economies was more akin to house-building as a form of economic organization than any capitalist enterprise proper. See Moreland, *India at the Death of Akbar*, 1920, pp. 185–86.

[51] *Modern Asian Studies*, 19(3), pp. 389–90.

[52] *Feudalism and Non-European Societies*, p. 248, fn. 13. Mukhia appeals to S. Bhattacharya's work. I am not sure, however, if Bhattacharya has been rightly interpreted by Mukhia.

[53] C.A. Bayly omits to attach any importance to this small detail in his *Rulers, Townsmen and Bazars: North Indian Society in the Age of British Expansion, 1770–1870*, Cambridge, 1983. The closest he comes to it is when he says, 'The Europeans [!] did well enough out of India; but not as well as they intended', p. 464.

of indigenous capitalism (Marx's 'regeneration') it sought to suppress it once it had been born, resulting in a stagnation that concealed not 'continuity' but a seething, fundamental contradiction between colonialism and national liberation.

It may fairly be said that the significance of Marx's concept of primitive (or primary) accumulation of capital has not often been fully appreciated.[54] Such accumulation had a double aspect: in the first place, it was a transfer of wealth, originating from non-capitalist sources (that is, from outside of capitalist production); and, second, it implied the coming into being of certain new conditions, such as the creation of the proletariat within the proto-capitalist economy of the colonizing country, for otherwise the transferred wealth could not be transformed into capital. Maurice Dobb rightly stressed the second aspect; but his interpretation of the first seems rather weak.[55]

In any case, both Dobb and his critics appear to have accepted Marx's primitive accumulation as a purely pre-industrial phenomenon, particularly by reading a chronological (not logical) meaning into Marx's statement about primitive accumulation 'preceding capitalistic accumulation; an accumulation not the result of the capitalist mode of production, but its starting point'.[56] What Marx means to say here is simply that primitive accumulation, having proceeded outside capitalistic production, becomes the 'starting point' of the circuit (or, should we rather say, a new, independent circuit) of capitalist production. There is no reason to believe that primitive accumulation would immediately cease once capitalist production begins and develops. Certainly, within the capitalist country itself the range of primitive accumulation would in due course contract as capitalistic production becomes general, or universal, for at the end of that process, there would be no non-capitalistic sectors left, wherein primitive accumula-

---

[54] One may cite as an illustration the rather casual reference to primitive accumulation in Eric R. Wolf's stimulating work, *Europe and the People Without History*, Berkely, 1982, p. 109.

[55] Dobb, *Studies in the Development of Capitalism*, London, 1946, pp. 177–86. Sweezy criticized some elements of Dobb's conception of primary accumulation in the famous symposium, *Transition from Feudalism to Capitalism*, edited by R. Hilton, London, 1976, pp. 55–56; Dobb's reply, ibid., pp. 65–66. But these criticisms did not relate to the points at issue here.

[56] *Capital*, I, p. 736.

tion could originate. Thus Marx recognized in 1867 that 'in Western Europe, the home of political economy, the process of primitive accumulation is more or less accomplished'. But then he adds: 'It is otherwise in the colonies'; and he cites a contemporary instance of how 'the English Government for years practised this method of primitive accumulation' in the colonies.[57] In other words, primitive accumulation continued to be an important means of transforming wealth gained from the non-capitalist world into capital simultaneously with the expansion of capitalist accumulation proper. As colonies expanded in the eighteenth and nineteenth centuries, primitive accumulation grew in absolute size and relative to the GNP of the entire colonial and semi-colonial world. If it shrank in any sense, this was only in relation to the aggregate capital formation of the metropolitan countries generated by the tumultuous increase in capitalist industrial production.[58]

Marx saw the tribute from India as a typical form of primitive accumulation in the colonies;[59] and from 1853 down to two years before his death, he continued to express his indignation at the drain of wealth from India, estimating in 1881 that it then amounted to 'more than the total sum of income of 60 million of agricultural and industrial labourers of India'.[60] By that time England, of course, had long been a capitalist nation, with no scope left for primitive accumulation within its own shores.

The 'tribute' in its earliest phase after Plassey was one of

---

[57] Ibid., pp. 790, 799.

[58] Rosa Luxemburg in *The Accumulation of Capital*, English translation, London, 1951, pp. 364–65, precedes Dobb in believing that to Marx the processes of primitive accumulation were merely 'travails by which the capitalist mode of production emerges from a feudal society'. In the next paragraph she distinguishes between the continuing 'augmenting [of] the material elements of constant and variable capital' from non-capitalist sectors, which, as we have seen, is Marx's primitive accumulation, and accumulation 'through realization of surplus value' by marketing capitalist products among non-capitalist strata, p. 365. The point has been discussed by Sayera I. Habib in 'Rosa Luxemburg's Contribution to the Marxist Theory of Imperialism', unpublished paper read at the Marx Centenary Seminar of *Social Scientist*, Delhi, 1983.

[59] *Capital*, I, p. 777.

[60] Letter dated 19 February 1881 to F. Danielson. I collected Marx's statements on the tribute in *The Marxist*, I (1), pp. 116–27; pp. 14–58 of this volume. My collection has not been exhaustive.

sheer plunder of accumulated treasures and revenues of Indian potentates by the East India Company and its servants (gainers in the famous 'Plassey plunder' and the Carnatic debts). But it came to be established as a constant imposition when the East India Company treated
its taxation revenue in the conquered territories as gross profits out of
which it could 'invest' in Indian goods to be sold throughout the
world, the proceeds to be its own net profit. Here was profit obtained,
without the investment of a single penny, except for the original cost
of conquest which too had been immediately recovered through plunder. To this were all the time added the incomes of the Company's
servants in India, from salaries, bribes and booty, which swelled the
tribute. The picture that R.C. Dutt drew of the 'drain'[61] has been richly confirmed by Holden Furber, much as he dislikes Dutt.[62]

Considering the 'prime costs' of the goods that were exported from the Company's possessions in India in payment of tribute,
together with coins exported mainly to China, the total drain has been
estimated by Furber at £1.78 million a year during the decade 1783–
84 to 1792–93.[63] In case we attach any weight to estimates of total
annual value of the gross production of the Company's possessions
during 1784–89, this scale of drain would amount to 9 per cent of the
estimated GNP![64] In terms of scale prices, the tribute from India at
about £4.2 million around 1801 amounted to over 2 per cent of the
British national income, or nearly 30 per cent of the net British domestic investment at that time.[65]

Let us first pause to examine the effects of this tribute on the
Indian economy during the first phase, when it was paid mainly out
of exports of Indian craft products, which lasted, formally speaking,

---

[61] R.C. Dutt, *The Economic History of India under Early British Rule*, sixth
edition, London, n.d., especially pp. 35–53.

[62] H. Furber, *John Company at Work*, Cambridge (US), 1951, especially pp.
303ff.

[63] Ibid., pp. 313–16.

[64] My calculations in 'Colonialization of the Indian Economy', *Social
Scientist*, III (8), p. 28; pp. 296–335 of this volume.

[65] Ibid., p. 29. Also see Sayera I. Habib, 'Colonial Exploitation and Capital
Formation in England in the Early Stages of the Industrial Revolution',
*Proceedings of the Indian History Congress*, Aligarh Session (1975), pp.
xxi–xxvii. And yet Furber can say that the drain 'did not reach vast
proportions'! *John Company at Work*, p. 310.

till the Charter Act of 1813.[66] What the mode of primitive accumulation here amounted to in essence was to fasten on to the pre-colonial
tax-rent to finance exports. Furber argues—and many writers seem
to agree silently with him, to judge from that weighty tome, the *Cambridge Economic History of India,* Volume II—that this annual despatch of Indian wealth to the metropolitan country caused no injury
to India. On the contrary:

> There is at least a possibility that the indirect results of European
> activity within India between 1783 and 1793 were tending to create
> wealth rather than to destroy it. . . . The immediate result of the
> stoppage of the 'drain' in piece-goods from Bengal would have been
> unemployment for one-sixth of the weavers and spinners in
> Bengal. We cannot know whether India as a whole would have been
> happier or wealthier in the late eighteenth century if Europeans had
> not sought fame, fortune and power there.[67]

The notion seems, at first sight, to be convincingly simple.
The large part of the Indian revenues that was set apart for 'investments' was, after all, not sent out in gold and silver; had that been the
case, no one would have found employment.[68] What the Company
and the English officials did, however, was to buy Indian cotton
goods, silk, etc., thus providing employment to numerous weavers,
silk-winders, etc. Had the pre-colonial rulers survived and had they
spent an equivalent sum from their revenues, they would not have
been able to give employment to more people. Where was there, then,
any loss to India?

---

[66] See the notable insights of Marx in his article in *Tribune* date-lined 24 June
1853, in *On Colonialism,* Moscow, n.d., p. 47; and Engels' letter to
Conrad Schmidt, 27 October 1890, in Marx and Engels, *Selected
Correspondence,* edited by Dona Torr, Calcutta, 1945, pp. 420–21.

[67] *John Company at Work,* pp. 311–12. The curious use of the word
'European' for English or British may be noted. One finds a similar use in
another American scholar, Kingsley Davis, *Population of India and
Pakistan,* Princeton, 1951, where he speaks of the beneficial 'European
influence', e.g., pp. 25–26.

[68] Furber tilts at windmills when he disputes the 'notion that India was
paying a tribute of gold and silver to her European [!] conquerors'. *John
Company at Work,* p. 310. One fails to find such a notion in the pages
of R.C. Dutt or any serious Indian writer on the subject.

What Furber forgets, first of all, is that India lost use values, together with exchange values, when these products went out of the country with no return received for them. Had they been used in India, the numerous resultant users of cloth and silk would have certainly been 'happier' and even 'wealthier' in material terms. But, forgetting the loss of use values, let us turn to the question of employment. We suppose, with Furber, that the pre-colonial rulers by an equivalent amount of expenditure maintained, in the first instance, the same number of artisans. To keep close to the hypothetical argument, we further assume that they bought no more than the same quantities of cloth, employing the same number of weavers as the English did. Now once the purchases had been made, they would have large quantities of cloth in their hands. Not being merchants, they could begin issuing such cloth in payment of wages (not, in fact, a rare practice with Mughal potentates). The result: the cloth, by such distribution, would give livelihood to a further class of persons paid through this means. The case would be no different had the Indian potentates simply sold the cloth on the market and employed retainers or bought other commodities (thereby giving employment to their producers) out of the proceeds: employment would have been given to a large number of people in addition to the weavers already employed. It is easily seen that the argument is not affected if the Indian potentates actually bought goods different from what the English invested in. The very retention of those goods in India would enable employment to expand, whenever these were sold or paid out in the form of wages. The picture of increasing unemployment of artisans and troopers that Ghulam Husain Tabatabai[69] drew in 1781 is, therefore, far more plausible than Furber's hypothesis.

The diversion of revenues into the Company's 'investments' not only affected employment; it also hurt Indian commerce. There was a substantial shift from the inland commerce handled by Indian merchants to external commerce controlled by the East India Company. In 1790 Cornwallis was right to speak of 'the languor' thrown upon 'the general commerce of the country' as a major consequence of the 'heavy drain of wealth'.[70] There is little basis for C.A. Bayly's

---

[69] *Siyaru-l Mutakhirin*, II, Kanpur, pp. 836–37, 840–41.
[70] Cornwallis, Minute of 3 February 1790, *Fifth Report*, II, edited by K. Firminger, p. 542.

soothing assurance that what took place was 'the redeployment of merchant capital within India, not its destruction'.[71]

## 1813–58

As the initial stage of the Industrial Revolution in England reached completion by the early years of the nineteenth century, the British colonial relationship with India entered its second or 'opium' phase. Losing world markets for its craft products, India could no longer pay the tribute by the export of its manufactures. This sudden alteration of India's position in world commerce brought about a crisis in the process of realization of the tribute. William Bentinck drew attention to this in an eloquent Minute in 1829.[72] India could not even pay in indigo and cotton in the face of West Indian and US competition, a failure marked by the fall of agency houses in the 1820s. The ultimate solution was found in opium and in the imposition of that drug on the Chinese people. The Company's employment of weavers, which Furber had found to be such a beneficial gift of the drain in its first phase, disappeared, without leaving a trace; and what 'happiness' and 'wealth' the Indian people could derive from the drain was now in the form of an extension of the cultivation of opium, proclaimed by John Crawfurd (1837) to be 'a great national advantage'.[73]

This new, opium phase of primitive accumulation continued to rely totally on tax-rent extraction, of which, as Eric Stokes has shown so well, James Mill and the Utilitarians became the foremost exponents.[74] The attempt to discover in this phase any kind of 'growth'—or, as the title of the volume edited by K.N. Chaudhuri

---

[71] *Rulers, Townsmen and Bazars*, p. 462.

[72] Report of Select Committee on East India Company's Affairs, 1831–32, *British Parliamentary Papers*, I.U.P., Colonies, East India 5, General Appendix, pp. 275–76.

[73] K.N. Chaudhury (ed.), *Economic Development of India under the East India Company*, Cambridge, 1971, pp. 251–52. The editor himself in his introduction passes by in silence the major feature of India's 'economic development' under the Company, viz. the rise of opium to the position of the premier item of Indian trade, accounting in 1858 for nearly a third of the value of Indian exports.

[74] Eric Stokes, *The English Utilitarians and India*, Oxford, 1959, pp. 81–139.

styles it, 'economic development'—is difficult to sustain by any conceivably acceptable measure. I have argued elsewhere that the processes of de-industrialization and de-urbanization postulated for this period have much more support in the evidence, descriptive as well as statistical, than has been allowed foi in recent writing, either of the continuity school or of Morris D. Morris and like-minded scholars.[75]

As the tax-rent extraction intensified (outside the Permanent Settlement areas), and there was a shift to an absolute imposition of money rent, with no allowance made for payments in kind (as under the earlier regimes), commodity relations continued to be extended and the old customary community relationships, hitherto sustaining a limited 'natural' economy, were blown asunder. The extending commodity relations, under fiscal pressure, created markets for British goods as agriculture-based crafts collapsed. Marx pointed out in a little-read article of 1859 that the failure of China to absorb British goods was due to its misfortune in not having come under British rule. In India, on the other hand, the British had been able to '. . . forcibly convert part of the Hindoo self-sustaining communities into mere farms, producing opium, cotton, indigo, hemp and other raw materials in exchange for British stuffs.'[76] Primitive accumulation thus laid the basis for a market for British industry just as it continually fed it with a stream of tribute capital.

At the same time, rent accumulation absorbed much of local usurer and merchant capital. The very fact that moneylenders and merchants began extensively to buy land, or foreclose mortgages on *zamindaris*,[77] meant that their capital ultimately passed as land revenue into the hands of the Company. The moneylenders' and bankers' entry into the ranks of the *zamindars* represented a curtailment of merchant capital rather than its penetration of land or agriculture.

[75] Irfan Habib, 'Studying a Colonial Economy', *Modern Asian Studies*, 19(3), especially pp. 359–68.
[76] Karl Marx, *On Colonialism and Modernization*, edited by Shlomo Avineri, p. 498. The point is more briefly made in *Capital*, III, pp. 328–29.
[77] For this phenomenon in N.W. Provinces (UP), see Stokes in *Cambridge Economic History of India*, II, pp. 46–47, 49, 52.

## 1858–1900

Just as the triumph of the cotton textile industry in England closed the initial phase of British colonialism in India, so the triumph of railways in England in the 1840s began another phase, that of the 'imperialism of free trade', with fundamental effects on the pattern of primary accumulation and the entire economic structure of India The spurt of wars, annexations and conquests (1839–56), the Rebellion of 1857 and the abolition of the rule of the East India Company (1858) marked the arrival of the 'free trade' stage in the colonialization of India.

Railway construction was the kingpin of the free trade regime. British capital was used to build major railway lines (with state-built railways also of sizeable length), and the capital was guaranteed a minimum return, which cost the Indian tax-payer Rs 568 million between 1849 and 1900.[78] The cost of state railways, aided by the raising of loans in London, imposed a further burden. At the same time the costs of 'good government' continued to rise, constantly swelling the 'Home charges'. There was thus a steady increase in the drain, marked by recurring trade surpluses for which the country received no return. The annual drain during this period has been estimated for various years by writers such as Dadabhai Naoroji, Y.S. Pandit and S.B. Saul; and now A.K. Banerji has gone into the whole question once again.[79] Taking estimates based on the balance of payments alone, Saul's figure for 1880 amounts to 4.14 per cent of the Indian national income as estimated by A. Heston for the year 1882–83.[80]

Banerji has been right in asking that economic theory should be concerned with the question of what happens to a country which year in and year out loses such a sizeable part of its GNP to another country, as India did during the entire period 1858–98 (and, in fact, right from 1757).[81] The fact that India had to have a rate of saving of 4 per cent of its national income just to pay the tribute must be borne in mind when economists speak of the lack of internal capacities for

---

[78] John M. Hurd, ibid., p. 743.
[79] A.K. Banerji, *Aspects of Indo-British Economic Relations, 1858–1898*, Bombay, 1982.
[80] *Modern Asian Studies*, 19(3), pp. 376–77.
[81] A.K. Banerji, *Indo-British Economic Relations*, pp. 207–14.

development, or the low per capita income base, from which the British could not lift the Indians, however much they tried.[82]

The drain was met in considerable part (notably the 'Home charges') by taxation. Since it so heavily bore down on the total national income, it is not surprising that the British government sometimes found it a difficult task to raise taxes without the increase being counter-productive. The considerable increase in prices in the latter half of the nineteenth century, the new post-Mutiny policy of befriending the *zamindars,* and the long intervals between the 'settlements' resulted in a gradual decline of the real burden of the land tax (though it still remained substantial and extremely regressive for the poorer tax-payers). But this decline was accompanied by an increase in the burden of other, largely indirect, taxes. The total annual revenue was lifted heftily from Rs 360.6 million in 1858–59 to Rs 514.1 million in 1870–71, while the share of land revenue in total revenue declined from 50 per cent to 40 per cent.[83] The total revenues rose again from Rs 619.7 million in 1877–78 to Rs 1145.2 million in 1901–02, while land revenue rose only from Rs 198.9 million to Rs 274.3 million.[84] Adjusted to price changes, the total burden of taxation increased by 75 per cent between 1870–71 and 1901–02,[85] but, according to the most optimistic (and undoubtedly exaggerated) estimate of national income growth, the total net national product in terms of constant prices rose by less than 31 per cent between 1868–69 and 1901–02.[86] When McAlpin argues that land tax had no role to play in the

---

[82] See Morris D. Morris' argument based on India's inability to develop owing to its low per capita income in the nineteenth century, *IESHR,* V (1), pp. 1–16, and his recent contribution in *Cambridge Economic History of India (CEHI),* II, especially p. 601n.

[83] Table in *CEHI,* II, p. 916, based on S. Bhattacharya, *Financial Foundations of the British Raj,* Simla, 1971.

[84] Table in R.C. Dutt, *Economic History of India in the Victorian Age,* seventh edition, London, 1950, p. 595.

[85] The results are very close whether one uses Moni Mukerji's table of changes in price-levels, 1850–1949 in V.B. Singh (ed.), *Economic History of India, 1857–1956,* Bombay, 1965, p. 685, or K. Mukerji's table of working-class cost of living index, 1857–1957, ibid., pp. 657–60.

[86] Alan Heston's estimates as tabulated in *CEHI,* II, pp. 397–99. For a criticism of these estimates as overstating national income growth see my essay, 'Studying a Colonial Economy—Without Perceiving Colonialism', *Modern Asian Studies,* 19(3), 1985, pp. 368–76.

impoverishment of the peasant, since its burden actually lightened,[87] she simply overlooks, in her haste to condemn Dutt, the enormous increase in indirect taxation.

Clearly, primitive accumulation was in full swing still, the simple tax-rent extraction reinforced by opium monopoly, salt duty and other direct and indirect taxes.[88] The dire consequences of this scale of fiscal exploitation of the Indian people for the purposes of tribute could be seen in the 1890s when India was compelled to export 2 to 3 million tons of wheat in years in which her own people died in millions.[89]

### British Capitalist Accumulation and India

Once a capitalist sector has been established initially through primitive or primary accumulation, capital begins to expand by virtue of surplus value generated by capitalist production itself. A part of the surplus value, taking the form of profits, is converted into additional capital ('extended reproduction').[90]

The surplus value contained in the value of the product of capitalist production is 'realized' when the product is sold. Thus continuing capitalist accumulation requires continuous expansion of the market for capitalist products.[91] This implies a corresponding contraction of the market for products of non-capitalist sectors of production, especially of what Marx called 'the petty producer' (artisan and peasant). Petty producers were previously forcibly expropriated through

---

[87] Michelle B. McAlpin, *Subject to Famine*, Princeton, 1983, pp. 198–205.

[88] In 1870–71 opium accounted for 16 per cent and salt for 12 per cent of the total British-Indian taxation (*CEHI*, II, p. 916)—shades of the France of Louis XVI!

[89] McAlpin takes cudgels against nationalists who advocated a ban on foodgrain exports in famine years. Her argument: if the foodgrain exports were forbidden, prices would decline, and food production would contract (*Subject to Famine*, pp. 204–5). In other words, famines, by raising prices, were the best thing that could have happened to Indian agriculture. But if 'neo-classical' economics is to be pursued at this level, one could argue that falling prices would mean falling costs, and so agricultural production need not have contracted at all. In more practical terms, there could be a legitimate expectation that resources previously used to produce export wheat would shift to producing coarser grains, such as barley and millets.

[90] Marx's classic treatment of this subject is in *Capital*, I, Part VII.

[91] *Capital*, III, English translation, Moscow, n.d., pp. 239–40.

measures of primitive accumulation;[92] but once capitalist accumulation begins, it immensely enlarges their 'expropriation', by driving out their products from the market and converting the petty producers into proletarians, available for employment as wage labourers.[93] This, in a sense, completes the conversion of surplus value into capital, because there can be no employment of capital without wage labour. In other words, within the homeland of capitalism, the extending market for capitalist goods facilitates the rapid extension of capitalist relations within the country.

But what happens when the market for capitalist products is situated in another country, between which and the producing country, there is no mobility of labour? It is Rosa Luxemburg's special merit to have drawn attention to this question, though she formulated it differently.[94] To her it appeared that capitalist accumulation required the continuous extension of the market for capitalist goods in non-capitalist sectors; otherwise there could be no 'extended reproduction' within the capitalist economy. It follows that it was essential for capitalist countries to export goods to non-capitalist or colonial countries. While one may not agree with Rosa Luxemburg's insistence on the essentiality of the non-capitalist market for all enlargement of capital, there is no doubt that sale of capitalist products in non-capitalist (including colonial) markets (once the non-capitalist sectors in the metropolitan countries had been more or less eliminated) was a major factor in maintaining the tempo of capitalist accumulation.[95]

It may be urged, as Sweezy does, that the sale of capitalist goods in non-capitalist markets is but a mere act of exchange, and cannot, therefore, contribute to any addition of capital in the capital-

[92] *Capital*, I, pp. 786–89.

[93] Marx touches on this conversion of artisan into wage labourer under the competitive impact of machinery in *Capital*, I, pp. 427–49.

[94] Rosa Luxemburg, *Accumulation of Capital*. This translation has a very instructive introduction by Joan Robinson.

[95] Marx stated as much when he wrote in 1853: 'at the same rate at which the cotton manufacturers became of vital interest for the whole social frame of Great Britain, East India became of vital interest for the British cotton manufacture'. Marx and Engels, *On Colonialism*, Moscow, n.d., p. 48.

ist country at the expense of the colony.[96] Marx, however, points out that external trade forms a special case for considering gains out of exchange.[97] He puts forward the concept of what is now called 'unequal exchange'. Both countries benefit from the trade in an immediate, direct sense, but the industrially advanced country benefits more: 'the favoured country recovers more labour in exchange for less labour, although this difference, this excess is pocketed, as in any exchange between labour and capital, by a certain class'.[98] Thus, though unlike the realization of tribute, the capitalist country's trade with colonies would exhibit parity between the visible values of exports and imports, this parity nevertheless conceals a 'surplus profit', i.e. an additional dose of accumulation of capital for the metropolitan country.[99] In other words, 'the richer country exploits the poorer one'.[100]

The imports of British manufactures into India, then, meant larger 'use values' in return for the same exchange values for their buyers and, therefore, enlarged consumption of goods (e.g., of cloth in India). It called forth the ruin of Indian artisans who previously produced goods that were now thrown out of the market by competing imports: 'millions of workers had to perish in the East Indies [India] so as to procure for the million and a half workers employed in England in the same [textile] industry, three years' prosperity out of ten'.[101]

Unlike the tribute it is difficult to measure the 'surplus profits' that British capitalism thus derived from India. The necessary statistical effort has yet to come. When it comes, British capitalism's gains by this means may well be found to match those achieved

---

[96] Paul M. Sweezy, *The Theory of Capitalist Development*, London, 1962, p. 205.

[97] *Theories of Surplus Value*, III, English translation, Moscow, n.d., p. 105.

[98] *Capital*, III, p. 28.

[99] Ibid.

[100] Marx, *Theories of Surplus Value*, III, pp. 105–6. Also see Bukharin, *Imperialism and the Accumulation of Capital*, English translation, edited by K.J. Tarbuck, New York, 1972, pp. 244–45.

[101] Marx, *The Poverty of Philosophy* (1847), English translation, Moscow, n.d., p. 113. Morris D. Morris has been disputing whether this actually happened in the nineteenth century. My criticism of his views will be found in 'Studying a Colonial Economy', pp. 359–64.

through tribute. In 1900–01 textile manufactures, hardware, machinery and mill work accounted for 46.5 per cent of value of all merchandise imported into India;[102] the imported (almost entirely British-made) cloth amounted to 1,875 million yards, while domestic cloth production the same year was an estimated 1,067 million yards only.[103]

Though large numbers of Indian artisans were ruined, the 'realization of surplus value' by British capitalism through capture of the Indian markets was not a simple process of wealth transfer from India. The market was captured because, with the steady rise of industrial productivity in Britain, the values of its products fell continuously. These imports (besides the needs of tribute) had to be paid for by India in raw materials and wage goods (cotton, jute, oilseeds, wheat, tea, animal skins), where, however, there was no fall in costs and whose values, therefore, did not fall as fast as those of imported manufacturers.[104] In such a situation, one would naturally expect to find an overall shift in the terms of trade in favour of agriculture between 1861 and 1910, a phenomenon which McAlpin is so pleased to discover.[105]

This shift must have increased the real income of certain classes of the rural population. To identify these, we may begin by a process of elimination.

Landless labourers did not sell any agricultural produce on the market, and they remained unaffected by the market gains of agriculture. The official *Prices and Wages* show practically no secular movement in real wages of agricultural labour at the all-India level,

---

[102] Source: Tables in R.C. Dutt, *Economic History of India in the Victorian Age*, London, 1950, pp. 530, 533.

[103] A.K. Bagchi, *Private Investment in India*, Cambridge, 1972, p. 226.

[104] Canal irrigation might have increased productivity in agriculture in some areas, but expansion of cultivation would, on the other hand, bring about dimishing returns.

[105] *CEHI*, II, pp. 894–95. A transitory improvement in terms of trade for undeveloped countries' primary products took place all over the world at the time. According to a table given by Michael Barratt Brown, *Economics of Imperialism*, 1974, p. 251, the unit value of developed countries' manufacturing products was 98 in 1876–80, with 1913 as base, =100, but the unit value of underdeveloped countries' primary products had been as low as 69 in 1876–80, with the same base year (1913).

between 1873 and 1900.[106] Dharma Kumar, indeed, finds a positive decline in the real wages of agricultural labour in six out of the seven reporting districts of the Madras Presidency in the last quarter of the nineteenth century[107]—this despite the fact that there was an element of understatement in the rates of the earlier years.[108] Similar conclusions have now been offered for Bombay-Deccan.[109]

What of the peasantry? Except for tea, the other major agricultural items of export were produced by peasants, who could sell their produce on the market. The peasants can be divided into two groups: (1) those who cultivated on landowners' lands with no restrictions on rent, i.e. who were tenants-at-will, and (2) those who paid revenue directly to the state (and rent to none) or paid rent that was fixed, or could be increased only within limits fixed by law. The two categories resulted from historical circumstances as well as the shape and form of the British revenue settlements. It is very difficult to determine the size of the two categories, and sometimes one shaded into the other.

In UP, whose records were often more complete than in other provinces, tenantry-at-will was found to be more widespread in Awadh, where it accounted for the bulk of the peasantry, than in

---

[106] See calculations by M. Mukerji, *National Income of India—Trends and Structure*, Calcutta, 1969, pp. 88–89 (simple averages of district figures in *Prices and Wages*). These represent the most reliable data available. Unluckily, Mukerji's flair for combining miscellaneous data leads him to construct a table (p. 91) where he gives a very low wage rate for 1857 (source unstated): it should not at all have been put alongside actual all-India averages. Goldsmith accepts this table and taking the 1857 figure to stand for 1860, asks us to accept an increase of 250.5 per cent between 1860 and 1913 (linking with Sivasubramonian's data for 1900–13) and 100.0 per cent between 1860 and 1880, while the cost of living rose only by 98.4 per cent in the longer and 27.8 per cent in the shorter period. See *Financial Development of India, 1860–1977*, New Haven, 1983, p. 15. Had he looked closely at Mukerji's table on p. 91, he would have seen that almost all the increase in real agricultural wages occurred between 1857 and 1868–69; he would, then, perhaps have had second thoughts about the validity of the 1857 rate for agricultural wages.

[107] *CEHI*, II, p. 238. Also see the same author's *Land and Caste in South India*, Cambridge, 1965, pp. 163–67.

[108] Atchi Reddy in *IESHR*, XV(4), p. 466.

[109] Sunanda Krishnamurty, 'Real Wages of Agricultural Labourers in the Bombay Deccan, 1874–1922', *IESHR*, XXIV(1), pp. 81–98.

other parts of the province, but the land cultivated by it was nowhere much lower than half at the beginning of this (20th) century.[110] It was equally extensive in the areas of the Permanent Settlement (Bihar, Bengal and Orissa), but precise figures do not appear to be available.

It is difficult to see how the tenant-at-will could in the long run benefit from the larger value borne by his produce, since rents would increase correspondingly. We could suppose that rents increased more where the export market exercised a larger pull, and less where its pull was relatively weak, and where the terms of trade had not, therefore, shifted as greatly in favour of agriculture. Where rents rose more, the value of landed property would also rise proportionately. Granted these assumptions, rents and land values should have risen more in the Punjab and UP (which raised cotton, wheat and

[110] The following table derived from some volumes of the UP *District Gazetteers*, edited by H.R. Nevil, is illustrative of the extent of the land under tenants-at-will:

*Land under tenants-at-will in Awadh (as % of total cultivated land)*

| District | Year | Per cent |
| --- | --- | --- |
| Lucknow | 1896 | 74.86 |
| Sitapur | 1893–97 | 86.50 |
| Hardoi | 1897–98 | 75.30 |
| Bara Banki | 1898 | 79.05 |
| Unao | 1896 | 72.00 |
| Fyzabad | 1895 | 63.64 |
| Rai Bareli | 1897 | 82.33 |
| Sultanpur | 1898 | 67.53 |
| Bahraich | 1892 | 90.27 |
| Gonda | 1902 | 72.27 |

*Land under tenants-at-will in UP, Awadh excluded (as % of total cultivated land)*

| District | Year | Per cent |
| --- | --- | --- |
| Saharanpur | 1906–07 | 46.01 |
| Aligarh | 1908 | 41.98 |
| Shahajahanpur | 1906–07 | 37.58 |
| Pilibhit | 1906–07 | 48.84 |
| Kanpur | 1907 | 25.05 |
| Gorakhpur | 1907–8 | 41.80 |
| Basti | 1905 | 46.13 |
| Bijnor | 1895–1902 | 42.20 |

oilseeds) than in Bihar and Bengal (where the major peasant-grown export crop was jute, but cotton, sugarcane and, then, opium and indigo were in retreat).[111]

Given our limited information, the hypothesis is fairly well confirmed. The direct information on rents is often suspect because these were understated either to avoid revenue enhancements at new settlements or to escape provisions of the rent acts. Still, if Saharanpur district represented the conditions of the Punjab and western UP, we can see that rents here rose considerably: the 'recorded rents' from tenants-at-will in the district rose by 46 per cent between 1886–87 and 1906–07 as against a rise of 23 per cent in rents levied on protected or privileged tenants.[112] Rents rose far more sluggishly in Bengal: the total estimated income from rents (and not simply rent rates) increased from Rs 13 crore in 1876–77 to Rs 16.8 crore in 1900–01, i.e. by about a quarter in twenty-five years.[113] In Orissa the rents on *pahis* or non-resident transitory cultivators rose by 40 per cent between 1836 and 1896, thus failing to keep pace with prices; on *thanis* or permanent cultivators they even declined marginally.[114]

The same pattern is reflected in land-values. In the Punjab the average land price rose from 31 times the annual revenue in 1875 to 127 times in 1910.[115] In UP the value of land was estimated at 5 years' revenue in 1861; but the average value for the province was 28 years' revenue in 1899–1900. This is reinforced by the prices given in terms of multiples of annual revenues that Stokes gives for Aligarh district: 7.5 in 1859–60, 15 in 1869–78, and 22 in 1879–88.[116] The increase

[111] Rajat K. Ray in *IESHR*, X(3), pp. 250–51, cites the case of Midnapore district, where rice was raised in 75 per cent of the cultivated area in 1803, the remainder being under cash crops like cotton, sugarcane, oil-seeds, tobacco, vegetables, etc.; but rice occupied 94.32 per cent of the cultivated area in 1910–18. Sugarcane cultivation, important until 1822, was pursued for local consumption only after 1835.

[112] *Saharanpur District Gazetteer,* Lucknow, 1921, p. 133.

[113] B. Chaudhuri in *CEHI*, II, pp. 134–42.

[114] Ibid., p.135.

[115] Goldsmith, *Financial Development*, p. 5, Table 1–24, col. 5, derived from H. Calvert, *The Wealth and Welfare of the Punjab,* Lahore, 1922, p. 299. The value-tax ratio in the Punjab was exceptionally high, and Goldsmith errs grievously in trying to calculate all-India land values by applying the Punjab ratio to all-India land tax figures.

[116] *CEHI*, II, p. 59.

is all the more remarkable for two reasons: first, that land revenue itself went on being enhanced, and, second, that the land valued also included land under protected tenants, where the rise in rent income was moderate. Land values in Bihar and Bengal, on the other hand, showed no increase, when stated in multiples of annual revenue, in spite of the fact that the Permanent Settlement prevented revenue enhancements.[117]

*Land prices as multiples of annual revenue*

|                          | *Bihar* | *Bengal* |
|--------------------------|---------|----------|
| 1874–75 to 1878–79       | 14.63   | 7.43     |
| 1879–80 to 1883–84       | 18.24   | 4.92     |
| 1884–85 to 1888–89       | 11.68   | 4.45     |
| 1889–90 to 1893–94       | 11.59   | 4.19     |

Clearly, rents and land values rose substantially only where higher export prices mainly cast their bounties; and there was thus a close correlation between the raw-material exports to Britain and the intensification of landlord-rent extraction. The tenant-at-will himself could make hardly any gains.

Circumstances would seemingly be otherwise with our second category of peasants, the revenue-paying *ryot* and the protected tenant. The Bombay Presidency, whose agriculture was perhaps the most heavily dominated by exports, especially of cotton, also possessed a '*ryotwari*' system bequeathed to it by Elphinstone. Conditions in the Presidency could illustrate best what happened to those who, in legal terms, were practically peasant proprietors.

Here, in the first place, substantial revenue enhancements came in the wake of rising prices.[118] These, like the rise in rents on occupancy tenants in UP, partly ate into the larger gross money income of the peasant. And then came the moneylender. While rural indebtedness already existed in the Deccan as in the rest of the country, it underwent a great expansion the moment large portions of the

---

[117] Data given by B. Chaudhuri in ibid., II, pp. 104–5.
[118] R.C. Dutt, *Economic History*, pp. 330–32; V.D. Diwekar in *CEHI*, II, p. 194.

peasants' produce began coming to the market.[119] Even the larger
peasant proprietors, borrowing upon expected returns from their
crop, fell into the net of the moneylender, whose object was '. . . to
keep the *ryot* in nominal possession of the land and to take the difference between what it produces and what is absolutely required for
the support of the cultivator.'[120] The moneylenders did here to the pro
prietary peasants what the landlords did to the tenants-at-will, viz.
deprived them of their expanded income from sale of produce. The
peasant riots of 1875, which shook the Bombay administration, were
entirely directed against the moneylenders and underscored the latter's increasing dominance.[121]

In the Madras Presidency, the home of Munro's *ryotwari*,
agricultural mortgages increased by 60 per cent between 1899 and
1910;[122] and in 1895 the total rural indebtedness was estimated at
Rs 45 crore, of which Rs 20 crore were on mortgages.[123]

The capture of markets in India by British capitalism, then,
had consequences different from those of its capture of the internal
market in Britain. There it immensely expanded the sector of capitalist production. In India, on the other hand, it essentially enlarged two
pre-capitalist forms of accumulation, rent extraction and usury. The
only partial exception was offered by tea plantations, where British
capital was served by wage labour, often of a semi-servile kind. The
near-total subjugation of the Indian market by British capitalism thus
generated only a very weak impulse towards true capital formation
within India. In other words, while it created a proletariat by destroying Indian crafts, it did not correspondingly generate capital that
could give it even partial employment.

[119] Dietmar Rothermund, *Government, Landlord and Peasant in India, 1865–1935*, Wiesbaden, 1978, pp. 15–19.
[120] Official report, Poona district, 17 July 1875, quoted by Neil Charlesworth in *Modern Asian Studies*, 6 (4), p. 409. For the general tendency of peasants, including 'the wealthiest cultivators' to fall into debt, see ibid., pp. 402–3.
[121] On the riots, see Ravinder Kumar, *Western India in the Nineteenth Century*, London, 1968, pp. 151–88. After giving much evidence of the moneylenders' increasing power owing to commercialization, Charles-worth treats the riots as a 'non-event', just because the rioters did not kill anyone, or because the actual land transfers had been few. 'Myth of the Deccan Riots of 1875', *Modern Asian Studies*, 6(4), pp. 401–21.
[122] Goldsmith, *Financial Development*, p. 46 n.
[123] Ibid., p. 44.

### Beginnings of Capitalist Accumulation within India

In colonial India, indeed in all countries other than the first industrial nation, Britain, capitalist accumulation could conceivably begin from either of two starting points: (a) import of capital from Britain or other countries where capitalist production had already established itself, and (b) conversion of indigenous wealth into capital—a species of 'primitive accumulation'.

The export of capital from the industrially advanced countries of Europe occupied a prominent place in the analyses of modern imperialism by J.A. Hobson (1902), Rosa Luxemburg (1913) and Lenin (1916). The outward flow of capital from advanced countries undoubtedly became a marked feature of world capitalism in the latter half of the nineteenth century; and the relationship of this phenomenon with the development of the 'monopoly' phase of capitalism was of primary interest to Lenin. For our present purpose, it is important to focus on what the exported capital did in the receiving countries, rather than on why it came to be exported at all.

Capital imported into a country could theoretically take four distinct forms:

(i) Loans to governments utilized for non-productive purposes. This was initially import of money capital, resulting in import mainly of products of Department II (consumer goods) and not of Department I (capital goods) of the capital-exporting country.[124] Returns on such investments accrued to the creditor basically from the borrowing country's tax resources; and, in the case of colonies and semi-colonies, the returns constituted a species of primitive accumulation for the benefit of the creditor country.[125] No capitalist accumulation could be generated within the borrowing country by import of such money capital. A large part of the Indian debt in Britain was composed of such borrowings, the amount raised being used to pay for wars and costs of administration.

(ii) Investments in commerce. These represented a flow of

---

[124] Marx divides the process of 'social production' into two departments, Department I producing 'means of production', and Department II 'articles of consumption'. See *Capital*, II, Moscow, n.d., p. 395. This division is most important for him in studying both the simple and complex reproduction of capital.

[125] Marx: 'The public debt becomes one of the most powerful levers of primitive accumulation.' *Capital*, I, p. 779.

merchant capital and did not again involve transfer of capital goods. In the case of India, British capital of this kind sought to capture those channels of commerce by which British manufactures were sold in India, and raw materials and wage goods were exported. The investments thus essentially carried forward the process of British industrial dominance of India.

(iii) Investments in creating infrastructures for capturing the internal market for the ruling country's industries. Railway investment was the characteristic form of this kind of capital imports together with investments in the extraction of coal which was essential for running the railways. Such investment required import of capital goods, and, to that extent, generated capitalist accumulation in the importing country. Yet there was always a hot-house air about such investment, since, as in the case of India, it required special guarantees to the railway companies from the Indian exchequer, or it came via state-raised loans. There was a gulf between the real value of the necessary capital goods and technology imported and the actual amount of money capital expended under the guarantee system, which was much larger.[126] It was thus a very expensive import of capital.

Marx in 1853 had hoped that the railways would become the harbinger of modern industry in India:[127] if this prophecy took time to be realized, it was surely because the railways became the kingpin of the imposition on India of what Marx himself called 'the monopoly' of 'the Manchester Free-Traders'.[128] The railways eliminated the possibility of any isolated regional markets for prospective local modern industries.

(iv) The final form that imported capital could take was investment for duplicating Departments I and II of the lending country in the receiving country, for the purpose of obtaining a higher rate of profit. This was the classic way in which capital moved from Britain to the United States. What motivated such movement was the possibility of gain from cheaper raw materials and higher labour

---

[126] R.C. Dutt, *Economic History*, pp. 353–60. The Indian tax-payer paid out Rs 568 million to the private railways to meet guarantee obligations between 1849 and 1900. J.M. Hurd in *CEHI*, II, p. 743.

[127] Shlomo Avineri (ed.), *Karl Marx on Colonialism and Modernization*, p. 136.

[128] Ibid., p. 374.

productivity (in relation to wages paid) and, in the case of migration
into independent countries, of gain from protective tariffs. In such
situations, while the initial capital transfer involved import of capital
goods into the receiving country, subsequently both Departments I
and II would be established there. The imported capital would itself
become indigenous, if the capital owners also migrated (a notable
feature of the British-US relationship).

This form of capital import remained very rare in India, the
only major exception being, perhaps, the capital invested in the
Calcutta jute mills in the nineteenth century.[129] And this too was in
Department II alone. India was an absolute, total colony: no tariff
walls protected its industries. Government and railway policy was to
discourage local supplies and to 'buy British'.[130] British capital did
not need to flow into Indian industry since the returns from it could
not be higher than from simple exports to India.[131]

There are many estimates of the seemingly large size of
foreign (mainly British) capital invested in India, steadily rising from
small beginnings before the Mutiny.[132] But it was not actually built
up of capital imports alone, as Goldsmith seems to assume in his
calculations of capital inflow.[133] Much of it came out of the incomes
of British officials in India: they had large salaries and could convert
their savings into tea plantations or shares in European business.[134]
This was surely a kind of primitive accumulation within India. Indian
savings too were transformed into British-controlled capital through
the operations of the Exchange and Presidency Banks, which were
entirely European controlled and provided an important source of

---

[129] Here too, as we shall note presently, much British-owned capital was
raised locally, so that to that extent there was no real movement of capital
from Britain.

[130] Even Morris D. Morris admits, 'official policy did not strongly support
the development of an iron and steel industry [in India] before 1900'.
*CEHI*, II, p. 587. For the railways' policy of buying from Britain, see Hurd
in *CEHI*, II, p. 479.

[131] R.P. Dutt, *India Today*, Bombay, 1947, p. 116, makes the point that, as
appears from Sir George Paish's estimate of total British capital in India
and Ceylon in 1909–10, very little seems to have been invested in industry.

[132] Ibid., pp. 116–17; Goldsmith, *Financial Development*, pp. 17–18.

[133] Goldsmith, *Financial Development*, p. 18.

[134] Bagchi, *Private Investment in India*, pp. 159, 165, 168.

short-term finance to British firms.[135] Finally, the system of European managing agencies enabled Europeans to control capital raised from Indian investors in the managed firms.

The British owners of capital that had been raised in India, tended to return to Britain, expecting the profits to be sent to them. Here was, therefore, a situation opposite to the British-US relationship; the capital was not imported, but the profits were expatriated, representing a further loss to the Indian economy.[136]

For the rest, the capital raised from European residents in India had practically the same pattern of investment as that of imported capital. It went into plantations, import and export, trade and finance, and only very rarely into industry. From the point of view of capitalistic development of India, most of the primitive accumulation that stood behind European capital, could, then, be regarded as so much waste.

The last source of capital formation left was primitive accumulation by Indian proto-capitalists. Clearly, as we can see now, the field for this was extremely limited. Landlord rent extraction was being intensified and, thus, instead of landlord wealth getting transformed into capital, even merchants tended to turn into landowners, as could be seen in the 'emergence of a limited number of large-scale *vaishya* landholders' in UP.[137] Usury fed on itself and there was little to attract the moneylender to industry. Finally, there were no high paid Indian officials with salaries comparable to those of the British, who could turn their savings into capital.

Indigenous industrial capital, therefore, originated mainly out of merchant capital. This can be seen from the information supplied by Amiya Bagchi on the social origins of Indian businessmen.[138] In 1911, of the 433 factories owned by Indians in the Bombay Presidency, as many as 277 were owned by members of the mercantile communities—Banias (125), Parsis (85), Bohras (40), Memons (13), Khatris (9) and Jews (5). The Parsis who dominated the cotton textile industry of Bombay in its earlier phase 'accumulated their capital

---

[135] Ibid., pp. 165, 171–74.
[136] Ibid., pp. 159–60.
[137] Stokes in *CEHI*, II, p.61.
[138] Bagchi, *Private Investment*, p. 184.

first from the opium trade and then from the cotton trade, particularly during the American Civil War'.[139]

It needs to be recalled that ever since Plassey, Indian merchant capital had been under pressure. The old pattern of domestic and foreign trade had been destroyed; the most profitable lines of commerce had been captured, first by the East India Company, and then by European private firms. Indian merchant capital receded into pockets, such as Bombay, where trade in Malwa opium and Deccan cotton offered some opportunities of survival and growth. Thus, if Indian industrial capital was chiefly to come out of merchant capital, its size could only be small, its germination confined to western India and its field of action to the cotton textile industry of Bombay and Ahmedabad. India's low per capita income or the quality of her entrepreneurship had little to do with the limited size and slow growth of indigenous capital.[140] On the one hand, the low per capita income did not deter the realization of the tribute; on the other, the example has yet to be offered where entrepreneurs have emerged in any country, despite a lack of availability of capital.

Colonialism thus created a dual and contradictory situation: it created first, the objective conditions for the emergence and spread of capitalist accumulation—the enlargement of a labour reserve army, modern transport, and modern education—phenomena which led Marx in 1853 to look forward with hope towards industrial development of the country. Simultaneously, however, by extraction of tribute, by intensifying non-capitalistic modes of accumulation and by a deliberate policy of free trade, colonialism greatly narrowed the limits within which capitalist accumulation could in fact develop. The limits were still narrower for indigenous capital.

The biographer of Badruddin Tyabji, president of the third session of the Indian National Congress, tells us how the young barrister made one of his first two political speeches at a big public meeting

---

[139] Ibid., p. 209.

[140] The factor of low per capita income has been repeatedly stressed by Morris D. Morris, most recently in  CEHI, II, p. 601 n. The insistence on deficiencies of Indian entrepreneurs has an older tradition: 'as Indians were unfamiliar with the conduct of modern business, entrepreneurs and capital had to be imported'. D.H. Buchanan, The Development of Capitalistic Enterprise in India, New York, 1934, p. 143. Cf. Bagchi, Private Investment, p. 157 n.

on 3 May 1879 organized by 'the mercantile community' of Bombay
to protest against the abolition of import duties on Lancashire goods.
It was no accident that Tyabji's elder brother was the chairman of the
board of directors of the textile mills belonging to Morarji Gokaldas,
who made the inaugural speech at the same meeting.[141] Incidents such
as this suggest direct links between the travails of Indian capitalism
and the rise of the National Movement. But the small size of indigenous capital should remind us that, despite undoubted links, there
was little correspondence between the slow accumulation of capital
and the much faster and broader spread of bourgeois ideology, finding expression in economic nationalism and swadeshi.[142]

It is not within the scope of this essay to discuss the impetus
that indigenous capitalism in turn derived from the National Movement. In dealing with this immensely complex theme, one can, however, now invoke the benefits of hindsight: for we know the end to
which events led, viz. the creation of an independent India and its
emergence as a bastion of capitalism in Asia.

[141] Husain B. Tyabji, *Badruddin Tyabji*, Bombay, 1952, pp. 127–28.
[142] The classic treatment of the economic thought of the early Indian
nationalists is in Bipan Chandra, *The Rise and Growth of Economic
Nationalism in India*, Delhi, 1966, reprinted 1969.

# Colonialization of the Indian Economy 1757–1900

For all students of modern Indian history, the colonialization of the Indian economy under British rule must remain a theme of overriding importance. Here was the first, the classic capitalist power, creating, and transforming, the largest colony in the world. Marx was greatly interested in this phenomenon, and called attention to the role of India as a source of primary accumulation of capital and as a market for the industries of the colonizing power. He studied, too, the destructive and the regenerative effects of British rule upon the Indian economy.[1] Since then, and especially since R.C. Dutt's splendid two volumes of *Economic History* at the beginning of the century,[2] much has been written on the subject. Monographs on the various regions and on individual aspects of economy and administration during the period have naturally multiplied. There is, indeed, now a danger that the major strands may be overshadowed by the minutiae that detailed research always turns up. A recent debate[3] did much to focus interest back on some of the important issues of the

---

[1] Marx's writings on India are conveniently collected together in Marx, *Articles on India*, second Indian edition, Bombay, 1951 (containing an introduction by R.P. Dutt); and also in Karl Marx and Frederick Engels, *On Colonialism*, Moscow, n.d. R.P. Dutt's own *India Today* contains an indispensable elaboration of Marx's views on India.

[2] *The Economic History of India under Early British Rule*, first published 1901; and *The Economic History of India in the Victorian Age*, first published 1903.

[3] Morris D. Morris' original paper, 'Towards a Re-interpretation of the Nineteenth Century Indian Economic History', published together with its critiques by Toru Matsui, Bipan Chandra and T. Raychaudhuri in *Indian Economic and Social History Review* (*IESHR*), V(1); Morris' rejoinder in *IESHR*, V(4)

main theme; and this paper is written with the same intention.

An attempt is here made to offer (or, mostly, restate) a number of propositions about the process of colonialization of the Indian economy from 1757 to about 1900. I have a feeling that the different stages of colonialization, each with its own specific features, need to be distinguished; and that there is need also to take into account a number of factors which in general discussions, at any rate, have seemed to escape notice. I hope that this paper would induce research workers, more qualified to speak on the subject, to enter the debate and help to reconstruct an acceptable framework for studying the economic processes of these hundred and fifty years.

I

In order to study these processes, it is imperative to keep in mind two given starting points. The first is the mode of production, especially the system of extraction of surplus (or, to use the more convenient term, exploitation) existing in India on the eve of the British conquests. The other is the nature of British imperialism, which was itself subject to change as the British economy was transformed under the impact of the industrial revolution.

On the first of these points, I shall presume, in order to save time, to summarize the conclusions that I have been led to, from the basic arguments set out in some detail in two earlier papers.[4]

The primary method of surplus extraction throughout India had come to be the levy of land revenue on behalf of, or in the name of, the sovereign ruler. This institution had come about not by 'immemorial usage', as British administrators were inclined to think,[5] but as the result of a historical process which can be studied[6] and which would appear to belie the theory of unchangeableness of pre-colonial societies. Whatever its origins, however, it was now the cardinal

---

[4] 'Distribution of Landed Property in Pre-British India', *Enquiry*, New Series, II, 3 (1965), pp. 21–75 (pp. 59–108 of this volume); 'Potentialities of Capitalistic Development in the Economy of Mughal India', *Enquiry*, NS, III, 3, pp. 1–56 (pp. 180–232 of this volume).

[5] Holt Mackenzie spoke in his famous Minute of 1 July 1819, of 'the property vested in government by immemorial usage of $^{10}/_{11}$ of the net rental of the country.' *Selections from the Revenue Records of the North-West Provinces,1818–20*, Calcutta, 1869, p.62.

[6] One attempt to do so is made in my paper in *Enquiry*, NS, II, 3.

principle of the Indian agrarian system, that land revenue should embrace the bulk of the surplus above the peasant's needs of subsistence.

The way in which the claims to land revenue were assigned, that is, how this share of the surplus was distributed among members of the ruling class (by way of *jagir* as in the Mughal empire) defined the basic elements of polity. Upon the expenditure of this vast surplus by the ruling class was based the urban economy of pre-colonial India, with its large craft production, large volume of long-distance trade and considerable development of commercial capital.[7]

Subordinate to the land revenue, and nominally forming a part of it, was a share in the surplus that went to a heterogeneous hereditary or semi-hereditary class of superior right holders over the land, to whom the Mughal clerks gave the convenient designation *zamindars*. Their nominal share varied from one-tenth of the land revenue in northern India and Bengal to one-fourth in Gujarat. It might actually have amounted to more than these proportions, but the recorded sale prices of *zamindari* rights suggest that the income expected from them was always small compared to the land revenue paid on the same land.[8]

One should remind oneself that cash-nexus (payment of land revenue in cash by peasants) was quite general in India;[9] and that sales of *zamindaris* were quite common.[10]

A considerable degree of stratification existed within the peasantry.[11] The village was usually the unit of assessment of land revenue and the upper strata of the peasants (*muqaddams* and the like), often shading off into small *zamindars*, imposed various rates

---

[7] *Enquiry*, NS, III, 3, pp. 22ff.
[8] See Irfan Habib, *Agrarian System of Mughal India*, Bombay, 1963, pp. 136–89.
[9] Ibid., pp. 236–40. 'In general, throughout Bengal, the rents are paid by the ryots in money.' Sir John Shore, Minute of 18 June 1789, para 226, in *The Fifth Report*, II, edited by Firminger, Calcutta, 1917, p. 54.
[10] *Agrarian System*, pp. 157–59.
[11] See Satish Chandra, 'Some Aspects of Indian Village Society in Northern India during the Eighteenth Century', *Indian Historical Review* (*IHR*), I(1), pp. 51–64. See also Choksey's description of various strata within the village community in *Economic History of the Bombay Deccan and Karnatak (1818–1861)*, Poona, 1915, p. 63.

on the peasants below them, in order to make up the revenue demanded from the whole village. This, together with a financial pool for 'village expenses' and certain customary payments to village artisans and servants, formed the basis of the village community.[12] It seems that rather than being the self-sufficient republic conceived of by Marx,[13] the Indian village community was a mechanism of subsidiary exploitation of the lower strata of the peasantry and the village labourers by the upper strata. The ruling class, and perhaps the *zamindars* as well, found this system quite convenient, since by permitting an unequal distribution of the revenue burden, they ensured its fuller collection.

Beneath the peasantry, a large rural proletariat was to be found, largely consisting of the menial and untouchable castes. The *zamindars* and the upper peasants had their farms or *khwud-kasht* holdings cultivated by labourers, who were paid wages in cash as well as grain, and who were held in conditions of semi-bondage.[14]

## II

This was the kind of economy of which the English became masters in Bengal and southern India during the decade and a half following the middle of the eighteenth century. They stepped into the shoes of the sovereign power by virtue of acquisition of *diwani* in Bengal and *jagirs* in the Northern Circars and elsewhere. The legal forms which concealed these conquests are not material except in so far as they provided rationalization for the main acquisition: the power to levy and collect land revenue and other taxes.

The East India Company, which obtained this power, was controlled by the great merchant-capitalists of London. These merchants had so far conducted a trade, based on the import of Indian piecegoods (muslin, calico, chintz), silk, indigo and spices, that was financed mainly by the export of treasure. Now, suddenly, they found in their conquests the ultimate bliss that every merchant dreams of:

---

[12] *Agrarian System*, pp. 122–36, 230–36.
[13] *Articles on India*, pp. 26–28; *On Colonialism*, pp. 35–36; and *Capital*, I, pp. 350–52.
[14] *Agrarian System*, pp. 121–22. See Dharma Kumar in *Comparative Studies in Society and History* (CSSH), IV(iii), pp. 337–63; also her *Land and Caste in South India*, Cambridge, 1965, pp. 29ff.

to be able to buy without having to pay, and yet be able to sell at the full price. This could be achieved by treating the entire revenues of the country as gross profits. From these the expenses necessary for maintaining government and army, and law and order—the costs of maintenance of the existing system of exploitation—had to be deducted in order to yield the net profits. These could, in turn, be invested for the purchase of Indian commodities, the so-called 'investments'. The purchase of these commodities in conditions where the buyer had a monopoly, and their sale in markets throughout the world, further enlarged the profits before the 'tribute'—a word freely in use for it at the time—was finally received in England. The revenues from the conquests dwarfed the amounts in bullion that had once financed English trade; and, accordingly, the exports of Indian commodities underwent an enormous increase. British imports originating in 'East India' increased from £1.5 million in 1750–51 to 5.8 million in 1797–98, from 12 per cent of total British imports to 24 per cent. In contrast, the British exports to East India rose only from 6.4 per cent to 9 per cent of total British exports.[15] Unlike the later imperialists, fighting for markets in the colonies, these pre-industrial conquerors were hunting for colonial commodities, which had the whole world as their market.[16]

The source of the conquerors' profits, however, lay not in commerce but in land revenue. Maximization of land revenue was necessary for the maximization of profits. It was this that led to the unrelenting pressure upon the *zamindars* in Bengal and to the system of temporary revenue farms auctioned to the highest bidders. The actual collection of revenue from the '*diwani* lands' in Bengal was

[15] P. Deane and W.A. Cole, *British Economic Growth, 1688–1959*, Cambridge, 1962, table on p. 87. The figures for 1750–51 are of English imports and exports only.

[16] This distinction does not strike many writers on English eighteenth century colonialism, who tend to speak as if the colonial conquests at that time were also the consequence of a struggle for markets. See, for example, E.J. Hobsbawm, *Industry and Empire*, Pelican Economic History of Britain, Vol. III, 1969, p. 54: 'We defeated them in the East. . . . And we did so for the benefit of *British* goods.' (Emphasis in the original.) But see Engels, Letter to Conrad Schmidt, 1890, extract in Marx, *Articles on India*, p. 97.

[17] Shore, Minute of 18 June 1789, para 68, *Fifth Report*, II, edited by Firminger, p. 18.

pushed up from Rs 64.3 lakh in 1762–63, under the *Nizamat*, to
Rs 147.0 lakh in 1765–66, the first year of the Company's *diwani*.[17]
And, according to another set of figures, the revenues of Bengal
increased from Rs 2.26 crore in 1765–66 to Rs 3.7 crore in 1778–
79.[18] Such was the pressure that a famine which in 1769–70 carried
off a third of the cultivators of Bengal, caused no decline in revenue
assessments.[19]

This tremendous pressure upon revenue payers, peasants as
well as *zamindars*, could not but create a crisis in Bengal; and it is
this crisis that forms the background to the controversy among the
English administrators, preceding the Permanent Settlement. One
group, represented by James Grant, argued that the land revenue
could yet be considerably increased.[20] The other, of which Cornwallis
became the spokesman, saw that the terrifying results of the tribute
so far extorted left no alternative but to offer a compromise to the
*zamindars*, whereby the Company might be protected against a fall
in its revenues, by resigning claims to any increase in land revenue
beyond a figure now to be finally settled.[21] Sir John Shore took an
intermediate position. But Cornwallis, backed by his alarmed masters, won the day, and Permanent Settlement was proclaimed in 1793.

Whatever the intellectual origins of the Permanent Settlement,[22] and however profusely the word 'proprietor' might be used

---

[18] R.C. Dutt, *Economic History of India under Early British Rule* (sixth
London edition), pp. 46, 69. Figures reconverted from sterling at 1=Rs 10.

[19] W. Hunter, *The Annals of Rural Bengal*, 1897, p. 39.

[20] 'Historical and Comparative Analysis of the Finances of Bengal', April
1786, in *Fifth Report*, II, pp. 159–477. Grant sums up his views on pp. 159–
60, when he says that there was a 'defalcation' of half a crore of rupees
yearly in the Northern Circars, and two crores in Bengal, i.e. the Company
could raise its collections further by these sums. See his table on p. 476.
See also Grant's 'Political Survey of the Northern Circars, 1784–1786',
*Fifth Report*, III, edited by Ferminger, pp. 1–118.

[21] Cornwallis sounds the alarm upon 'the consequences of the heavy drain
of wealth' being severely felt and 'the langour which has thereby been
thrown upon the cultivation and commerce of the country', and declares
that unless its 'inhabitants' (read, *zamindars*) were given 'some prospects
of private advantage to themselves', they could not be expected to exert
themselves. This was necessary to enable Bengal 'to continue to be a solid
support to British interests', i.e. to continue to furnish tribute. Cornwallis,
Minute of 3 February 1790, *Fifth Report*, II, p.542.

[22] Ranajit Guha, *A Rule of Property for Bengal*, Paris, 1963.

for the *zamindar* by Shore and Cornwallis,[23] all this did not convert him into a real landlord. The bulk of the surplus went to the Company. The share of the *zamindar*, to begin with, was fixed at only an eleventh part of the land revenue expected to be assessed on the peasants. The *zamindars* were thus really cast in the role of little more than hereditary revenue farmers with fixed leases. In 1789 Shore estimated the total surplus of Bengal at Rs 3.25 crore, of which the Company exacted no less than Rs 2 crore while the remainder went to *zamindars*, other intermediaries and holders of 'alienated lands'.

Moreover, the position of the *zamindars* worsened on the morrow of the Permanent Settlement.[24] It is possible, though I have not found it suggested anywhere, that the immediate cause for this lay in the behaviour of prices. Cornwallis had expected the rate of silver gradually to fall, and so the prices to rise; but, if Brij Narain's series of prices of coarse rice in Bengal is to be trusted, prices fell disastrously. From 1780 to 1789, the price of coarse rice had remained stable at an annual average of Rs 1.51 per maund; and for the next five years, 1790–94, the average remained nearly the same, at Rs 1.56. But in 1795 the price fell and remained low for the next fifteen years, the annual average being only Re. 0.85 per maund during 1795–99, Rs 1.02 during 1800–04, and Rs 1.09 during 1805–09.[25] Faced with this fall in prices, which kept them at barely 65 per cent of the level maintained before 1793, it is not surprising that many of the *zamindars* could not collect rents from the peasants at the old rates in order to meet the fixed revenue demand of the Company, and had no choice but to sell out or see their right auctioned off to other bidders. It was at this time that a number of *zamindaris* passed by foreclosure of mortgage, sale or auction to bankers and merchants.[26]

[23] Shore, Minute of 18 June 1789, *Fifth Report*, II, pp. 27–29.

[24] N.K. Sinha, *Economic History of Bengal*, II, Calcutta, 1962, pp. 177–78.

[25] Brij Narain, *Indian Economic Life, Past and Present*, Lahore, 1929.

[26] N.K. Sinha, *Economic History of Bengal*, II, pp. 177, 223. For the entry of merchants and bankers into the ranks of *zamindars* in the Banaras region, another permanently settled area, see B. Cohn, *Land Control and Social Structure in Indian History*, edited by R.E. Frykenburg, pp. 80–84. This does not, of course, mean that all or even most of the new *zamindars* (the auction-purchasers and other buyers) were bankers and merchants. See Ratna Ray, *IESHR*, XI (1), pp. 1–2.

This was not, however, a transfer of capital from commerce to land;[27] but really an indirect annexation of that capital by the East India Company.

Thus, irrespective of intentions, there was no relaxation of pressure against the *zamindars* (and through them, upon the peasantry). What this pressure yielded was 'the drain of wealth' to England. It is naturally not easy to compute the total amount of this drain or its annual flow. Much would depend on whether the calculation is on the basis of 'prime costs' in India, naturally depressed owing to the Company's monopoly, or on sale prices received by it on the Indian commodities; and whether one would consider only the 'investment' in the China trade, fully financed from Bengal, or the entire return on that investment. Taking the drain through the official channels of the Company alone, the drain from Bengal and Bihar would have amounted in 1779, by one criterion, to £ 737,651; but, by the other, to £ 1,823,407(at £ 1=Rs 10).[28] Keeping to the conservative criteria, Furber estimates the total drain (including private remittances by Englishmen, often through the other European companies) at £ 1.78 million per annum during the decade 1783–84 to 1792–93.[29] One way, again, of estimating the amount of tribute is by looking at the balance of trade between Britain and 'East India', although this would exclude the drain through Europe. According to the customs house figures, there was a spectacular increase in the excess of imports from East India over exports thereto, between 1789–90 and 1797–98. In the earlier year the excess amounted to £ 1.16 million; in the later, £ 4.15 million.[30] The year 1797–98 might, however, have been an exceptional year.[31] Taking the years 1797–1801, the excess of the value of imports works out at £ 2.81 million per annum; and during the years 1799–1803, at £ 2.58 million.[32] Let

[27] N.K. Sinha, *Economic History of Bengal*, p. 223: 'Cornwallis succeeded in diverting native capital to land.'

[28] James Grant in *Fifth Report*, II, p. 281

[29] H. Furber, *John Company at Work*, Cambridge, Mass., 1951, pp. 112–16.

[30] Deane and Cole, *British Economic Growth*, table on p. 87.

[31] See table in B.R. Mitchell and P. Deane, *Abstract of British Historical Statistics*, p. 331.

[32] Ibid.

us then assume that £ 2.70 million represents approximately the annual excess in value of imports over exports. Since the customs house recorded the prices at prime costs, or even simply accepted declarations as to prices prevailing in the country of origin, the imports were greatly undervalued. The official prices need to be multiplied by a factor of about 1.75 in order to be brought up to real prices.[33] One has also to take smuggling into account.[34] One should therefore put the total gain of Britain at the expense of India to well over £ 2 million in 1789–90 and over £ 4.70 million about 1801. This enormous transfer of wealth could not but have significant consequences for both India and England.

It is difficult to estimate the GNP of the British possessions in India which directly contributed the tribute. Grant in his calculations grossly overestimated the agricultural produce of Bengal.[35] Applying Shore's more reasonable estimate for the total agricultural produce of Bengal[36] to the British Indian possessions as a whole, in proportion to the land revenue they contributed,[37] we get a figure approaching Rs 15 crore. To this we may add Rs 5 crore as value added by manufactures, enlarging proportionately the estimate of Rs 3 crore given by Grant for Bengal.[38] The total GNP of Bengal, Bihar, Banaras, the Northern Circars, etc., should therefore have been under Rs 20 crore per year during the period 1784–89, to which the calculations of Grant and Shore relate. Taking Furber's estimate (based on prime cost in India) for the drain during 1783–84 to 1792–93, we find that the tribute amounted to 9 per cent of the GNP—a crippling drain for any economy.

How this specifically affected the economy needs to be studied. It would seem that we should be looking for a two-fold effect. First, there must have been a considerable decline in Bengal in the

---

[33] On the nature of official valuation, Deane and Cole, *British Economic Growth*, pp. 42–43, 315–17. When converted into real prices, the total value of British imports in 1797–98 rises from £24.4 million to £43.1 million. Ibid., table on p. 44.

[34] Ibid., pp. 44–45.

[34] Grant in *Fifth Report*, II, p. 276. He put the agricultural product of Bengal alone at Rs 21 crore annually.

[36] Shore, *Fifth Report*, II, p. 27, estimated it at Rs 8.51 crore.

[37] Based on Grant's table in *Fifth Report*, II, p. 476.

[38] *Fifth Report*, II, p. 276.

kind of urban employment of troops, retainers, craftsmen in traditional luxury trades, servants and so on, which was supported by the previous appropriators of the surplus. This is exactly the burden of Ghulam Hussain Tabatabai's complaints in 1781.[39] Second, in so far as the transfer of wealth took the form of exports of eastern Indian commodities, this resulted in a radical disturbance of the entire trading pattern of India. In the previous century the principal exports of Bengal used to be transported overland eastwards: much of the muslin, and a third of the silk.[40] The great silk manufacturers of Gujarat prospered on silk imports from Bengal.[41] Now, however, of the Rs 3.30 crore worth of 'raw silk, cotton and silk manufactures' of Bengal, no less than Rs 1.68 crore worth was exported to Europe, 1.10 crore consumed locally, and only 0.60 crore left for export to other parts of India and the Middle East.[42] This great diversion of trade could not but have had its effect upon Gujarat and other craft centres so far dependent upon silk from Bengal. There must also have been an absolute decline in Bengal's commerce with the inland regions, thus causing merchant capital formerly employed in it to become idle—a complementary factor, undoubtedly, in the acquisition of *zamindari* by bankers and merchants.

At the cost of a short digression, a word on the role of the Indian tribute in the economy of England would not be out of order. Taking the amount of the tribute to be about £ 4.70 million on the basis of sale prices, we find that it amounted to over 2 per cent of the British national income, estimated at £ 232 million for 1801.[43] We must remember that the total rate of capital formation in Britain was probably no more than 7 per cent of the national income about this time;[44] and this means that, at this crucial stage of the Industrial

---

[39] *Siyar-ul Mutakhirin*, II, Kanpur, pp. 836–37, 840–41.

[40] J.B. Tavernier, *Travels in India, 1640–67*, II, translated by Ball, second edition revised by W. Crooke, London, 1925, p. 2. Of the silk, a third remained in Bengal, a third was sent to other parts of India and the Middle East, and a third was sent to Europe through the Dutch.

[41] Ibid.

[42] Grant in *Fifth Report*, II, p. 276.

[43] Deane and Cole, *British Economic Growth*, pp. 161, 281–82. The National Income estimate for 1801 is really an estimate of National Product and is also described as such by Deane and Cole.

[44] Ibid., p. 263. See also F. Crouzet (ed.), *Capital Formation in the Industrial Revolution*, London, 1972, p. 15 and n.

Revolution, India was furnishing her with an amount that was almost 30 per cent of the total national saving. The neglect of this factor in discussions of capital formation in England during this period is surprising. One would certainly have to assume a complete immobility of capital to suggest that this enormous accession of wealth in the hands of London merchants and the nabobs did not directly or indirectly channel capital into industry to any significant degree whatsoever.[45]

By 1800, England was on the threshold of completing the conquest of the cotton textile industry by the machine. During the next thirty years the extension of the machine to most other sectors was to be similarly accomplished, culminating in the construction of railways, a sector that was to dominate the British economy during the 1830s and 1840s. The need for capital not only continued, but increased. The annual rate of capital formation as a proportion of national income was maintained at about 7 per cent until 1830, whereafter it accelerated to reach 9 or 10 per cent.[46] This capital could not yet entirely be generated by 'capitalist circulation', and needed continuing primary accumulation. As against the rate of 9 per cent of national income for total capital formation reached during 1821–31 to 1831–61, net *domestic* capital formation accounted for only 7.4 per cent of the national income.[47] This meant that the pressure for tribute could not be relaxed.

But simultaneously, another aspect became increasingly important: the progressive subjugation of the Indian market for English industry. The British cotton textile industry consumed 16.1 million lbs of raw cotton in 1784–86; 99.7 million lbs in 1815–17; and 1050 million lbs in 1859–60. The enormous increase could not be sustained by the home market. The proportion of the output exported to total output during the successive periods rose from 16 per cent in 1784–86 to 58 per cent in 1815–17, and 63 per cent in 1859–61.[48] Not only would these exports destroy the worldwide market for Indian textiles, but it would become necessary for Lancashire to

[45] See.Deane and Cole, *British Economic Growth*, pp. 34–35, who offer extremely inconclusive remarks on the whole question.
[46] Ibid., pp. 263–64; Crouzet, *Capital Formation*, p. 15 and n.
[47] Kuznets, cited in Crouzet, p. 15 n.
[48] Deane and Cole, *British Economic Growth*, pp. 185, 187.

invade India's own home market. A similar urge governed other new industries as they came up with mass products.

This dual economic assault upon India marks the second stage of British colonialism in India, set by the progress of industrialization in England. The duality was not without its own contradictions, complicating the realization of the tribute as well as the conquest of the Indian market—contradictions that we will comment upon presently.

### III A

At the end of the eighteenth century, the official doctrine seemed to be that a limitation of revenue demand was desirable in order to create private property in land, which would in turn lead to extension of cultivation and growth of commerce. What the Company was denying to itself by way of land revenue would be more than compensated in time by the enlargement of revenue from taxes on commerce.[49] Cornwallis had picked on the *zamindars* as the future proprietors; Munro, the architect of the *ryotwari* system, thought a limitation of land revenue to a third of the produce would render land an article of saleable property for the cultivating *ryots*.[50]

But very soon a different view became dominant: the view that neither the *zamindars* nor the peasants deserved to be proprietors. Any part of the surplus left in their hands was wasted; it must belong to the Company; and the business of land administration was to find out the cost of production so as to appropriate the net product in the form of revenue. The proponents of the doctrine were the Utilitarians, the ideological spokesmen of triumphant capitalism.[51]

This doctrine was essentially a rationalization of the economic pressures already at work. The Directors of the Company had become dissatisfied with the Permanent Settlement, even before James Mill had uttered a word on the subject. They flatly repudiated, in 1811, the Permanent Settlement that had been promised to the

---

[49] Cornwallis, Minute of 3 February 1790, *Fifth Report*, II, p. 541.

[50] Thomas Munro's report, 15 August 1807, in *Fifth Report*, III, pp. 501–2.

[51] The outstanding study of utilitarian views in respect of Indian land revenue and agrarian economy is by Eric Stokes, *The English Utilitarians and India*, Oxford, 1959, pp. 81–139.

*zamindars* of the Ceded and Conquered Provinces (modern Uttar
Pradesh, excluding Oudh) in 1803 and 1805. They then probably
thought that waiving claims to revenue due upon extension of cultivation was unwise; but the rise in prices which took place in the
second and third decades of the century must have set a seal upon
their distavour. The rise in prices was such that the price level around
1830 was over 50 per cent above what it was in 1800.[52] Most of the
benefit from this went to the *zamindars*, who could enhance the rents
from the *ryots*, while their own obligation towards the company
remained fixed in terms of cash. From the Court of Wards accounts
of Bengal, before 1832, it appears that the *zamindars'* profits now
equalled or exceeded slightly the government revenue.[53] Here lay the
basis for the growth of true landlordism in the permanently settled
areas: in Banaras, permanently settled in 1795, the average price paid
for *zamindaris* in 1837 was fifteen times the annual revenue demand
on the land involved.[54]

But the permanently settled areas of eastern India were to
remain an exception, and the transformation of its *zamindars* into
landlords cannot be held to be characteristic of the position of the
*zamindar* class as a whole during this period. The characteristic
operation of imperialism of this stage was seen only partially in the
*ryotwari* settlements. It appears in its true fullness in the *mahalwari*
system of the Ceded and Conquered Provinces (annexed 1801,
1803). The *ryotwari* was a permanent arrangement only in so far as
the land occupied by the *ryot* at the time of the settlement was concerned; even here it provided for a mechanism to adjust revenue to

[52] I rely upon Brij Narain's series of prices of coarse rice in Bengal. The average annual price during 1800–09 was Rs 1.05 per md.; during 1810–19,
Rs 1.22; during 1820–29, Rs 1.66; and during 1830–39, Rs 1.43. This trend
was not confined to Bengal or to rice. The price of wheat at Farrukhabad
(UP) was on an average Re 0.91 per md. during 1801–10, Rs 1.13 during
1811–20, Rs 1.21 during 1821–30, and Rs 1.33 during 1831–40. Brij
Narain, *Indian Economic Life, Past and Present*, pp. 113–14.
[53] Out of the 'farmers' rent' of Rs 11.75 lakh collected in the Court of Ward
estates throughout Bengal, government revenue accounted for Rs 5.74
lakh; the remainder, Rs 6.01 lakh, formed the 'Zamindar's Profit'.
Statement furnished by Holt–Mackenzie, *Parliamentary Papers, 1831–
32, Colonies: East India*, 9, Irish University Press, p. 255.
[54] B. Cohn in *Land Control and Social Structure in Indian History*, edited
by R.E. Frykenburg, Madison, 1969, p. 112.

prices. The wasteland remained with the government to be given later upon terms of its choosing. In the *mahalwari* and Bombay systems, there was never a permanent settlement; only short leases, at first, and then settlements for 20 or 30 years, in the 1830s and 1840s.

In studying the various principles and methods of assessment that were employed, one is struck by the divergence between what should, at first sight, have happened and what actually resulted. On paper, in the Ceded and Conquered Provinces, the land revenue was reduced from 91 to 83 per cent of the total 'rental' in 1822, to 75 per cent by the Regulations of 1833, and to 66 per cent by the Directions of 1844. In 1855 for future settlements it was reduced to 50 per cent by the so-called Saharanpur Rules. Pringle claimed that but 55 per cent of the rental was taken as land revenue in Bombay.[55] Similarly, the insistence that settlement officers work out costs of production and vary the rates according to soils tends to suggest that the 'rental' was assessed properly, and the reductions of land revenue to lower and lower proportions should have reduced the revenue demand per acre.

It is best to remember that these measures for theoretically scaling down the land revenue were accompanied by others that had the opposite effect. The land revenue under the preceding Indian regimes was fixed as a share of the crop, and varied according to the crop cultivated. The land revenue under the British, whether directly imposed on the *ryots* or assessed on the *zamindars*, was a true tax on land. The assessment was on the basis of what and how much it ought to produce, not on what crop it actually raised. The Anglo-Indian land tax had, therefore, still less to do with actualities of production than the tax it was replacing. Secondly, the more scientific land surveys increasingly made it impossible for any land to be concealed and so to escape assessment, a feature quite common under earlier administrations. There were also large-scale resumptions of lands hitherto held revenue-free. Thus the actual incidence of demand per acre would increase simply because of more efficient survey, as well as owing to resumptions. When the notion of fixing the revenue on the basis of 'rents' prevailing between primary cultivators and revenue payers was increasingly invoked, this too did not help because these

[55] E. Stokes, *English Utilitarians and India*, p. 134.

'rents' themselves were determined by the magnitude of land revenue previously in force. Moreover, under Bird in the Ceded and Conquered Provinces, and Wingate in Bombay, the practice of first fixing the total demand on an area, and only then undertaking its distribution upon lower units (village, field), rendered the assessment to be governed by what was assessed previously. Beyond all this was the ability of the Company to collect what had been assessed, an ability to some degree denied to its predecessors.[56]

It is, therefore, essential to consider the total land-revenue collections, in order to see whether the fiscal pressure upon the revenue payers increased or not. Unfortunately, territorial alternations make valueless certain statistics of revenue collections in the Ceded and Conquered Provinces (or Agra Province). But a comparative statement for the Provinces explicitly excluding Banaras, Ghazipur and Jaunpur (permanently settled) and all acquisitions made after 1806–07, puts the total land-revenue demand at Rs 2.10 crore in 1806–07, Rs 3.06 crore in 1819–20 and Rs 3.60 crore in 1829–30, which means an increase of over 70 per cent in twenty-three years.[57] A set of figures of actual revenue receipts shows that they rose in the Agra Province from Rs 4.96 crore in 1834–35 to Rs 5.60 crore in 1844–45, an increase of 15 per cent in ten years.[58] According to another set of figures given by a witness conscious of the effects of territorial changes, the land revenue of the same provinces amounted to £3.33 million in 1826–27 and £ 3.25 million 1831–32.[59] These statistics suggest an overall increase of about 88 per cent in the land-revenue demand during the forty years following 1806–07. Were we able to consider the statistics for revenue collection for the same period, the increase would be still larger.

---

[56] In 1838–39, the amount assessed in the North-Western Provinces (old Ceded and Conquered Provinces) was Rs 4.6 crore, the collection Rs 3.6 crore. In 1847–48 the respective figures were Rs 4.3 and Rs 4.2 crore. See R.C. Dutt, *Economic History of India in the Victorian Age*, London, 1950, p. 46. The figures have been reconverted at £ 1=Rs 10

[57] *Parliamentary Papers, 1831–32, Colonies: East India*, 9, IUP, Appendix, pp. 4–5.

[58] *Parliamentary Papers, 1852, Colonies: East India*, 12, IUP, pp. 481–82. Figures for subsequent years are not comparable because of the addition of Cis- and Trans-Sutlej Territories in 1846–47.

[59] *Parliamentary Papers, 1871, Colonies: East India*, 19, IUP, p. 84.

The prices during this period increased at the beginning, but became stable after 1818. The following prices are taken from Brij Narain.[60]

*Average price of wheat, Farrukhabad*

| Year | Price (Rs per md) |
|------|-------------------|
| 1801–10 | 0.91 |
| 1811–20 | 1.13 |
| 1821–30 | 1.21 |
| 1831–40 | 1.33 |
| 1841–50 | 1.03 |

The price data collected by Asiya Siddiqi for the same region for the period 1813 to 1840,[61] also broadly discount any possibility of a large increase in prices after 1820: on the contrary, there appears to be a distinct tendency towards depression in wheat prices, and quite a noticeable decline in jowar and bajra. The behaviour of rice prices varied sharply from place to place. It is thus quite obvious that the increase in land revenue in the Ceded and Conquered Provinces was a substantial increase in *real* terms, by nearly as much as 70 per cent during the first half of the nineteenth century, at constant prices.

In Bombay, the land-revenue assessments immediately after the annexation (1818) were pushed up to the maximum levels ever reached under the Peshwa's regime.[62] Pringle's assessments which followed in 1825 were acknowledged to have been devastatingly high.[63] These methods were supposed to have been moderated by the

[60] *Indian Economic Life, Past and Present*, pp. 113–14.

[61] A. Siddiqi, *Agrarian Change in a North Indian State*, Oxford, 1973, pp. 187–94.

[62] R.D. Choksey, *Economic History of the Bombay Deccan and Karnatak*, pp. 24–25. The land revenue collection, Rs 0.69 crore in 1817–18, was pushed up to Rs 1.82 crore by 1820–21. R.C. Dutt, *Economic History of India in the Victorian Age*, p. 65.

[63] Its results were thus described by the Administrative Report of the Bombay Presidency (1872): 'Numbers abandoned their homes and fled into the neighbouring states. Large tracts of land were thrown out of cultivation; and in some districts no more than a third of the cultivable area remained in occupation.' Quoted by Choksey, *Economic History of the Bombay Deccan and Karnatak*, p. 92n.

survey which commenced under Goldsmith and Wingate, in 1835. Yet the moderation did not affect the total collection. In 1837–38 the land-revenue collection in Bombay Presidency stood at £ 1.86 million, a figure that had only once before been exceeded (in 1826–27).[64] In 1842, it touched £ 2 million.[65]

There was no justification for the maintenance of collections of this magnitude in the movement of prices in Bombay Presidency. With the exception of some years, there was continuous decline in the prices of jowar and bajra, the staple foodcrops of the region, from 1820 to 1832;[66] and a very great decline in the prices of foodcrops occurred during the 1840s, the low levels continuing until after 1855.[67]

In Madras Presidency, settlements were carried out under Sir Thomas Munro during 1820–27. The old assessments had been very heavy, and the new were by no means moderate.[68] The total land-revenue collections in Madras Presidency amounted to £3.79 million in 1819–20 and to £ 3.43 million in 1837–38.[69] The collections during the next decade increased considerably.[70] But prices declined

---

[64] R.C. Dutt, Economic History of India under Early British Rule, pp. 403–5.

[65] Parliamentary Papers, 1871, Colonies: East India, 19, IUP, p. 8.

[66] Choksey, Economic History of the Bombay Deccan and Karnatak, pp. 93–94.

[67] Statement of Prices at Bombay, Poona, Belgaum and Ahmedabad (1824–1863) for wheat, jowar, rice, ghi and firewood, in Parliamentary Papers, 1871, Colonies: East India, 19, IUP, pp. 617–18.

[68] The conclusions Nilmani Mukherjee arrives at, after a detailed study of the economic consequences of the ryotwari arrangements during the period 1792–1827, are: 'The high assessments caused great suffering to the ryots. There was a marked shrinkage in the volume of agricultural output.' Ryotwari System in Madras, 1792–1827, Calcutta, 1962, p. 313.

[69] R.C. Dutt, Economic History of India under Early British Rule, pp. 403–5.

[70] Dharma Kumar (Land and Caste in South India, Cambridge, 1965, p. 114) says the annual average collection of land revenue during the first ten years of the nineteenth century was Rs 384 lakh, and in the decade ending 1849–50, Rs 395 lakh (the decimal points placed in these figures in Kumar are obvious misprints). The figures for the last decade represented full recovery from a decline that had occurred during the preceding two decades. Rs 10 were then worth £ 1. The acquisition of the small principality of Karnul in 1842 could not have had a more than marginal effect on the total revenue collections of the entire Presidency.

substantially over the whole period: the average annual price of common rice was Rs 1.47 per maund in 1813–19, Rs 1.53 in 1819–23, Rs 1.33 in 1828–32, and Rs 1.13 in 1841–53.[71] A set of index numbers of food prices compiled for Madras Presidency show that with the prices during the decade 1801–02 as base, =100, the average annual prices during the succeeding decades were 88.5 (1811–12 to 1820–21); 98.2 (1821–22 to 1830–31); 91.4 (1831–32 to 1840–41); and 69.0 (1841–42 to 1850–51).[72] Thus the total revenue collections in Madras Presidency appear to have moved in a direction opposite to the movement of prices.[73]

The general picture, then, is that from about 1820 to 1850, the total revenue collections increased substantially in all the three major zones outside the permanently settled territories. Among these zones the highest increase undoubtedly occurred in the North-Western Provinces (Ceded and Conquered Provinces). The only factor which might relieve the pressure on the agrarian economy exerted by real taxation on such scale, could be a substantial increase in population, causing a dramatic extension of cultivation and therefore a decline in the incidence of land revenue per acre as well as per capita.

'All authorities [!] agree', in the words of a cautious spokesman of the official British view, on all matters, 'that a great increase [in population] took place between the beginning of the nineteenth century and the first [but incomplete] census of 1872. . . .'[74] It is, indeed, true that official or semi-official estimates suggest an increase in population from 134 million in 1820 to about 255 million in

---

[71] Dharma Kumar, *Land and Caste*, p. 91.

[72] A. Sarada Raju's table and index (unweighted) in her *Economic Conditions in the Madras Presidency, 1801–50*, Madras, 1941, pp. 228–29. The averages for decades have been calculated by me from her index. Also see Dharma Kumar, *Land and Caste*, p. 84: from the table of Index Numbers of Food Prices reproduced by her, it can be seen that the average price for the years 1841–42 to 1850–51 was only 66.5, when the 1816–25 prices are taken as base, = 100.

[73] Other evidence for the heavy incidence of land revenue in the Madras Presidency during the first half of the nineteenth century is furnished in A. Sarada Raju, *Economic Conditions*, pp. 49–52.

[74] V. Anstey, *The Economic Development of India*, London, 1957, p. 38. The first edition of her work appeared in 1929.

1871.[75] But the wonderful thing about these figures is that they exhibit an almost stable population from 1820 to 1844—indicating, in fact, a decline from 134 million to 131.8 million. It is only after 1844 that a dramatic rise occurs, to 151.9 million in 1852,[76] 180.9 million in 1855 and 190.9 million in 1865, before 255 million are reached in 1871, a feat only possible at a rate of growth of 5 per cent per annum during the last six years. But as soon as the censuses properly begin, with 1871, there is a sudden fall to a rate of growth of just 0.39 per cent per annum for the next thirty years, the population in 1901 being only 281 million.

Davis attempts to deal with this statistical 'embarrassment of riches' for the period 1844 to 1871, yielding a rate of increase of about 3 per cent annum (a demographic monstrosity), by suggesting that the increase is wrongly spaced in the contemporary estimates, and that the earlier estimates are right, but the middle ones are, inexplicably, gross underestimates. 'The best policy seems to be . . . to assume that the population remained at this point [125 million] for one and half centuries more [after 1600], after which a gradual enhancement of growth began, accelerating as 1870 approached'.[77] This is clearly not an attempt at interpreting the demographic evidence, but at subverting it altogether, in order to maintain one's assumptions about the economic benefits of British rule.

The stability of the population between 1820 and 1850 is quite remarkably corroborated by such detailed districtwise estimates as we have. The population of Madras Presidency, according to Dharma Kumar's figures, increased only from 13.48 million in

---

[75] D. and B. Bhattacharya, *Census of India, 1961: Report on the Population Estimates of India*. See also Kingsley Davis, *Population of India and Pakistan*, Princeton, 1951, p. 25. Davis's figure for 1800 in his table of contemporary estimates is really his own, having practically nothing to do with the figure given by the source from which it is ostensibly abstracted.

[76] *British Parliamentary Papers, 1852, Colonies: East India*, 12, IUP, pp. 334–39. The other figures are abstracted from D. and B. Bhattacharya, *Census of India*.

[77] Kingsley Davis, *Population of India and Pakistan*, p. 26. The figure for 1600 is Davis's own revision of Moreland's estimate (itself weakly based) of 100 million. The latest estimate for 1600 is 144 million by Shireen Moosvi in *IESHR*, X (2), pp. 180–95.

1823 to 13.97 million in 1839.[78] I worked on certain data available for various districts of eastern India and found a *total* increase in population of about 15 per cent between 1812 and 1852, giving a rate of annual increase of about 0.35 per cent at the compound rate.[79] In the case of both Dharma Kumar's tables and my own, a remarkable increase takes place during the two decades preceding 1871-72.[80]

While all this would be sufficient to rule out a fall in land revenue per capita during 1820–44, there is the strong probability that the population increase between 1844 and 1872 is also ephemeral. In UP (excluding Oudh), there were fairly efficient censuses conducted in 1853 and 1865. Selecting ten districts at random, I found a total increase of just 10 per cent during the nineteen years between 1853 and 1872, yielding an annual rate of increase of about 0.5 per cent.[81]

What seems likely, therefore, is that the estimates and even some of the 'censuses' like the 1847 census in the North-Western Provinces, before the 1871–72 census, gave grossly low figures for the population, by probably heavily under-enumerating the rural population. As such, the entire evidence becomes suspect. But such as it is, it certainly gives no ground for postulating any increase of population much beyond 15 per cent during the first half of the century, and 10 per cent during the next twenty years: the population of India was probably slightly less than 200 million in 1801 and about 230 million in 1851.[83]

[78] Dharma Kumar, *Land and Caste*, pp. 120–21.

[79] Note on Indian Population, 1800–72 (unpublished) presented at the seminar on the Colonization of the Indian Economy, Aligarh, 1972, table I.

[80] The year after 1839 for which Dharma Kumar offers figures is 1851–52, with population at 22.01 million, growing to 31.60 million in 1871. My table showed a similar increase from a population of 19.60 million *c.* 1852, to 31.14 million in 1872.

[81] See my Note on Indian Population, table II.

[82] When the 1868 census of Oudh (part of the 1871–72 census) returned a population of 11.22 million, the confession was made that 'we [had] always underestimated it, and nobody imagined that the population was so dense till there was a regular census taken.' *Parliamentary Papers, 1871, Colonies: East India*, 19, IUP, p. 98.

[83] This fits in with M. Mukerji's revision of the official population figure for 1856 to 227 million, by multiplying the original figure by 1.256, the factor implied in Davis's revision of the 1871 census, on account of underestimation and incomplete geographical coverage. M. Mukerji in *Economic*

If, then, we consider the actual incidence of land revenue, it becomes clear that by 1850 the basic pillar of British colonialism was still the direct appropriation of the agricultural surplus; and that, unrelieved by any decline in per capita terms, this appropriation was pressing hard upon the producer just as Marx had visualized it.[84] It is obviously difficult to document the decline in material conditions of life of the peasantry. What one can say from portrayals of the diet of the rural classes of northern India, such as the one quoted by Crawfurd,[85] is that the ultimate in poverty had seemingly been reached.

The pressure upon the peasantry was seen by Marx as involving the destruction of the Indian village communities.[86] Marx had undoubtedly obtained a rather idealized picture of the village community from his reading of some of the official reports. A closer scrutiny suggests, as I have earlier indicated, that the village communities really concealed considerable stratification and dominance of a body of upper peasants and small *zamindars* over a number of cultivators and landless labourers.[87] As the British sought to maximize land revenue and had far greater power of control, they could disregard the village as a revenue-paying unit in a manner that had been impos-

---

*History of India, 1857–1956*, edited by V.B. Singh, Bombay, 1965, pp. 667–68. It is not clear, however, whether the 1856 estimate had overlooked the areas excluded by the 1871 census.

[84] Rent, says Marx, 'may assume dimensions which seriously imperil reproduction of the conditions of labour, the means of production themselves, rendering the expansion of production more or less impossible and reducing the direct producers to the physical minimum of the means of subsistence. This is particularly the case when this form is met with and exploited by a conquering commercial nation, e.g. the English in India.' *Capital*, III, Moscow, 1959, pp. 776–77. See also Marx's article of 19 July 1853, reprinted in *On Colonialism*, pp. 72–75.

[85] John Crawfurd in *The Economic Development of India under the East India Company 1814–58*, edited by K.N. Chaudhuri, Cambridge, 1971, p. 234. The description is of the year 1826. Speaking of 'the food of the lower classes in the villages' of Hindustan, the observer says, 'their earnings rising only from 4s. to 6s. [Rs 2 to 3] per mensem, forces a recourse to the vilest food. The more scrupulous castes are obliged to mix with coarse grains above mentioned wild roots, herbs and insects; while the outcastes as the numerous race of Chumars, Kanjars, Dusads, etc., scruple not to eat vermin, dead fish, carrion, etc.'

[86] *Articles on India*, p. 21; *On Colonialism*, p. 36.

[87] See Section I of this article.

sible for the earlier regimes.[88] They could then press upon the upper elements that had so far been favoured with lower rates; and gradually the smaller *muqaddams* of the *mahalwari* system and the *mirasdars* of Bombay, the kingpins of the old communities, tended to be levelled with the lower strata of the peasantry.[89] On the other hand, it is less easy to consider what happened to the agricultural labourers. In so far as they depended upon wages from the upper peasantry, its woes were naturally passed on to them in an intensified form. At the same time, the weakening of communal control probably enabled certain landless labourers of lower castes to set up as cultivators.[90] But there is little evidence that this was of more than marginal significance; and where, as in Malabar and Canara, agrestic bondage prevailed, the Act of 1843 had little actual effect in altering the condition of the bondsmen.[91] It is possible that the population of landless labour increased by emigration of unemployed urban labour; but the evidence for this too has not yet been brought out.

A significant fact, quite often missed, is that up till the middle of the eighteenth century, outside the permanently settled regions of eastern India, the pressure upon the *zamindars* tended to be extremely heavy. The official statements regarding *zamindars* in the light of proprietors and even conceiving them as allies of British power, had little significance in the actual world of revenue collections. Their position was naturally the worst in the *mahalwari* areas of northern India where the collections had been most relentless. It was officially acknowledged in 1882–83, with reference to the pre-Mutiny assessments, that

---

[88] See my *Agrarian System of Mughal India*, pp. 230–36.

[89] For the *mahalwari* areas, see A. Siddiqi, pp. 108–9. For the opposite view, see Sulekhchandra Gupta in *Contributions to Indian Economic History*, I, edited by Tapan Raychaudhuri, Calcutta, 1960, pp. 21–45. This is not the place to discuss his arguments, but it seems to me that he gives inadequate attention to the realities of the revenue pressure and the actual behaviour of prices, in suggesting that the intermediaries and the upper strata strengthened themselves during this period. For the fate of the *mirasdars*, see Choksey, *Economic History of the Bombay Deccan and Karnatak*, pp. 115ff.

[90] See A. Siddiqi, *Agrarian Change in a North Indian State*, pp. 112–13; Nilmani Mukherjee, *The Ryotwari System in Madras, 1792–1827*, pp. 295–96.

[91] Dharma Kumar, *Land and Caste*, pp. 74–76.

the proportion of the rental left to the proprietors by the old
assessments in the NW Provinces was much less than was absolutely necessary to provide for the support of themselves and their
families, bad debts, expenses of management, and vicissitudes of
season. . . . it is only since the late revision that they have been left
a sufficient margin to live at all and count with certainty on meeting
their liabilities to the state.[92]

In one district (Aligarh) 50 per cent of the land changed
hands between 1839 and 1858, and 'the moneylending and trading
classes' enlarged their share of the landholding of the district, by
means of purchases, from 3.4 per cent in 1839 to 12.3 per cent in
1868.[93] In another district (Muzaffarnagar), a quarter of the land
changed hands between 1841 and 1861, and the proportion of the
land held by the 'non-agricultural classes' increased from 11 per cent
of the total area in 1840 to 19.5 per cent in 1860.[94] These conditions
remind one of what had happened to the Bengal *zamindars* immediately
after the Permanent Settlement. The sale price of *zamindari* in private
sales and mortgages in the Aligarh district during 1839–48 was but
three-and-a-half times the amount of land revenue.[95] The price relative to land revenue had certainly improved since before the 1820s,
when it was not even at par.[96] But this improvement was probably
owing to the speculative factor introduced by the thirty-year settlement: and the gulf that divided the *zamindars* of this region and the
permanently settled areas is indicated by the fact already noted, that
the price of *zamindari* was fifteen times the annual land revenue in
Banaras in 1837.

Yet immediately upon the annexation of Oudh in 1855, it
was decided to extend to Oudh the selfsame system of Agra Province,

[92] Administration Report of NW Provinces, 1882–83, quoted in E. Stokes,
*English Utilitarians and India*, p. 133.

[93] E. Stokes in *Elites in South Asia*, edited by E. Leach and S.N. Mukerjee,
Cambridge, 1970, p. 20.

[94] E.T. Atkinson, *Statistical etc., Account of the North-Western Provinces
of India*, III, Meerut Division, part ii, Allahabad, 1876, p. 552.

[95] Ibid., II, Meerut Division, part i, Allahabad, 1875, p. 469.

[96] *Parliamentary Papers, 1831–32, Colonies: East India*, 9, IUP, Appendix,
pp. 152–53. The figures are given for the Ceded and Conquered Province
for the years 1817–18, 1818–19 and 1819–20.

'which had brought unexampled prosperity to that region'.[97] The Mutiny of 1857, which rook place in precisely these two regions, must be regarded, in one of its principal aspects, as a peasant revolt led by the *zamindars*, against the main agrarian exploiter, the British regime.[98]

### III B

We have said that during the period, about 1800 to 1850, the colonial objective changed from seizing Indian commodities to seizing the Indian market. The changed objective not only made the East India Company's monopoly over Indian internal commerce and overseas trade obsolete, but positively required free trade. The Charter Acts of 1813 and 1833 largely accomplished this change.

The English exports of manufactures, textiles in the first place, not only practically wiped out the Indian exports of cotton goods, but also entered India to challenge Indian manufactures, in their home market. The exports of cotton goods from the United Kingdom to India increased from 0.80 million yards in 1815 to 45.00 million yards in 1830, 51.78 million yards in 1835, and 100.05 million yards in 1839; and cotton twist from a mere 8 lbs in 1814 to 4.56 million lbs in 1828 and 10.81 million lbs in 1839.[99] The value of British cotton goods entering India was £ 2.29 million in 1839; that of cotton twist was £ 0.64 million.[100] In 1855 they reached the values, respectively, of £ 5.40 million and £ 1.27 million.[101] The

---

[97] Jagdish Raj in *Contributions to Indian Economic History*, I, edited by Tapan Raychaudhuri, Calcutta, 1960, p. 50.

[98] See however 'Talmiz Khaldun' in *Rebellion: 1857, A Symposium*, edited by P.C. Joshi, Delhi, 1957, p. 52, where the Mutiny is characterized as 'a peasant war against indigenous landlordism and foreign imperialism'. The best discussion of the agrarian elements in the Mutiny is by E. Stokes in *Elites of South Asia*, pp. 16–32. See also Sulekhchandra Gupta in *Enquiry*, 1, pp. 69–98. Any full characterization of the Mutiny must include a definition of the role of the unemployed urban artisans and the sepoys of the Bengal army, a modern force in an otherwise medievalist upsurge.

[99] *British Parliamentary Papers: East India Company Affairs, Colonies: East India*, 8, IUP, pp. 511 and 517. Meghnad Desai, *IESHR*, VIII (4), pp. 346–49, based on J. MacGregor (1848).

[100] Meghnad Desai in *IESHR*, VIII (4), p. 349.

[101] R.C. Dutt, *Economic History of India in the Victorian Age*, p. 161.

exports of Indian cotton manufactures declined dramatically. During the decade 1794–95 to 1803–04, the East India Company's sale of Indian piecegoods amounted to £ 2.42 million annually;[102] in 1849 the value of cotton goods, twist and yarn export from India was no more than £ 0.69 million.[103]

The effects of these imports of English manufactures on the largest craft industry of India have often been discussed. Crawfurd in 1837 disputed the complaint of adverse effects on the Indian textile industry by claiming that the British cotton goods imported into India accounted for a mere 6 per cent of the total value of India's domestic textile production.[104] But inasmuch as the competition of British manufactures had also wiped out Indian textile exports of a value of well over £ 2 million, the total fall in the value of Indian production should have been about 11.5 per cent. Speaking in terms of quantities, British manufacturers seem to have annually furnished 1.2 yards of cloth per Indian family in 1835 and 2.3 yards in 1839.[105] Working back from the estimated Indian per capita consumption of 9.80 yards per family per year in 1900–01,[106] and assuming at least a 100 per cent increase in consumption between 1839 and 1900, in view of the relative fall in prices of cotton goods, one arrives at the maximum of 24.5 yards per family per year in 1839. This would mean that British manufacturers were supplying as much as 9.4 per cent of the cloth annually consumed in India by 1839. Even if we adjust Ellison's estimate for 1856–60 to our inferences about the size of the Indian population at that time, the proportion of Indian cloth consumption supplied by Britain would seem to have risen threefold, to over 27 per cent, by 1860.[107]

---

[102] I. Durga Parshad, *Some Aspects of Indian Foreign Trade, 1757–1893*, London, 1932, p. 212 (table).

[103] R.C. Dutt, *Economic History of India*, p. 162.

[104] *Economic Development of India under the East India Company*, edited by K.N. Chaudhuri, pp. 239–42.

[105] For the quantities of British cotton manufactures exported to India in 1835 and 1839, see the preceding paragraph. I have assumed the Indian population to have been roughly 215 million and each family to consist of 5 persons.

[106] H. Fukazawa in *Economic History of India, 1857–1956*, edited by V.B. Singh, p. 238 (table).

[107] Ellison estimated the proportions to be 3.9 per cent in 1831–35 and 35.3 per cent in 1856–60. He assumed the population to be 150 million and 182 million in the respective years, and fixed Indian cloth consumption at 21

Morris has alleged that this vast influx of British cotton goods did not harm India's domestic industry because Indian demand for cloth was 'fairly elastic', and there was an increase in cloth consumption arising from 'changes in custom'. He has also suggested that the import of yarn strengthened the competitive position of the Indian weaver.[108] These arguments have been dealt with by Bipan Chandra[109] and Meghnad Desai[110] and a few comments here should suffice. While it is true that the low prices of imported manufactures increased the total quantity of cloth consumed, the further implied assertion that the total *value* of cloth consumption in India also increased substantially, at any rate by a higher percentage than that of the value of imported cloth to that of previous total consumption, is quite baseless. In the initial phase, with such extreme pressure for tribute, there could hardly have been much scope for demand to expand. On the supply side, Desai has shown that in order to maintain their position against competing British cloth, the Indian weavers, even after shifting to cheaper British yarn, needed to increase their productivity by 43 per cent between 1818–21 and 1829–31, unless they accepted a corresponding diminution in their income or wages.[111] The fact that Indian weavers were being forced to shift to imported twist in order to survive, is only an argument for the larger destruction of the Indian spinning industry, and hardly one for the prosperity of the Indian weaver. It would seem that initially British cotton goods

---

lb. per capita. Cited by Desai, *IESHR*, VIII (4), pp. 353–54. It is likely that cloth consumption, estimated at 21 lb. during the 1880s, was much less thirty years earlier. In that case, Ellison's original estimate of the share of Indian cloth consumption supplied by Britain might really be the right one.

[108] *IESHR*, V (1), pp. 8–9.

[109] Ibid., pp. 52–63.

[110] *IESHR*, VIII (4), pp. 317–61.

[111] Ibid., p. 358. Such an increase in productivity was, of course, impossible without technological innovation. Thus, the result was an enormous fall in the income of the weaver. According to the District Collectors' reports, 'in Vizagapatam, the price of Punjum cloth of the Company's assortment fell from Rs 6 per piece in 1815 to Rs 3–8–0 in 1844, and the profits of the weaver from 1 or 2 rupees to 8 or 4 annas. In Bellary, prices in the case of the inferior varieties diminished 35 per cent and the net income by 75 per cent.' A. Sarada Raju, *Economic Conditions in the Madras Presidency, 1800–1850*, p. 180. (1 rupee = 16 annas.)

mainly hurt the weaving of the fine and medium varieties, and therefore affected the hitherto better situated urban weavers far more than the rural weavers producing coarse cloth for the poorer part of the populaton.[112]

Alongside cotton goods, English exports to India of iron (bar and bolt as well as cast and wrought), together with hardware and cutlery, guns, glass, and 'machinery', had increased enormously by 1828.[113] They continued to grow during the following years and naturally caused a slump in the corresponding crafts in India.

There was thus ample cause for the 'de-industrialization' of India which marks the second phase of British rule. The urban decline, initiated by the diversion of the surplus from the Indian ruling classes to the Company, spread quite naturally wherever the East India Company's sovereignty extended. It was compounded many times over by the urban unemployment forced by English manufactures. This urban decline seems not only to have been in relative terms (percentage of urban population to total), but in absolute terms as well. Taking the same districts of eastern India whose population I studied for 1812, 1852 and 1872, I found that the populations of eight major towns in those districts had declined from 923,344 around 1812 to 866,749 in 1872.[114] Since the towns included Calcutta, the capital of British India, whose population had increased by nearly 270,000 during the period, the overall decline is remarkable. The population of Patna fell from 312,000 in 1812 to 158,900 in 1872;[115] and there was no town in Bihar in 1872 which could even remotely be said to approach Patna in population, so that there was no question here of compensatory growth elsewhere. Examples of spectacular decline in populations of individual towns can be multiplied, for example Dacca, Murshidabad, Lucknow (after annexation, 1856). Detailed regional studies would be necessary before the precise magnitude of the decline in urban population can be indicated, but of the process itself there can be no doubt.

[112] See D.R. Gadgil, *The Industrial Evolution of India in Recent Times*, London, 1944, p. 43.

[113] Statistics showing the increase between 1814 and 1828 are given in *Parliamentary Papers, 1831–32, Colonies: East India*, 8, p. 511.

[114] Note on Indian Population, 1800–72, table III.

[115] A census of 1837 put its population at 284,132. See Hunter, *Statistical Account of Bengal*, XI, pp. 32–34.

### III C

The two-pronged assault of imperialism, the extraction of tribute and the seizure of markets of Indian manufactures, could not proceed independently. One reacted on the other.

The difficulty which the extraction of tribute placed in the way of Lancashire's capturing the Indian market was that by denying a large share in the agricultural surplus to classes that could buy the imported wares, it limited the scope of effective demand. An optimistic air with regard to the consequences of free trade had pervaded the parliamentary enquiries preceding the Charter Act of 1833. Free trade and the curbing of the direct and indirect commercial activities of the Company would, it was hoped, unleash a massive and continuous expansion of British exports to India. But in practice, serious lags were encountered within the general process of expansion. Thus the total value of British cotton goods imported in India in 1849 (£ 2.22 million) proved to be less than the value imported in 1839 (£ 2.29 million).[116] Partly, the reason lay in the undeveloped means of transport. But the main factor was that British products had to deal with a severely restricted market labouring under a huge direct economic burden.[117]

Conversely, the de-industrialization of India, as it proceeded, seriously affected the entire mechanism of the transfer of wealth from India to Britain, and raised serious obstructions to the realization of tribute.

Hitherto the realization of tribute from India had taken the form of export of Indian manufactures; and this, as Dundas proclaimed in 1799, was the best thing for everyone. Britain obtained 'wealth and capital', and India, 'prosperity, industry, population and revenue'.[118] But as 'a severe check' was put to these exports by the competition of British manufactures themselves, the happy days of mutual

---

[116] For the 1839 figure see Meghnad Desai, *IESHR*, VIII (4), p. 349; for 1849, see R.C. Dutt, *Economic History of India*, p. 161.

[117] See Karl Marx, 'The East India Company' (1853), *Articles on India*, p. 50; *On Colonialism*, pp. 48–49.

[118] He added prophetically: 'The manufactures of that country would be reduced to very deplorable circumstances if any severe check was to be given to the usual investment and exports from India.' *A Selection from the Despatches, Treaties, and Other Papers of the Marquess Wellesley, K.G.*, edited by S.J. Owen, London, 1877, p. 697.

convenience were over. Theoretically, India, losing the market for manufacturers, could have diverted its raw cotton to the English factories. But this proved impracticable for Indian cotton was too short-stapled for the English factories which came to be supplied mainly from America. A shortlived demand from England after 1815 soon ceased, and only limited quantities could be sent to China.[119] The other articles were indigo and silk. As English cloth production expanded, the demand for indigo grew correspondingly. The European agency houses in Bengal flourished on the indigo trade after the Charter Act of 1813 had brought in the private English merchants. But West Indian competition destroyed the hopes of continuous expansion of indigo exports, and this brought about the crash of 1832–33, consuming the principal agency houses.[120] Raw silk, as raw material for English silk-weaving factories, could not similarly compete with Chinese and Italian silk; and its exports remained limited.

By 1830, therefore, the 'realization' problem had become quite acute. It was about this time that the solution was found in opium. During 1816–17 only 3,210 chests of Indian opium had been exported to China; in 1830–31, no less than 18,760 chests; and the value rose from $ 3.66 to $ 12.90 million.[121] Opium advanced to the position of the premier article of export of India, exceeding £ 5.7 million in value in 1849 and £ 9.1 million in 1858, easily dwarfing the other items of export, and accounting for nearly a third of the total value of Indian exports.[122] Under this impetus, the cultivation of poppy during the twenty years preceding 1837 is said to have multiplied fourfold.[123] Opium had this merit, that it had hardly any bulk and could be transported from the most distant places inland without

---

[119] N.K. Sinha, *Economic History of Bengal*, III, Calcutta, 1970, pp. 14–17; A. Siddiqi, *Agrarian Change*, pp. 153–56, cotton prices on pp. 190, 192–93. Also see R.C. Dutt, *Economic History of India*, pp. 131–32.

[120] See the account in A. Tripathi, *Trade and Finance in the Bengal Presidency, 1793–1833*, Calcutta, 1956; and S.B. Singh, *European Agency House in Bengal*, Calcutta, 1966.

[121] *Parliamentary Papers, 1831–32, Colonies: East India*, 9, IUP, p. 250. See also ibid., 8, pp. 512–13.

[122] R.C. Dutt, *Economic History of India*, table on p. 162, and table on value of imports and exports on p. 160. See also table on commodity composition of Indian exports, 1814–15 to 1857–58 (selected years) given by K.N. Chaudhuri in *Economic Development of India*, p. 26.

[123] Crawfurd in ibid., p. 251.

the need of roads or railways. Here was 'commercialization' of agriculture without any investment worth the name; and Crawfurd could only regret that the Company's monopoly should restrict the free expansion of its cultivation and thus sacrifice 'a great national advantage'.[124]

The 'national advantage' (of Britain, of course) lay in the export of this vast quantity of opium to China. The prospects of this commerce seemed limitless as one contemplated the progressive conversion of larger and larger strata of the Chinese people to the newly introduced wonders of the poppy world.[125] The beauty of the arrangement was that China would in return furnish tea and silk; and thus the tribute would be realized in an enlarged form. In 1855, England consumed tea and silk of China to the value of £ 8.5 million, while exporting a mere £1 million worth of goods to that country.[126] The balance was sheer gain obtained through Indian exports of opium, which in 1855 amounted to £6.23 million.[127]

*British trade with Asia (in £000,000)*

| Year | Imports | Exports | Re-exports | Excess of Imports over Exports |
|------|---------|---------|------------|--------------------------------|
| 1854 | 23.0 | 12.0 | 0.6 | 11.0 |
| 1855 | 24.3 | 13.1 | 0.5 | 11.2 |
| 1856 | 29.8 | 15.4 | 0.6 | 14.4 |
| 1857 | 33.8 | 16.8 | 0.7 | 17.0 |

[124] Ibid., pp. 251–52.

[125] *Parliamentary Papers, 1831–32, Colonies: East India*, IUP, p. 251 (Q. No. 2190).

[126] Thomas Toke in *Economic Development of India*, p. 171.

[127] R.C. Dutt, *Economic History of India*, p. 162. In 1836–37 India had exported to China goods of the value of Rs 6.72 crore and imported to the value of Rs 0.53 crore in goods and 1.24 crore in treasure, leaving a favourable balance of Rs 4.96 crore. The balance was smaller in the next two years. K.N. Chaudhuri, *Economic Development of India*, table on p. 49. It ought to be borne in mind that Indian customs house figures for exports at this time used to be gross under-valuations. Crawfurd, ibid., pp. 245–46.

The results of this triangular relationship appear from the trade statistics. The table on the previous page gives the figures for the British imports from, and exports to, Asia (excepting Turkey and the Middle East).[128] These figures thus show a continuous annual net inflow of imports of £11 million to £17 million without any return payment.

This indicates the magnitude of the tribute; and tribute was what the Opium Wars of 1840–42 and 1856–58 were about. Any refusal of the Chinese people to consume opium would bring down the entire fabric of tribute realization that had been built up. This, the most powerful-ever mafia in the world could hardly be expected to tolerate.[129]

The consequences of imperialism in the first half of the nineteenth century were that irreconcilable contradictions existed between the imperialist power on the one hand, and the Indian peasantry and artisans on the other; and further, that in the relations between imperialism and the *zamindars* (not yet landlords in any true sense), contradictions held primacy, and accommodation was secondary. Another characteristic of this stage was that the dominance over China had become indispensable for the economic exploitation of India.

## IV

About the middle of the nineteenth century, a new stage set in for English capitalism. Capital investment at home reached saturation point with the complete victory of machine industry in every branch of production and the construction of the basic network of railways, the greatest absorbent of capital so far known. Once this point had passed, the export of capital began in earnest. British 'net foreign investment' was already equal in size to 42 per cent of the net domestic capital formation in fixed assets during 1860–69. After a trough during the next decade and a half, it reached 114 per cent

---

[128] B.R. Mitchell and Phyllis Deane, *Abstract of British Historical Statistics*, Cambridge, 1962, p. 318.

[129] See Dadabhai Naoroji, *Poverty and Un-British Rule in India*, first Indian edition, pp. 188–89, for a passage written in 1880 and containing an indignant criticism of the opium trade as an infamous form of realization of the Indian tribute.

during 1905–14.[130] British capitalism gradually transformed itself into monopoly capitalism; and faced by competition from other rising industrial giants, notably Germany and the USA, the international supremacy of British imperialism gave place to a protectionist colonialism, particularly after 1870.[131] These developments characterize the third, and the full blown, phase of British imperialism.

The major new characteristics of this stage were the export of capital and the intensified race for markets. In the case of India, the two aspects were closely interrelated. The capital exported was pre-eminently for railway construction; and the railways enabled Britain to carry her conquest of the Indian market to its maximum extent.

By 31 March 1872 British capital invested in Indian railways at a guaranteed rate of interest (around 5 per cent per annum) had risen to £ 94.73 million.[132] In the meantime, the British Indian government also borrowed in London to lay out 'state railways', and so the 'Indian' debt in England mounted from £ 15.09 million in 1858–59 to £ 55.40 million in 1876–77, an increase of £ 40 million.[133] 'From 1857 to 1865 the major movement of British capital was to India.'[134]

While the extraction of tribute continued on the old basis (in 1872 the excess of the value of British imports from Asia over exports thereto amounted to £ 17.7 million),[135] here was a partial reversal of the flow of wealth that had so long gone in one direction only. The reversal was, of course, only superficial: the principal and returns on this capital belonged to Britain, and not India, and would only swell, in time, the size of the Indian tribute.[136]

---

[130] Deane and Cole, *British Economic Growth*, p. 266 (table).

[131] See Maurice Dobb, *Studies in the Development of Capitalism*, London, 1946, pp. 311–12.

[132] R.C. Dutt, *Economic History of India*, p. 359.

[133] Ibid., pp. 373–74.

[134] L.H. Jenks, *The Migration of British Capital, to 1875*, London, 1963, p. 207; quoted in A.G.L. Shaw (ed.), *Great Britain and the Colonies, 1815–1865*, London, 1971, p. 21.

[135] Mitchell and Deane, *Abstract of British Historical Statistics*, p. 318. The excess in value of Indian exports over imports in trade with all countries in 1871 was almost the same, viz. £17.6 million. R.C. Dutt, *Economic History of India*, pp. 343–44.

[136] The burden was increased substantially also because the guaranteed capital was so wastefully employed. According to Dadabhai Naoroji

By 1871 the railway mileage in India exceeded 5,000 miles, and the main trunk lines to the inland regions had been laid. The mileage approached 10,000 in 1881; and then another spurt in construction took it to 19,555 by 1895. India, perhaps the poorest country in the world, now rivalled the richest in railway mileage. But while in western Europe and America, the railways served as the catalyst of the industrial revolutions, in India they served as the catalyst of complete colonialization.

The influx of imports from Britain that came on the heels of the railways can be described by citing a few data from trade statistics. The import of cotton manufactures doubled between 1859 and 1877, and rose by nearly half as much again between 1878 and 1887. Imports of silk goods, less than one-fifth in value compared to cotton goods in 1859, rose by about four times between 1859 and 1877, and by 50 per cent again between 1878 and 1887.[137] Import of wool manufactures similarly increased. The heavier products of British industry, such as metal manufactures (hardware, cutlery, etc.) and machinery and tools now began to be imported in large quantities.

The railways thus helped Britain to retain India still more securely as one of her principal markets. Britain's exports to India accounted for 9.15 per cent of her total exports during the period 1846–55. The proportion was 12.6 per cent in 1876–85.[138] India's role in sustaining Lancashire's exports was still more significant. In 1849 British export of cloth and yarn to India amounted to 11.7 per cent of total British exports of these items. By 1875 the proportion

---

(*Poverty and Un-British Rule in India*, p. 121, also p. 31), the annual drain of wealth from India to Britain increased from £ 8.7 million during 1855–59 to £ 31 million during 1870–72. While Naoroji certainly stood on the right side of the barricades, the principles on which he based his calculation are not above criticism. See Bipan Chandra, *Rise and Growth of Economic Nationalism in India*, New Delhi, 1966, pp. 645–48. The large increase in the annual drain exhibited in Naoroji's figures is partly to be explained by the exceptional capital-flow to India during the late 1850s and early 1860s which had reduced the excess of Indian exports over imports during that period, and so concealed the real size of the Indian tribute.

[137] See table in R.C. Dutt, *Economic History of India*, II, pp. 345, 530.

[138] These calculations have been made from the statistical tables given in Mitchell and Deane, *Abstract of British Historical Statistics*, pp. 283, 324–25.

had risen to 27 per cent.[139] In so far as capital invested in railways helped to subjugate the Indian market for British industry, it inhibited the export of capital for investment in other sectors. The tariffs were so manipulated as to make India an utterly unprotected economy;[140] and apart from plantations and the jute industry no other branch of the economy could attract British capital with any expectation of high returns.[141]

The old craft industries could not but have suffered greatly from this onslaught of imports. In 1872 the quantity of cloth imported into India crossed the figure of 1,000 million yards; in 1887, of 2,000 million yards.[142] In 1900–01, the total Indian production (mill and handloom) barely exceeded 1,000 million yards.[143] Ellison estimated that in 1880–81 Britain supplied as much as 58.4 per cent of the total consumption of cloth in India.[144] By 1887 the proportion must have gone up to much above 66.6 per cent. It is quite likely that by the 1880s the process of de-industrialization had been more or less completed. As Thorner puts it, 'the scope which remained for any subsequent "de-industrialization" was decidedly limited'.[145] But even his rearranged figures from the censuses show a decline in employment

---

[139] Based on tables of imports into India in R.C. Dutt, *Economic History of India*, II, pp. 161, 345, and tables of British exports in Mitchell and Deane, *Abstract of British Historical Statistics*, pp. 303–4. It would have been better to take both sets of figures from British trade statistics. But the result is unlikely to be very different. Meghnad Desai estimates the share of India in Britain's total textile export to have been 15 per cent during 1821–30 and 30 per cent during 1871–80. See *IESHR*, VIII (4), p. 339.

[140] The classic account is in R.C. Dutt, *Economic History of India*, II, pp. 401–16, 537–44.

[141] Of a total of £ 365.3 million of British capital invested in India by 1909–10, government debt accounted for £ 182.4 million, railways and other transport for £ 141.5 million and plantations for £ 24.2 million. Investments in electricity and power, etc., minerals and oil, and commerce and industry, all together, amounted to no more than £ 12.7 million. Sir George Paish's estimate, adapted and cited by Arun Bose in V.B. Singh (ed.), *Economic History of India, 1857–1956*, p. 494.

[142] Meghnad Desai in *IESHR*, VIII (4), p. 351 (table).

[143] Amiya K. Bagchi, *Private Investment in India, 1900–1939*, Cambridge, 1972, p. 226 (table).

[144] Meghnad Desai in *IESHR*, VIII (4), pp. 353–54.

[145] Daniel and Alice Thorner, *Land and Labour in India*, Bombay, 1962, p. 77.

in manufacturing, mining, construction and trade, from 18 per cent in 1881 to 16 per cent in 1901.[146]

The railways did not simply assist imports by transporting them cheaply. Their ability to furnish exports in return was at the root of the expansion of imports. The entire composition of Indian export changed as bulk no longer remained a barrier to transport. In 1871 opium was still the principal item, but foodgrains and raw cotton each closely approached it in total value, and oilseeds were not very far behind. In 1901 foodgrains, raw cotton, jute, and hides and skins had raced ahead of opium, while oilseeds and tea were practically at par with opium in value, though the decline in the value of opium had been less than 25 per cent. The total value of exports had risen between 1878 and 1901 from Rs 67.43 crore to Rs 121.95 crore.[147] There was thus a real shift in Indian agriculture to production of raw material for England; a shift in relative acreage from foodgrains to non-food crops;[148] and, of course, an enlargement within the acreage under foodgrains of the portion devoted to crops for export.

This vast change in Indian agriculture (sometimes called 'commercialization') had a polarizing effect on the rural population. As the quantity of food available for the home market declined—and it declined as fast as the railway network extended—famines repeatedly ensued. It had been the expectation of the proponents of the railways that these would help to banish famines, by bringing in supplies. But the very opposite took place: the supplies went out! This is not the place to chronicle famines,[149] which has in any case been done often. Suffice it to say that they steadily increased in frequency and scale, culminating in the great famines of 1896–97 and 1899–1900, when millions perished.[150] Moreover, the real wages of agri-

[146] Ibid., pp. 78–79 (table).
[147] R.C. Dutt, Economic History of India, tables on pp. 529 and 533.
[148] See table in B.M. Bhatia, p. 224, and Amiya K. Bagchi, Private Investment in India, p. 95. The tables relate to the last decade of the nineteenth century and the earlier years of this century. Agricultural statistics of this kind are not available for earlier periods.
[149] A chronological table is furnished by Bhatia, p. 343.
[150] Ibid., pp. 242, 250, 261.

cultural labourers exhibit absolutely no increase over the entire period 1873–1900.[151]

While the conditions of the poorer peasantry and rural proletariat became more and more critical, the extending production of commercial crops laid the basis for extensive landlord and rich-peasant agriculture. In 1891 the smaller proprietors cultivated 54 per cent of the cultivated area in the Punjab; in 1900, only 45 per cent.[152] Writing in 1903, R.C. Dutt was led to exclaim, 'every true Indian hopes that the small cultivation of India will not be replaced by landlordism. . . .'[153]

There was an increase, conversely, in the numbers of the landless labourers. Surendra J. Patel has set out the census evidence on this.[154] The evidence is certainly not foolproof: it is as difficult to accept a decline in the relative number of agricultural labourers between 1871–72 and 1891, as it is to accept a doubling of it between 1891 and 1901. But the general trend towards increase is unmistakable. Dharma Kumar in her study of south India finds that the proportion of agricultural labourers to the total agricultural population increased from the 15 or 17 per cent to 27 or 29 per cent during the course of the nineteenth century.[155] The fact that there was probably no important shift of population from the non-agricultural to the agricultural sector between 1881 and 1931[156] does not affect our conclusion at all, because we are postulating a swelling of the ranks of the rural proletariat by influx mainly from the pauperized strata of the peasantry, rather than from unemployed artisans. This situation furnished the setting in which a new basis was laid for the relationship between imperialism and the *zamindars*.

The abolition of the Company's rule in 1858 was brought

---

[151] M. Mukerji in V.B. Singh (ed.), *Economic History of India, 1857–1956*, pp. 678–79 (table); Bhatia, pp. 349–51 (tables). Dharma Kumar finds a substantial decline in real wages of agricultural labourers in the Madras Presidency between 1875 and 1900; *Land and Caste*, pp. 165–67.

[152] R.C. Dutt, *Economic History of India*, p. 471.

[153] Ibid., pp. 518–19.

[154] Surendra J. Patel, *Agricultural Labourers in India and Pakistan*, Bombay, 1952, pp. 1–20.

[155] Dharma Kumar, *Land and Caste*, pp. 168–82. She declines to see in this increase a 'radical transformation of the agrarian economy'.

[156] Daniel and Alice Thorner, *Land and Labour in India*, pp. 70–81.

about by an alliance of British industrial interests, ever more dominant in Parliament since the Reform Act of 1832. Direct government
of India would give both Lancashire and the railway interests a much
greater authority over what concerned them in India. Under the new
regime the emphasis shifted from the levy of direct tribute through
land revenue to the exploitation of India as market and as source of
raw materials.[157] This change had an immediate impact on the policy
of British imperialism towards the *zamindars*.

    After the Mutiny, Thornhill, a local officer, urged the gov-
ernment to 'throw itself on [the side of] the larger proprietors and
repress the peasantry'.[158] He was correctly anticipating, or interpreting, the new policy of imperialism. In part this policy was forced upon
it by the Mutiny itself, which had shown how dangerous it was to be
left without faithful allies. It therefore needed to be proclaimed by the
Queen in 1858 that: 'We know, and respect the feelings of attachment
with which the natives of India regard the land inherited from their
ancestors, and we desire to protect them in all rights connected there-
with, subject to the equitable demands of the state.' But the new policy
could not have been put into effect had the same dependence of
imperialism upon land revenue continued.

    There was another factor, too, that greatly helped its imple-
mentation. This was a general rise in price during the second half of
the nineteenth century.[159] Official price indices cover the period from
1861, but other sources enable us to trace earlier price movements.
In the table that follows, the figures in columns A and B are calculat-

---

[157] Marx summed up the divergence between the old and new 'lines' of
imperialism in his reference, in 1853, to a parliamentary speech of Bright,
'whose picture of India ruined by the fiscal exertions of the Company did
not, of course, receive the supplement of India ruined by Manchester and
Free Trade'. *Articles on India*, p. 36; *On Colonialism*, p. 29. The ambitions
of Lancashire with regard to India were given full expression during the
parliamentary controversy over the renewal of the East India Company's
Charter in 1853. The construction of railways was a major plank in the
Manchester programme for India, and the guarantee system for railway
capital was vigorously supported. R.J. Moore, 'Imperialism and Free
Trade Policy in India, 1853–1854', in A.G.L. Shaw (ed.), *Great Britain
and the Colonies, 1815–1865*, pp. 181–96.
[158] Quoted by E. Stokes in *Elites in South Asia*, p. 25.
[159] See D.R. Gadgil, *Industrial Evolution of India in Recent Times*, London,
1942, pp. 21–22.

*Average annual prices*

| Decade | A Coarse Rice: Bengal Rs per md. | B Wheat: Farrukhabad Rs per md. | C Common Rice: Madras Rs per md. | D General Prices: India 1919 50=100 |
|---|---|---|---|---|
| 1841–50 | 1.35 | 1.03 | 1.13* | — |
| 1851–60 | 1.62 | 1.43 | — | — |
| 1861–70 | 2.23 | 2.22 | 3.12 | 15.84 |
| 1871–80 | 2.83 | 2.11 | 3.30 | 16.22 |
| 1881–90 | 2.67 | 2.67 | 3.41 | 15.73 |
| 1891–1900 | 3.65 | 3.33 | 4.60 | 19.18 |

* Average annual price for 1841–53.

ed from tables in Brij Narain,[160] in column C from Dharma Kumar,[161] and in column D from official statistics as presented by M. Mukerji.[162] It is clear that foodgrain prices rose about three times between 1850 and 1900.

The increase in prices naturally led to enhancements in rents while the land revenue due to be paid by the *zamindars* remained stationary for the whole period of the settlements. Even when new settlements were undertaken, the increase in the assessments in UP was on a very limited scale, being set far below what would have been justified by the ascent in prices. But in Bombay Presidency, where it was the peasants mainly, and not *zamindars* and *taluqdars*, who paid the revenue, the new settlements in the 1870s were so high as to lead to agrarian disturbances.[163] This was yet another application of the Thornhill principle.

[160] Brij Narain, *Indian Economic Life: Past and Present.* The movement of wheat prices at Farrukhabad is corroborated by the detailed price–data for Meerut collected and analysed by Toru Matsui in *Memoirs of the Institute of Oriental Culture,* University of Tokyo, No. 64, March 1970, pp. 97ff (tables). Toru Matsui's prices begin from 1845, or more often, 1848.

[161] Dharma Kumar, *Land and Caste,* p. 91 (table).

[162] M. Mukerji in V.B. Singh (ed.), *Economic History of India 1857–1956,* p. 685 (tables). See also tables of prices from the same source in Bhatia, p. 348.

[163] See A. Colvin's Memorandum of 8 November 1875; extracts quoted in R.C. Dutt, *Economic History of India,* pp. 330–32.

The result of increasing rents and a relatively stationary revenue demand was that the *zamindars'* share of the 'rental' as compared with the land-revenue expanded considerably. The Saharanpur Rule of 50 per cent share of the proprietor now set the minimum rather than the normal or maximum standard. This was the basis of the formal conversion of the *zamindar* into the modern Indian landlord. The long series of tenancy acts, beginning with the Bengal Rent Act of 1859, merely extended recognition to his new position, and to the subsidence of the bulk of the Indian peasantry into mere tenantry-at-will.

The role of usury during this entire process was of considerable significance. Usury had strong roots in the preceding Indian agrarian economy.[164] It now greatly facilitated the subversion of small peasant cultivation and the growth of landlord and rich-peasant agriculture. At the same time, usury was also a parasitical growth feeding upon this very process. The moneylender stood forth as a claimant to a large share of the rural surplus, sometimes even rivalling the landlord. It often suited the British administration to proclaim 'rural indebtedness' as a source of all evil that befell the peasant.[165] But the phenomenal growth of usury was an inseparable aspect of the transformation of the Indian agrarian economy brought about by colonialism itself.

To sum up, it was during the second half of the nineteenth century that the modern Indian landlord was created and an alliance formed simultaneously between him and imperialism. Yet such were the factors inherent in this very phase of imperialism that it also gave birth to two new classes in Indian society, the bourgeoisie and the industrial proletariat. This was a prospect that Marx had seen when contemplating the projected construction of railways in India.[166] The connection between the changes that Britain wrought in India and the rise of the Indian bourgeoisie has already been so well analysed by R.P. Dutt, for example, that even the briefest description would be

---

[164] See my article, 'Usury in Medieval India', *Comparative Studies in Society and History*, VI, 4, The Hague, pp. 394–98.

[165] See Bipan Chandra, *Rise and Growth of Economic Nationalism in India*, p. 466 and n.

[166] Karl Marx, 'The Future Results of British Rule in India', 1853; *Articles on India*, pp. 70–72; *On Colonialism*, pp. 79–81.

useless repetition. Here at last was the one great 'regenerating' effect of colonialism which had so far only pitilessly attacked and shattered a vast, civilized society.

The irreconcilable contradictions that emerged between imperialism and its junior ally, the landlords, on the one hand, and the bulk of the Indian people, including the bourgeoisie, the working class and the peasantry, on the other, laid the seeds of the struggle for national liberation. The whole epoch that followed, spanning the first half of this century and ending with the withdrawal of British imperialism and the parting of the ways of the Indian bourgeoisie and the proletariat, constituted the fourth and final stage of colonialism in India. But it would undoubtedly need a revolution in India before the vestiges and survivals of colonialization are altogether removed.

# Studying a Colonial Economy—
# Without Perceiving Colonialism

From the size of India's population alone the economic history of India constitutes an important segment of the economic history of mankind. But with the middle of the eighteenth century, it assumed a further, special significance: subjugated by the first industrial nation of the world, it offered a classic case of the colonial remoulding of a pre-modern economy. Not surprisingly, the changing nature and consequences of this process and all its surrounding conditions have formed the constant theme of a long and continuing debate.

To the editors of *Cambridge Economic History of India,* Volume II,[1] the debate has apparently been an exercise in irrelevance. They refer condescendingly to 'the sturdy classics—Dutt, Gadgil, Anstey, Naoroji'—their worth being not even sufficient to justify the editors taking the trouble of placing them in the correct order. Dutt and the others have been rendered 'out of date', the editors say, because 'over the previous decades', 'scholars have enhanced our understanding of the historical experience of specific regions and communities and illuminated aspects of economic activity but lightly touched upon previously'. As far as increase in information is concerned, the editors are on safe enough grounds. But going by their description, the field for which new information has been gained is different from that with which Naoroji and Dutt were concerned. In other words, the editors set out to dispense not only with the 'classics', but also with

[1] Dharma Kumar (editor, with assistance from Meghnad Desai), *Cambridge Economic History of India*, Vol. II, Cambridge, 1982, henceforth referred to as *CEHI*. References to this work appear in parentheses in the text.

the questions raised there. They seem determined to read modern Indian history without looking at colonialism.[2]

This becomes obvious from the plan of the volume. Part I, comprising more than half the book, is entitled 'The Land and the People' In this part we first have a chapter on India in the mid-eighteenth century, whereafter the country is chopped up into four regions. The agrarian relations of these regions are studied separately up to 1947 in four sections; and then there are four separate studies of their 'economies', upto 1857 only. With a characteristic defiance of chronology (the region subjugated earlier by Britain should surely have come first) the study in each chapter begins with the north-western and central regions. These regional studies are followed by three chapters on national income, population and occupational structure, all the three basically concerned with the post-1857 period. From these we are led to Part II, styled 'The Beginning of the Modern Economy'. This begins with a chapter on the growth of large-scale industry. There is next a single chapter on irrigation and railways (a pairing for which it is difficult to find a reason, unless it lies in both of these being treated as 'public works'). Chapters follow on foreign trade, price movements and the fiscal system. Part III consists of two chapters on 'Post-Independence Developments', one on India, the other on Pakistan.

I beg to be forgiven for setting out the list of contents like this, but this is necessary to show that such a plan of chapters practically precludes a whole series of the most crucial questions from being taken up. Where can one study the tribute or drain of wealth, let us say in the 'mercantilist' phase, 1757–1813? Or the process of 'de-industrialization'? The editors say disarmingly that there ought to have been a chapter on handicrafts, though curiously enough they allow Morris D. Morris, who writes on large-scale industry, to have a full say on small-scale industry as well (pp. 668–76).

The editors themselves hasten to add that they wished there were a separate chapter on the theme simply because of 'the continuing importance of handicrafts', lest someone might think that they

---

[2] Characteristic of the editors' outlook is their avoidance in their preface of any reference to colonialism or Britain's exploitative relationship with India. The closest they come to it is in their allusion to literature on underdevelopment and development policies.

have had 'de-industrialization' in mind. There is similarly no space provided to discuss the process of the late nineteenth-century commercialization of agriculture; and the question of growth of landless labour is suitably tucked away among the 'regions'. The whole issue of the 'imperialism of free trade', which since the Gallagher-Robinson essay should have gained a place in 'current literature',[3] eludes both the editors and the contributors.

If the straitjacket of the editors' scheme was not sufficient, the contributors themselves, with a few exceptions, have succeeded in setting a course which suggests that to them economic theory came to a close with free trade and comparative advantage. Explicitly, and most often implicitly, they are out to demolish the nationalist criticism of exploitation and impoverishment under colonial rule. It is worth some reflection that there is little in this volume by which official annoyance could have been aroused even before 1914.

In this paper, I take up what I think have been important aspects of the colonial impact on the Indian economy (up to the beginning of the twentieth century) that are either overlooked in *CEHI* or receive treatment on which one may have considerable reservations. It should be understood that I do not pretend to be more knowledgeable than the editors and authors of *CEHI*, and that I note and raise particular questions simply because *CEHI*'s way of dealing (or not dealing) with them has proved so disappointing to me.

### The Tribute, 1757–1813

In so far as the East India Company and its servants saw their conquests in India as commercial acquisitions, the seized treasuries and tax income appeared to them as nothing but gross profits. The 'Plassey plunder', where enormous individual fortunes were made, was followed by a continuous extraction of wealth, through taxation, monopoly and corruption, generating a stream of exports from India, without any corresponding imports. Those who decry 'scholarship-by-quotation' and crave for statistical data have here quantitative evidence of great value to estimate the 'drain' in terms of both prime

---

[3] John Gallagher and Ronald Robinson, 'The Imperialism of Free Trade', *Economic History Review*, second series, VI, 1953, pp. 1–15, and the large body of subsequent writing on the theme.

costs in India and sale proceeds in overseas markets. They can compare the size of the total wealth transferred from India with the estimated gross national product of the Company's dominions (for which they can use estimates of production by Grant and Shore[4]), and with estimates of British national income. With Furber's work already decades old,[5] and the convenient presentation of British historical statistics by Mitchell and Deane,[6] so much quantitative evidence could have been laid out, and the ground cleared for enquiring as to how the transfer affected India and benefited Britain. This was, after all, the main economic aspect of the colonial relationship in its initial phase; and the drive for revenue which it set afoot is basic to any understanding of the Permanent Settlement. Yet *CEHI* has no room for all this; and the only place where an allusion to it occurs is in K.N. Chaudhuri's chapter on foreign trade. He begins by telling us that

> . . . the far more important characteristic of the half a century following the revolution of 1757 [a euphemism for Plassey] was the fact that the Indian trade still continued to flow along the *traditional* channels and its composition was based on an *exchange* of fine textiles, foodstuffs and other raw materials for precious metals and certain manufactured products. (p. 806; emphases added)

The description is surprisingly inaccurate: the end and purpose of the 'revolution of 1757' was to disrupt altogether the 'traditional channels' and to enable Britain to obtain Indian goods without any export of treasure in return.[7] Indeed, Chaudhuri himself, while

---

[4] James Grant in *The Fifth Report*, II, edited by W.K. Firminger, Calcutta, 1917, p. 276, and Shore, in ibid., pp. 27–28.

[5] Holden Furber, *John Company at Work*, Cambridge, Mass., 1951, especially pp. 112–16. One searches in vain for any reference to this work in *CEHI*.

[6] B.R. Mitchell and Phyllis Deane, *Abstract of British Historical Statistics*, Cambridge, 1962, especially pp. 309ff (col. for trade with Asia). The statistics have been used for calculating the drain by Sayera I. Habib, *Proceedings of the Indian History Congress*, Aligarh Session, 1975, section IV, pp. xxii–xxiv.

[7] See what S. Bhattacharya says, *CEHI*, p. 289. From Chaudhuri's own Table 10.2 B on p. 819 it can be seen that the Company's export of silver to India ceased after 1757–58.

speaking of Bengal before the Company seized its revenues, shows how the influx of bullion had led to 'an expansion of the economy of Bengal' and how this stream dried up after 1765 (p. 814).[8] But he holds back from drawing a converse picture of what must have happened to the commerce and crafts of Bengal when it ceased receiving any recompense for its exports. His entire assessment of the consequences of the new phase suddenly narrows down to two rather secondary phenomena: the inflationary pressure of demand for textiles and the monetary disturbance created by the export of Bengal silver to China.[9] The effects on the crafts and internal trade of Bengal that the author of the *Siyaru-l Mutakhirin* wrote about and Cornwallis referred to in justification of his scheme of Permanent Settlement[10] are all silently passed over, as if these are not even hypotheses that should be tested. S. Bhattacharya does cite Steuart for the statement that Bengal's export trade with countries other than Britain suffered as a result of the English Company's claims on export goods (p. 289); but, unfortunately, he too quickly passes on to other matters, and the implications of this enormous commercial diversion for both Bengal and the regions previously trading with it are left unexplored.

### 'De-industrialization'

The Charter Act of 1813, in so far as it dismantled the East India Company's monopoly of Indian trade, opened the country to the industrial products of England, notably the textiles of Lancashire. A reader of writers as diverse as Marx and R.C. Dutt can see how this

[8] One may recall how in his *Trading World of Asia and the English East India Company, 1660–1760*, Cambridge, 1978, p. 462, Chaudhuri attributed 'industrializing' qualities to the influx of bullion under the aegis of the Dutch and English Companies; the 'coastal provinces of India' were turned into a 'major industrial region'.

[9] Even here Chaudhuri's argument needs qualification. Since the English Company purchased cotton textiles out of the revenues of Bengal, Bihar and Orissa, it did not put more currency into circulation; it only diverted it. Thus the 'inflation' was nothing but a rise in prices of goods in which it 'invested'; of other goods no longer in demand the prices should have fallen. Moreover, export of silver to China should have had a deflationary effect.

[10] Ghulam Husain Tabatabai, *Siyaru-I Mutakhirin*, II, Kanpur, pp. 836–37, 840–41; Cornwallis in *Fifth Report*, II, edited by Firminger, p. 542.

added a new and major element in the economic disruption of India.[11] Previously, the 'drain' or revenues by diverting a large portion to export goods had destroyed such avenues of employment as were sustained by the demand of the deposed ruling classes and their dependents. After 1800, textile exports, the mainstay of the eighteenth-century tribute realization, could not withstand the competition of English factory-produced cottons in the world market. After 1813 Lancashire invaded India as well. Tribute realization could now only take place in the form of export of raw materials and agricultural products, like indigo and raw cotton, but the ultimate answer, found by the second quarter of the nineteenth century, lay in opium. The entire process constitutes part of what has come to be called 'de-industrialization'.

This 'received' view obtains partial support here and there from some individual contributions in *CEHI*. But the general tone of the volume is in sharp opposition to it. The spirit is manifest in Tom Kessinger, when he discounts the critical view held by Asiya Siddiqi and C.A. Bayly towards the tribute-induced 'growth' before 1857. Kessinger assures us that '*all* of the evidence points to expanded employment in agriculture, processing and transportation in a period of little or very gradual population growth' (p. 269; emphasis added). The evidence that Kessinger himself presents is not of much weight, and, in respect of towns at least, his pronouncements must be treated with the greatest caution, as we shall see. We may also note here the resort to a useful device, viz. speculative demography. Kingsley Davis postulates a very rapid population growth for the nineteenth century by assuming conditions of prosperity brought about by that noble phenomenon, 'the European influence';[12] now his compatriot, Kessinger, seeks to establish the very same economic prosperity by assuming a very slow population growth.

---

[11] Marx's articles bearing on India are best collected in Karl Marx, *On Colonialism and Modernization*, edited by Shlomo Avineri, New York, 1969, I have summarized his views in *The Marxist*, I(1), Delhi, 1983, pp. 116–33; pp. 14–58 of this volume.

[12] Kingsley Davis, *The Population of India and Pakistan*, Princeton, 1951, pp. 25–26.

These comments are made in passing. The main theoretician against 'de-industrialization' is Morris D. Morris (pp. 668-76), and it is his propositions that need to be scrutinized the most closely. On this theme we have already the benefit of reading his two previous essays;[13] but it will be best to confine attention to what he now says in *CEHI*.

He begins by deprecating the emphasis usually placed on the textile industry as the index of the fortunes of Indian handicrafts: 'Despite the importance of the enormously varied handicraft activities and the considerable—sometimes overwhelming—detail that is available about them, the only one to which scholars have paid much attention is the textile industry' (p. 668). But Amiya Kumar Bagchi met this objection long ago, through a notable paper, 'De-industrialization in Gangetic Bihar, 1809–1901', in which he compared the data on craft employment in certain Bihar districts given in Buchanan's surveys and the figures of the 1901 census. Bagchi found that the 'industrial' segment of the population in these districts contracted from about 18.6 per cent of the total to about 8.5 per cent in the course of the ninety years following 1809.[14] It is difficult to understand Morris' silence over this paper, since his fellow contributor, S. Bhattacharya, duly notices it and accords it much importance (pp. 290–91).

Coming to the textile industry, to which Morris himself devotes his main attention, he argues that the imports of Lancashire goods initially affected the spinners only, and not the weavers, since imported yarn enabled weavers to compete with imported piece-goods. He ignores here the pertinent criticism levelled by Meghnad Desai, himself an editor of *CEHI*, that even after shifting to cheaper British yearn, Indian weavers would have had to increase their productivity by 43 per cent or accept a corresponding diminution of their income, between 1818–1821 and 1829–1831, in order to compete

[13] *Indian Economic and Social History Review (IESHR)*, V (1), pp. 1–16, and V (4), pp. 319–88.

[14] *Essays in Honour of Prof. S.C. Sarkar*, New Delhi, 1976, pp. 439–522. A subsequent controversy between him and Marika Vicziany in *IESHR*, XVI (2), April–June 1979, pp. 107–62, enabled Bagchi further to defend his evidence.

with British cloth.[15] Morris also admits that contemporary witnesses spoke of the distress of the weavers; but this was because, unlike Morris, they did not know that the distress was really being 'caused by weather instabilities which periodically caused crop failure, by declines in agricultural incomes, and by steep falls in local demand for cloth' (p. 669). Such ignorance on the part of contemporaries should surely excite wonder. It is true, however, that the initial assault of the powerloom was on the Indian weaver manufacturing for export, as can be seen from William Bentinck's Minute of 30 May 1829.[16] Yet in 1837 Crawfurd (defender of the Lancashire imports as well as the opium trade) estimated that English manufactures had by then replaced about 6 per cent of the Indian production of cloth (not yarn) for the domestic market, besides eliminating Indian textile exports.[17] The destruction of exports alone must have hurt a large number of weavers. At the close of the eighteenth century 40,000 looms worked for the Company in the Madras Presidency; and these amounted to no less than one-sixth of the number of looms working in that Presidency about sixty years later.[18]

Though Morris overlooks these pre-1835 misfortunes of the weaver, he concedes that between 1835 and 1870, 'we would expect to encounter the great competitive squeeze on handloom weavers' (p. 669). Apparently, this modifies his previous rejection of such a squeeze even when confronted with a decrease in the price of British woven cloth.[19] But the effect on weavers is still doubted by Morris, though for a new reason altogether, namely, the lack of 'pubic attention' paid to it 'during these years' (p. 669). With easy neglect of

[15] *IESHR*, VIII (4), p. 354.
[16] Report of Select Committee on East India Company's Affairs, 1831–32, *British Parliamentary Papers, Colonies: East India*, 5, IUP, General Appendix, pp 275–76. One would like especially to refer to this, because Morris and a 'distinguished Bentinck scholar' could not trace a quotation given by Marx from Bentinck, *IESHR*, V(4), p. 383n. Here Bentinck says the same thing in the same vigorous language.
[17] *Economic Development of India under The East India Company*, edited by K.N. Chaudhuri, Cambridge, 1971, pp. 239–42.
[18] This is calculated on the basis of data provided by Dharma Kumar in *CEHI*, II, p. 369 and n.
[19] Bipan Chandra in *IESHR*, V(1), pp. 55–57; Morris' reply, *IESHR*, p. 380n.

chronology, he places Marx among the pre-1835 critics of Lancashire, while in actual fact Marx first referred to the sufferings of the
Indian weavers only in 1847; he thereafter returned to the theme
repeatedly in 1853 and the subsequent years of that decade, and references to it appear in *Capital*, Volume I, published in 1867.[20] He thus
incessantly called 'public attention' to the matter throughout the
period defined by Morris. If there was less open official concern with
the sufferings of the weavers, this was undoubtedly due to the fact
that with the export of opium to China the problem of tribute realization had been solved; and there was little ground any longer for that
anxiety on this score which had been manifested by Bentinck while
writing in 1829 on the destruction of Indian textile exports.[21] Besides,
free trade was now an article of faith in Britain, and officials could
hardly have expected to get a hearing if they contested its wisdom.
Thus, there is sufficient reason for any official reticence which might
now have developed about the fate of the Indian weaver: it is no proof
that what the officials were reticent about did not exist.[22]

Morris goes on to restate his dictum about the 'shift to the
right of the demand curve' for cloth,[23] but he does so now in more
measured terms:

> The dramatic decline in cloth prices . . . should have stimulated a
> substantial rise in cloth demand. We do not know whether demand
> elasticity and population growth after 1835–40 increased the
> market rapidly enough to enable Indian producers to retain their
> absolute share of the market, but these factors certainly seem to
> have cushioned some of the impact. (p. 669)

Let us put the matter in simple terms: if the Indians spent the
same amount in value per capita on cloth as they did before the Lancashire imports, then, at lower prices prevailing now, they would be

[20] The 1847 reference is in *The Poverty of Philosophy*, Moscow, n.d., p. 113;
and the 1853 statement in articles in *New York Daily Tribune* for which
see Avineri (ed.), *On Colonialism*.

[21] Report of the Select Committee (see note 16), pp. 275–76.

[22] In *New York Daily Tribune*, 22 June 1853, Marx said of a speech by Bright
that his 'picture of India ruined by the fiscal exertions of the Company
and Government did not, of course, receive the supplement of India ruined
by Manchester and Free Trade'. Avineri (ed.), *On Colonialism*, p. 79.

[23] *IESHR*, V (1), p. 9.

able to consume larger quantities of cloth. Ellison thus erred in supposing that the Indian consumption per capita had all along remained the same (set by him at 2.5 lb) as it was in 1880–81 (when British imports had captured much of the Indian market); fifty years earlier the consumption should have been much smaller. Thus, if we take Ellison's table,[24] and assume a per capita consumption of cloth in 1831–35 at 1.5lb only, and the population then at 222 million (as estimated for 1833 by Morris,[25] as against 150 million accepted by Ellison), the per capita domestic production would have fallen only from 1.44 lb (and not 2.4 lb) in 1831–35 to a little above 1.00 lb in 1880–81. If the per capita consumption in 1831–35 had been smaller than even 1.5 lb, the domestic production would have been still smaller at that time. And yet that domestic production must have accounted for about 97 per cent of the total value of cloth consumed per capita in the early 1830s, while the domestic production of 1880–81 accounted for only 41.6 per cent of the same amount, assuming that the value of cloth consumed per capita had remained constant. Thus the spinners and weavers together would have had not only to face a contraction of production, but also to suffer a very large fall in real earnings per unit of product.

The situation would have been different only if there was a shift 'to the right of the demand curve' and if the total value laid out on per capita cloth consumption had increased. Of this there is not the slightest proof. The increase in cloth consumption supposedly due to moral admonitions of missionaries (p. 369), and changes in fashion, can all be accommodated within the expansion of cloth consumption owing to the lowering of prices along the same old demand curve. Indeed, one may theoretically argue that if cloth prices fell, wages might also fall and rents increase, to cover the reduction in the costs of subsistence: in the case, the demand curve might well have shifted to the left!

.It is worth noting that some of the specific evidence presented by two other contributors CEHI does not accord with Morris' line of interpretation. Dharma Kumar finds for southern India that 'the unit value of cloth output certainly declined sharply in many districts

[24] Thomas Ellison, *The Cotton Trade of Great Britain* (originally published, 1886), London, 1968, pp. 62–63.

[25] *IESHR*, XI (2–3), p. 311.

and probably also the incomes of certain classes of weavers' (p. 370).
She is less sure about a decline in the number of looms, but there is
no plausible ground for rejecting Dodwell's estimate of 400,000
looms in the Madras Presidency in 1800, when it is rather reasonably
worked out on the basis of the number of looms working for the Company, assumed to be a tenth of the total. About 1857 there were
225,000 looms in that Presidency, and there was a noticeable shift
to inferior cloth (pp. 369–70; 369n).

For western India, Divekar's finding is the same as that of
Dharma Kumar: the weavers' real earnings fell 'considerably' between the 1820s and 1840s. He also finds a decline in the number of
looms though he gives numbers for only one place in Bijapur district
(p. 349).[26]

A more definitive result emerges from Amalendu Guha's calculations. He makes an attempt to estimate handloom production by
estimating raw cotton production, reduced by the volume of exports
and consumption in weaving factories. He finds that the net availability
of cotton yarn (including imported and machine-spun yarn) for the
handloom industry declined from 419 million lb in 1850 to 240 million lb in 1870 and 184 or 221 million lb in 1900.[27]

[26] Unluckily, in his survey of eastern India, S. Bhattacharya does not give
data for either real earnings of weavers or numbers of looms during this
period, though he says that weaving 'showed surprising survival capacity'
(p. 292). Kessinger does not seem to have come to grips with the question
in his survey of northern India, though he does give interesting data on
the disappearance of the supply of piece-goods from the Upper Provinces
to Calcutta between 1812–13, when they composed 41 per cent of the
total trade, and 1835–36, when their share had dwindled to 2 per cent (pp.
253–54).

[27] Paper (cyclostyled) presented at a seminar on the Transformation from
Medieval to Colonial Economy, Aligarh, 1972. Amalendu Guha's
conclusion can also be supported by the figures on India's raw cotton
exports to Britain. From 145 million lb in 1855 these climbed to 443 million
lb in 1872, constituting 16 per cent of total British raw cotton imports in
1855, and 31 per cent in 1872; see Peter Harnetty, *Imperialism and Free
Trade: Lancashire and India in the Mid-19th Century*, Manchester, 1972,
p. 49. Unless the Indian per capita cotton production also increased on such
a dramatically high scale, the per capita availability of cotton within the
country must have undergone an enormous decline. The force of M.B.
McAlpin's studies has been to deny such an increase in per capita cotton
acreage during this period; *Journal of Economic History (JEH)*, XXXIV,
1974, pp. 662–84; and *IESHR*, XII (1), pp. 43–60.

In the twentieth century there happens to have come about a stability and some revival of the handloom; and much of Morris' own theorization seems to be projection of this phenomenon back into the nineteenth century.[28] This apparent reversal in the fortunes of the handloom is noticed by Gadgil, who says, reasonably enough, that 'at a certain stage' in the decline of handicrafts under the pressure of modern industry 'a point of equilibrium was reached in the competition between the two industries; and that 'this point was [only] reached towards the end of the last century'.[29] Bagchi, too, has examined the reasons behind this revival of the handloom, and he notes the lag in the development of the weaving departments in Indian factories, the application of the fly-shuttle to the loom, and, not the least, the swadeshi movement.[30] A twentieth-century recovery (ultimately to be a passing phase) owing to these and other factors, thus cannot by itself persuade us to disbelieve in the eclipse of the handloom during the preceding century.

### De-urbanization

As the Indian ruling classes were deposed and the revenues which they appropriated were transferred to the Company, the cities and towns which depended on the supply of articles of consumption and services to the older ruling classes and their households, courtiers and retainers rapidly declined. The assault of free trade after 1813 devastated centres of handicrafts, notably textiles, and a fresh process of urban decay began. Gadgil summed up the argument in his cautious manner and postulated a 'slight' relative fall in the urban population in the course of the nineteenth century.[31]

One would have thought that this was a fairly important matter to be gone into at some length in a 1,074-page textbook on modern Indian economic history. L. and P. Visaria in their chapter on population briefly refer to Gadgil's conclusion, but the only comment

---

[28] See *IESHR*, V(4), p. 378, where Morris takes as his starting point the existence of 3.1 million handlooms in India and Pakistan in 1950–51.

[29] D.R. Gadgil, *The Industrial Evolution of India in Recent Times, 1860–1939* (fifth edition), Delhi, 1971, p. 180.

[30] Amiya Kumar Bagchi, *Private Investment in India, 1900–1939*, Cambridge, 1972, pp. 220–28.

[31] Gadgil, *Industrial Evolution of India*, pp. 144ff.

they make themselves is that 'the level of urbanization [in India] has *always* been very low' (pp. 519–20).[32] The Visarias' implicit scepticism about a nineteenth-century decline in the relative size of the urban population is shared by S. Bhattacharya, who, dealing with eastern India in the nineteenth century, puts a question-mark after 'De-urbanization' in a section-heading, and also pursues in the text the indefinite course that the heading presages (pp. 275–77).

Kessinger's heading, 'Growth of Towns', for the same period is firm, and his conclusions absolutely definite. In the British territories 'the expansion of economic activity' brought a 'period of rapid growth to the cities and towns of the Ganges valley'. In the native states the situation was at variance with this: 'None of the court cities, not even Lucknow, show the kind of dynamic growth related to commercial centres in British territories. Awadh in fact had a relatively small number of towns in its territories at the same time of annexation in 1854 [*sic*]' (pp. 265–66).

Kessinger's specific statements about Lucknow and Awadh need to be checked. First, Lucknow: there is no doubt as to an immense increase in its population under the Awadh kingdom. In 1799 its population was estimated at half a million,[33] and in 1858 at a million, so that it should then have been larger than Calcutta.[34] Even Kessinger admits that Lucknow became 'probably North India's largest city' (p. 266). He offers no argument why such growth is not 'dynamic', while the much more modest increase in the size of some towns in British territories deserves such characterization. More, the moment Lucknow passed under British control with the annexation of Awadh in 1856, a steady decline began. The depopulation must have been heavy after the British seizure of Lucknow during the rebellion of 1857–58;[35] but the decline continued till 1911, as the successive censuses show (see table on facing page). Thus Lucknow

---

[32] But see ibid., pp. 142–43.

[33] Tenant, *Indian Recreations*, II, p. 401, quoted in H.R. Nevill, *Lucknow: a Gazetteer*, Lucknow, 1922, p. 149. In 1824, Heber 'guessed' that the pupulation was 300,000. R. Heber, *Narrative of a Journey Throughout the Upper Provinces of India*, London, 1828, p. 90.

[34] William Howard Russel, *My Indian Diary*, edited by Michael Edwardes, London, 1957, p. 59.

[35] J. Nevill, *Lucknow District Gazetteer*, p. 63.

*Population of Lucknow, 1869–1911*

| 1869 | 284,779 |
|------|---------|
| 1881 | 261,303 |
| 1891 | 273,028 |
| 1901 | 261,049 |
| 1911 | 259,798 |

*Population of major towns in Southern Awadh*

| District | Year | Number of towns of 5,000 (in censuses, of 4,500) and above | Total population of the towns |
|----------|------|------------------------------------------------------------|-------------------------------|
| Unao | 1838 | 9 | 103,000–114,000 |
| | 1869/72 | 5 | 37,842 |
| | 1881 | 5 | 38,467 |
| | 1911 | 5 | 37,809 |
| Rae Bareli[a] | 1838 | 13 | 96,000 |
| | 1869/72 | 4 | 29,218 |
| | 1881 | 4 | 38,379 |
| | 1911 | 4 | 40,545 |
| Sultanpur | 1838 | 5 | 39,000 |
| | 1869/72 | 1 | 5,708 |
| | 1881 | 1 | 9,374 |
| | 1911 | 1 | 9,519 |
| Pratabgarh[b] | 1838 | 11 | 102,000 |
| | 1869/72 | 1 | 6,240 |
| | 1881 | 1 | 9,756 |
| | 1911 | 2 | 16,041 |
| Fyzabad[c] | 1838 | 5 | 134,000 |
| | 1869/72 | 3 | 55,635 |
| | 1881 | 6 | 111,773 |
| | 1911 | 3 | 82,569 |

[a] The 1881 population for Salon not being available, it has been assumed to be the mean of the 1869/1872 and 1891 figures (5,699).
[b] Bela and Pratabgarh counted as one town.
[c] Ayodhya and Faizabad (Fyzabad) counted as one town.

would seem to have lost all its dynamism once it passed under British rule.

As for the supposedly small number of towns in Awadh before annexation, it is not clear from where Kessinger derives his information. One major detailed survey of the southern districts of Awadh by Butter in 1838 gives estimates of population of a large number of towns; these may be compared with the results of censuses beginning with 1869/1872. For this comparison, I have taken towns to which Butter assigns a population of 5,000 or more,[36] and then located them in the later British districts. From the modern censuses, I have taken all towns with a population of 4,500 or more (the lower size for the census towns is to offset any rounding in Butter's estimates). The results are tabulated in the table on the previous page.

In these five districts of Awadh, then, the number of towns containing estimated populations of 5,000 and above was 43 in 1838; but the 1911 census counted no more than 15 such towns (even including those of 4,500 to below 5,000). The total population of the towns stood at an estimated 374,000 to 385,000 in 1838, and at only 186,483 in 1911.

Kessinger's statement that Awadh contained only a small number of towns before annexation is thus totally at variance with the quantitative evidence we have access to. Even if we allow for a large margin of error in Butter's estimates, the general tendency is still clear enough: towns in Awadh declined sharply in total population after the territory became subject to the benefits of direct British rule.

S. Bhattacharya's hesitation in accepting a decline of urban population in eastern India is also not easy to understand, since he has had before him Durgaprasad Bhattacharya's detailed work on pre-census population estimates of eastern India, which contains a very revealing table comparing estimates for individual towns during 1811–30 and the population counted in 1872.[37] The trend towards decline is quite unmistakable. The only city which shows a large

---

[36] Donald Butter, *Outlines of the Topography and Statistics of the Southern Districts of Oudh,* 1839, reprint (photo reprod.), edited by Safi Ahmad, Delhi, 1982, pp. 143–44; also pp. 100–16.

[37] D. Bhattacharya, *Report on the Population Estimates of India,* Vol. III, 1811–20, Pt. A, Eastern Region (*Census of India 1961*), pp. xvii–xviii.

increase is Calcutta, growing from 179,917 in 1821 to 428,328 in
1872. But this growth was more than counterbalanced by the decline
registered in the populations of almost all the other major cities:
Dacca declined from an estimated 200,000 in 1800 to 68,595 in
1872; Murshidabad from 165,000 in 1815 to 46,182; and Patna
from 312,000 in 1811–12 to 158,900.[38] Bhattacharya suggests that
the earlier estimates tended to be inflated because of the large area
the Indian towns occupied (p. 278, quoting Rennel). But the estimates
we have used were based on house or hut-counts, such as the one for
Patna made by Buchanan in 1811–12, and thus should not have been
influenced by the extent of land falling within the city limits.[39]

It is not my intention to supply further demographic information which should have appeared in *CEHI*. What I have offered is
only by way of illustration: the case for de-urbanization in the nineteenth century has a much stronger basis in descriptions and statistics
than the *CEHI* editors and contributors have allowed for.

### Per Capita Income

While *CEHI* may be parsimonious in the space it devotes to
matters such as the tribute, handicrafts, or urban populations, one
cannot have any quarrel with it on the generosity with which the
estimation of national income is treated, in full 87 pages (pp. 376–
462). Heston's industry in setting out the detailed calculations is
commendable; and one wishes one could as forthrightly commend
the calculations themselves.

Heston's conclusion, which he states close to the beginning
of his chapter, is that the per capita income rose by at least 35 per cent
between 1860 and 1920, implying an increase in real national income
by over 70 per cent (p. 379). One basic premise on which Heston
builds his series to achieve his result, is a firm assumption that crop-
yields have remained absolutely constant, an assumption which sets

---

[38] I have checked these figures with the volumes of Hunter's *Statistical
Account of Bengal*; they diverge slightly, in the case of the 1872 census,
from the figures given by D. Bhattacharya, ibid.

[39] Francis Buchanan, *An Account of the Districts of Bihar and Patna in
1811–1812* (The Patna-Gaya Report), Patna, n.d., p. 61. Buchanan fixed
a ratio of 6 persons to a house on the basis of trial enumerations, the house
were estimated to number 52,000.

him against all the previous official crop-estimators, and against Blyn, Sivasubramonian and other statisticians, who have accepted long-term declines in crop-yields per acre as a plausible phenomenon.

Heston says frankly enough that if we were to accept official yields, the output of principal crops per capita between 1901 and 1946 would rise by a meagre 7 per cent as against 23 per cent, which he gets by taking the crop-yields to be constant. He had elsewhere argued, especially with reference to the Bombay Presidency, that official estimates of crop-yields tended to be inaccurate before crop-cutting methods came to be employed in the early 1950s.[40] But Ashok V. Desai took issue with him over this wholesale rejection of the official data.[41] In *CEHI* itself McAlpin uses these very data to establish an association between price movements and variations in output of various crops (pp. 880–84).

Even if the official yields are sometimes suspect, the adoption of constant yields is a totally arbitrary procedure. It is not to be supposed that there should have been an upward movement in yields from extension of irrigation and shift to more profitable crops. This is because the yields for irrigated and 'dry' land are separately given in the statistics, and the acreages of the principal crops are also separately specified. Thus, an upward movement in total output per acre could well occur even if there was a decline in the yields.

Heston, on the other hand, insists that these yields themselves were being pressed upwards through a number of factors. The most important was 'the more intensive use of land due to more workers per acre' (pp. 880–84). But this does not agree with Michelle McAlpin's finding that the cultivated acreage per capita did not fall between the 1860s and 1901.[42] The other factors which Heston specifies, viz. 'increased use of improved seeds, implements and chemical fertilizers, improved dry-farming methods and rotations', can also hardly have had much significance in nineteenth-century agriculture. During that period, Heston's own list of contrary factors was all the more important: 'the general expansion into lower quality lands, the

---

[40] *IESHR*, X(4), December 1973, pp. 303–32; XV (2), April–June 1978, pp. 173–86.

[41] *IESHR*, XV (2), pp. 173–86.

[42] *IESHR*, XII (1), pp. 55–57.

substitution of better quality foodgrain lands for cash-crops and the decline in natural fertilizers, particularly oilseeds cakes that were exported and cowdung which was increasingly used as fuel as deforestation accelerated' (p. 390).

In the light of these factors, it is even less possible than otherwise to accept a projection of constant yields from 1952-55 to as far back as 1875, and to give credence to the increase in per capita income which Heston derives from such projection.

Heston again strives to obtain the same result by, first, postulating a very large relative size for the income from animal husbandry, and then, assuming a very high rate of growth for that income. In respect of the first he has been criticized by Angus Maddison, who would assign to animal husbandry an income equal only to 25.15 per cent of the income from crops in 1900–01; in Heston the corresponding figure is 36.4 per cent for 1899–1900 (table 4.3A, p. 397).[43] An inflated size of pastoral income would naturally exaggerate the effect of its growth upon per capita national income. This growth Heston puts at no less than 58.7 per cent between 1868–69 and 1899–1900, implying an increase of 40.8 per cent per capita.[44]

Such a dramatic increase in pastoral income is opposed to almost all that we know about the conditions of animal husbandry of the period. The steady reduction in grazing lands and the disappearance of breeding grounds of cattle, owing to the expansion of cultivation, adversely affected the supply of fodder and the quality of breeds. The Royal Commission on Indian Agriculture, 1928, laid stress on the fact that a mere increase in cattle population could not,

---

[43] See A. Maddison, 'What did Heston Do?', unpublished note circulated at the conference on *CEHI*, Cambridge, 1984, where the original version of this paper was also presented. Maddison puts the income from crops substantially above the estimates of both Sivasubramonian and Heston for good enough reasons (table 6 in the note). For Maddison's own original estimates, which Heston seems to dismiss rather too casually, see his *Class Structure and Economic Growth: India and Pakistan since the Moguls*, London, 1971, pp. 166–67.

[44] Heston explicitly assumes a 57 per cent increase, but the figures he conjectures show one of 58.7 per cent; the discrepancy is left unexplained (pp. 397, 440). To convert this into increase per capita, I have used the population tables constructed by Morris D. Morris in *IESHR*, XI(2–3), p. 312.

under such circumstances, add to the total efficiency of livestock.[45] Heston ignores the circumstances as well as the admonition: he proceeds on the assumption that an increase in the number of livestock must have enlarged the pastoral product in an exact proportion (p. 440). He then goes on to suggest an increase in the number of cattle by 60 per cent and of sheep and goats by 45 per cent between 1868–69 and 1899–1900 (p. 440). He assembles estimates of varied coverage and doubtful reliability which, however, do not necessarily support his thesis of a population explosion among cattle (pp. 438–39).[46] Such a phenomenon would be truly astonishing in the face of a dwindling fodder supply; and Heston, too, is none too sure of his cattle 'censuses'. He, therefore, tells us that 'the main reason' for his argument in favour of a large increase in pastoral income is 'the expansion in the exports of hides and skins from Rs 5 million in 1859 to Rs 115 million by 1901' (pp. 439–40). But the moment we convert these figures into those in terms of 1946–47 prices, in which Heston states all his figures in his Table 4.3A, we can see how weak even this 'main reason' is. In terms of those prices, the value of skins and hides exported annually rose by Rs 385 million between 1859 and 1901. Heston, on the other hand, conjures up an increase of no less than Rs 2,504 million in the income from animal husbandry between 1868–69 and 1899–1900![47]

About 67.7 per cent of the increase in national income that Heston estimates for the last thirty-two years of the nineteenth century is accounted for by agriculture and animal husbandry; and we have just seen how illusory are the data of growth that he offers us for

---

[45] *Report of the Royal Commission on Indian Agriculture*, London, 1928, pp. 198–200. See also W.H. Moreland, *Agricultural Conditions of the United Provinces and Districts*, Allahabad, 1913, pp. 26–31; and Vera Anstey, *The Economic Development of India*, fourth edition, London, 1952, p. 172.

[46] Atkinson counted 101.6 million heads of cattle in British India in 1895; the official *Agricultural Statistics* reported only 76.7 million in 1896–97, implying the disappearance of a quarter of the cattle population within a year. For the whole of India Sivasubramonian estimates 153 million heads in 1900–01. A comparison with the *Agricultural Statistics* would make one infer that over half the cattle were to be found in the princely states.

[47] For converting the increase in value of exports of hides and skins into 1946–47 prices, I have used Moni Mukherjee's table on price levels in *Economic History of India 1857–1956*, edited by V.B. Singh, Bombay, 1965, p. 685.

these sectors. It is difficult to pursue him in detail the rest of the way, but let us note that he has no authority for a 4 per cent increase in employment in the small sector between 1875 and 1895 ('I would not defend the figures . . . very stoutly'; pp. 396,451); nor for an increase in productivity per worker in that sector during the same period by 11.5 per cent (p. 451). Such assumptions need substantiation, since the conditions of small-scale industry at the time were hardly conducive to growth. (See the preceding discussion on 'De-industrialization' in this paper.) Heston's fellow-contributor, J. Krishnamurti finds that the work force in this sector kept declining in absolute numbers after 1900 (pp. 538–41, especially tables on pp. 534–5); that it followed an opposite trend during the thirty years preceding 1900 cannot therefore just be taken for granted. For the increase of productivity Heston has no evidence from the small sector itself, but he invites us to accept it because productivity increased in agriculture (given his own assumption of constant yields), in large-scale industry and in the railways![48] He even assigns the same increase in productivity to domestic service—'where one might suppose there were no gains in productivity' (p. 451)!

Such is the substance from which Heston weaves an increase in per capita income in the heyday of free trade. Beyond his own effort, Heston had appealed in an earlier paper to Moni Mukherjee and Morris D. Morris as two other proponents of the same view.[49] Of these, Mukherjee looms fairly large in Heston's chapter in *CEHI*, which quotes from him this disarmingly illogical sentence: 'It is somewhat difficult to believe in a continually declining sequence of per capita real income in as large, as varied and as great a country as India.'[50]

---

[48] Heston gives a table (4A.II) on p. 445 (where the column headings are a little misleading), which he describes on p. 450. This consists of Moni Mukherjee's real-wage indices for agriculture and industry (as recalculated by Heston) and his own indices of productivity per worker for agriculture and large-scale industry and an index of output per worker in railways. The real-wage series of Radhakamal Mukherjee, Kuczynski and K. Mukerji (all of which show declines in real wages) are ignored. It is this table which forms the basis for Heston's supposition of an increase in craft productivity (p. 451).

[49] *IESHR*, X(4), p. 330n.

[50] From M. Mukherjee's chapter on 'National Income' in V.B. Singh (ed.), *Economic History of India*, p. 703; quoted in *CEHI*, p. 404.

Given this basic philosophy, Mukherjee links the estimates of the earlier writers in such a manner as to produce a rise in per capita income in the second half of the nineteenth century. First of all, he takes F.T. Atkinson's two estimates, one for 1875 and the other for 1895. Both had an upward bias because Atkinson was responding to nationalist criticisms. Yet when Mukherjee reduced them to common (1948–49) prices, Atkinson's two figures displayed a very slight change: a bare 3 per cent increase in twenty years (Table IV, p. 672).[51] Mukherjee, therefore, went to Dadabhai Naoroji's estimate of 1867–68, which was based on different assumptions than Atkinson's and relative to his, had a markedly downward bias. Atkinson's estimate for 1875 was therefore naturally a hefty 21 per cent higher than Naoroji's (even after its being raised by V.K.R.V. Rao) (p. 672). Mukherjee converts this difference into an increase in per capita income during the intervening seven years (pp. 686–87). His further refinements consist, first, in building an annual series in which the indexed per capita income is made to rise from 169 in 1867 to 210 in 1876 (p. 689), and, second, in transforming the annual series into a table of nine-year moving averages, which results in artificially spreading this increase over a longer period, and so screening the sudden jump (pp. 701–2, see also column 5 in Table 4A.I on p. 442, and Heston, p. 418.

Heston does express some reservations about Mukherjee's use of the point estimates (pp. 384, 418–20); but his reader never obtains the means of realizing how arbitrary Mukherjee's linking of Naoroji's and Atkinson's estimates is, and how, in effect, evidence has been artificially pressed to prove what had previously been assumed. If one rectifies this, and restricts Mukherjee to Atkinson's two estimates, which follow a common method and basis of calculation, then, rather than a rise in per capita income, 'stability [stagnation?]' over the period 1875 to 1900 would be the consequence.[52]

[51] This results when Atkinson's figure for 1895 has been scaled down by 20 per cent (following V.K.R.V. Rao) and the 1875 figure by 15 per cent. There is little justification for the latter, except that 'a smaller scaling down would entail a drop in real per capita income between 1875 and 1895, an unlikely contingency' (p. 672).

[52] See Mukherjee's table in V.B. Singh (ed.), *Economic History*, pp. 689–90. There is an actual decline, from 202 in 1875 and 210 in 1876 to 188 in 1900. The words in inverted commas are from Heston's comment on p. 418.

*Average life expectancy (in years)*

|  | Male | Female |
|---|---|---|
| 1872–81 | 23.67 | 25.58 |
| 1881–91 | 24.59 | 25.54 |
| 1891–1901 | 23.63 | 23.96 |
| 1901–11 | 22.59 | 23.31 |
| 1911–21 | 19.42 | 20.91 |
| 1921–31 | 26.91 | 26.56 |
| 1931–41 | 32.09 | 31.37 |

Morris D. Morris' belief in an increase in per capita income in the nineteenth as well as the earlier part of the twentieth century rests on the absence of 'Malthusian checks'. To him, the increase in population after 1921 implies a stability or increase in per capita income.[53] However, if the demographic argument is applied to the period before the first world war, with which we are here concerned, the opposite conclusion must follow: The average expectation of life at birth calculated from the decennial censuses, shows the pattern in the table above.[54]

Given the enormous decline in life expectancy between 1872 and 1921, the supposition of a rise in per capita income would be hard to justify.[55] Directly faced with this dilemma, Heston now tells us that the two are unrelated—'This seems anyway to be the Indian experience' (p. 414). But it is, of course, far more likely that the 'Indian experience' has not at all been such as Heston has pictured it, and that the per capita income and the expectation of life-span moved in the same (downward) direction before 1921.

One particular set of data which are significant, though not infallible, for checking the trend in per capita income, relate to real wages. Heston tabulates real-wage indices from Radhakamal Mukerjee

[53] *IESHR*, V(1), p. 14 and n.
[54] Kingsley Davis, *The Population of India and Pakistan*, Princeton, 1951, p. 62.
[55] As Heston puts it, 'Up to 1920 per capita income and perhaps food availability are rising, while mortality experience is not improving [!] at all', p. 414.

and K. Mukerji, and both indicate a substantial fall in real wages from 1857/1860 to 1916/1920 (134 to 100 in R. Mukerjee and 145 to 100 in K. Mukerji; p. 402, Table 4.5, columns 10 and 11). Jurgen Kuczynski's weighted real-wage index similarly shows a large continuous decline between 1880 and 1919 (127 in 1880–89 to 98 in 1910–19).[56] Dharma Kumar, the *CEHI* editor, herself speaks of official figures showing 'a marked decline in the real wage rates [of agricultural labourers] in six out of the seven districts [of Madras Presidency] covered in the last quarter of the nineteenth century' (p. 238).[57] How does this accord with the supposed rise in per capita income during the very same period?[58] Heston would replace these real-wage indices by a fresh one calculated by himself from Moni Mukherjee's figures for wages and prices (Table 4A. II, columns 2 and 5 and text, p. 450). The interesting point is that even these show a decline from 1880–81 to 1900–01, while an earlier rise demands scrutiny; and certainly the large deviations from the results of R. Mukerjee and K. Mukerji have to be explained.

This long discussion of Heston's estimates of per capita income has been necessitated by the seductive quality that detailed figures, percentages and indices have acquired today. Once it is realized that Heston's figures merely express quantitatively what had been assumed in order to reach these figures, it would become obvious that the precision of his estimates is deceptive. The estimates do not prove by any means that the conditions of life were improving; they have been made on the premise of improvement, that is all.

---

[56] V.B. Singh (ed.), *Economic History of India*, p. 611.

[57] See also the same author's *Land and Caste in South India*, Cambridge, 1965, pp. 163–67. The decline is all the more remarkable since the wage rates tended to be under-reported until 1887, whereafter the understatement was 'somewhat less'. M. Atchi Reddy in *IESHR*, XV (4), p. 466.

[58] Heston: '. . . we again seem to find for the nineteenth century divergent trends in the per-capita income and real wages, which is not a tidy result' (p. 408). A divergence between the two is, of course, possible if there is a radical change in the distribution of national income, as in period of rapid growth of industrial capitalism. Within the Indian economy the landlords apparently gained considerably in the half latter of the nineteenth century but essentially the process was one of 'the slow impoverishment of the mass [rather] than the enrichment of the few' (Stokes in *CEHI*, p. 65).

### The Drain and National Income

I now offer another illustration from Heston's array of figures, where these are apt to be quite misleading. National income is
the sum total of the value of goods produced and services rendered
internally plus income earned abroad, minus wealth transferred
abroad. Heston accordingly supplies a column on 'foreign earnings'
in his table on 'Net Domestic Product, 1868–1900' (Table 4.3A, p.
397). As may be expected, the figures are all negative, since India was
subjected to a continuous drain of wealth. Given in 1946–47 prices,
the figures suggest detailed calculation; but as Heston explains it, the
device by which they have been obtained is simplicity itself. He first
takes Sivasubramonian's figures for net loss by foreign trade in 1900–
01, and then proceeds backwards by assuming 1.5 per cent annual
growth in foreigners' earnings remitted from India. For this there is
the greater authority than Heston's own supposition that the annual
earnings of foreigners in India doubled between 1857 and 1900 (pp.
452–53).[59] Such an inspired short-cut dispenses with all the detailed
calculations of the drain by Dadabhai Naoroji, William Digby, Y.S.
Pandit and others.

The degree of accuracy that Heston with his simple device
achieves can be tested if we turn to Kirti Chaudhuri's chapter in
*CEHI*. Here we are told of S.B. Saul's estimate of Britain's favourable
balance of payments with India in 1880, viz. £ 25 million, equal at
the current sterling ratio, to Rs 300 million (p. 873).[60] Converted into
1946–47 prices, according to M. Mukherjee's table,[61] this gives us a
value of Rs 1,355 million. This sum is nearly three times the value
Heston enters for 1882–83 (there is no entry for 1880) under 'foreign
earnings'—a mere minus 484 million in 1946–47 prices. In 1882, the
surplus export of merchandise, which can serve as a floor-figure for
the net drain, amounted to Rs 1,237 million in 1946–47 prices.[62] This

---

[59] This is surely an area where 'hunches' of this kind have the least
justification, for the quantitative evidence is so rich. For the latest survey
of that evidence see A.K. Banerji, *Aspects of Indo-British Economic
Relations*, Bombay, 1982.

[60] A.K. Banerji, ibid., pp. 18–19, argues that Saul underestimates the extent
of India's net payments to Britain in 1880–81.

[61] V.B. Singh (ed.), *Economic History of India*, p. 685.

[62] See table on p. 873 for figures in current prices. By 'net drain' I mean the
total payments made to the British, less British capital exports to India.

accords with Saul's estimate for 1880 and is two-and-a-half times that
of Heston. Similarly, in 1898–99, according to Y.S. Pandit's estimate,
cited by K.N. Chaudhuri, India had a total net deficit of payments of
Rs 396.5 million, and an export surplus of Rs 355.6 million (p. 874),
equal to Rs 1,397 million in 1946–47 prices. In 1898 the Home charges alone amounted to Rs 244.8 million, that is Rs 961 million in
1946–47 prices.[63] Yet Heston's entire total for net foreign payments
in 1898–99 in 1946–47 prices, is just Rs 625 million.

The enormous inaccuracy in representing the size of the
drain is not cited just to score a point: the drain of wealth at Rs 1,355
million in 1882 would reduce Heston's total for 'net product' in
1882–83 to Rs 32,712 million, and the drain would then amount to
4.14 per cent of the national income at that time. Such a continuous
loss of savings would be crippling for any economy. Where would
investments come from to stimulate any expansion of the economy,
when the bulk of the possible savings was annually lost?[64] And yet
there is no discussion in the pages of *CEHI* of the basic quantities and
implications of the drain in this 'modern' phase of the Indian
economy.[65]

### Commercialization of Agriculture and Its Consequences

The railway construction of the second half of the nineteenth
century may be said to have completed the 'colonialization' of the
Indian economy, pulling all its erstwhile isolated segments inside the
net of British free trade. On the railways *CEHI* offers a very competent study by John M. Hurd (pp. 762–803), and the relationship of
prices and the expanding markets for agricultural produce is explored
by McAlpin (pp. 878–904). But from here the trail is abruptly abandoned. Starvation and famines of the utmost severity were a marked

[63] William Digby, *Prosperous British India: A Revelation from Official
Records*, London, 1901, reprint, New Delhi, 1969, pp. 217–18.

[64] It may be remembered that the total capital formation at the end of British
rule was no more than 5 or 6 per cent of the NDP. See Angus Maddison,
*Class Structure and Economic Growth*, p. 65; *CEHI*, p. 948.

[65] In her section on south Indian economy before 1857 Dharma Kumar does
recognize that 'the "economic drain" was large', but urges that it 'is not
clear that [this was] . . . accompanied by the impoverishment of the people'
(pp. 360, 375).

feature of the last quarter of the nineteenth century.[66] Was this simply due to a continuation of the older conditions (what then of the relief expected from the railways?) or to a decline in the availability of foodgrains as a result of the transfer of land to non-food crops and high-price grain (wheat), or, again, to 'a change in the distribution of income'?[67] None of these alternatives is discussed in *CEHI*: one looks in vain for data on growth of regional specialization, and relative crop-acreage; and on the distribution of rural income, especially the movement of rents. Thus the question as to who benefited from the rise in agricultural prices and an improvement in terms of trade in favour of agriculture (p. 894) is left high in the air.

Some of the *CEHI* contributors seem particularly anxious to avoid any suggestion that the expanding market and increasing differentiation could have enlarged the ranks of agricultural labourers. This anxiety may explain the slip that Eric Stokes makes at one place in his inimitable contribution on agrarian relations in northern India: 'The pressure towards reduction of the size of purely tenant holdings came from the increase of the numbers of the rural proletariat. The myth of the rise of the landless labourer . . .', etc. What is stated for a fact in one sentence becomes a myth in the next (p. 63).[68]

Similarly, Dharma Kumar writing in *CEHI* omits reference to her own important finding that in south India the proportion of agricultural labourers to the total population increased from about

---

[66] See the useful appendix to the chapter on population which tabulates famines, 1750–1947 (pp. 528–31). The most deadly famine was that of 1896–97, with 96.9 million affected and 5.1 million deaths.

[67] Michelle Burge McAlpin, 'Railroads, Cultivation Patterns and Foodgrain Availability: India 1860–90', *IESHR*, XII(1) (January–March 1975), pp. 43–60, the quoted words being from her conclusion (p. 58). Also see her earlier essay in *JEH*, XXXIV, 1974, pp. 662–84, where too she disputes the effects of railways on foodgrain availability. She ought, perhaps, to have treated acreage under wheat separately from other foodgrains: for it was really the coarse grain availability which was in question. Nor should one be so dogmatic about the fall in foodgrain availability. Even a 'small decline in the share of land planted with grain', plus foodgrain exports, could have had a devastating effect on a very large population permanently hovering upon the verge of starvation.

[68] What Stokes appears to be saying is that large numbers of agricultural labourers held small bits of land and were not totally landless. This would not be seriously disputed by anyone.

15 or 17 per cent to 27 or 29 per cent during the course of the nineteenth century.[69] Surendra J. Patel's pathbreaking book, *Agricultural Labourers in India and Pakistan* (Bombay, 1952), does not even find a place in the bibliography of *CEHI*. By such silence apparently are old 'classics' to be rendered obsolete.

### Imperialism and Indian Industry

Part II of *CEHI* opens with a long chapter by Morris D. Morris on the growth of large-scale industry (pp. 553–676). Set nearly in the middle, Morris's contribution dominates the volume, being the only one where full-scale theorization about India and the British regime has been offered. To this the reader can relate the conclusions in many of the other contributions whose authors explicitly or implicitly share Morris's early nineteenth-century, pre-List approach.

Morris begins by taking a swing at Karl Marx, who, he says, was 'excessively optimistic' in forecasting the development of modern industry in India. Not only was Marx wrong here but if Indian industry did not develop, there is no reason to put the blame on 'British policy which inhibited local initiative' (pp. 553–54).

It has been widely recognized that British tariff policy was mainly directed towards making India an unprotected market for Britain.[70] Morris immediately proceeds to contest this. Given conditions as they stood, he says, 'scholars are beginning to agree' that the effects of 'a vigorous protective tariff policy' would have been 'minuscule'. He argues that 'the jute and cotton textile industries not only grew swiftly without tariff protection but many of their most important markets were overseas where tariffs could not have helped' (p. 555).[71]

---

[69] *Land and Caste in South India*, pp. 168–82.

[70] Angus Maddison, *Class Structure and Economic Growth*, p. 56, for a recent statement.

[71] Among scholars who share his outlook on tariffs Morris might have in mind B.R. Tomlinson. In his *Political Economy of the Raj, 1914–1947*, London, 1979, p. 13 (also pp. 15–16), Tomlinson argues that for India's industrial development protective tariffs would have been less important than the transformation of 'the traditional institutions of the internal economy'. He refers us in turn to T.D. Rider's unpublished Ph.D. thesis on 'The Tariff Policy of the Government of India and its Development Strategy, 1894–1926'. I suppose if one can see an official development strategy in that period, one can see anything.

This last sentence is typical of Morris's arguments. First, it is illogical to lump jute and cotton industries together. The jute industry before 1914 was almost wholly British controlled and, therefore, had no serious tariff problems. As for exports, it is obvious that industries with protected home markets can often afford to accept lower profit margins in foreign markets; and so protection at home helps them abroad. In any case, according to Morris, 'the market for Indian cloth was almost entirely domestic' (p. 587). But, above all, it is the general logic of the formulation which is so weak. The textile industry was the *only* major industry which, owing to close access to cheap raw materials and a large home market, had some chance of growth. Other industries had no chance at all, and by imposing free trade, the British secured their total suppression or prevention.

Morris repeats his remarks in the succeeding pages as well;[72] and he finds his case so far proved to his satisfaction that he describes neither the tariff and excise nor the currency manipulation with which Britain tried to stifle the Indian cotton industry. Thus, a reader of Morris would not know that under Lancashire pressure all duties on imports into India were abolished in 1879 and 1882, ostensibly to remove unfair competition and in the interest of 'the native population', who would get cheaper cloth.

What happened in 1894 went even beyond the sweeping measures of 1879–82. A tariff of 5 per cent was now levied on imported cloth but a 'countervailing excise' was levied on Indian mill yarn competing with Lancashire. In 1896, in order further to protect Lancashire, such excise was levied on all Indian mill cloth. Gone was the pretence that free trade was intended to cheapen cloth for the Indian consumer. Morris cannot but notice the setback the Indian cotton mill industry suffered as a consequence, but the way he puts it is certainly odd: 'Between 1894 and 1896 tariff agitation generated considerable uncertainty' (p. 577).[73] What harmed the Indian industry was thus not the excise measures, but the Indians shouting themselves hoarse over them!

---

[72] 'Given the widespread impression that industrial development was impossible because of implacable British hostility to Indian competition, the career of the cotton mill industry seems particularly paradoxical.' (p. 573).

[73] Morris surely means the agitation in India over the countervailing excise, not over the tariff imposed on imports.

Elsewhere in *CEHI*, K.N. Chaudhuri wonders why the abolition of tariffs in 1882 did not overwhelm the Indian textile industry and refers, as a possible factor, to the continuous devaluation of the rupee owing to silver influx and free mintage (p. 868). But this loop hole, too, was plugged when in 1893 the Indian mints were closed.[74] One is gratified to learn from *CEHI* that this was done at the insistent demand of the Indians: 'There was considerable agitation in India for the closing down of the mints for the free coinage of silver and the ultimate adoption of the gold standard' (p. 770). A.G. Chandavarkar has apparently omitted to read the statement submitted to the Currency Committee, 1893, by that obsolete thinker, Dadabhai Naoroji, who opposed precisely the two measures which are here ascribed to an Indian agitation.[75] Nor does it strike him, as it did R.C. Dutt, that a revaluation on this scale (raising the rupee from 13.1 d in 1894–95 to 16 d in 1898–99) must have greatly imperilled the Indian cotton industry.[76] The rise in the value of the rupee naturally made exports to East Asia and the Middle East less competitive and cheapened British yarn and cloth in India.[77]

If the Indian textile industry still survived, it was not because of any lack of trying on the part of the British government. In other sectors its hostility to Indian industrialization was bound to be more, even fully, successful.

In his sub-chapter on railways, J.M. Hurd recognizes that the Government of India was 'interested not in India's financial and industrial development but in Britain's', and that it urged the railway companies to 'buy British' right down to 1924 (p. 749). Its refusal to utilize the capacity of Indian railway workshops to produce competitive locomotives, to which Hurd refers (p. 749), is dismissed

---

[74] This step is commended by Chaudhuri: 'the adoption of the gold exchange standard provided India with a really modern and automatic mechanism regulating the supply and demand for foreign exchange' (pp. 874–75).

[75] *Poverty and Un-British Rule in India*, London, 1901, reprint, Delhi, 1962, pp. 495–98. See Bipan Chandra, *The Rise and Growth of Economic Nationalism in India*, New Delhi, 1966, pp. 279ff.

[76] *India in the Victorian Age*, second edition, London, 1906, reprint, Delhi, 1976, p. 433.

[77] See, for a fall in the share of cotton goods in Indian exports between 1890–91 and 1900–1, *CEHI*, II, p. 844 (Table 10.11).

summarily in a footnote by Morris.[78] He has no time to consider the fact that owing to official policy, the railways failed to act as a stimulant for heavy and machine-building industries as they did elsewhere in the world. This judgement is left for Hurd to deliver: 'India's loss from the purchase policies of the railways was not limited to her lack of progress in developing heavy industry. She also failed to reap the benefits of the spread effects to industry which would have occurred. Instead, the spread effects stimulated the British economy.' (p. 749)

The farthest Morris would go is to acknowledge that 'of course, official policy did not strongly [!] support the development of iron and steel industry' (p. 587). Seemingly oblivious to the irony of it, he applauds the action of the government in pledging itself to buy 10,000 tons of iron from BISCO, if the price was 5 per cent *lower* than that of English iron upon its being landed in India (p. 586). If the iron and steel industry did not still develop before 1900, it was apparently the fault of 'entrepreneurial behaviour' (pp. 586–87).

Whatever else might have been responsible for the failure of Indian industry to develop, Morris exonerates the colonial regime from any culpability throughout. The real culprit, he finds, was India's low per capita income. It was only half that of Japan at the time of the Meiji Restoration: 'This suggests the inappropriateness of considering Japanese development as a model of what would have happened in India had political conditions been different' (p. 601n). It is extraordinarily difficult to compare the incomes of two pre-industrial countries so differently placed in respect of climate, diet and pattern of consumption; yet Morris boldly makes the comparison the cornerstone of a theory. The theory must imply an unrelieved pessimism for India, for, as Alan Heston stresses, it has a receding per capita income relative to the advanced countries (e.g., USA) (p. 415), and also, presumably, relative to the oil sheikhdoms. We have, or ought to have, therefore, no industrial future, whatever be our 'political conditions'.

This critique of the structure of contents and the dominant message of *CEHI* has necessarily been largely negative. It has addressed itself to showing that *CEHI* offers an interpretation of modern

---

[78] 'Railway workshops were important centres of large-scale production, but unfortunately this is an activity about which it is not yet possible to say much.' (p. 566n.)

Indian economic history which is both incomplete and tendentious. *CEHI* omits any serious scrutiny of colonialism and underrates its impact on Indian economy. To say this does not mean that the nationalist view of these matters as stated in the 'classics' is all that is required to reconstruct modern economic history; or that the nationalist view did not have flaws, such as too often ignoring internal contradictions within the Indian economy or (much less often) presuming an earlier golden age. But the nationalist undoubtedly had a case; that case cannot be dismissed by mere claims to superior knowledge or better doctrine. The opposite picture that *CEHI* constructs, pre-eminently through the contributions of Heston and Morris, has far less to recommend it: in so large a part here have mere impressions been transformed into statistics and assumptions made to predetermine conclusions. The purpose of the present critique would be served if the reader is sufficiently warned against accepting this picture as anything more than yet another speculative exercise by one side in the old great controversy.

# Index

Abdul Ghafur, 225
aboriginal and pastoral tribes, 71
Abu'l Fazl, 240
   *A'in-i Akbari*, 176, 250, 251, 252, 267
accumulation, 199, 259, 260, 263–65, 268, 270, 271, 289, 294, 295
   pre-colonial, 259-71
   primary (primitive), 8, 41, 42, 43, 44, 49, 182, 271-81, 282, 290, 292, 293, 296, 306
   socialist, 12
   *see also* capitalist accumulation
advances, system of, 220, 231, 269
Afghanistan, 65
Afif, 88
agrarian classes, 177
agrarian crisis, 257
agrarian economy, 313
agrarian exploitation, 81, 224, 231
agrarian relations, 66, 76, 337, 361
agrarian revolts, 7, 25, 200, 257, 271
   *see also* armed resistance
agrarian revolutions, 38
agrarian society (Aryan), 62
agrarian system, 249
agrestic bondage, 317
agricultural communities, 116, 119, 165
agricultural conditions, 115
agricultural labour, 71, 284, 285
agricultural labourers, 71, 201, 216, 317
agricultural produce, 284
   of Bengal, 304
   expanding markets for, 360
   great drain of, 239
agricultural production, 183, 190, 196, 267
agricultural products, 341

agricultural surplus, 184, 203, 205, 267, 323
agricultural technology, 129, 183
agriculture, 163, 166, 168, 183, 234, 235, 266, 285, 286, 288, 341, 354, 355
   commercialization of, 338, 360–61
   and craft, 34
   and handicraft, 26, 27
   cattle power in, 183
   commercialization of, 178, 360–61
   dyke-based, 114
   semi-servile relations in, 197
   pre-history of, 110
*ahimsa*, 168, 169
*aimma* grant, 100
*Aitareya Brahmana*, 64
Akbar, 33, 91, 95, 100, 209, 265
Alauddin Khalji, 81, 82, 84, 86, 87, 89, 90, 91, 171, 174, 262
Alberuni, 172, 173, 175
Alexander, 62
Altekar, 135
Althusser, 3, 11
Amin, Samir, 5, 261
*amlak* grant, 100
anarchy, 180
'ancient communal ownership', 19
Andhras, 166
animal husbandry, 353, 354
animal-killing *jatis*, 125
Anstey, 336
Antonova, K., 262
*antyajas*, 172
*araghata*, *see* Persian wheel
*ardha-sitikas*, *see* sharecroppers
aristocracy, 7, 29, 55, 89, 90, 91, 101, 114, 115, 119
armed resistance, 91, 242, 243, 244